Sketching
Outdoors

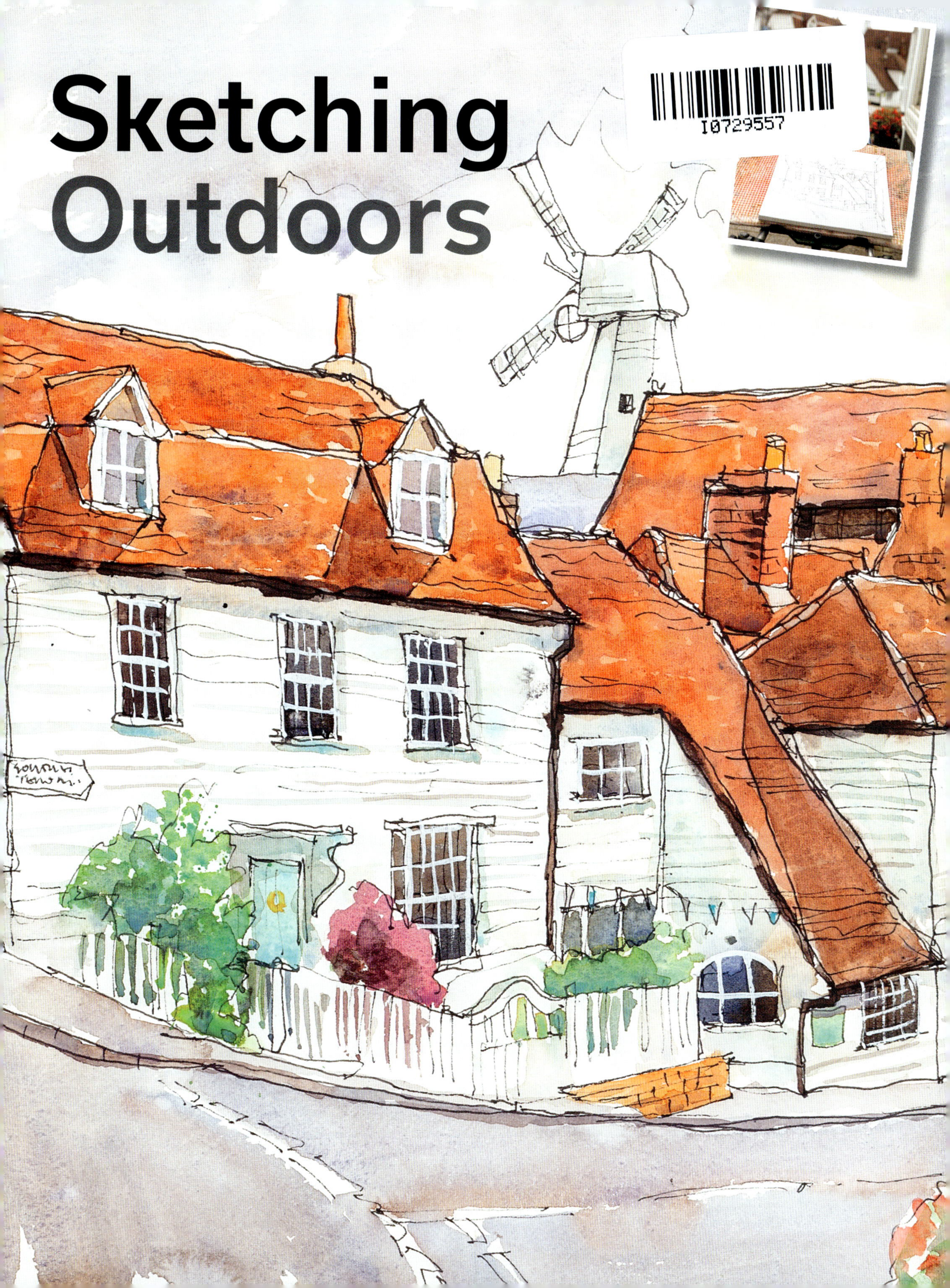

Dedication

To Sally, my long-suffering other half who has put up with me
disrupting the whole household while this book was in progress.

And of course Freddie, Boo, Lily Fig, Tim and our latest addition Joey,
who all try to get their muddy paws all over my artwork!

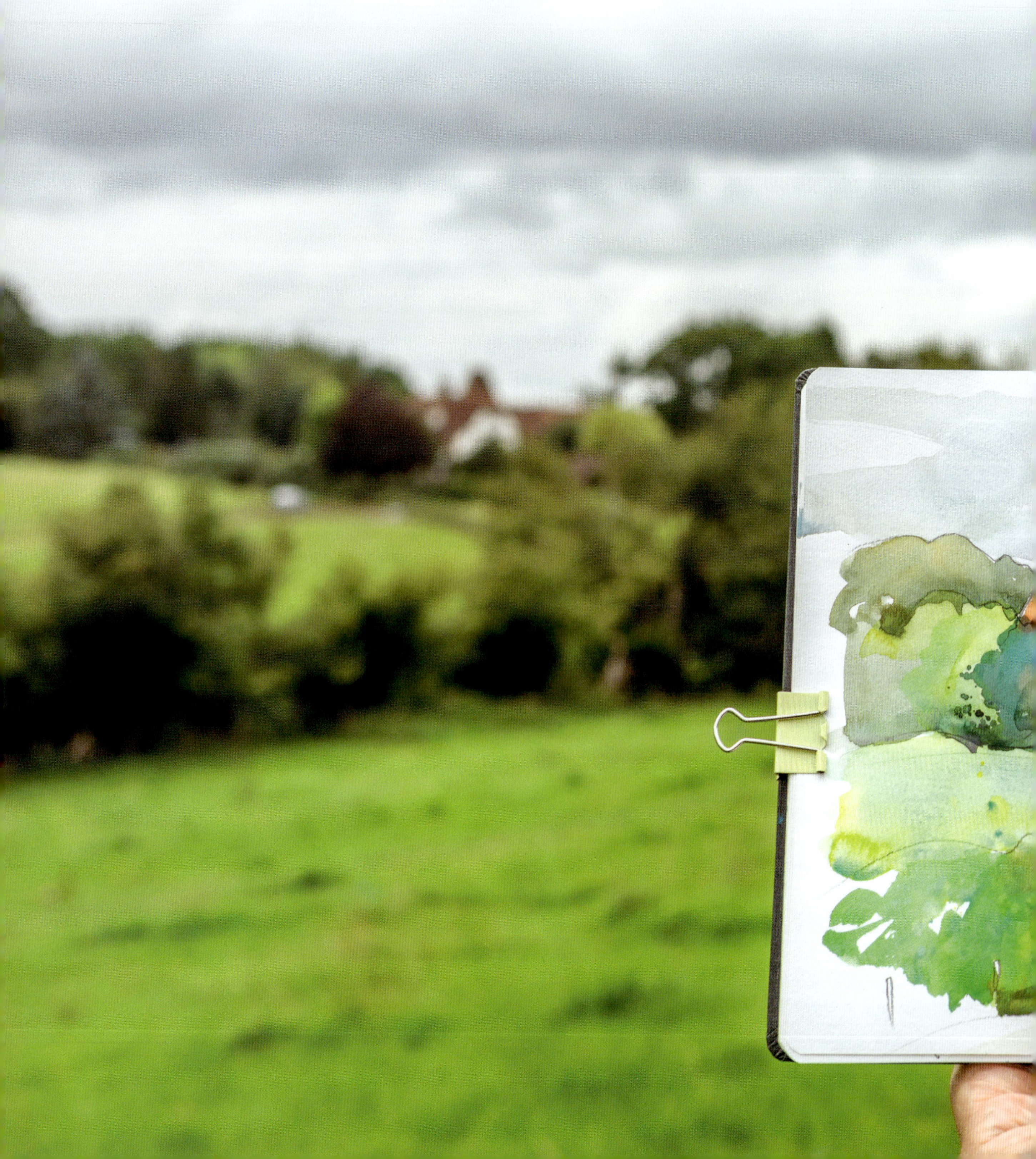

Sketching Outdoors

Discover the joy of painting outside

BARRY HERNIMAN

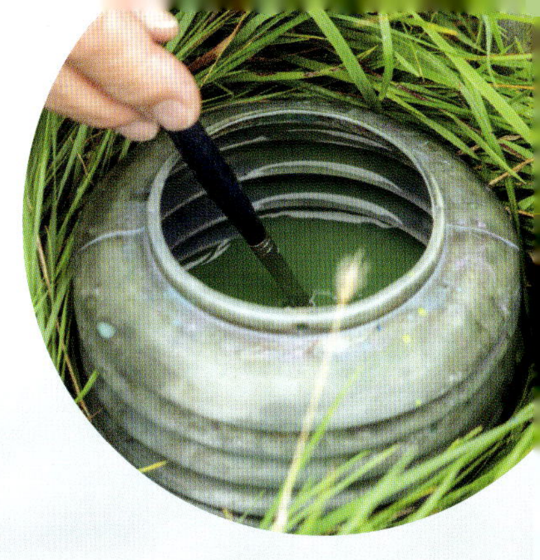

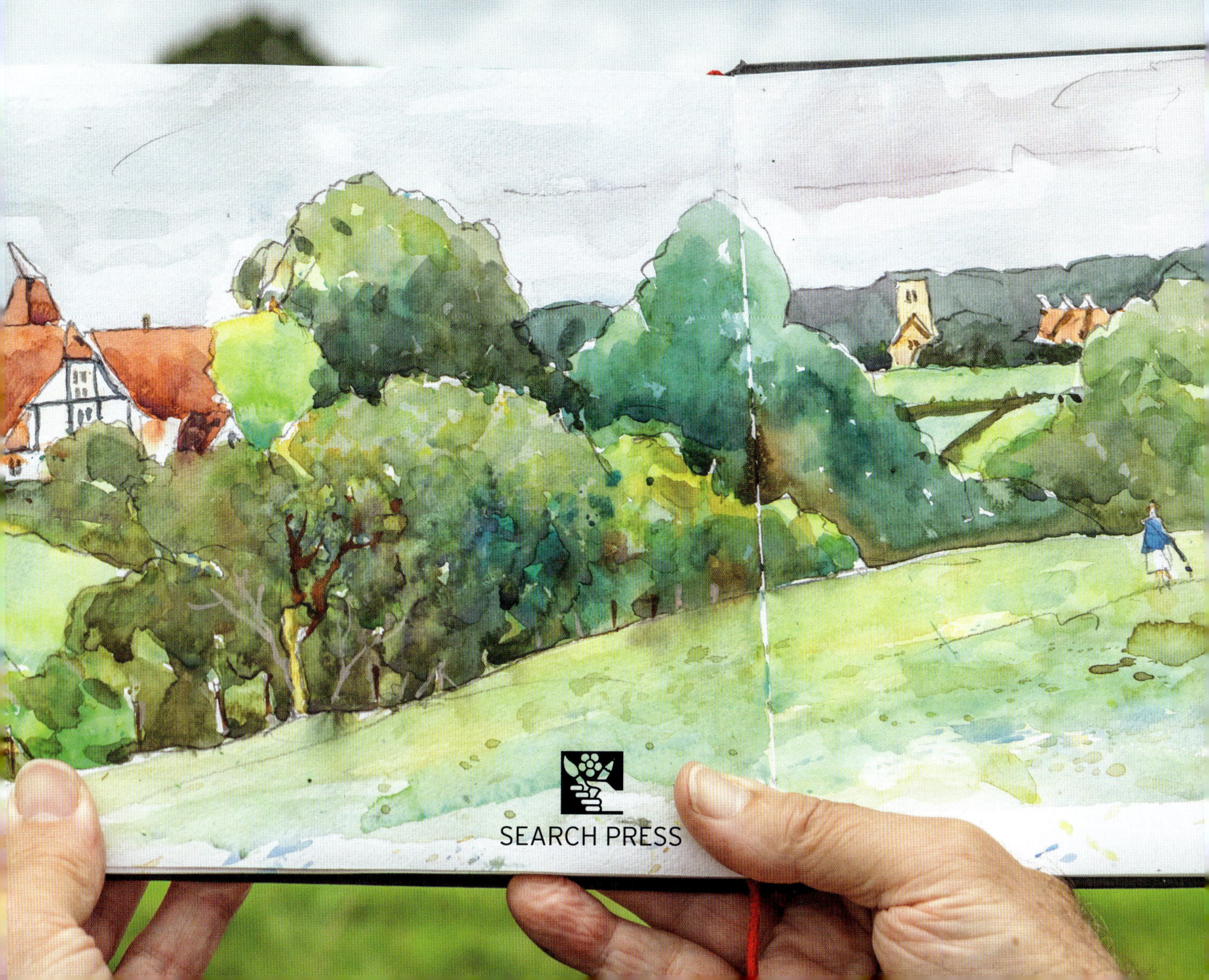

First published in 2023
Search Press Limited
Wellwood, North Farm Road,
Tunbridge Wells, Kent TN2 3DR

Photographs by Mark Davison at Search Press
Studios and on location

Photographs and design copyright ©
Search Press Ltd. 2023
Photograph on page 33 © Schmincke finest artists'
colours – Germany

ISBN: 978-1-78221-958-3
ebook ISBN: 978-1-78126-953-4

Suppliers

If you have difficulty in obtaining any of the
materials and equipment mentioned in this book,
then please visit the Search Press website for details
of suppliers: www.searchpress.com

You are invited to visit the author's website:
barryherniman.com

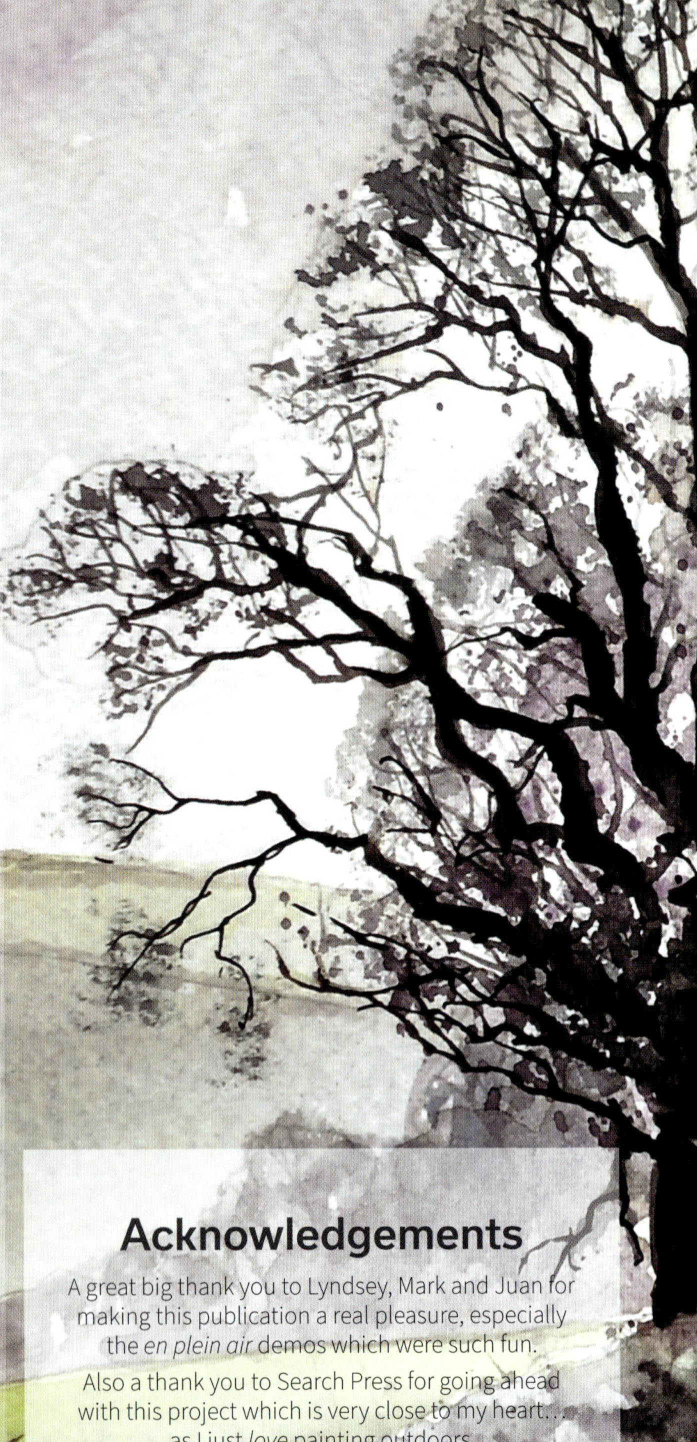

Acknowledgements

A great big thank you to Lyndsey, Mark and Juan for
making this publication a real pleasure, especially
the *en plein air* demos which were such fun.

Also a thank you to Search Press for going ahead
with this project which is very close to my heart…
as I just *love* painting outdoors.

Contents

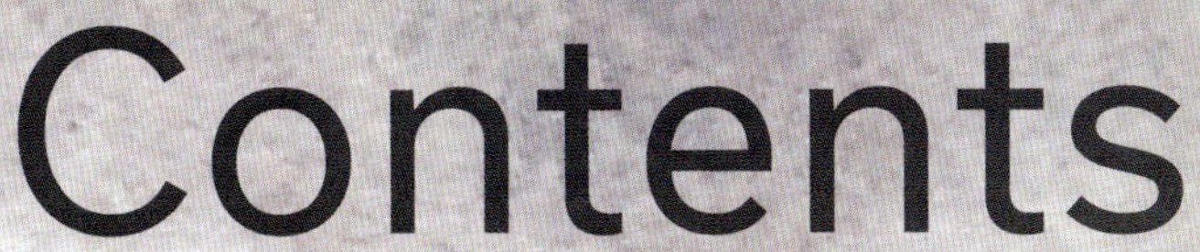

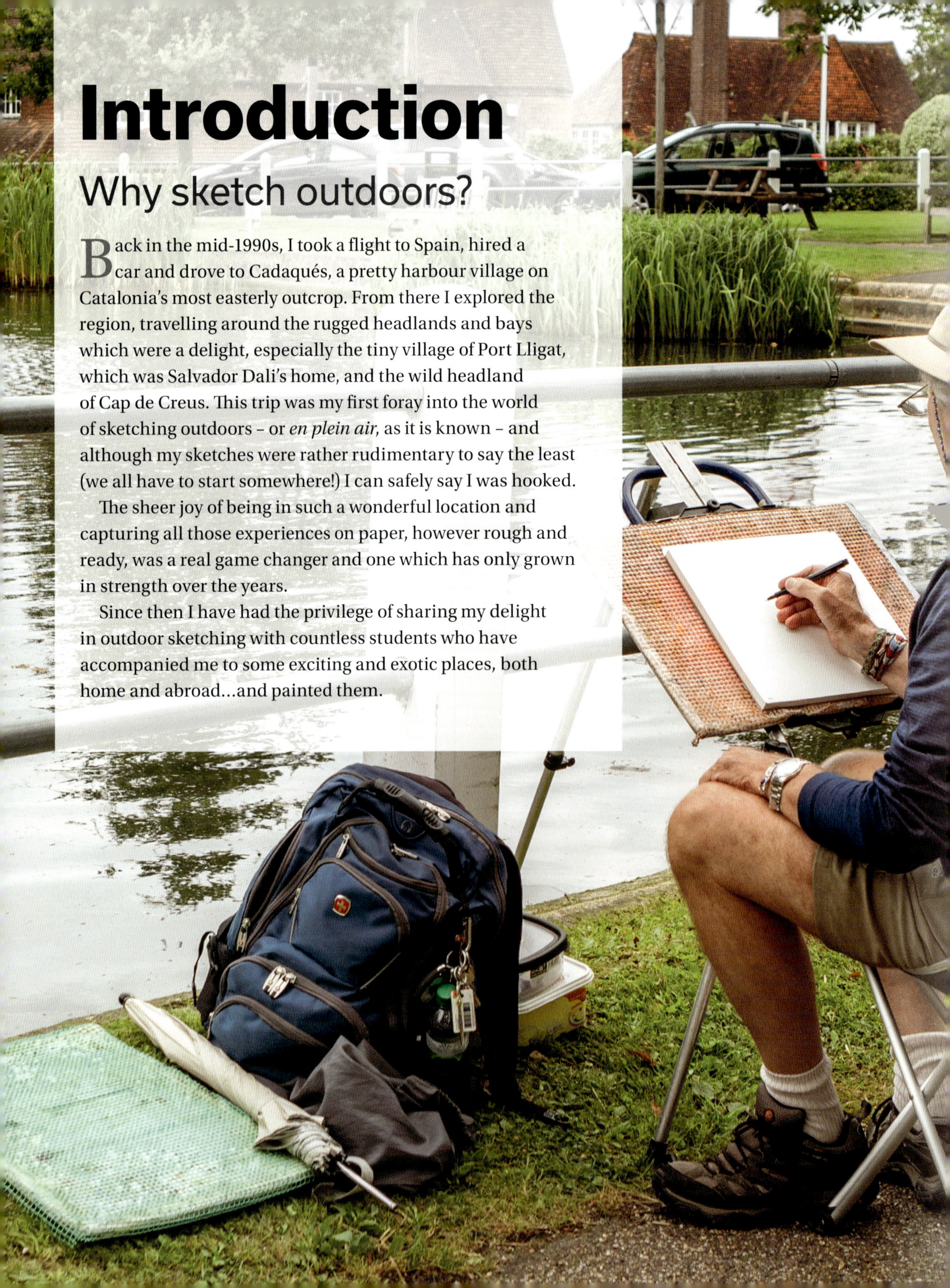

Introduction

Why sketch outdoors?

Back in the mid-1990s, I took a flight to Spain, hired a car and drove to Cadaqués, a pretty harbour village on Catalonia's most easterly outcrop. From there I explored the region, travelling around the rugged headlands and bays which were a delight, especially the tiny village of Port Lligat, which was Salvador Dali's home, and the wild headland of Cap de Creus. This trip was my first foray into the world of sketching outdoors – or *en plein air*, as it is known – and although my sketches were rather rudimentary to say the least (we all have to start somewhere!) I can safely say I was hooked.

The sheer joy of being in such a wonderful location and capturing all those experiences on paper, however rough and ready, was a real game changer and one which has only grown in strength over the years.

Since then I have had the privilege of sharing my delight in outdoor sketching with countless students who have accompanied me to some exciting and exotic places, both home and abroad...and painted them.

Today, with an ever-increasing body of artists taking up the challenge of painting *en plein air*, the spectre of being open to all the elements and the fear of the gaze of the general public seems to be evaporating, thank goodness. More and more people are experiencing the delight of organizations like Urban Sketching, whose manifesto states, 'We draw on location, indoors or out, capturing what we see from *direct* observation'; and this just about sums up how I feel about outdoor sketching.

I will be focusing on speed and efficiency in your sketching, so you will be able to produce quick and pleasing renditions of your chosen subjects without getting bogged down with detail overload. This way you will develop your own sketching 'shorthand', enabling you to turn out a satisfying sketch within any given timeframe. So saddle up your painting gear and get ready for an exciting experience. Your journey into the great outdoors starts now!

Don't get lost in the detail
A very quick on-site demo to show students how I go about producing a sketch without getting bogged down with detail. This was done with a waterproof felt pen and watercolour washes to show what can be produced in a very limited time. What it lacks in accuracy, I think you'll agree, it gains in vitality.

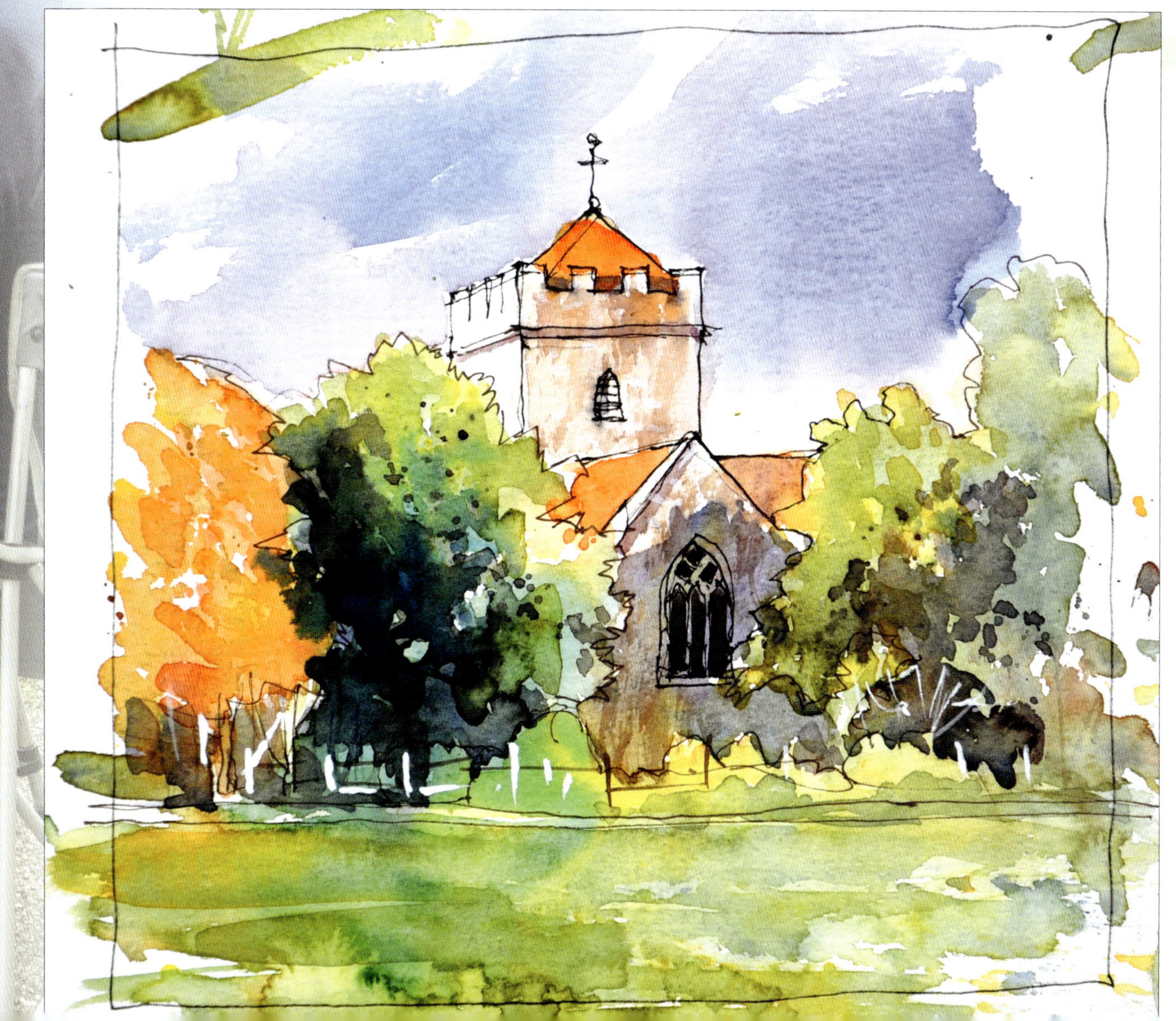

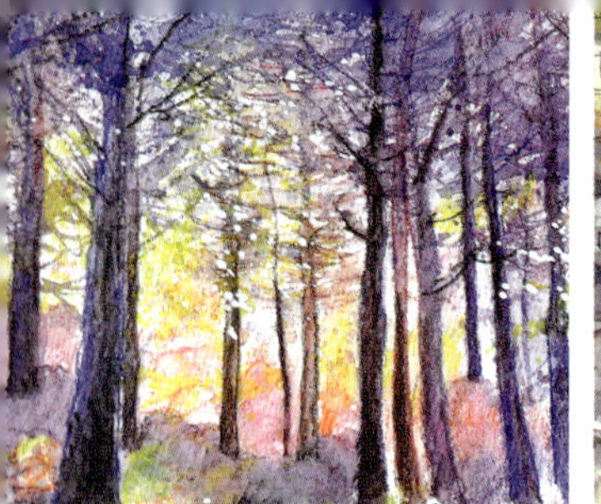
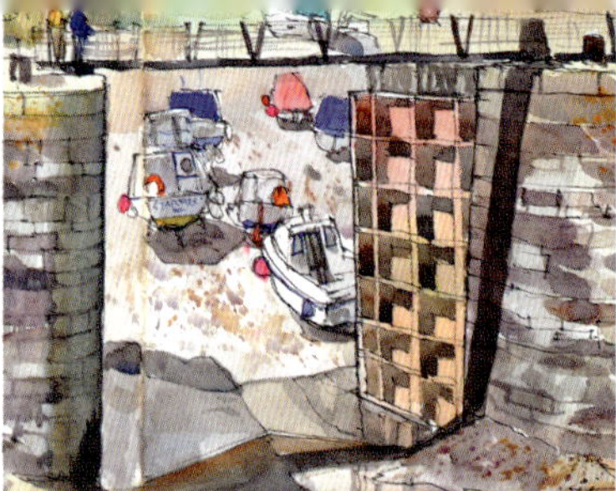
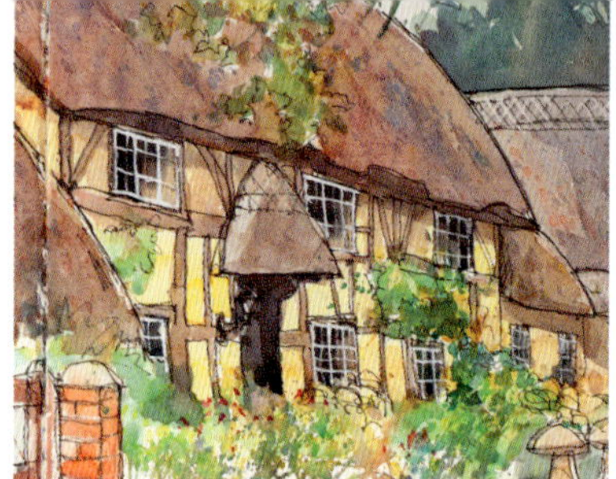
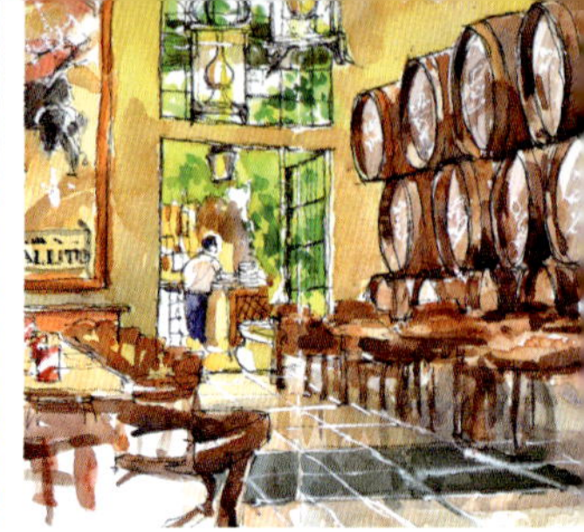

Experiencing the outdoors

Ever since my first ventures into the world of *en plein air* painting, I have been an advocate of the pleasures and skills that arise from being immersed in all the sights, sounds and visual stimuli that are afforded to the artist. Just taking time to do a 10-minute sketch will impart so much information about the scene to the senses, which can be recalled when painting at a later date.

Choosing a subject to paint or sketch can feel like a time-consuming and thankless task if you let it. I feel that too much time can be spent looking for that sublime 'picturesque' scene when a subject could be right in front of you. So if you are caught up in this web, repeat the mantra 'It's only a sketch' and get cracking with the first thing that grabs you. If you don't like it then move on to the next! It won't be long before you can see sketching possibilities at every turn.

I remember on a painting trip to Staithes in North Yorkshire I sat next to a couple from a local art group who looked rather bemused. When I asked them why they weren't painting they replied they 'couldn't see anything to inspire them'! I'm sorry, but if you can't find anything to inspire you in this wonderful coastal village perched on the hillside, then maybe *en plein air* is not your thing!

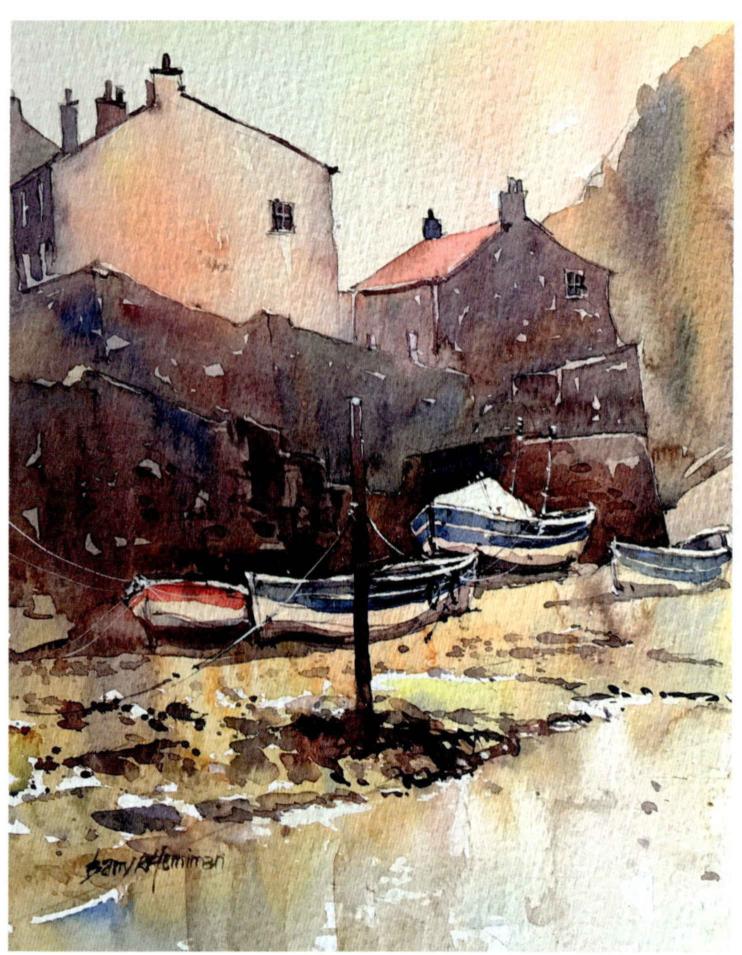

What inspires you?

One of the women who came on my painting breaks stated that she categorically 'did not do boats!' So if we were anywhere near a harbour scene, I would seek out an alternative for her to paint in the area. This also applies when you are setting off on a sketching trip: make sure you have a fair idea of what you might find to inspire you at your chosen location.

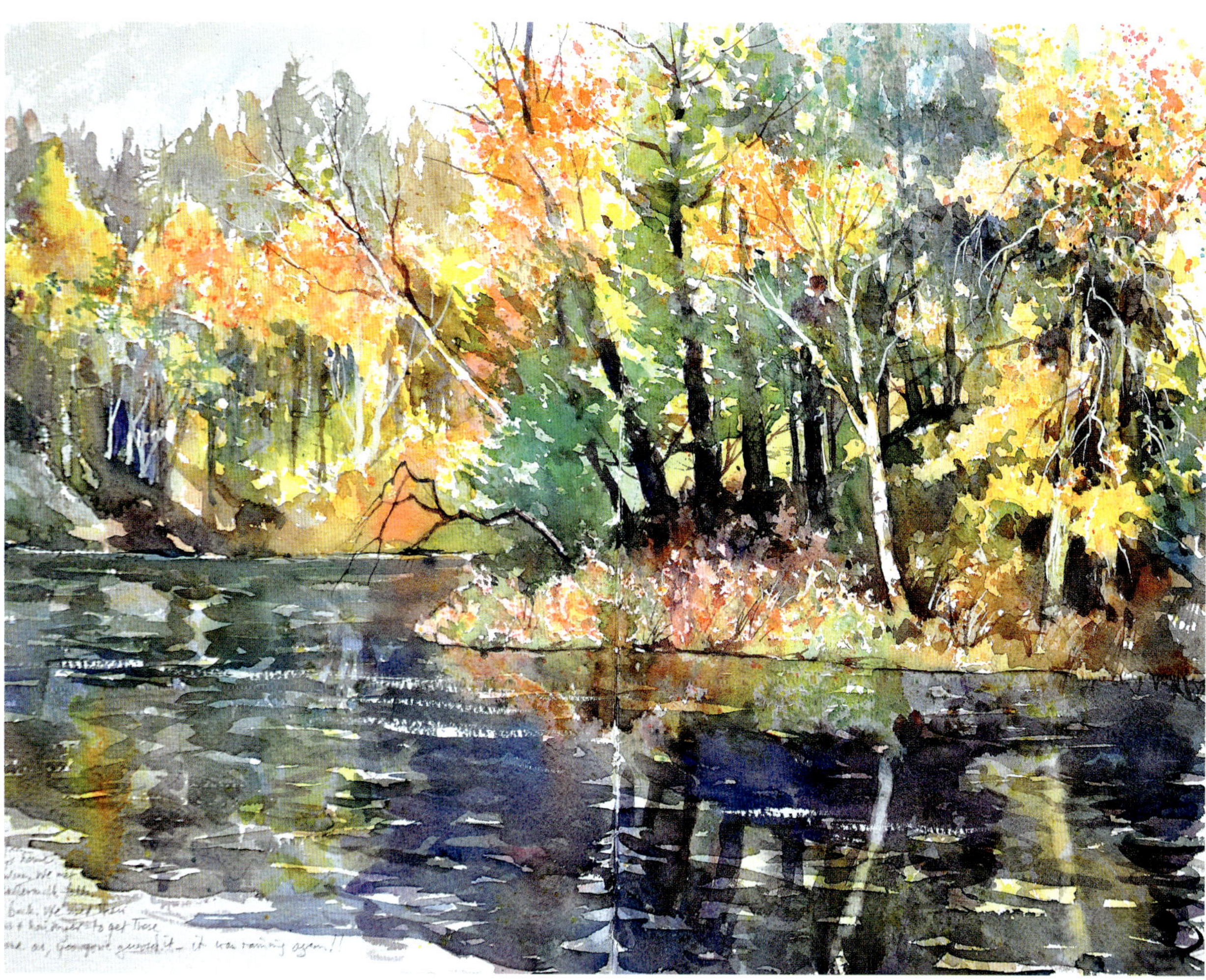

Colours of fall

For me, the wonderful fall colours never fail to inspire. My favourite place to find them is on the East Coast of America in the heart of New England. Our rented house in Vermont's Lake District is a short stroll down to the water's edge where there are painting subjects galore right on our doorstep so to speak. Midway between Lakes Pauline and Rescue is a perfect base and I have returned here year after year and never tired of the wonderful scenery.

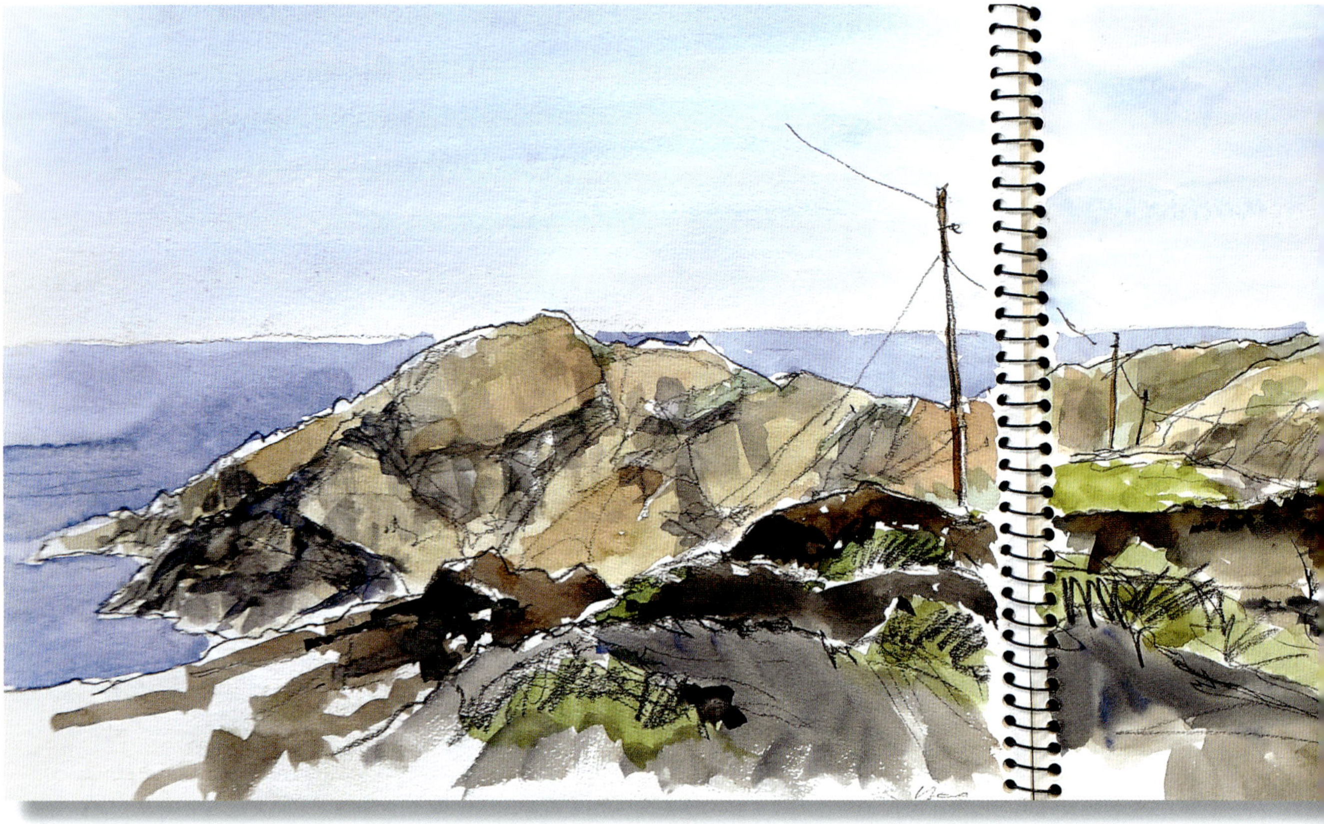

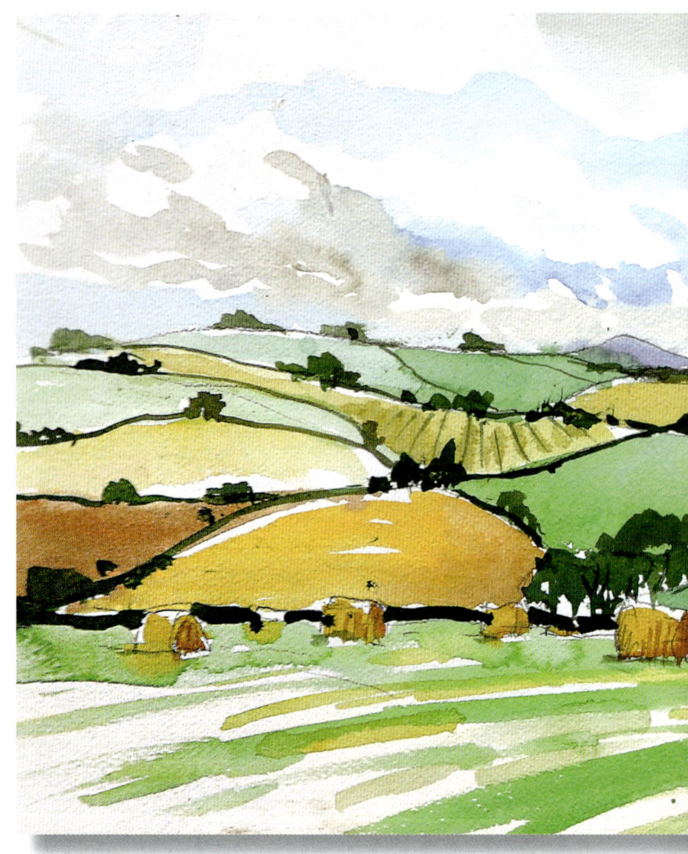

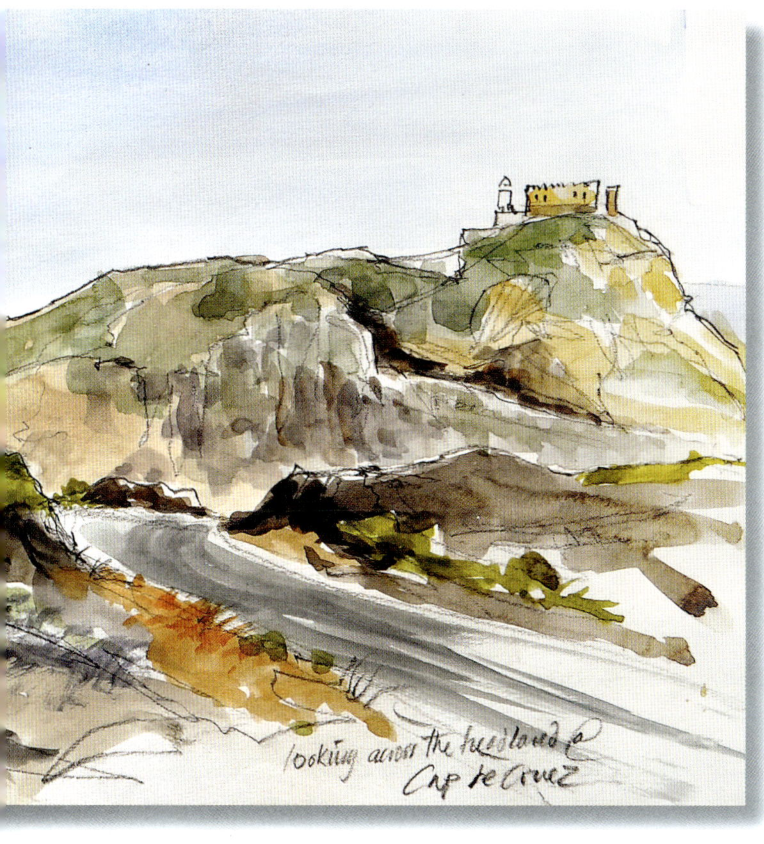

My early sketches outdoors
My very early forays into outdoor sketching at Cap de Creus in Spain (left) and a local scene across our fields in Herefordshire, UK, with hay bales (below). These early sketchbooks were spiral-bound and only contained cartridge paper, which wasn't the best for watercolours.

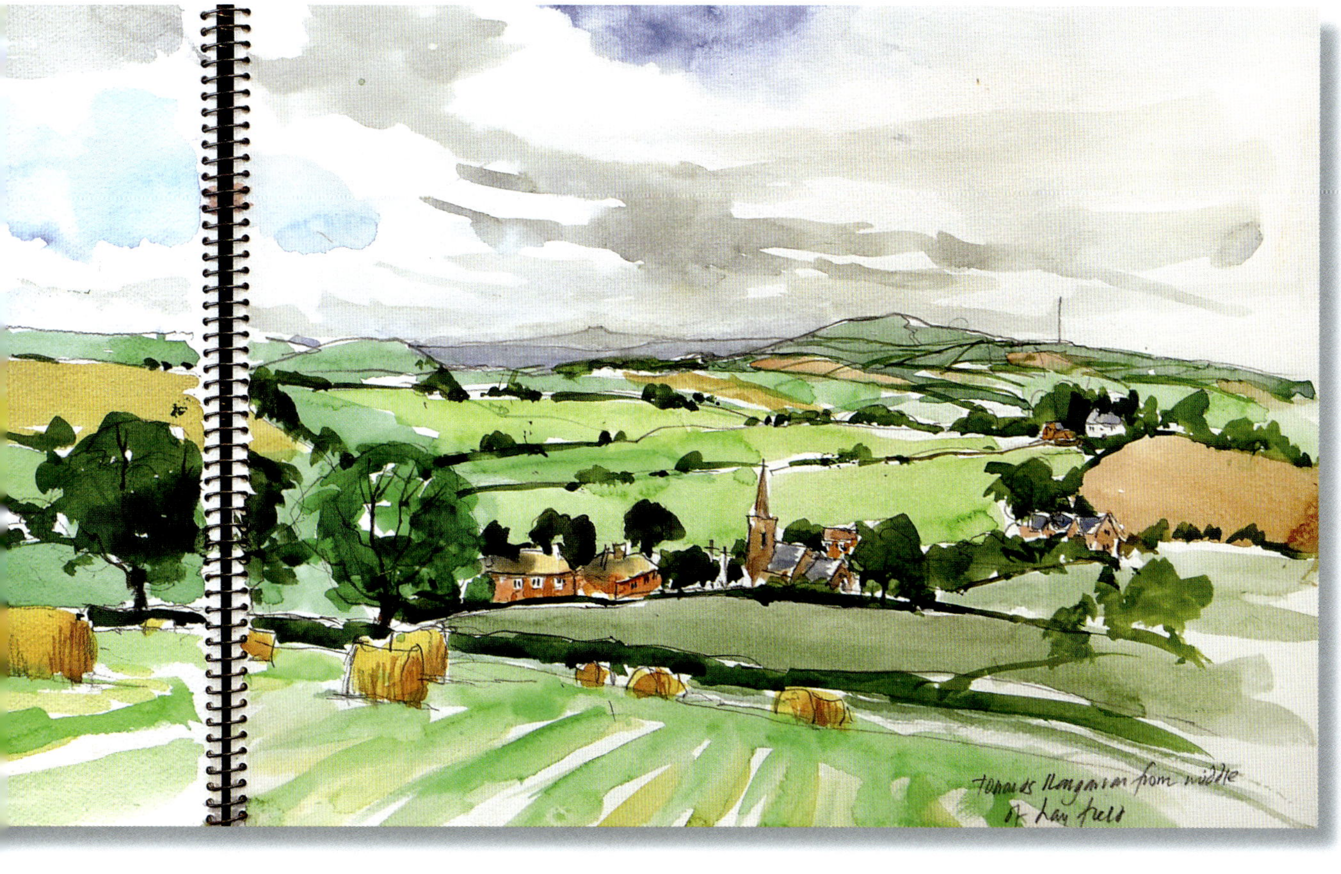

Working from photographs versus working *en plein air*

Should you work from photographs or from real life? This is always quite an emotive subject. Sketching outside, in front of your subject, gives your work an immediacy that is lacking in a studio piece worked from photographs. But it is not always possible, even with the best will in the world, to stop and sketch, so this is where the camera is invaluable.

One thing I would say is that when using a photograph for reference, don't follow it slavishly, just refer to it for information and inject some of your own feelings about the scene into your painting.

Taking reference photographs for future paintings

The camera is a great tool but it just cannot see all the different lights and darks or the tonal differentiation between them that we can observe with the naked eye. The camera does a great job of capturing the mid-tones, but the lights invariably turn towards white and the darks towards black. This happens more often when you are taking a shot of an overall scene that inspires you, but contains a lot of contrast.

To get a more representative exposure of that particular area, I take a series of shots of that same scene but zone in on some of the individual elements (see opposite).

I have chosen this bridge scene as a classic example of these extremes of exposure, as it has both a very light sky and also very dark shadows under the bridge arch.

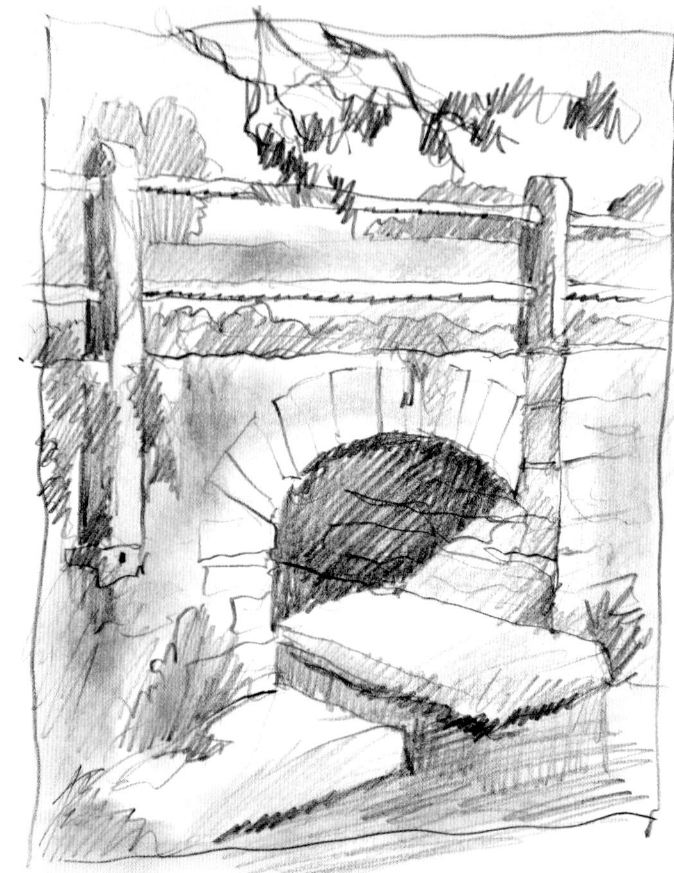

Sketch made using reference photograph opposite
A quick tonal sketch, created from the photograph opposite, no bigger than postcard size, will help to focus the mind on the different tones before you begin.

Overall picture

There is a small bridge on Garron Brook that runs under the lane into the hamlet of Langstone, Herefordshire, and I thought this would be a good example of how to photograph for reference purposes.

This is the overall view and as you can see, all the mid-tones are fine but the shadow under the bridge is almost black and the scene above the bridge is somewhat washed out.

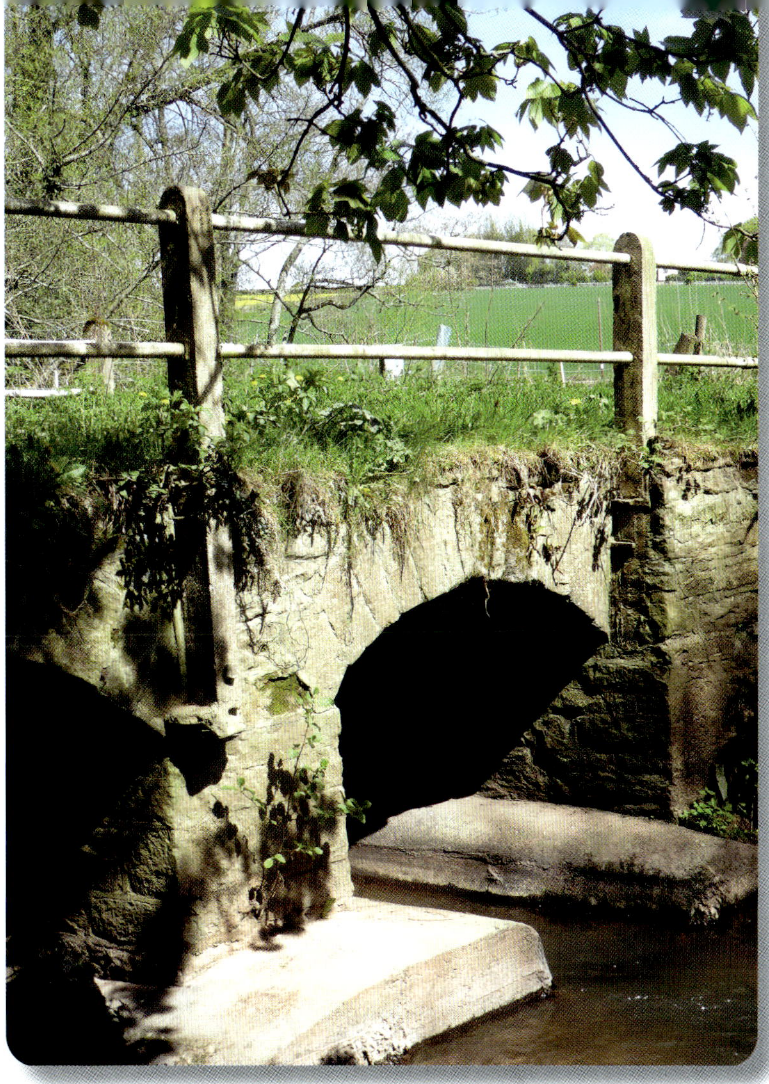

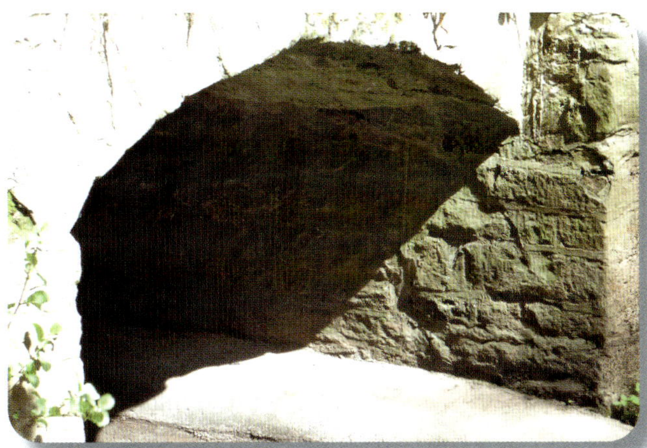

Detail of the darks

In this photograph I zoomed into the area under the bridge arch and the camera has exposed for that dark area so that you can now see the detail there.

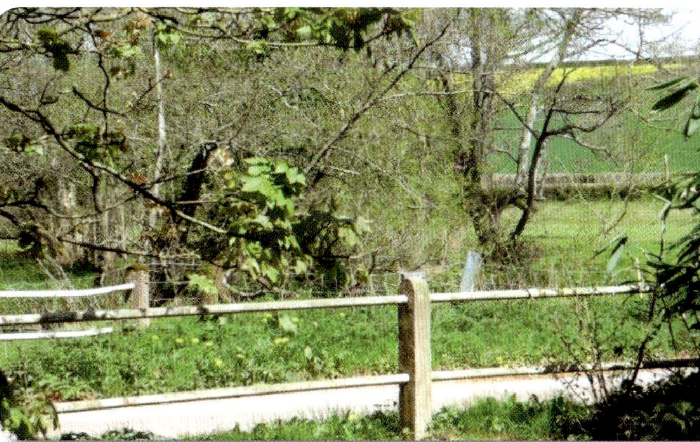

Additional detail

I also took some photographs of the areas above the bridge, just for extra reference should I need it.

Pros and cons of using a camera

I am a real advocate for 'experiencing' your surroundings when sketching, and being sensitive to changes in light, weather, and noise – what my photographer insightfully called 'living the picture'. In stark contrast to this is a photograph which is an *exact* moment in time, like a still from a movie, where you only get a snapshot of the whole picture. A fraction of a second captured by a camera just replicates what the camera sees and how it sees it, and this can be rather disappointing when referring back to it later. However, it is also here that the photograph comes into its own, for example, capturing a transient moment like the sun breaking through the clouds for a moment. This would be extremely difficult to recall from memory with any accuracy and detail, so a photograph is a perfect prompt.

Also, which lens is being used will determine how much distortion there will be to the scene. So many compact cameras and phone cameras these days have a somewhat wide-angle lens, which is great for getting in all that lovely view, but it compresses it considerably and bears little relation to what's seen with the naked eye. That lovely vista of background mountains is then reduced to a rather thin and ineffectual line across the photograph and you could end up asking why you took it in the first place (see my disappointing photograph opposite!).

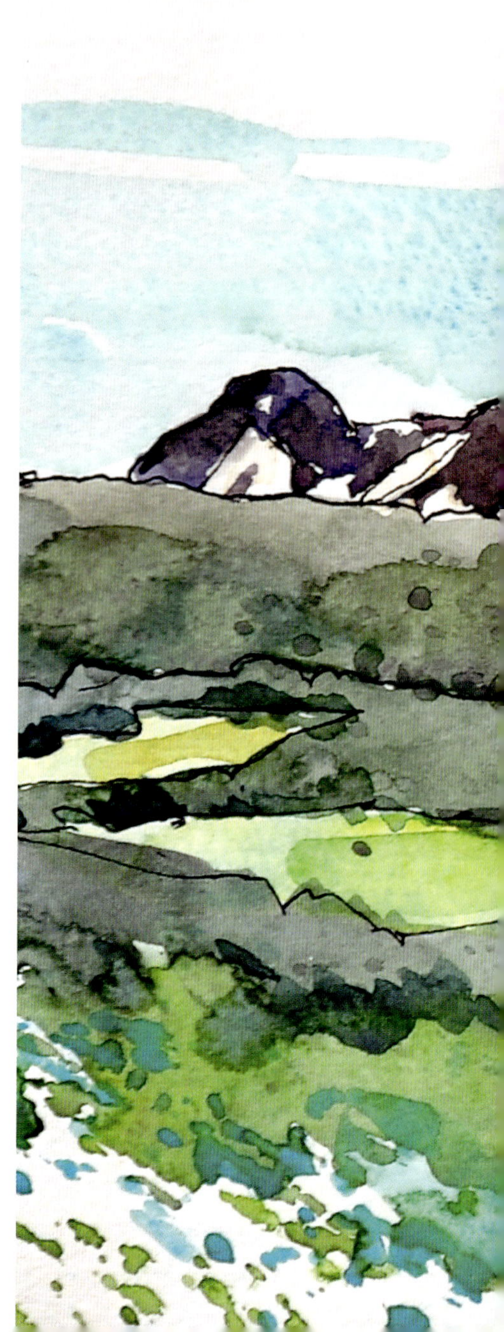

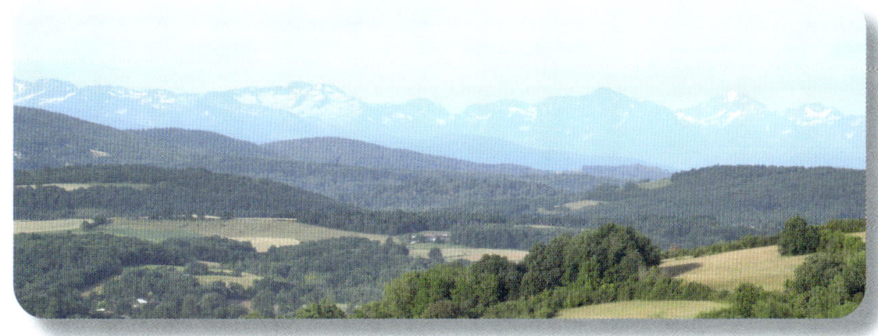

Manzac d'en Bas

For the first few days at Manzac, France, the Pyrenees were hidden behind a veil of cloud, but one morning it lifted and we got our first view of the snow-capped mountains. I took a panoramic photograph and then got the sketchbook out to capture the mountain vista. Checking my photographs later, I was really disappointed with the result, shown left. Thank goodness I had the foresight to sketch the view as I saw it rather than relying on what proved to be a very disappointing photograph.

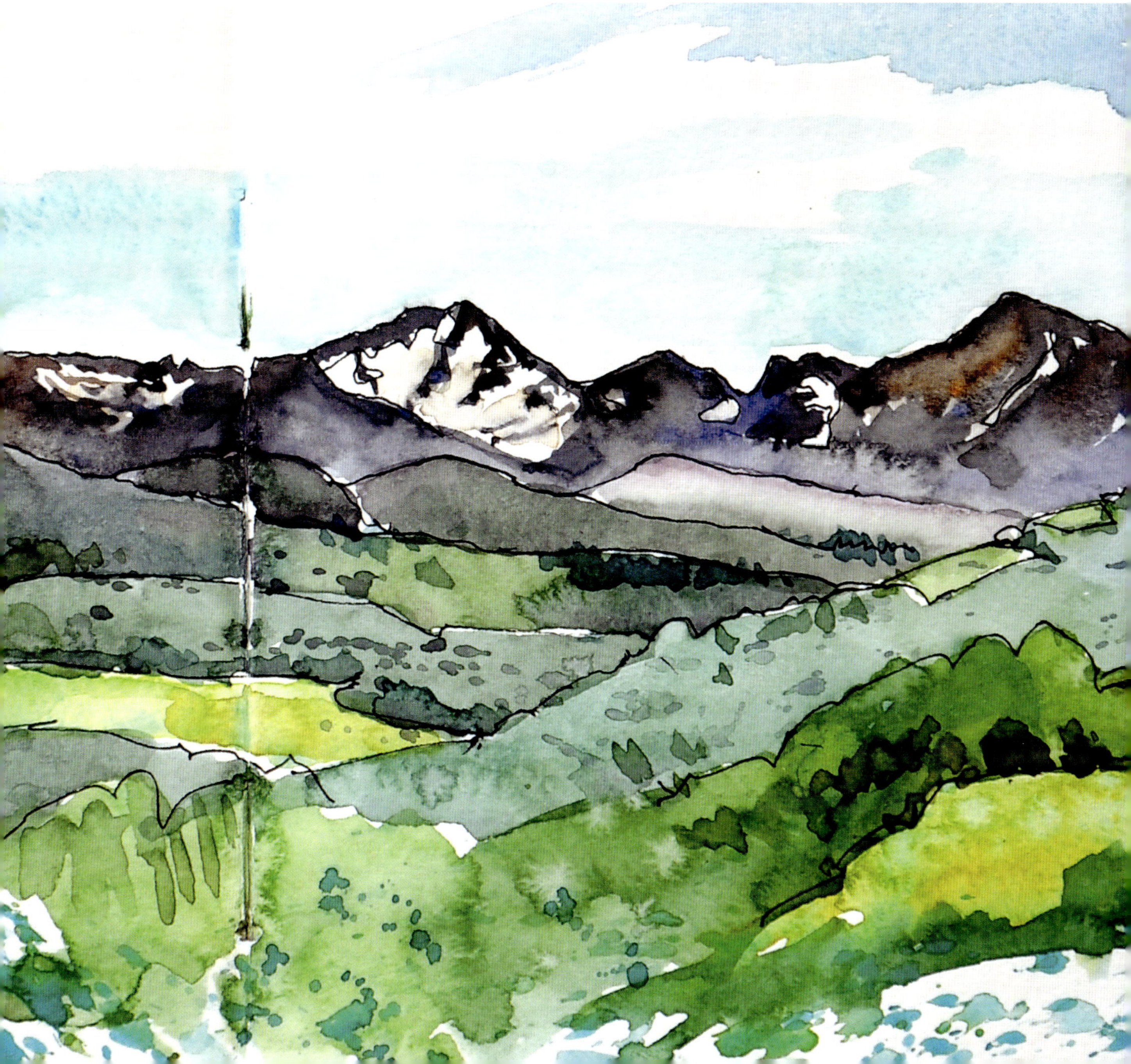

What do I need?

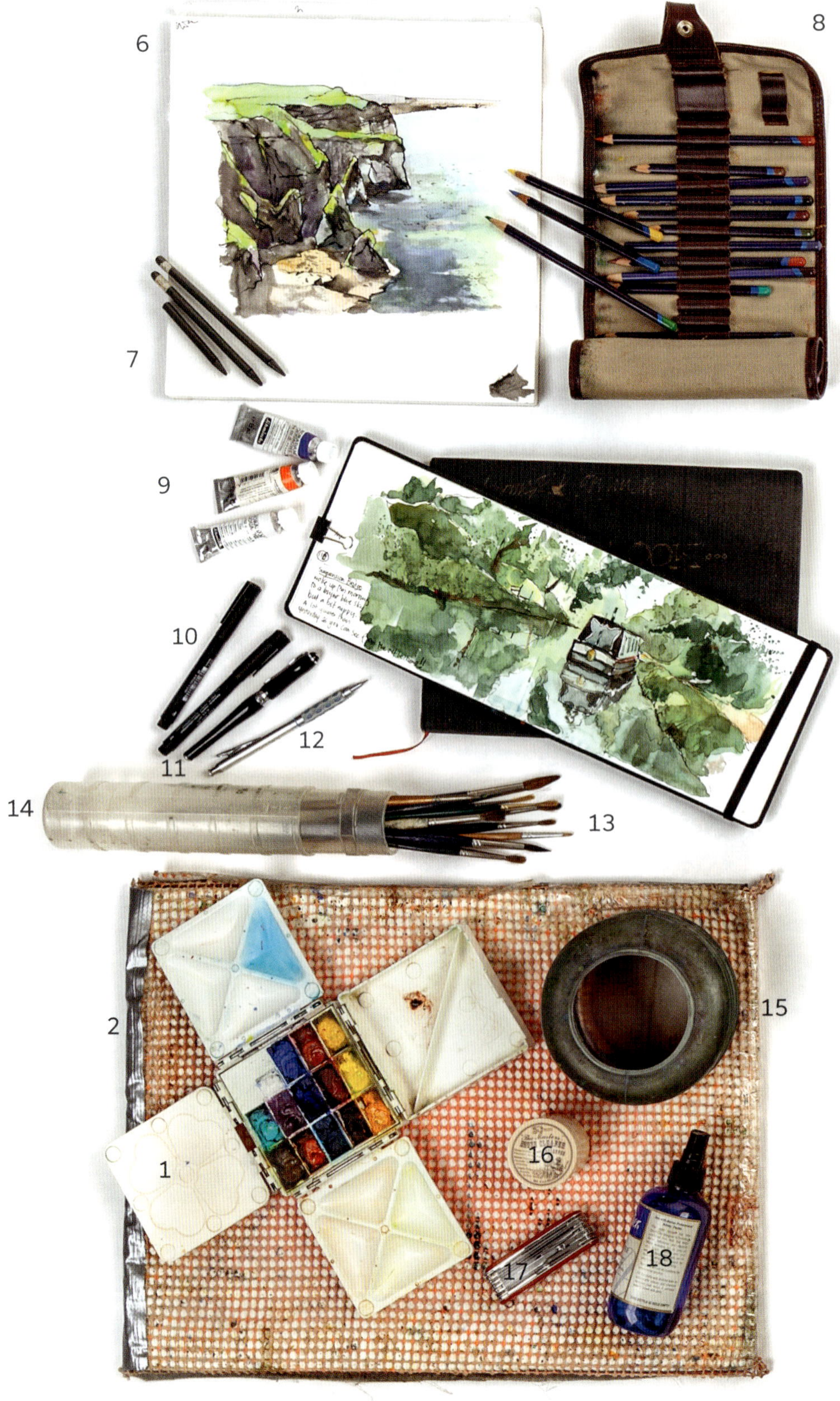

Over the years I have seen students loading up with everything but the kitchen sink and then having to lug it around all the painting venues. Obviously a lot boils down to personal choice (and, often, cost) but I suggest that you choose your essentials and leave the rest at home.

Here's the basic kit I take with me 'into the field'. It's all explained over the next few pages.

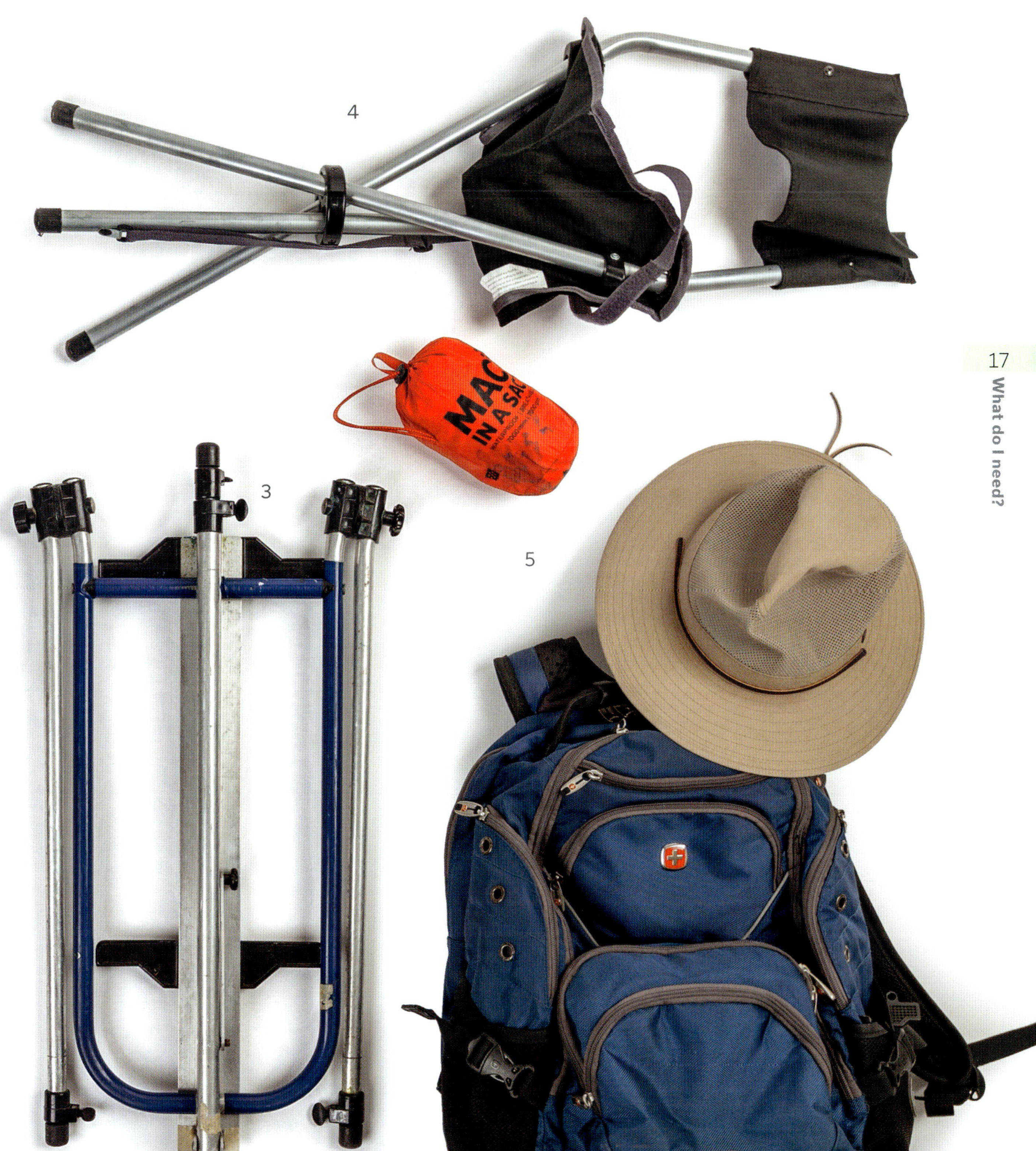

My basic travelling kit

My pared down kit for when I'm on the move includes my Cloverleaf Paintbox with my paint wells full of paint ready for the tour. I use Schmincke Horadam Artists' Watercolours which are pure pigment with the addition of gum arabic. This means that the paints never go hard like some brands. Just a quick squirt of water from your atomiser spray bottle and the paints are rejuvenated and ready for use. Because I know they can always be restored to their original juicy state, I always dry my colours off before travel – this stops wet pigment from migrating from well to well in transit.

On the following pages I have described my favoured pieces of kit to give you an idea of what I take out sketching with me. Hopefully this will provide a useful yardstick when deciding what you need for your sketching forays.

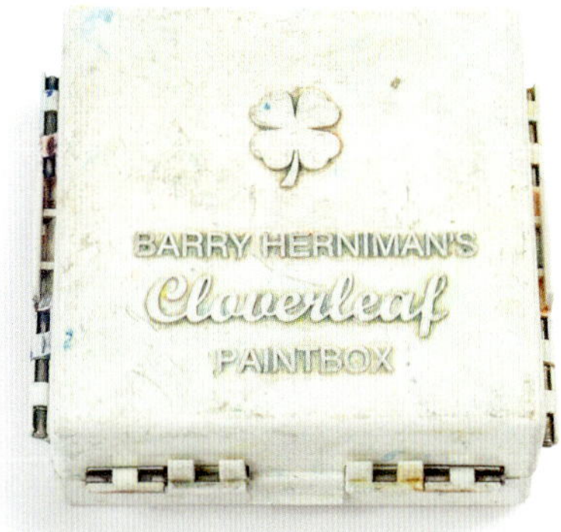

The Cloverleaf Paintbox

1 Paintbox and palette

Over the years I have gone through all possible assortments of paintboxes and palettes for when I'm painting outdoors. Nothing really came up to scratch until I bought a rather expensive, handmade metal folding box that was advertised in the magazines. I used this for years, even upgrading to the larger version, but when I was asked the price by interested students (around £250 at the last count, many years ago) a glazed look would follow and that was the end of that.

So I decided to design my very own paintbox. I teamed up with Shelley in Guernsey, one of my painting students, who thought it was a great idea. After doing a mock-up out of a cereal packet we took it to one of her local computer designers to produce a prototype and my 'Cloverleaf Paintbox' was born.

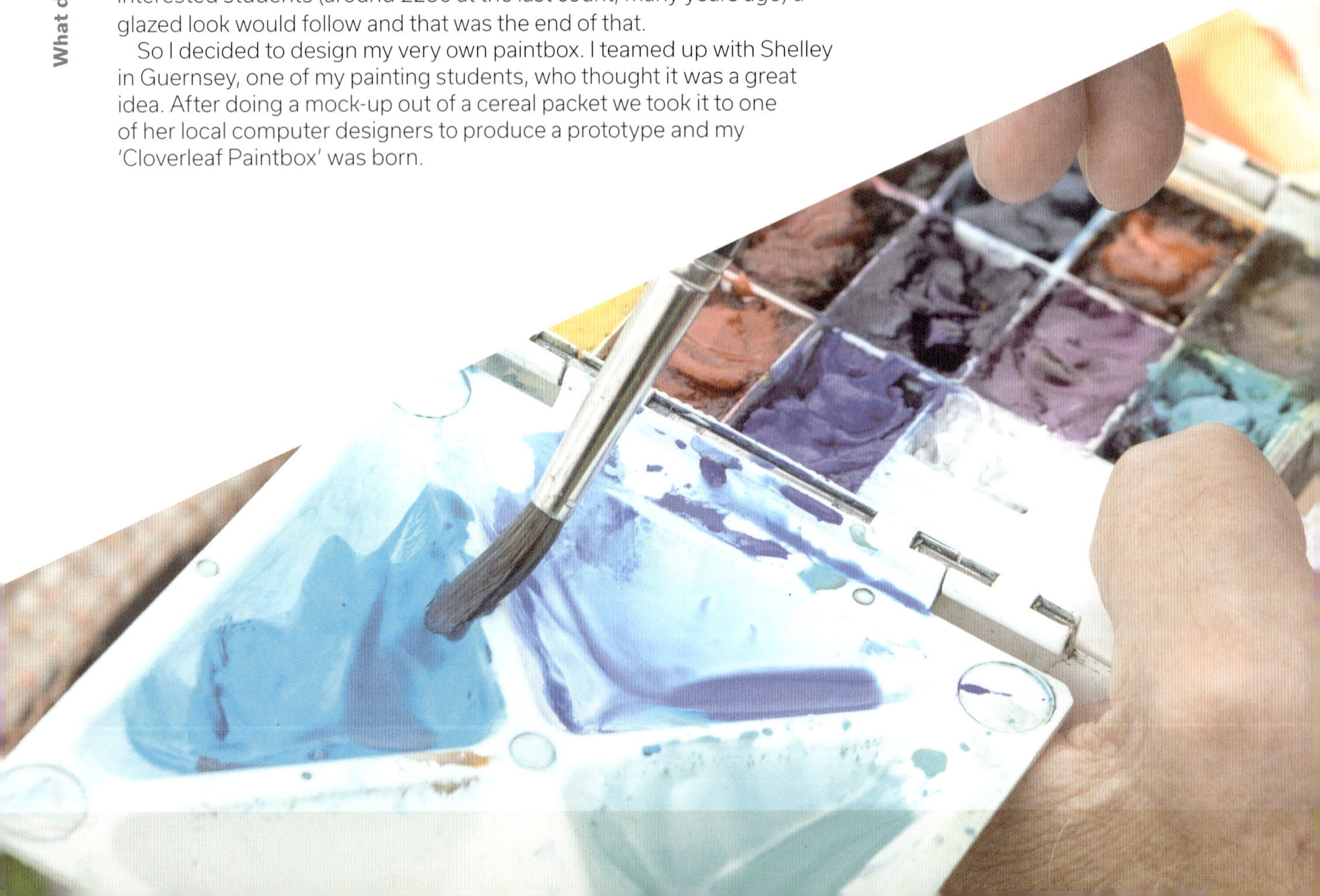

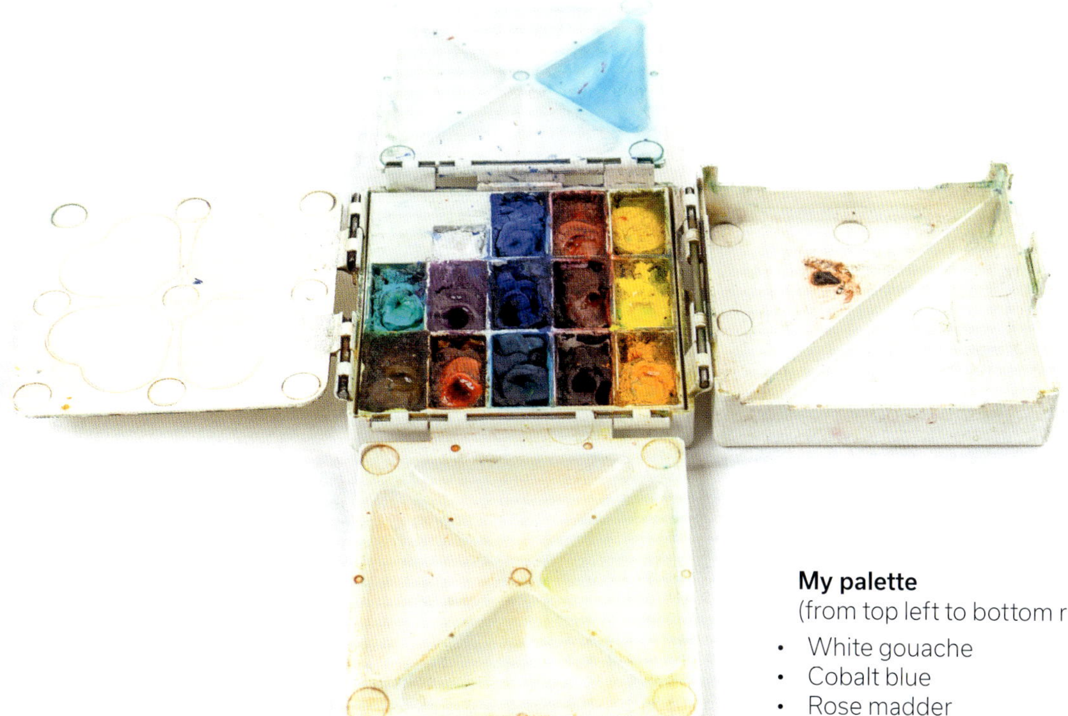

My palette
(from top left to bottom right)

- White gouache
- Cobalt blue
- Rose madder
- Pure yellow
- Cobalt turquoise (the only one that isn't transparent)
- Manganese violet
- Ultramarine
- Madder red dark
- Aureolin
- Schmincke yellow
- Schmincke orange
- Helio turquoise
- Madder brown
- Indian yellow

The Cloverleaf Paintbox has 13 deep wells, which will each take full pans, into which I squeeze a good amount of paint, enough for a week's painting at least! Over the years I have pared my colours down to those listed on the right which allow me to paint anywhere I choose to go, from the lush greens of an English wood to the sun-baked olive groves of Spain.

I have arrived at a palette of colours which are transparent or semi-transparent, to suit my way of painting with a series of transparent washes.

2 Lightweight drawing board

When sketching outside I tend to use my sketchbooks almost exclusively and I like to be able to move them about during the painting process, so I don't want them fixed to the easel. For this reason I have fashioned a *very* lightweight but surprisingly rigid and durable board made from 4mm (¼in) thick Foamcore covered with rubber non-slip matting. Using this board means I can place my sketchbook onto it and it will remain in position without my fixing it. It doesn't look very attractive, but it works a treat!

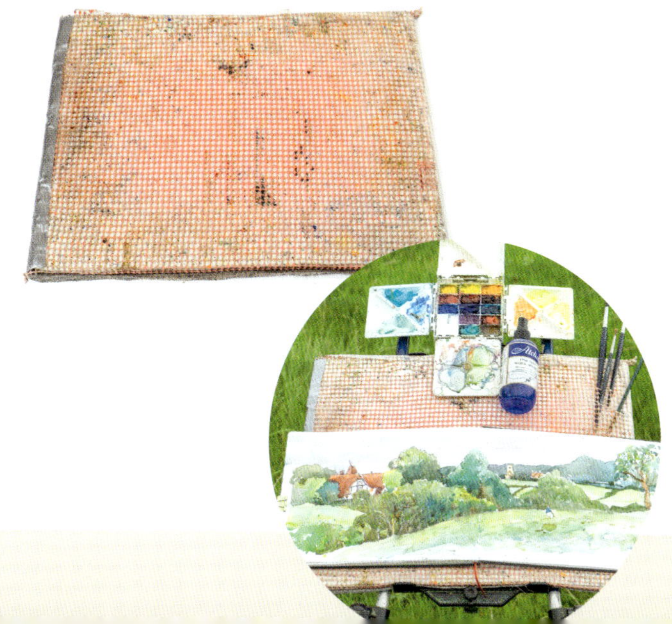

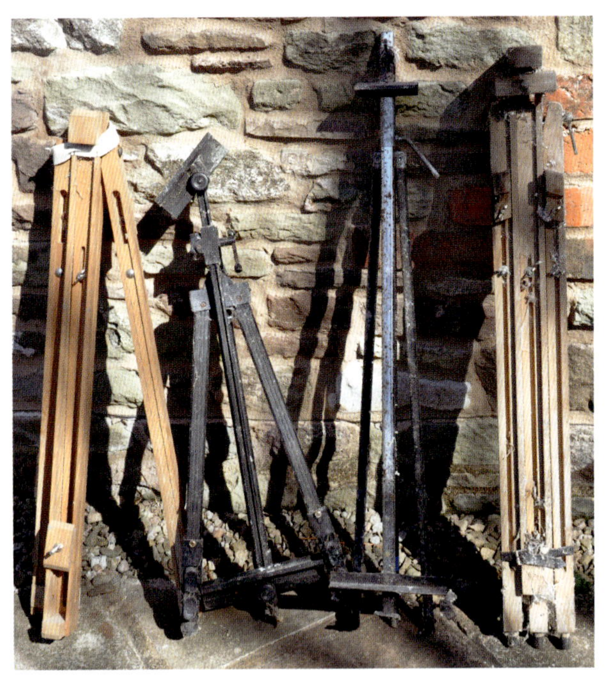

My graveyard of easels.

3 Folding easel

When painting outside I like to keep both hands free – one to hold the paintbox and the other the brush – and using an easel gives me this freedom.

Check that your easel actually does fold! This is very important for a watercolour artist. Easels are a bone of contention with many of my students who, over the years, have come up with all manner of heavy, unwieldy and in most cases highly inappropriate easels. I have seen them struggle with easels which can take over an hour to assemble. By the time they are set up, the rest of us have almost finished our sketch! However, I was also guilty of amassing a wide assortment of mediocre easels early on in my career until I was introduced to the Herring Versatile Easel (opposite) – and everything changed.

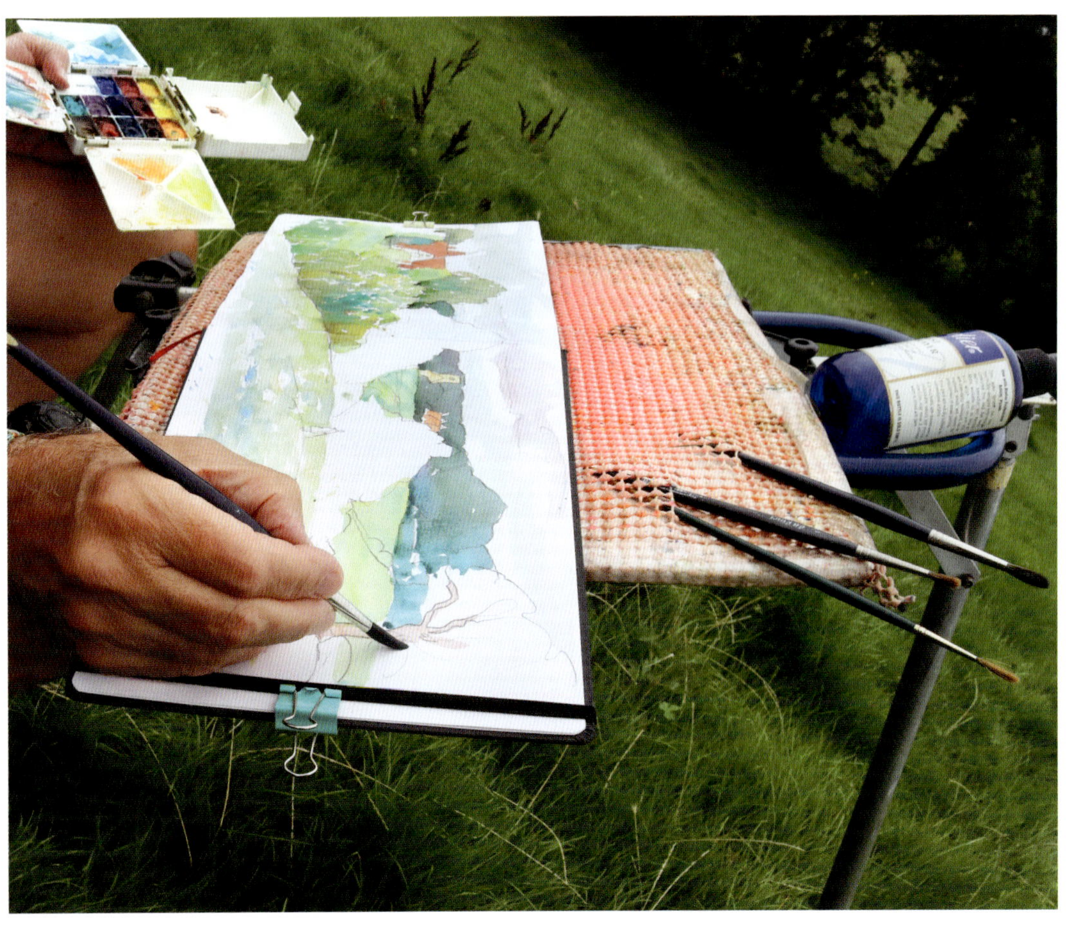

The Herring Versatile Easel
Don't struggle with a heavy, unruly
easel when you could use a compact
easel. This truly versatile easel can be
used flat for watercolours (see opposite)
and upright for oils and pastels. It is
lightweight with extendable legs for
various standing or sitting positions and
folds flat for ease of transportation.
Its approximate weight is 1.75kg (3¾lb).
Size closed: 70 x 35cm (27½ x 14in).

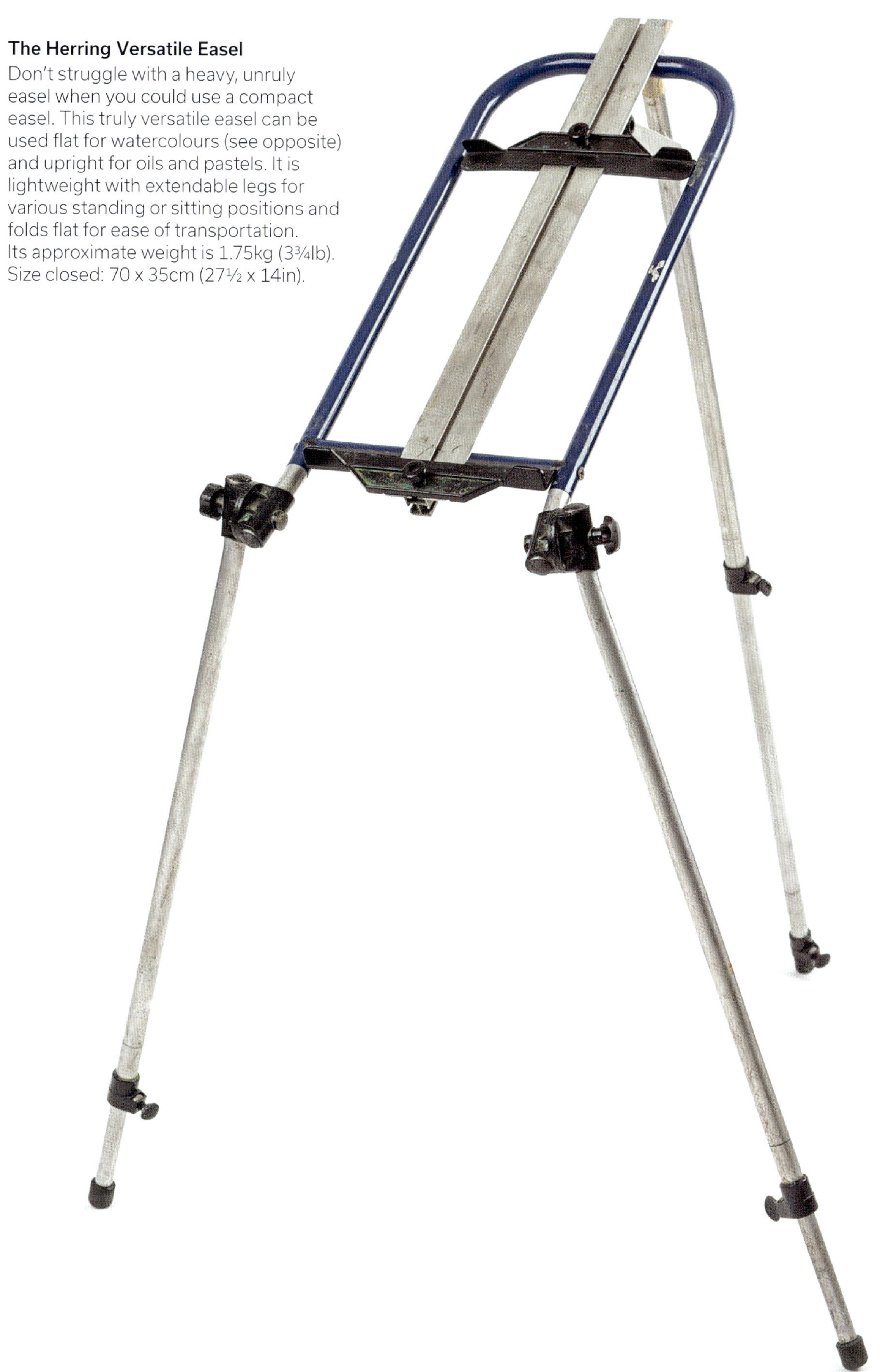

4 Seating

When I first started painting *en plein air*, the selection of portable, lightweight seating was rather limited. Not so today! By trawling the internet and visiting camping stores, I have been able to find an array of seats in all shapes and sizes to suit my needs.

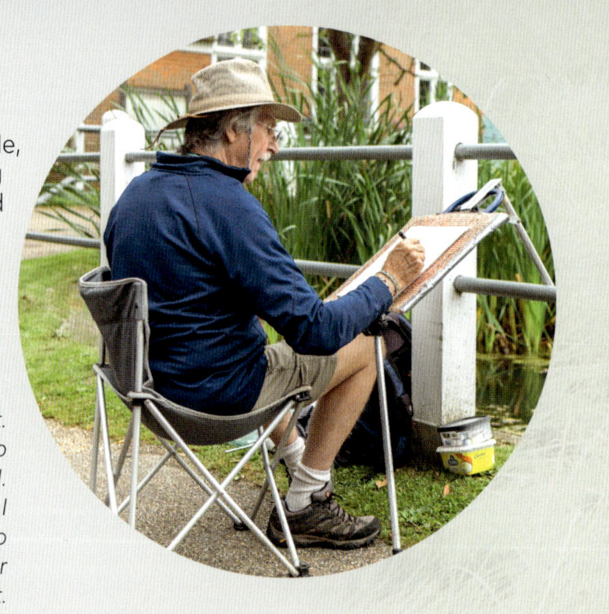

One prerequisite for me is a seat with a backrest. Many years ago I fell backwards out of a tree, trying to rescue our new kitten, and landed on a broken wall. I was lucky not to break any bones, but since then I find standing for any length of time quite arduous, so I need to sit when painting. I also need some lumbar support, so a backrest is paramount.

Large collapsible camping chair

A large and rather comfortable seat, made with a strong, tubular aluminium frame and a canvas seat and backrest. The one I have also has a folding side table attached, which is great for water pots and so forth. The two sides simply snap together when folded up for transportation. Because of its size, this chair is not ideal for field trips which entail a lot of walking, as it soon becomes rather cumbersome, but if I'm working on site then this is fine.

Compact folding camping chair

This is one of my favourite portable chairs for when I am working in the UK. The scissor design allows for the chair to be easily folded and stored in a carry bag with a shoulder strap for easy transportation.

This style of chair comes in all shapes and sizes and is easily obtainable from a variety of outlets.

Vango seat and backrest

I sourced this seat for when I was doing my 'travelling sketchbook' hiking/painting tour. I needed a very lightweight, collapsible seat with a backrest that could be easily attached to my rucksack and this fitted the bill. There's a myriad of lightweight folding stools out there but you try finding one with a backrest...

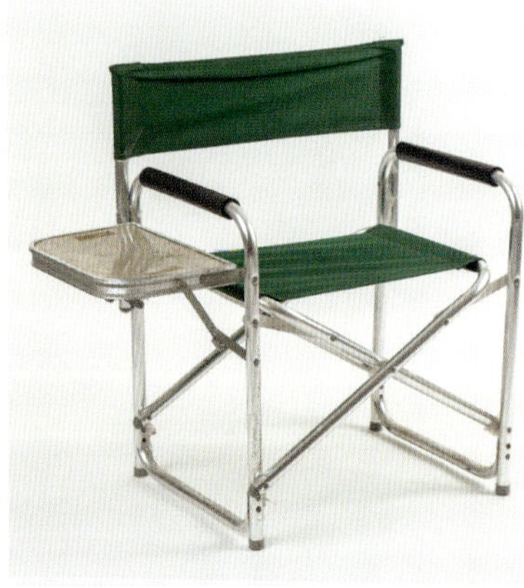

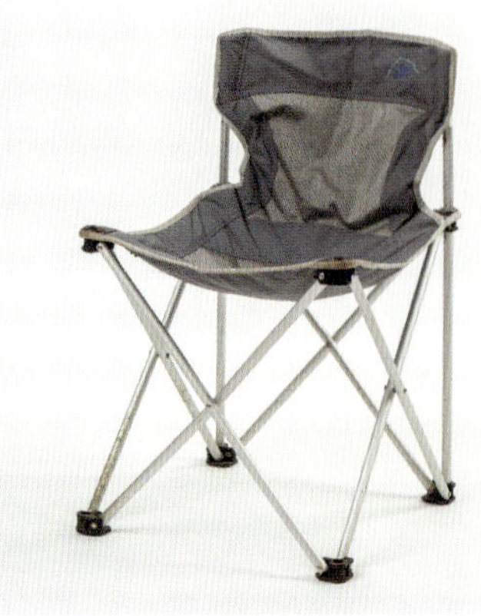

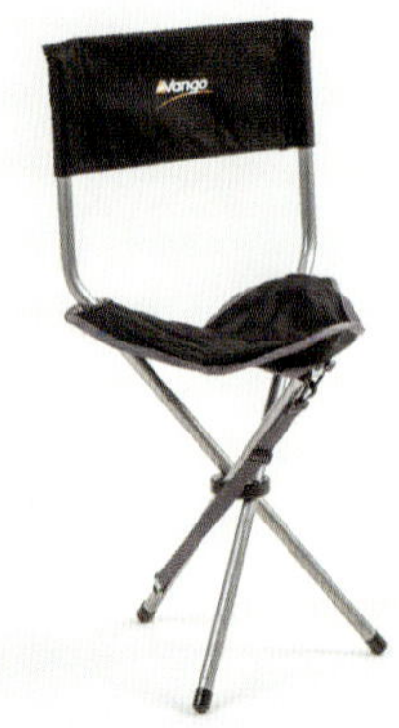

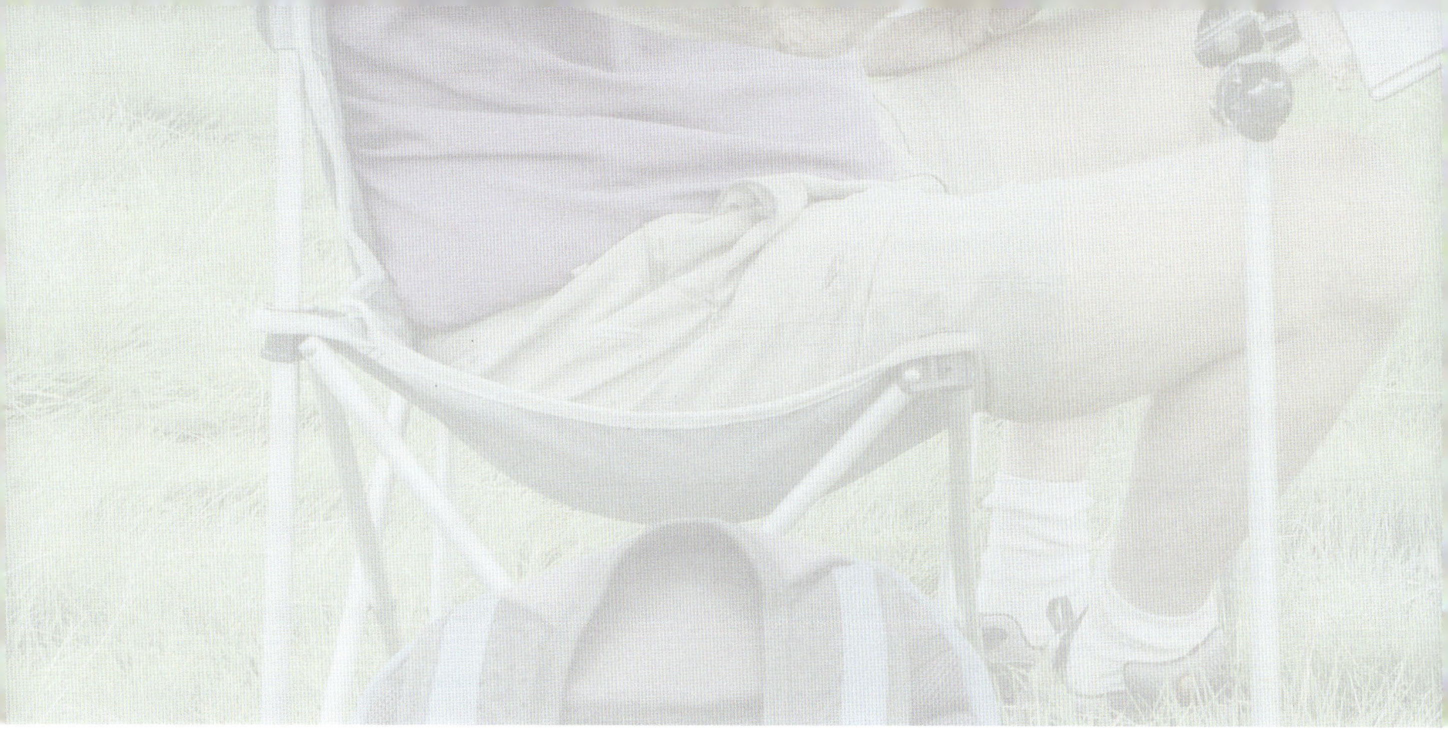

Trekology portable camping chair

This extremely light, strong and portable seat is just great for those trips abroad where baggage limitations are a concern. The frame of the seat is made up of aluminium poles connected by shock cords, which allow the whole frame to be 'broken' down and stored in its own small storage bag. The durable seating fabric is stretched between the four upright supports to provide a comfortable seat with an integral backrest, and it all weighs just 1.4kg (3lb).

Taope portable camping chair

This has a very similar construction and materials as the Trekology chair, the main differences being the seat height and the backrest. I found that the Trekology chair was great in terms of weight and compactness but with my long legs I needed a chair that stood higher off the ground and this chair fits the bill perfectly. It's also very lightweight, just 1.5kg (3¼lb).

Folding parasol

A great addition to the painting kit is a small parasol, complete with universal joint clamp which allows you to fix it anywhere on your chair/easel. I use this piece of equipment when it gets hot or when visiting sunnier climes. Keeping the baking sun off you and your work is a real plus and opens up a lot of potential painting locations that would otherwise prove too uncomfortable to work in. Often the best spot is somewhere exposed, and the last thing you want is heat stroke.

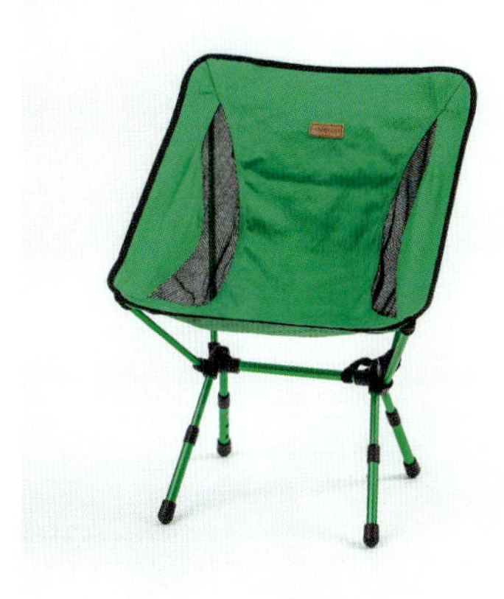

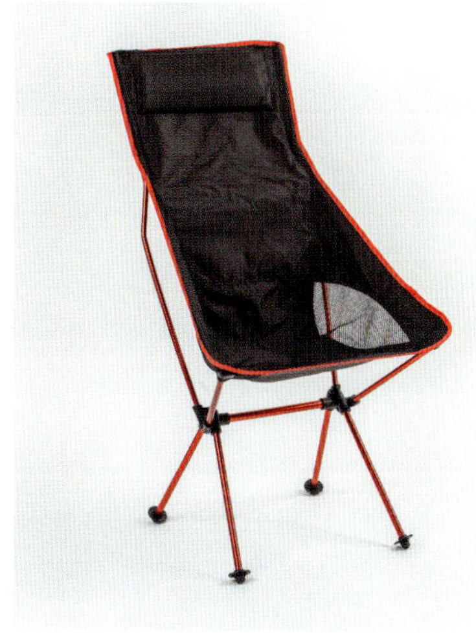

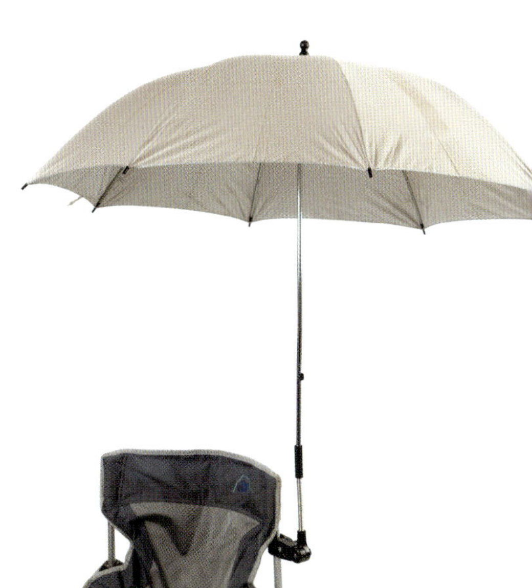

5 Clothing

This is a very personal subject and obviously very dependent on time of year and painting location, whether home or abroad. So I will keep this section to the minimum, just giving you a few tips on possibly the more essential items you might need.

Rainwear

The most obvious piece of equipment to take on excursions in places like the rainy UK is a suitable waterproof jacket with a hood as you just never know with the weather. Some warm gloves or mittens are also a boon for those rather chilly, overcast days, as it's rather unpleasant when your hands get really cold. Hiking trousers like Craghoppers are not only windproof and showerproof, with a host of pockets for your essentials, but they also dry really quickly. The latest styles are made from stretch material for extra comfort...and are available in men's and women's versions.

Footwear

I'm also careful what I put on my feet, as an outdoor stint could leave them getting cold or wet – or both. For that reason I am usually wearing my Merrell walking shoes, made of a GoreTex material which is not only waterproof but breathable as well. These are great for here and abroad. If you check out Cotswold Outdoor or GO Outdoors to name but a few, you'll get a great selection of styles, makes and prices.

   As I said, this is a very personal subject but there are a host of marketplaces out there that stock all sorts of specialist clothing and equipment, most of which are available online.

Rucksack

Over the years I have gone through a multitude of carrying bags, but I now use a Swissgear rucksack which has multiple compartments and pockets, and this really suits my needs. It is also very sturdy – which it needs to be as it gets rather rough handling during my painting sessions. It's also very comfortable when carried on your back with aerated padding and fully adjustable shoulder straps.

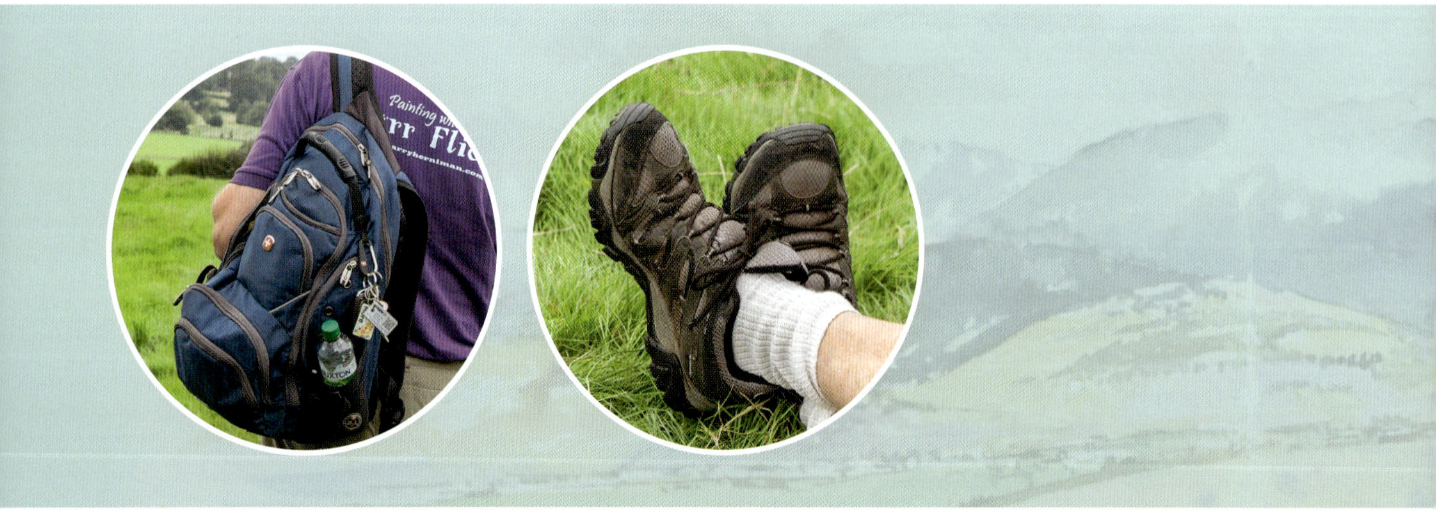

6 Watercolour paper blocks

These blocks consist of a number of pages of watercolour paper glued on all four sides, and they are great for outdoor work as you don't need to take a board or stretch your paper beforehand.

7 Graphite sticks

A great alternative to charcoal, these come in different grades of softness/darkness, are a lot less messy and don't need fixing.

8 Inktense watercolour pencils

These pencils contain an ink element which gives them a real glow when they are mixed with water. Great for producing those lightning full-colour sketches.

9 Gouache

There are many makes out there but my favoured brand is Schmincke Horadam Gouache. This brand uses the finest pigments with natural opacity without the use of white. As a result, you can work from almost transparent to opaque with just one medium!

10 Waterproof pens

I love working in line and wash (see page 126) and for this I need a waterproof ink so I can overpaint my line work with watercolour. There is a bewildering array of pens out there on the market in all nib thicknesses but do check that they are truly waterproof, as I have had a so-called waterproof pen run on me.

11 Fude bent nib drawing pen

A new addition to my sketching armoury is the Fude bent nib drawing pen. I was introduced to this rather unique pen by Matthew, one of my students, on a holiday abroad. He let me have a go with his pen and I was hooked. The bent nib enables you to make very thin lines right up to rather thick ones all in one stroke. Combined with waterproof ink, this is a really great sketching tool for all sorts of subjects.

12 2B pencil

This grade of pencil is the perfect balance of hardness and softness, making it versatile. A good all-round pencil. '2B, or not 2B, that is the question.'

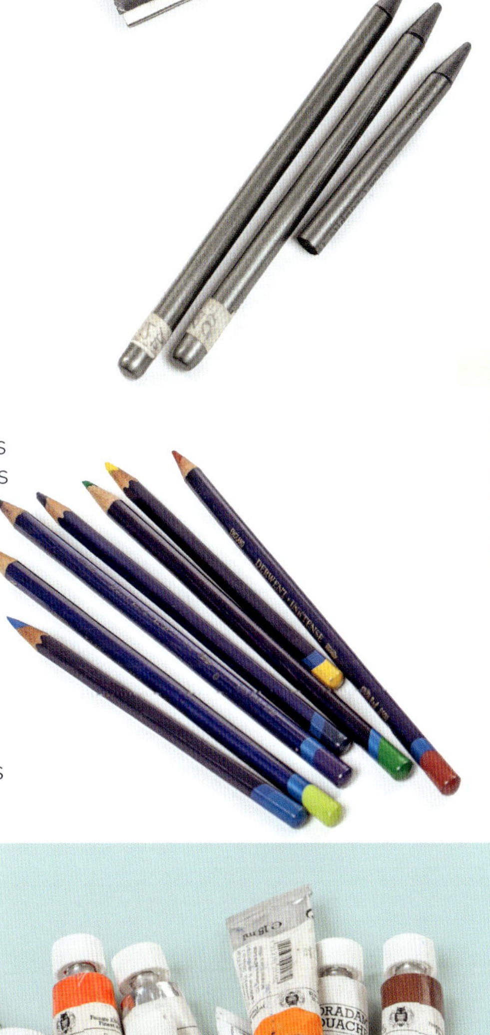

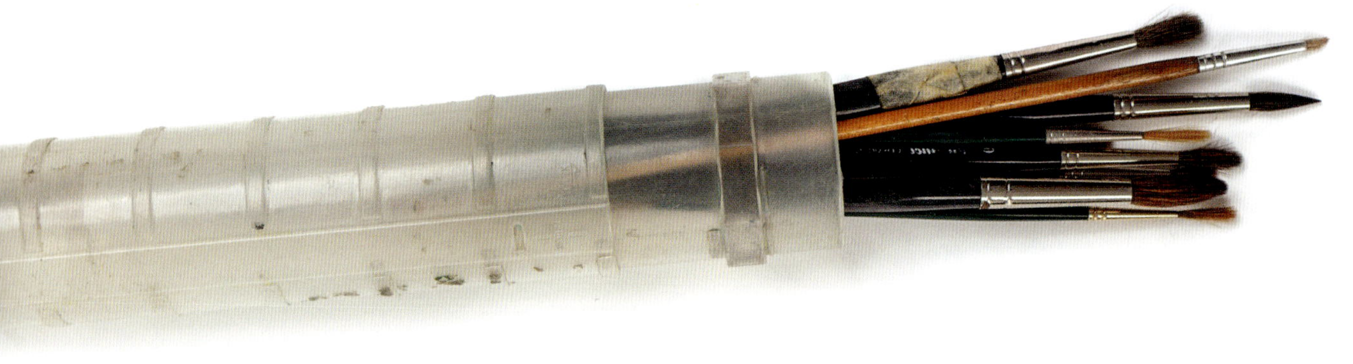

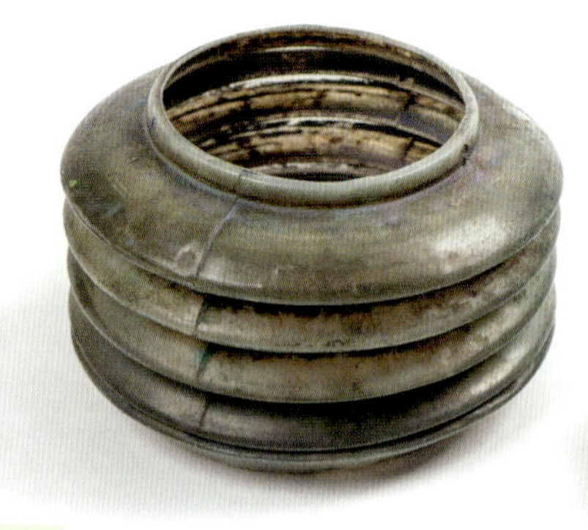

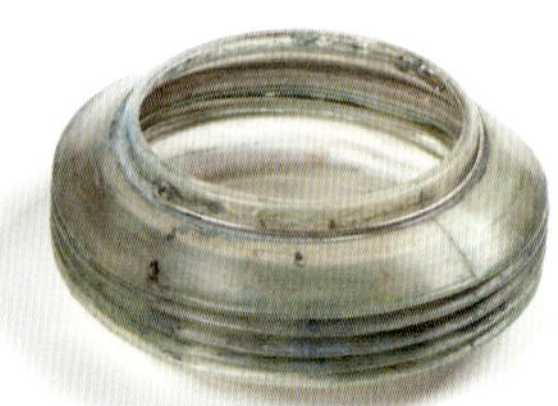

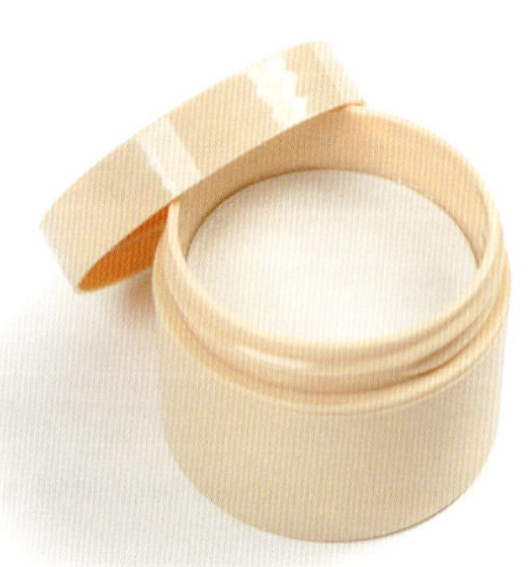

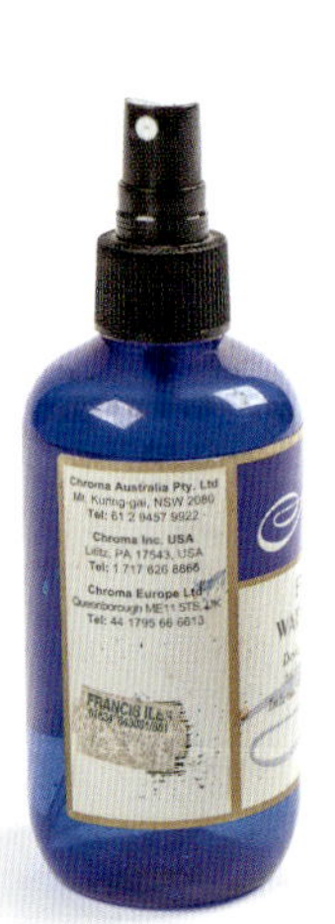

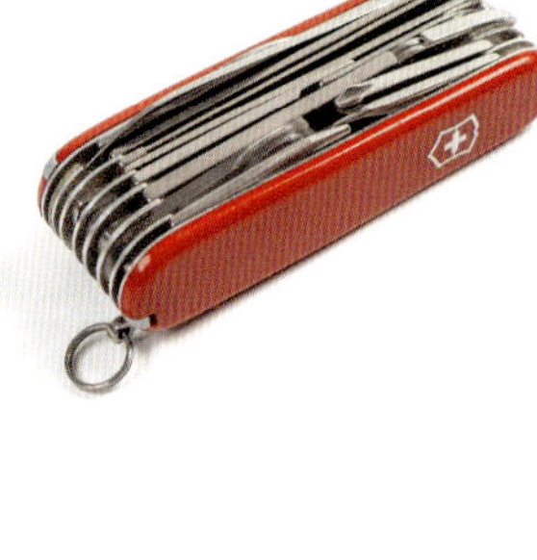

13 Paintbrushes

I tend to use rounds for my watercolours in different sizes to suit.

My travelling brush of choice is the hard wearing DaVinci Cosmatop range which has served me really well over the years. Made from a mixture of natural and synthetic hair, the natural hair in the belly of the brush gives good colour carrying capacity while the more resilient synthetic hair in the tip makes it sturdy. This enables me to mix up my colours but still retain a good tip for detail work all with one brush. Sable brushes are lovely to work with but are a lot less resilient, a lot more expensive and once you lose the tip...!

14 Brush tube

This holds my assortment of brushes, keeping them together and safe.

15 Collapsible water pot

I have two different sizes of this collapsible pot, which is very useful for travelling.

16 Brush cleaner

Give your brushes a good invigorating clean after your painting sessions to keep them in tip top condition. After all they are not cheap so look after them and they will reward you with long service.

17 Multi-tool

I use this for sharpening pencils and I use the pliers to take the tops off paint tubes.

18 Atomiser spray bottle

This little piece of equipment is a real must to keep your paints moist while painting. It's particularly handy in hot weather or hot countries.

My travelling kit for abroad

Paring down your kit to travel is always a difficult one, especially if you have only ever worked from home or in a studio set-up where all your favourite kit is on hand whenever you want or need it. Not so when you're on the move!

What to take and what to leave behind is always a tricky decision especially when travelling abroad with all the baggage restrictions that go with it. So here is an overview of the absolute minimum of kit that I take with me on my forays out of my home country:

- Folding easel/board
- Paints and pencils
- Brushes in tube/roll
- Folding paintbox/palette
- Collapsible water pot
- Collapsible seat/stool
- Backpack/rucksack
- Parasol

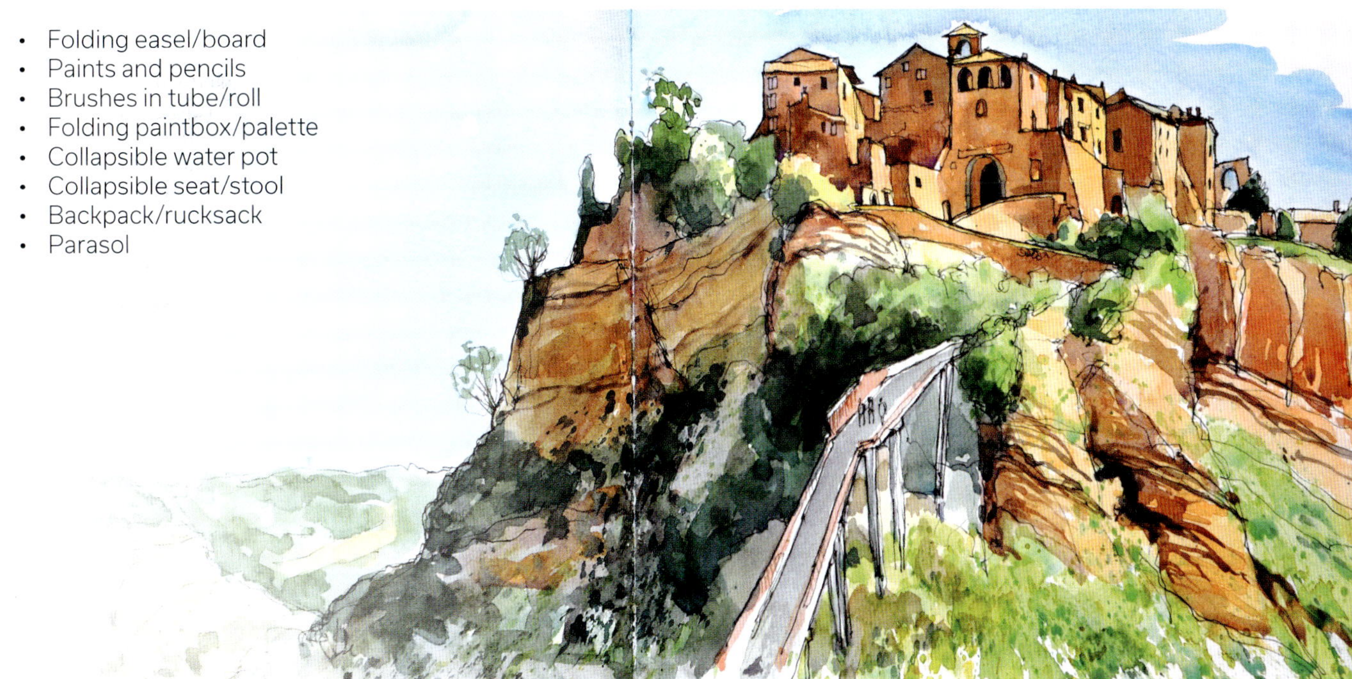

Painting in hot locations

I will personally *never* go out without a hat, preferably one with a brim to keep the sun off my neck. Wearing something like a baseball cap, with no neck protection can lead to sunstroke after a day's painting in the sun.

There is also a huge array of specialist shirts, shorts and so forth with UV protection. Some have insect repellent impregnation as well, so these work really well in hot countries.

Walking sandals are a real favourite with me for many reasons. They are not only really cool but also have cushioned insoles for comfort and great traction when walking.

Another super addition to your clothing list is a compact and breathable waterproof jacket which packs down neatly into its own tiny drawstring bag. This is really handy if you get caught out in a shower and it also provides protection against the wind.

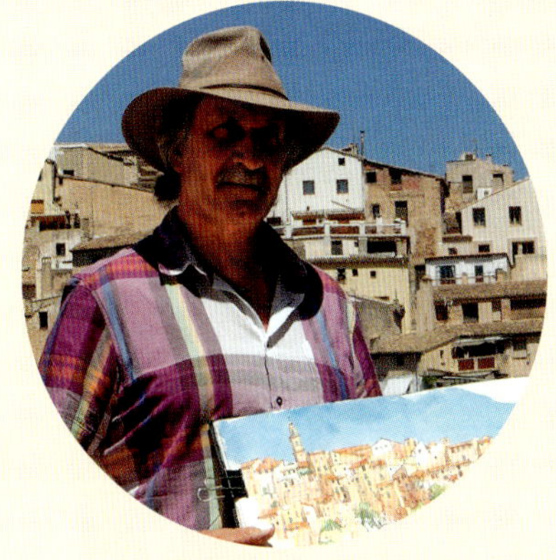

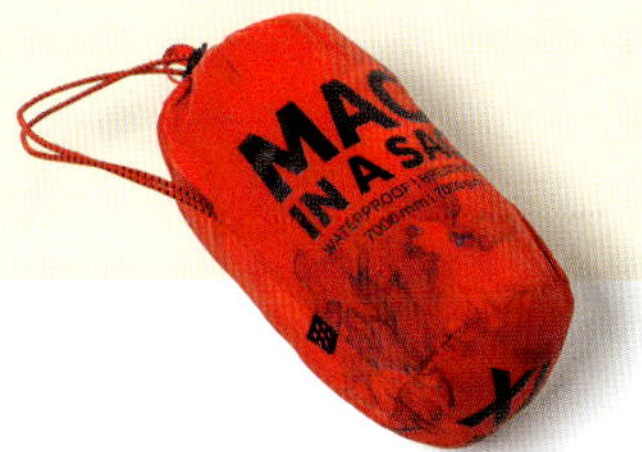

Which medium should I use?

Asking what media I need is like asking how long is a piece of string. With the huge array of different sketching media out there, this really comes down to personal choice and, to some extent, where one is going to sketch with the possible weight restrictions and transportation.

Here I will give you some basic information on some of the best 'transportable' media around and their advantages. Ultimately, that decision is yours to make, but here I tell you what I think the merits are of the different media.

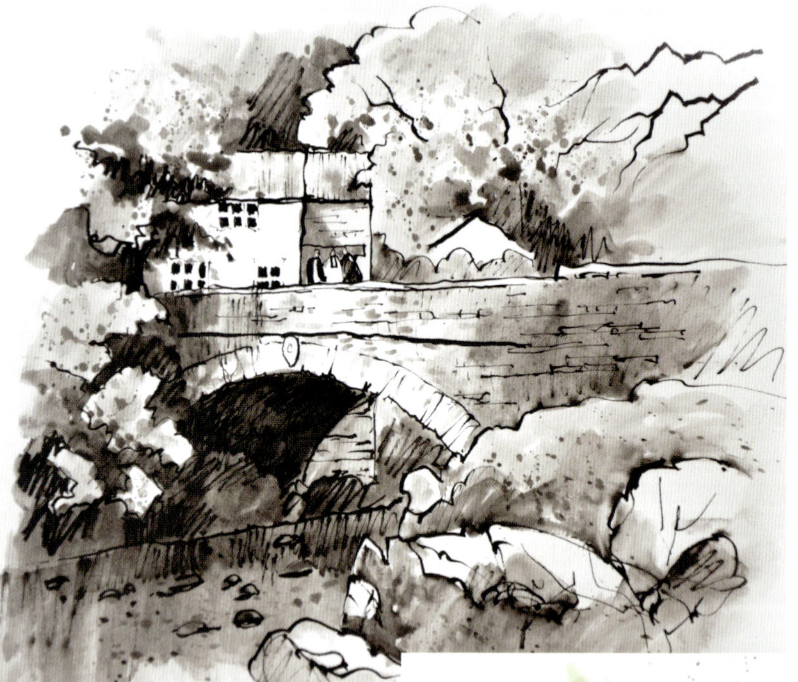

Pen and ink

For a quick study, or even a more considered piece, I find that pen work is ultimately satisfying in that you can produce lovely tonal sketches with the minimum of kit: a pen and paper.

The power of ink

I just love doing ink sketches especially as I now have the rather unique Fude bent nib drawing pen (see page 25) to work with. This sketch shows you how much you can produce using just ink.

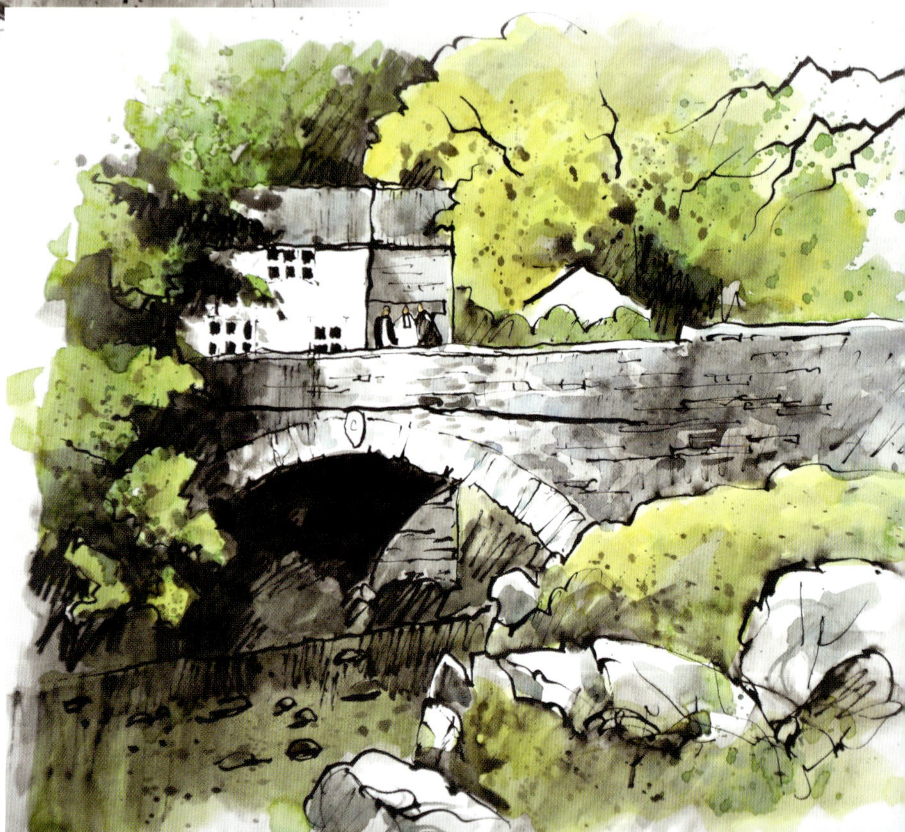

Adding colour

If you want to go a step further, and providing you use waterproof ink, you can overlay some simple watercolour washes.

Watercolour

This has to be my preferred medium. With the advent of the hard-backed watercolour book, I found myself working the majority of my *en plein air* practice in this medium as I took advantage of being able to produce vibrant watercolour sketches on lovely paper.

I originally used a more conventional watercolour approach in my sketchbooks but with the advent of the smooth HP paper sketchbook I moved onto 'line and wash' which is now my favoured mode of sketching. For the 'line' element I use a variety of waterproof artists' drawing pens, over which I lay my watercolours.

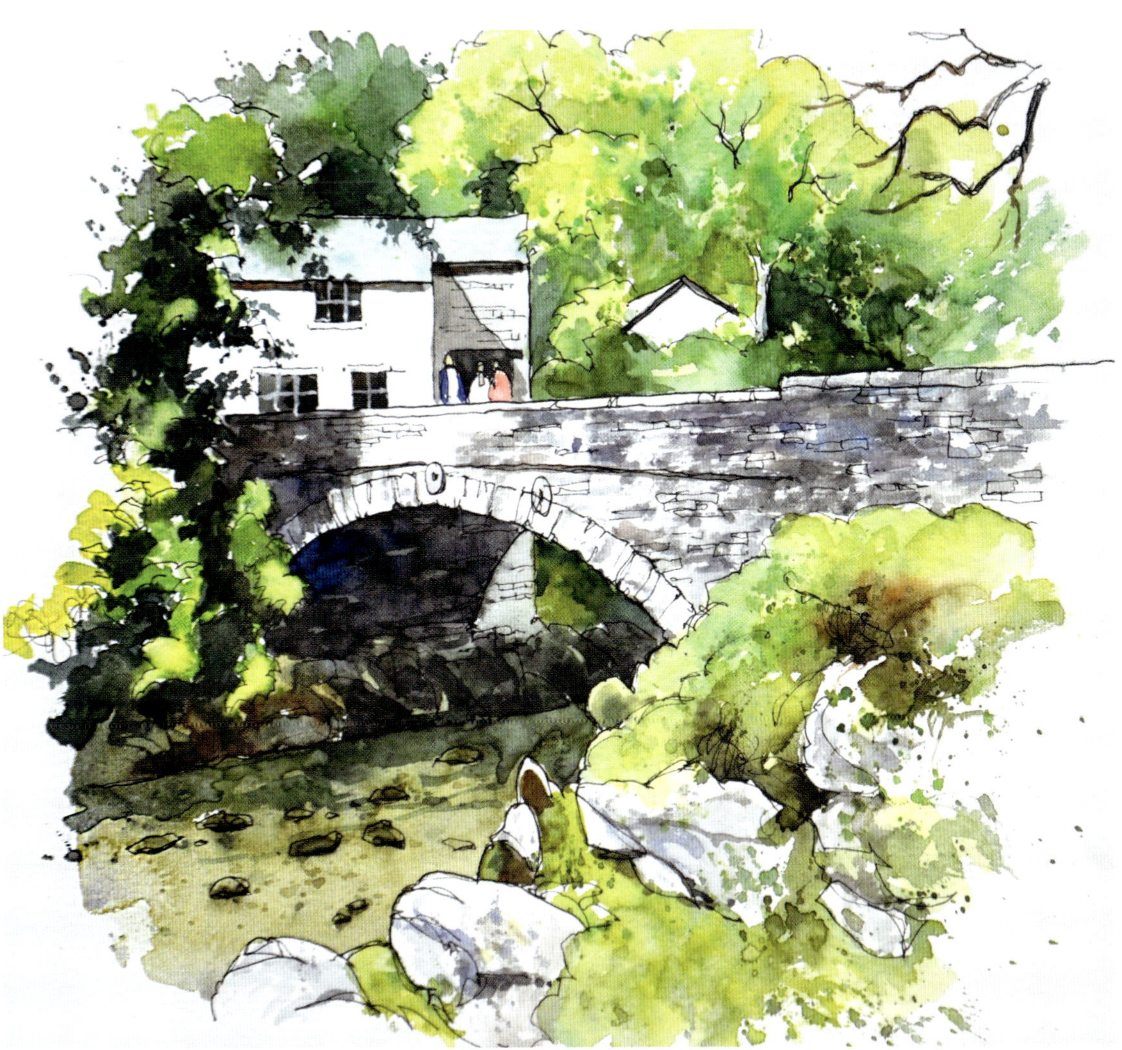

Adding more colour
*A line and wash watercolour just about
has it all and I have filled countless
sketchbooks with these renditions.
Using a fine waterproof felt-tipped
pen, roughly 0.5 to 0.7mm, I do the
main drawing and then go in with my
watercolour washes.*

Colour pencils and watercolour pencils

Colour pencils have been around for ages but now there are watercolour pencils which become liquid when water is added to them. Draw up your scene, then brush on water to produce a watercolour wash, which is really exciting. If you would like to work with a stronger medium, try the Inktense range of water soluble pencils. When mixed with water, the colours turn into vibrant ink.

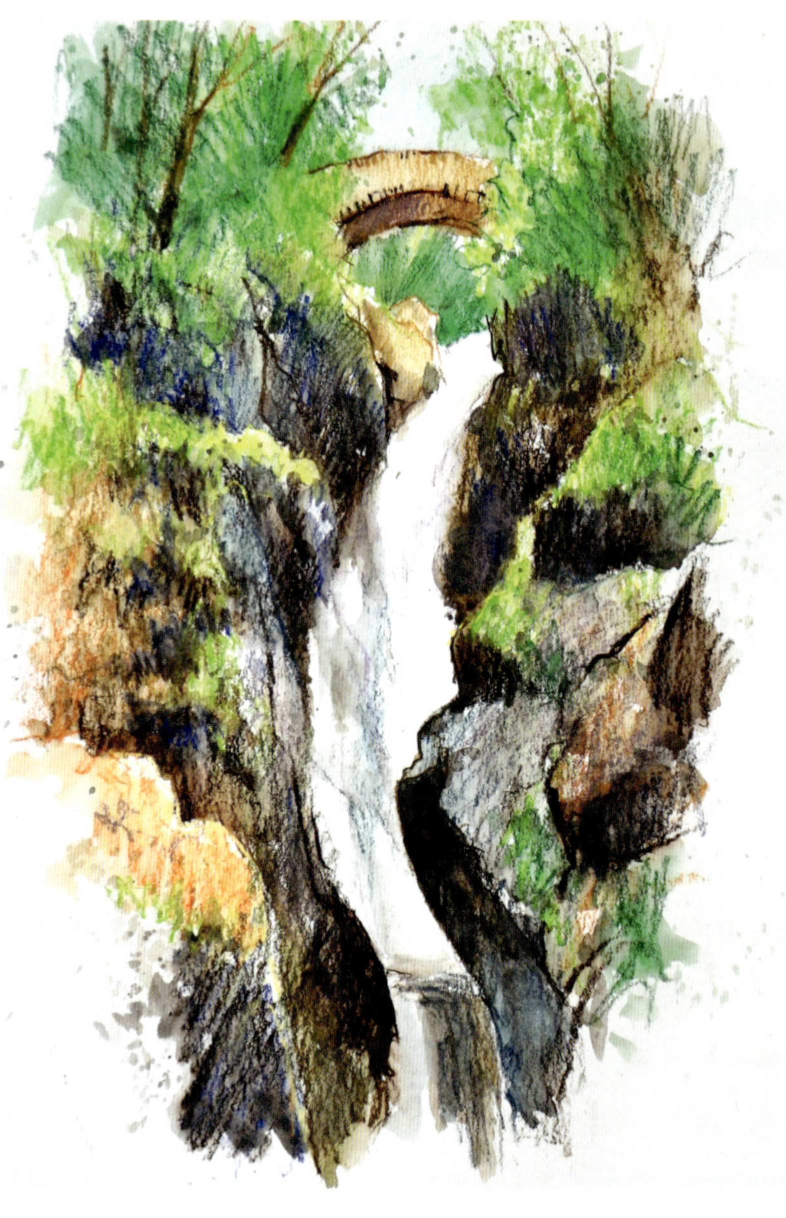

Watercolour pencils
These were my first introduction to water soluble pencils, which allow you to produce not only a coloured drawing, but with the addition of water, a watercolour sketch to boot.

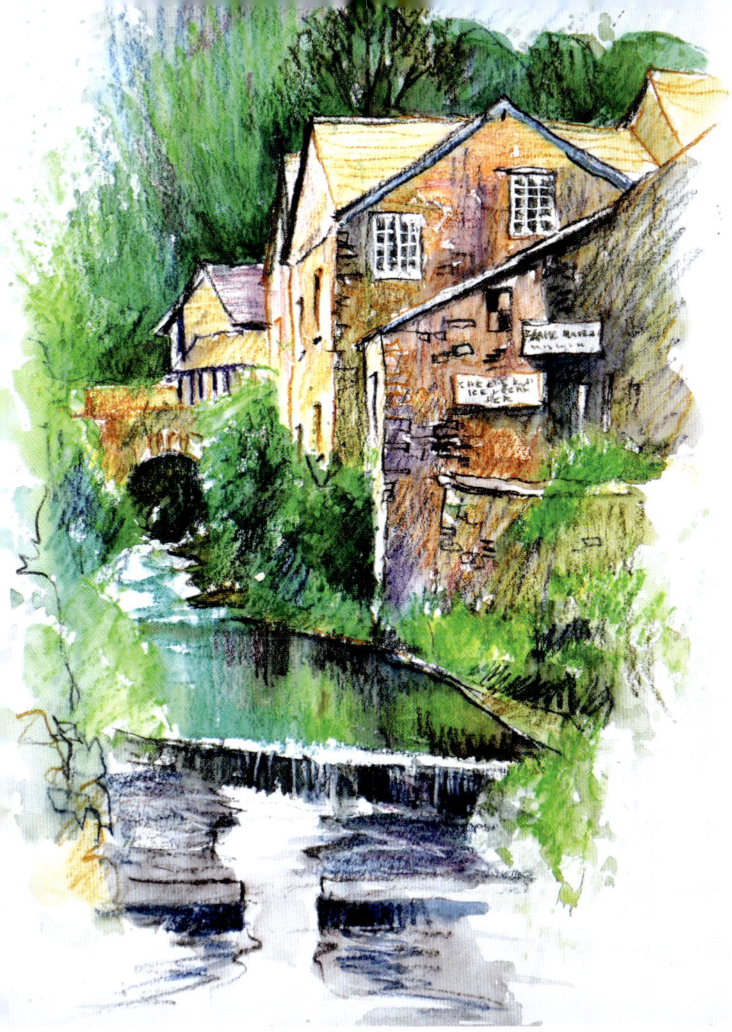

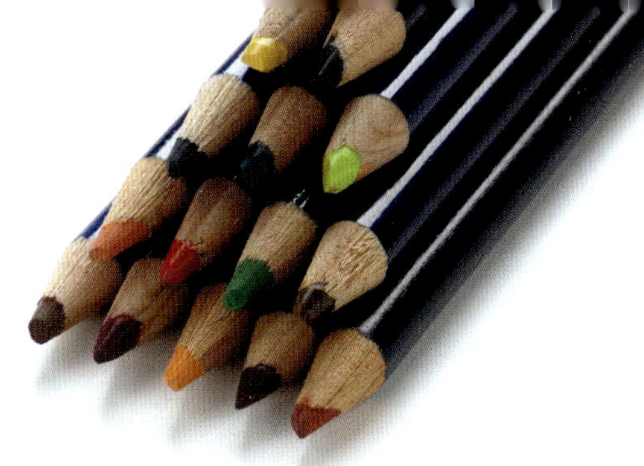

Inktense

Very similar to watercolour pencils but with an ink formula in the 'lead' which really comes to life when water is added. The colours are very vibrant and also waterproof once dry, which means you can safely work over them to build up colour or lay a wash.

*A demo of Ambleside in the
Lake District, UK, worked in Inktense.*

The difference a little water makes

When drawing with Inktense pencils, you will notice that the dry colours bear very little relationship to the wet colours, as can be seen from these two sketches. The left-hand one has all the line work and shading established and I'm just going in with the brush. On the right you can see the finished sketch and how the different colours perform when water is added.

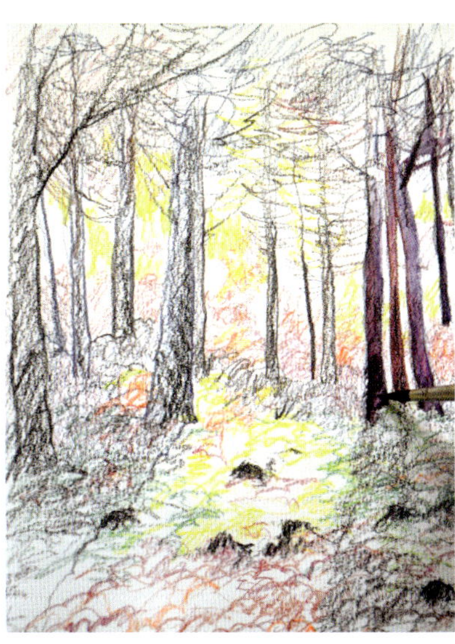

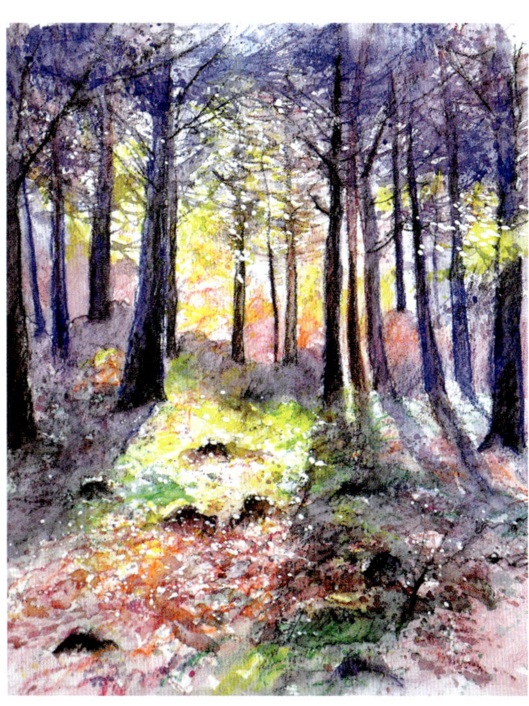

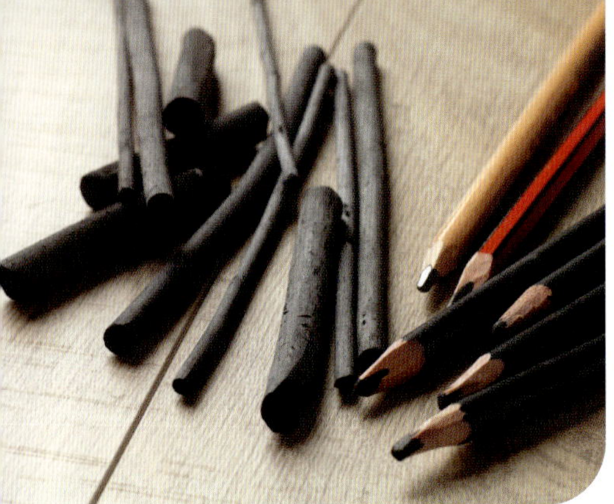

Pencil, charcoal and graphite sticks

As a basic sketching tool, what is simpler than the pencil? I tend to use 2B as a starting point as it is quite a dark lead and not overly smudgeable when producing your line work. I then go in with softer grades 4B/6B for those lovely darks. Rubbing your finger over a passage of graphite will produce some soft tonal areas and highlights can be lifted with a soft eraser.

Graphite sticks are also great as a sketching medium but they are not as workable as pencil, whereas charcoal is eminently smudgeable but quite messy and ideally needs fixing.

The benefits of using pencil
Sketching with the pencil is simple and enjoyable and you can get a great range of tones by using different grade pencils.

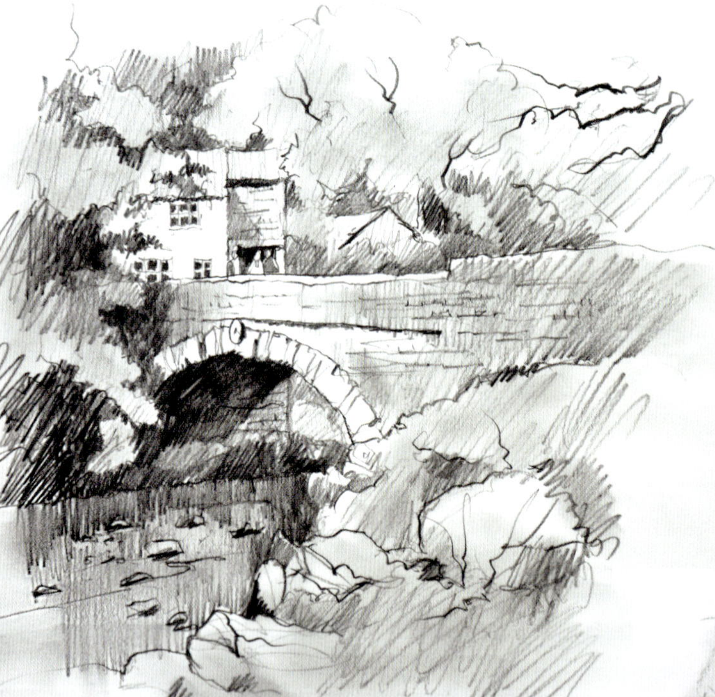

Using graphite sticks
There is not a great difference in the tonal values, but are a joy to use as you can get some lovely darks.

Pastel pencils

Another great addition to the sketching armoury. All the characteristics of pastels but in pencil form. I love pastels but because of their nature they really need fixing as they smudge easily, especially if in a sketchbook, so I personally don't use them outside.

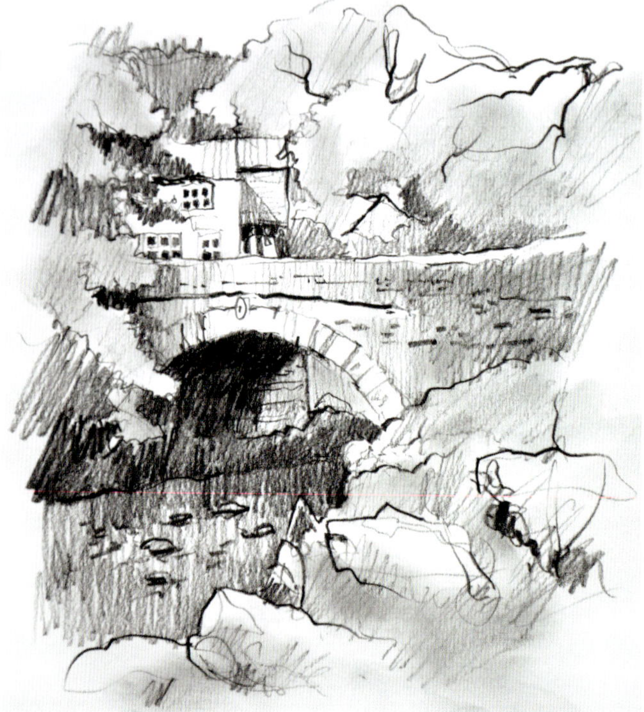

Gouache

What a totally underrated medium this is! I am even more convinced of
this now that I have discovered the fantastic range of Schmincke Horadam
Gouache. These wonderful pigments are naturally opaque, (not additionally
reinforced by adding white) so you are able to dilute them down to an almost
transparent wash. You can then overlay with opaque passages, all with just
one medium; and you can work from dark to light which you can't really do
with watercolour.

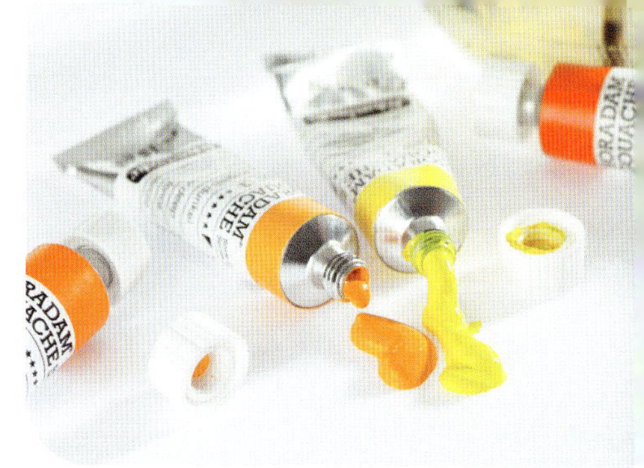

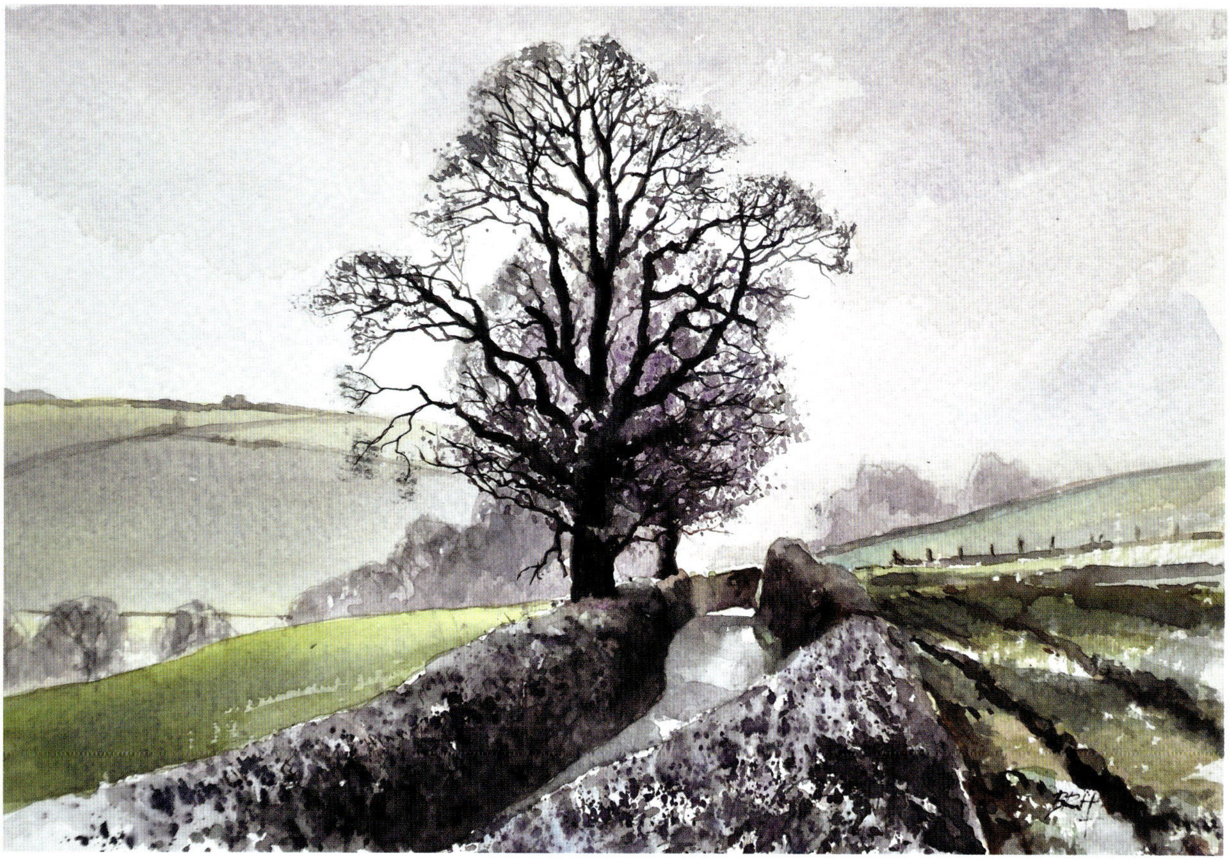

The effects of gouache
*Looking at this gouache sketch of
Ruxton Lane, Herefordshire, you
would be forgiven for mistaking it for
a watercolour. You can produce both
transparent and opaque passages all
with one medium: gouache.*

Acrylics and oils

I don't use these two media for outside work but I know people who
do and love them, so please do not be put off by my reluctance to
include them here.

Painting with acrylics in a studio is a pure joy but I find that out
in the open, the paints dry up too quickly both on the palette
and on the paper (and the tubes themselves are rather large and
obviously heavier).

There are also a lot of artists out there who paint oils *en plein air*
and have all the equipment like easels and pochard boxes for
carrying the painting equipment and the wet paintings. Believe me
I can get into enough mess throwing watercolour around, so I don't
dare think what would happen if I used oils!

The importance of a sketchbook

Without a doubt the most important addition to my outdoor sketching armoury is the sketchbook! Today's sketchbooks come in a bewildering array of different sizes, weights, binding and most importantly, paper content.

My first forays into the sketching world saw me using a variety of soft-covered spiral-bound affairs which, after much use, would start to come apart at the seams. I moved onto hardbound sketchbooks which were so much better and more hard-wearing, but still only contained cartridge paper or similar. These were fine for line work and pencils etc., but I always found my watercolour sketches came out rather dull and lacklustre as the colours would be absorbed by the paper.

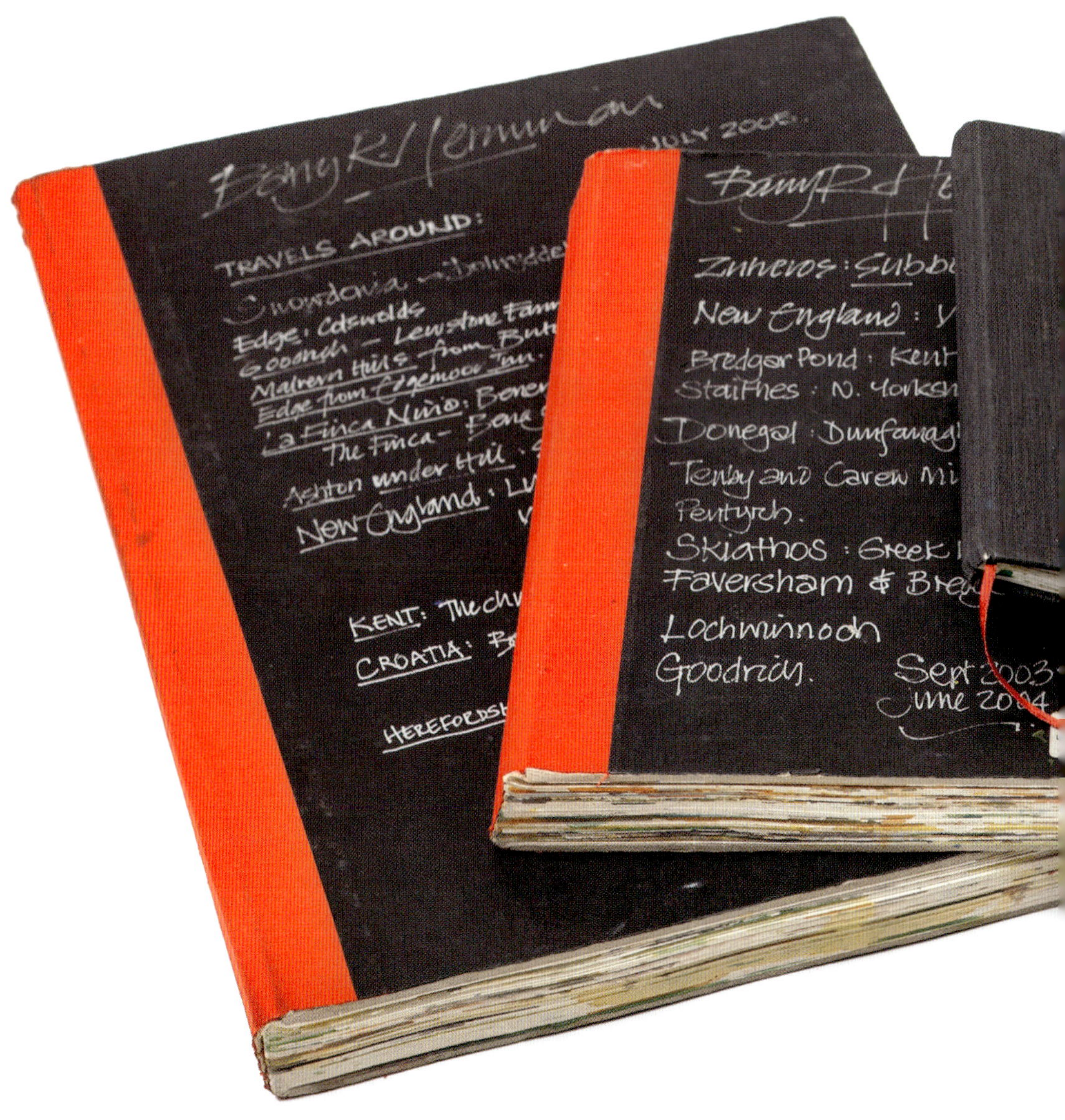

Then one day I happened upon an A4 (210 x 297mm/8¼ x 11¾in) hardbound sketchbook that contained 300gsm (140lb) Saunders Waterford watercolour paper...and that was a turning point. Now I could go to town, doing full-blown watercolours in the knowledge that they would remain as bright and vibrant as when I painted them.

I had even moved onto A3 (297 x 420mm/11¾ x 16½in) sized portrait sketchbooks which allow for A2 (420 x 594mm/16½ x 23½in) landscape panoramas over the two pages. Great fun to do, but not overly practical, especially with the growing weight and size restrictions being introduced by the airline companies. One particular sketchbook weighed nearly 2kg (4½lb), so you couldn't call it lightweight by any stretch!

My sketchbooks

*Here are the latest sketchbooks I have been using in recent years.
I usually label them for easy reference later.*

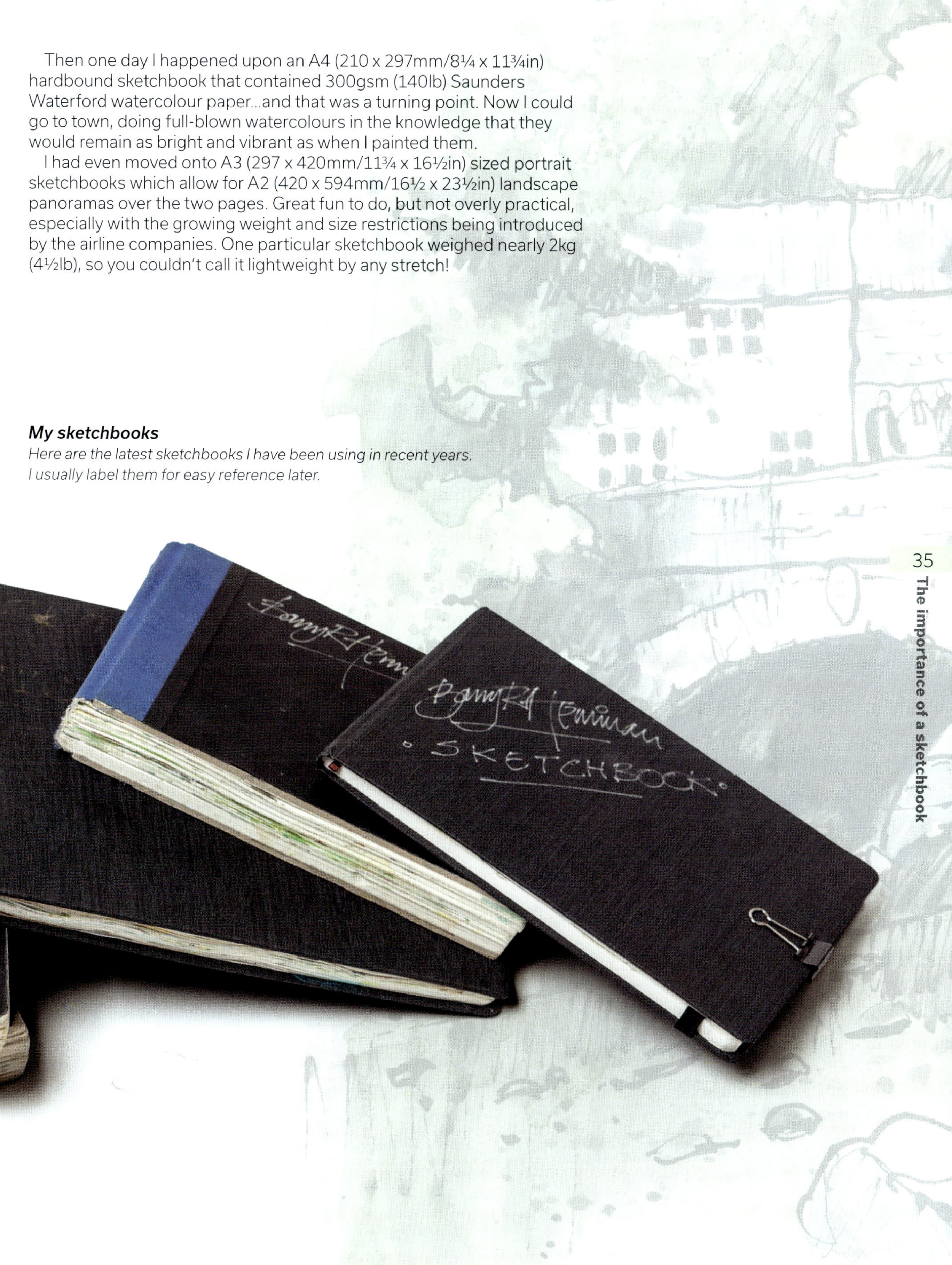

Saunders Waterford Rough and HP sketchbooks

These have been my sketchbooks of choice for several years and many of my students have followed suit and enjoy them as well. They are stitched and hardbound which means they will lay flat when opened and you are able to paint across the two pages for a panorama without a gap at the spine. My original sketchbooks were A4 (210 x 297mm/8¼ x 11¾in) and A3 (297 x 420mm/11¾ x 16½in) portrait format and contained Rough watercolour paper (see below).

I then came across a landscape format sketchbook which I used for many years. They are 28cm wide by 25.5cm deep (11 x 10in), contain 30 pages of 300gsm (140lb) Saunders Waterford watercolour paper and weigh just under 1kg (2¼lb) (see opposite). This landscape format lends itself to extensive panoramas which I now favour in my outside work.

Another first was the fact that I bought a book containing HP (smooth) paper as I just love doing ink and watercolour sketches and I found the the pen glides beautifully over the smooth surface. I discovered that I couldn't lay a flat wash as easily on this surface as with Rough or Not surfaces, so I have adjusted my painting techniques to complement this lovely surface and just go straight in with a variety of immediate brushstrokes.... After all, it is only a sketch!

The Saunders Waterford Rough sketchbook was one of the sketchbooks that really got me started painting outside with a vengeance! A4 (210 x 297mm/8¼ x 11¾in) portrait format (right image) open to produce an A3 (297 x 420mm/11¾ x 16½in) landscape panorama over the two pages. I also used a few A3 portrait format books (left image) that would afford me a huge A2 (420 x 594mm/16½ x 23½in) panorama when opened up!

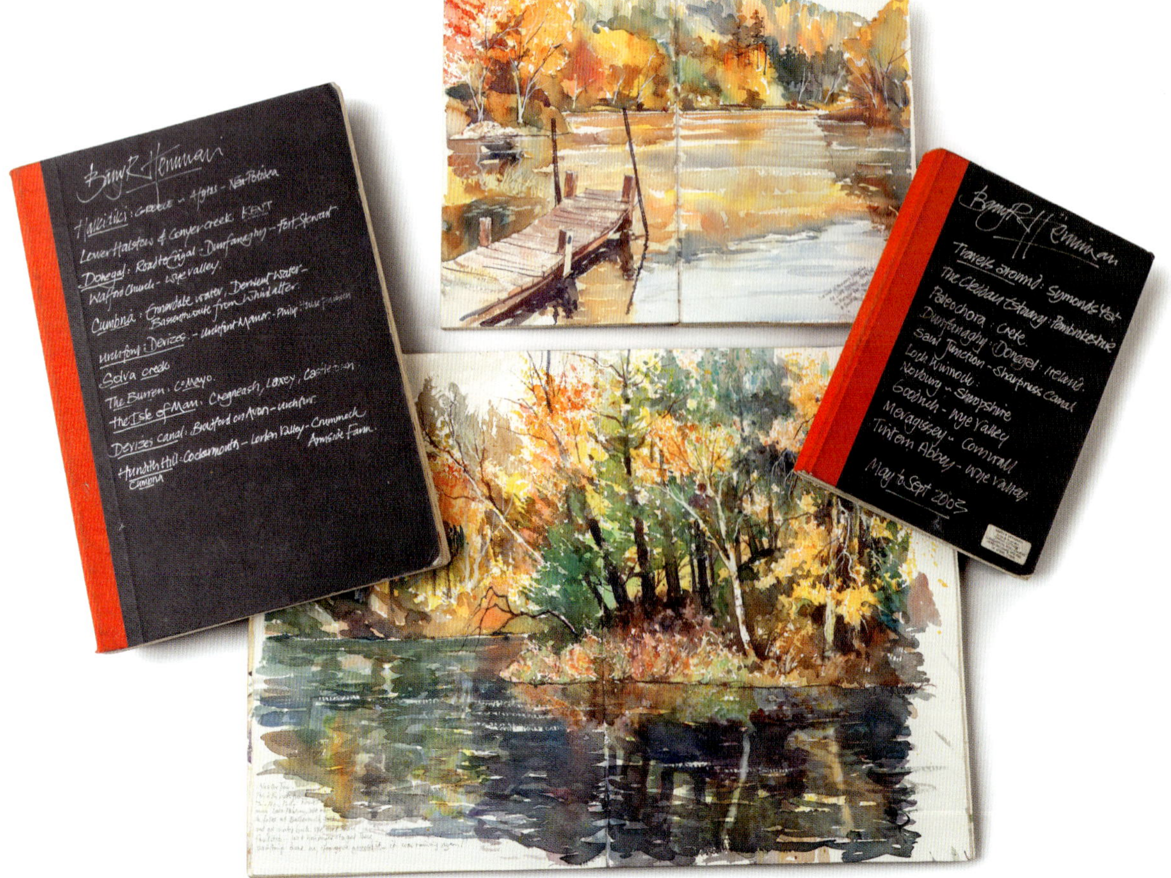

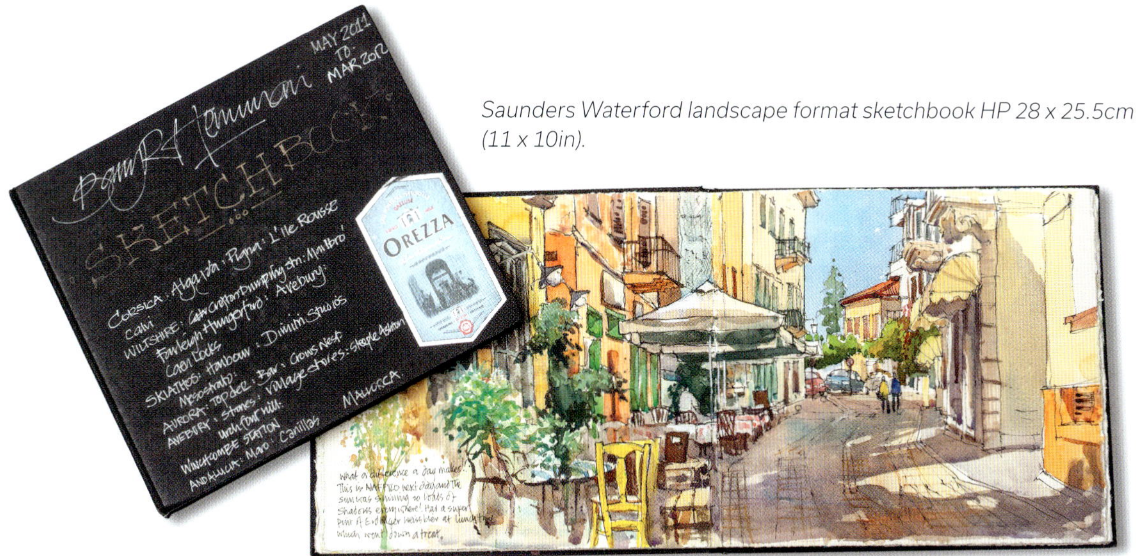

Saunders Waterford landscape format sketchbook HP 28 x 25.5cm (11 x 10in).

Hahnemuhle Watercolour Book sketchbook

After a visit to Patchings Art Festival, in Derbyshire, UK, a few years back, I came away with a couple of new sketchbooks from the Hahnemuhle stand and everything changed once again. I had an A4 (210 x 297mm/8¼ x 11¾in) and A5 (148 x 210mm/6 x 8¼in) landscape format hardbound sketchbook with 30 pages of 90lb (190gsm) fine-grained watercolour paper to try out and was pleasantly surprised with the results. I say this as I had been used to working on 300gsm (140lb) paper and worried that this lighter paper wouldn't stand up to consistent use, but my worries were unfounded. I could do full watercolour sketches on both sides of the paper with no show through and the colours would remain bright and vibrant as well. Other benefits are that it's half the weight of the Saunders Waterford book and almost half the price.

Once again I have just given you the sketchbooks I favour, but there are so many different types by different manufacturers now that you really are spoilt for choice. Just check out Jackson's Art Supplies for instance to see what is now readily available on the market.

Hahnemuhle watercolour books, A4 and A5 landscape format.

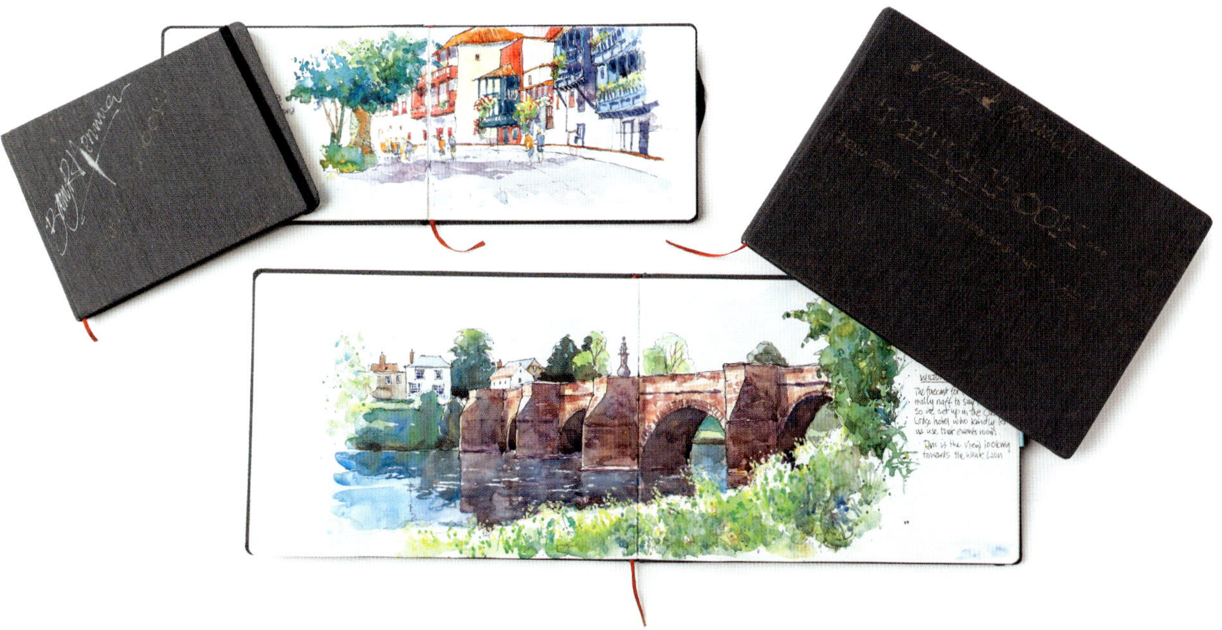

Different painting surfaces

Watercolour sketchbooks come with a variety of paper textures:

Rough watercolour paper is great for textures as you can create a myriad different ones just by dragging the brush over the surface at different angles and with varied colour dilution. My first sketchbooks contained Rough paper, which was fine when using pencil for my line work and getting all those textures.

Not or semi-Rough paper is a great inbetween surface, not too rough and not too smooth, so you get the best of both worlds.

HP (hot pressed) or Smooth paper is now my surface of choice when purchasing a sketchbook. It is great for pen work as the nib slides beautifully across the smooth surface – it's a joy to use.

Rough watercolour paper.

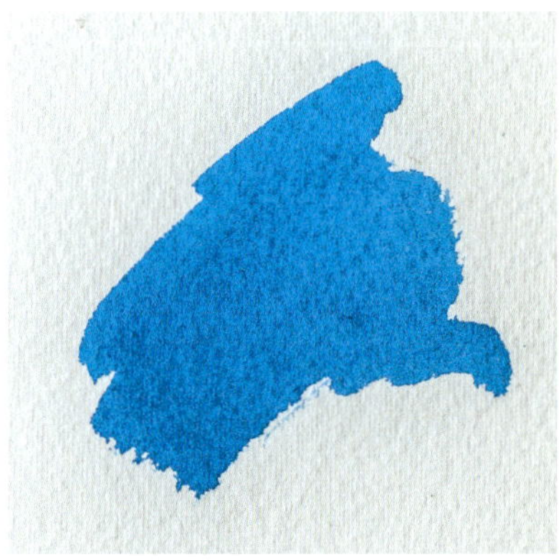

Not or semi-Rough paper.

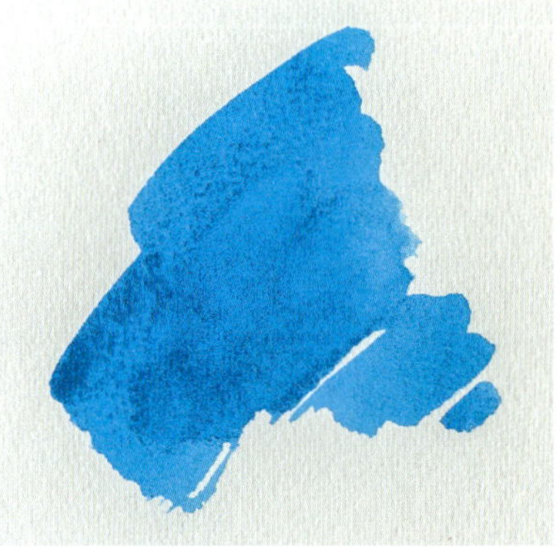

HP (hot pressed) or Smooth paper.

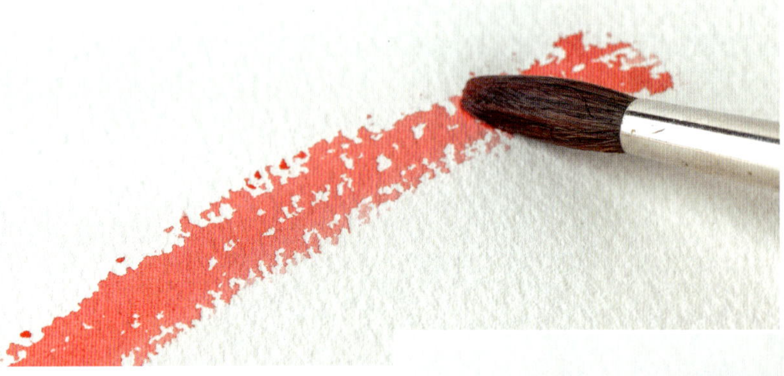

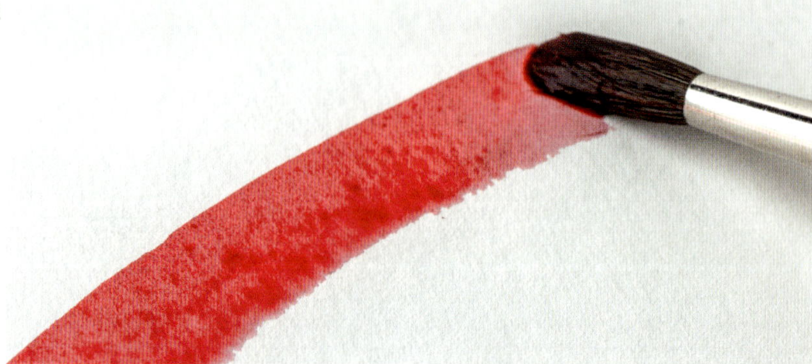

The two extremes of paper texture. Rough (top) and Smooth (bottom).

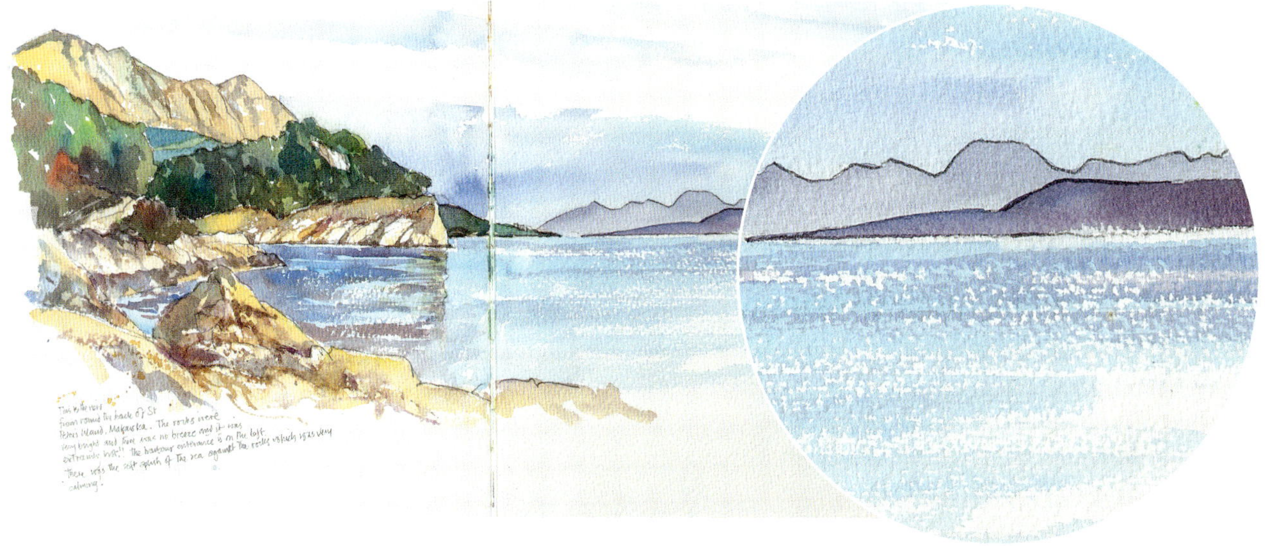

Sketch on Rough paper, with inset showing the texture created.

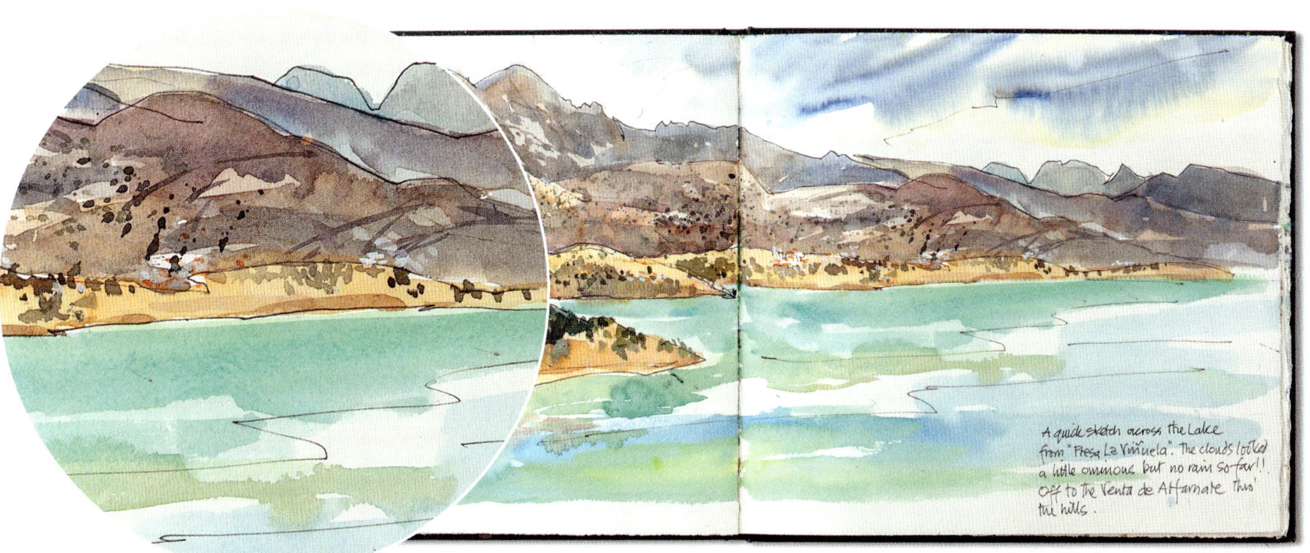

Sketch on Smooth paper, with inset showing the texture created.

Why use a sketchbook?

There are many reasons why using a sketchbook is so important. If you go out with a lovely piece of stretched watercolour paper on a board, the chances are you will be looking to do a full-blown painting to take home rather than a quick sketch. Don't get me wrong, doing a full painting *en plein air* is eminently satisfying, it's just that I want to concentrate on the sketching elements. How many times have you gone out and done quick studies on loose pieces of paper, only for them to be relegated to the bottom drawer, or the bin even, when you get home, sometimes never seeing the light of day again? With a sketchbook, nothing is wasted or ripped up because it wasn't deemed good enough, and that in itself is another reason to put everything into your book. It is also a great yardstick by which to measure your artistic improvement, as you can always refer back to previous work and gauge how you are progressing.

If you discard work you are unhappy with, you will only be as good as your last piece of work and will have nothing to compare it with.

The mere fact that you are using a sketchbook, as the name implies, gives you the liberty to just sketch without having to worry about producing a 'finished' piece of artwork. And it is so much fun! A sketch, doodle, scribble, call it what you will, is all about information gathering and it will ultimately become part of your painting repertoire and artistic improvement.

A note about notes

I also use my sketchbooks as a travelogue. They are a great reminder of places visited and experienced. I annotate each sketch with my notes on time and place to further aid recollection of the emotions of that day.

'Lightning' sketches

When time really is of the essence you have to get as much down as you can. These sketches show what you can achieve when pushed for time.

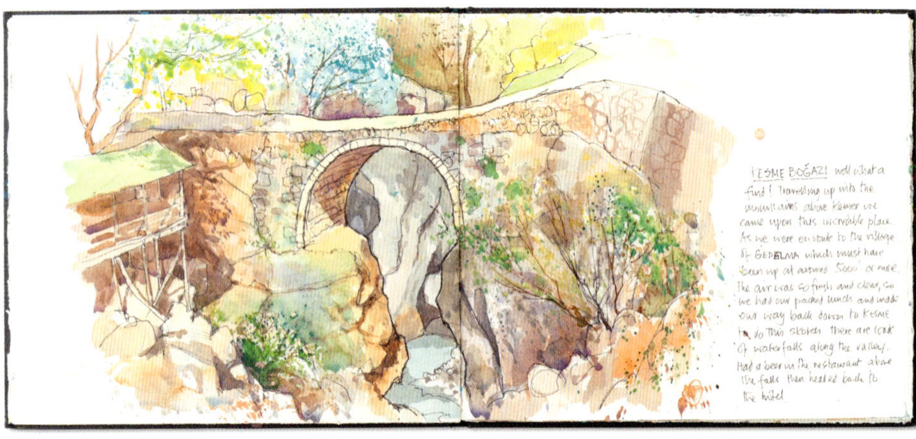

On one of my painting holidays to Turkey we took a bus up into the mountains in search of some interesting painting venues...and what a find this was! We came across this magnificent stone bridge straddling the wild mountain river and decided to spend the whole afternoon there. There was a small bar/café on the left of the picture so that was a bonus.

This derelict barn was in the heart of the Spanish countryside where we were dropped off for the duration. To say it was a hot day is an understatement and when we got out our packed lunches, we were plagued by wasps! Not one of my favourite painting spots I must say.

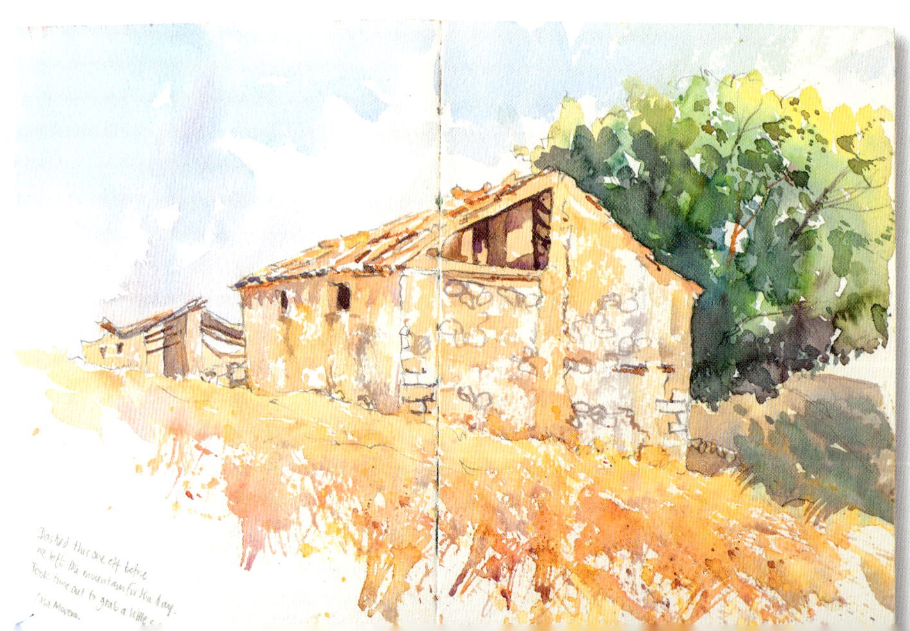

This pub at Wooton Rivers, Wiltshire, UK, was the last sketching venue of the day and we had only about a quarter of an hour before our coach had to go back. I didn't want to keep the rest of the coach waiting for me, so I rattled through this colourful sketch.

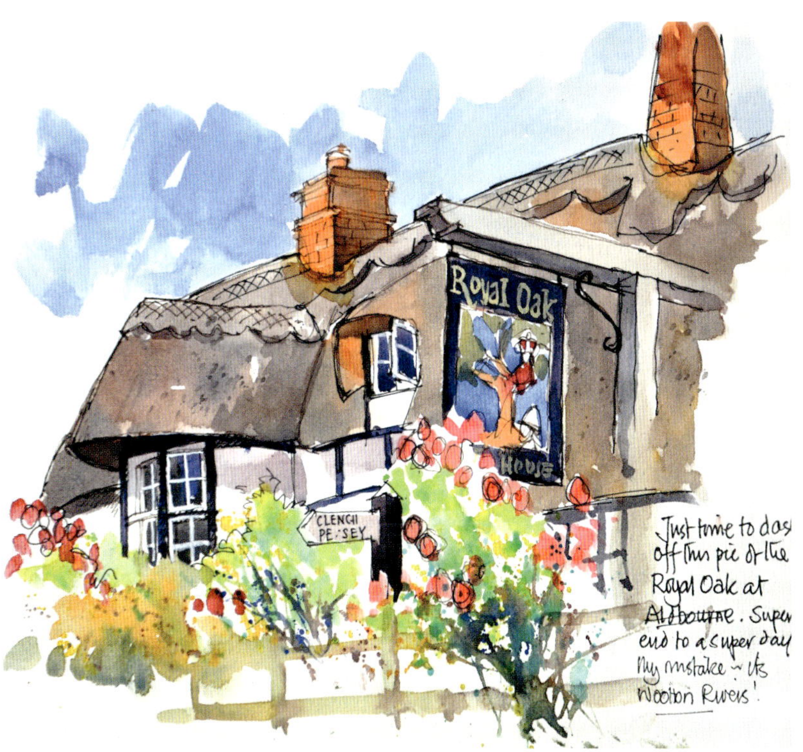

I set up my easel in Sovana, Tuscany to do a full double-page spread in my sketchbook but as I got into the swing of things the light went as the clouds gathered and I literally had to throw the paint at the sketch while it was all wet. This is as much as I got down on paper before we were rained off, and boy did it come down!

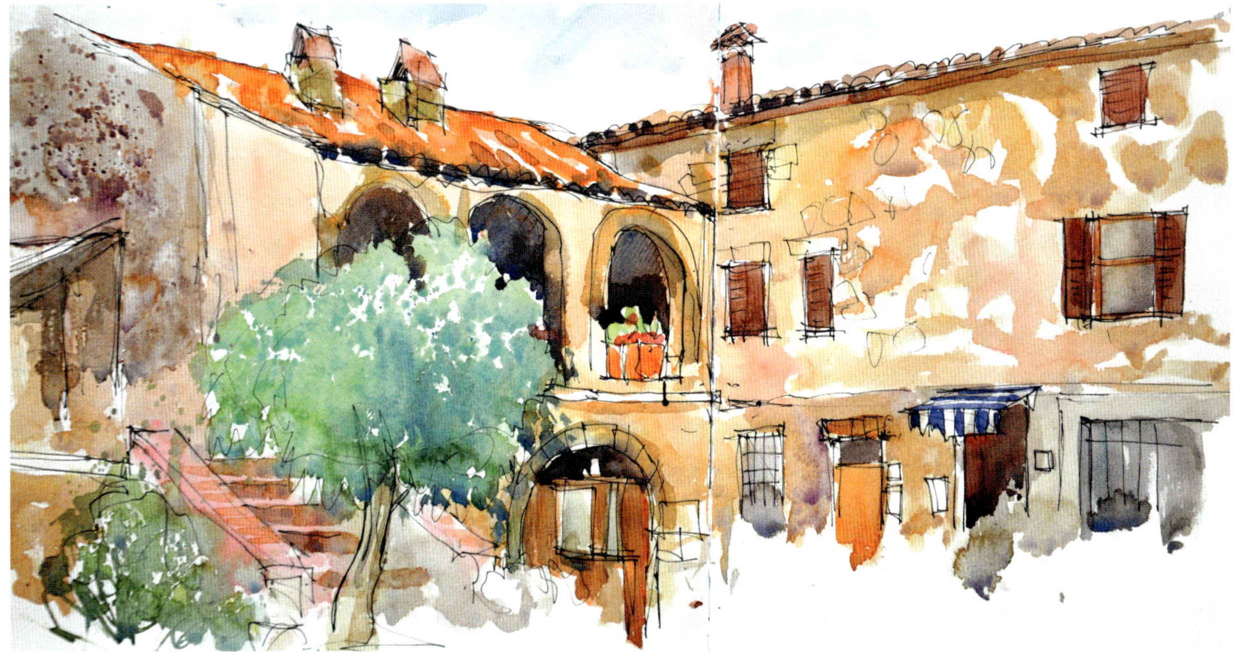

On one of our trips to Skiathos, Greece, my wife Sally and I decided it would be good to take a walk over the mountains towards the town. Our first trip took us to bus stop 9 but on subsequent trips we ventured all the way to the harbour where we had lunch and a bus trip back. This became one of our favourite jaunts so I decided to draw up a map of our route in my sketchbook to bring back happy memories.

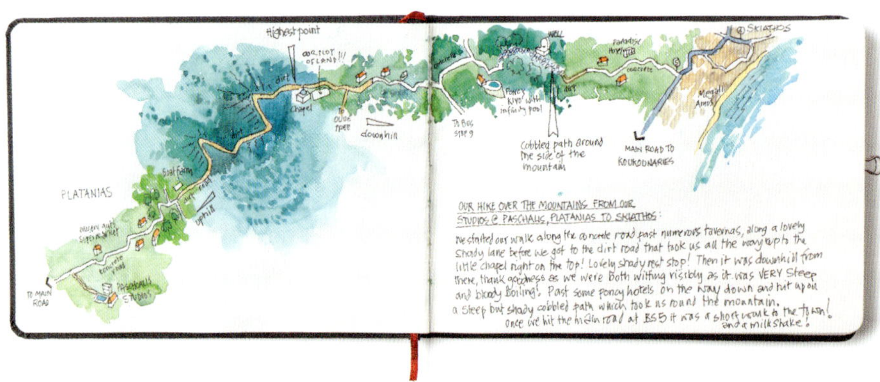

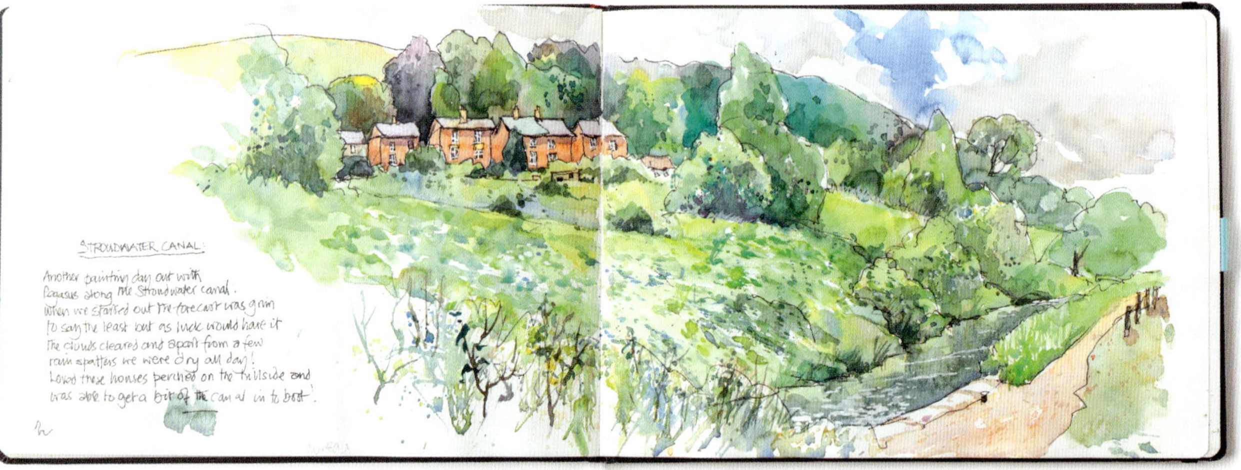

One of my painting days with Pegasus Art alongside the Stroudwater Canal. I rather liked the line of houses up on the hillside that were catching the sun. The canal is in the right-hand corner of the sketch.

What do I use it for?

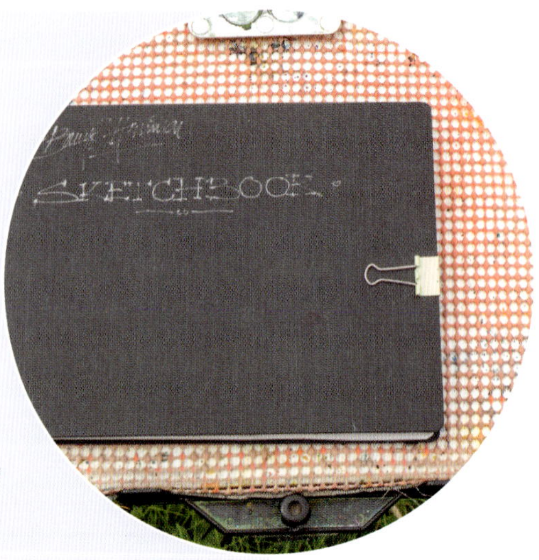

I urge students to put everything into their sketchbooks no matter how rudimentary as it will all be there to refer back to should needs be. Every sketch, doodle or colour swatch of a certain mix will be there for you to revisit and rediscover.

Another thing I urge students to do is to avoid the temptation to save the sketchbook for 'best' or for when they feel they are good enough. I have heard students say that it's such a lovely book and they don't want to spoil it!

Remember that this is *your* sketchbook and it's very personal, like a diary, so you don't have to show it to anyone if you don't want to. With that in mind, go ahead and let loose! I have had many students ask me proudly if I would like to see what they have been doing in their sketchbooks since we last met.

Should I use an easel?

I find trying to rest the sketchbook on my knees is very cumbersome especially on a windy day when it decides to move about or slams shut in the middle of a very fluid passage! To keep the pages from flapping about on the easel, I take a variety of bulldog clips with me to secure them while painting.

Lately I have taken to painting in a smaller A5 landscape sketchbook which is great for quicker sketches, when time is short or carrying the larger sketchbook is not practical. Because of its size, it's easier to work with it on your lap or propped up on a table or wall, whatever is at hand.

If you do use an easel, the obvious first consideration is the transportation. Where you are painting, how far you would have to carry it and if you are flying are all factors to consider before you decide to take an easel along.

As I mentioned earlier, there is an array of large, heavy and unwieldy easels which are totally unsuitable for the outside artist. Find an easel that allows you to paint almost horizontally – a must when painting fluid watercolours.

That is why I just love the Herring Versatile Easel: it's lightweight, sturdy, folds flat for transportation and can be used sitting down or standing and at any painting angle you desire. I take it everywhere I go and set it up in all manner of weird and wonderful locations so that I can rest my sketchbook on it and just concentrate on the painting at hand.

Ultimately, whether to use an easel or not is a personal choice – just make sure you find one that suits your way of working.

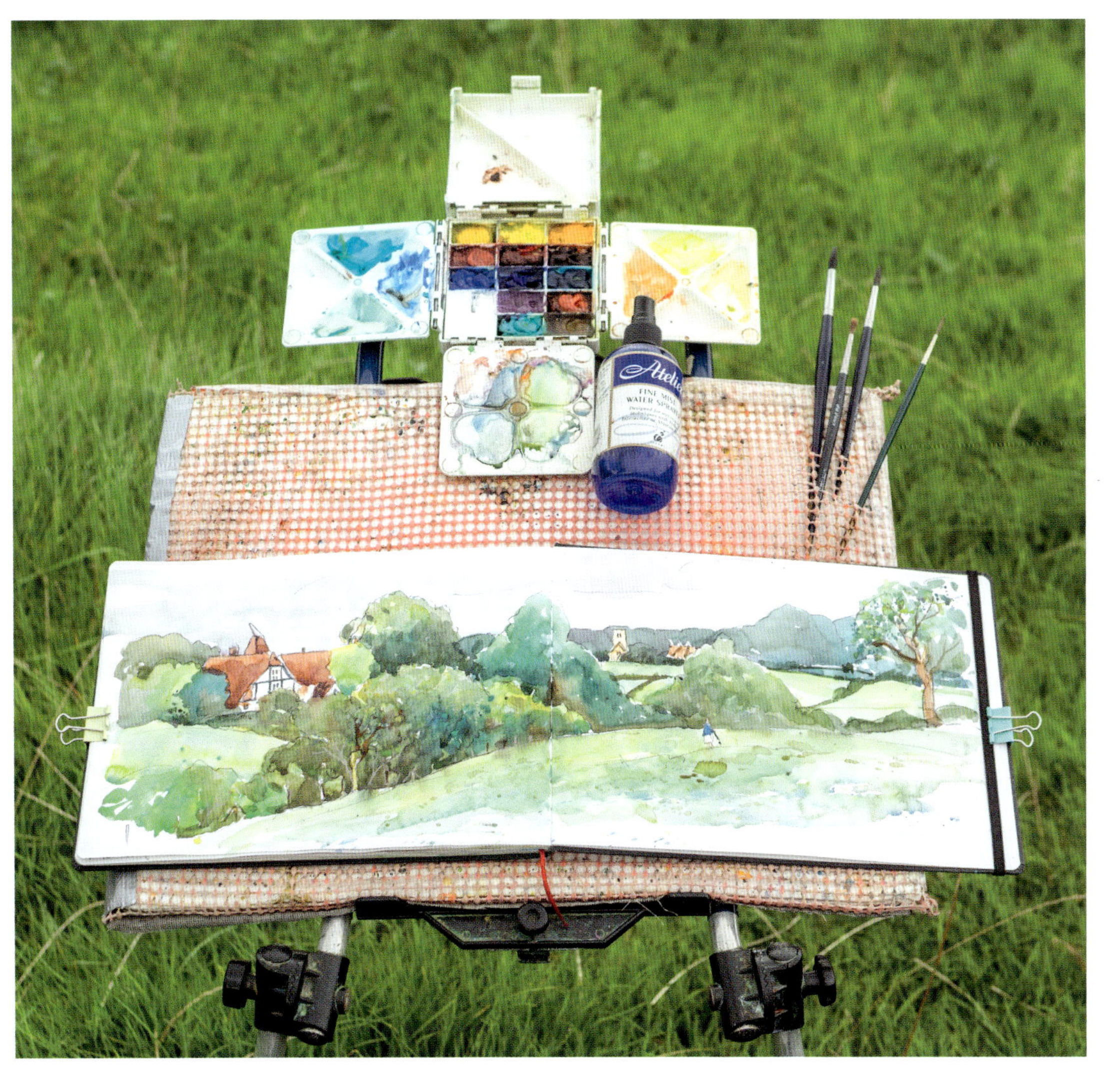

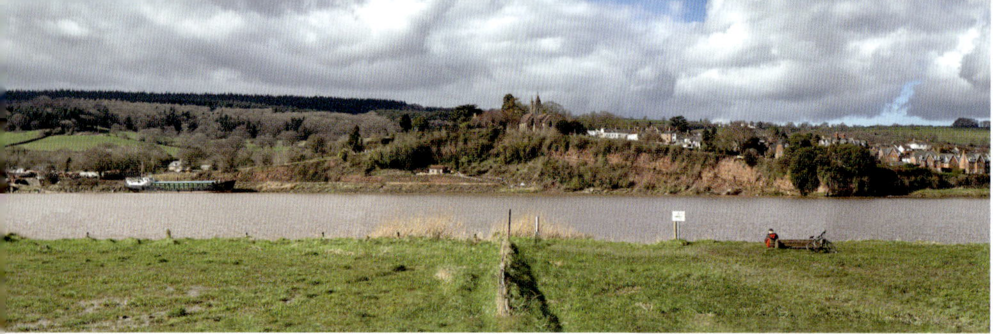
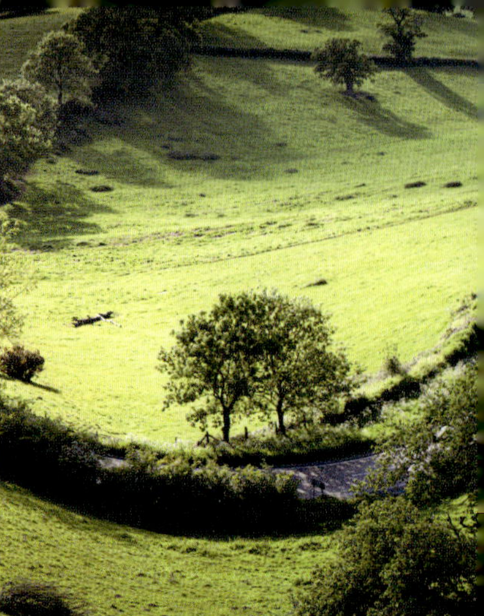

Where should I go nearby?

Choosing where to go to paint can be tricky. However, if you just head out with your trusty sketchbook, with no preconceived idea of what you'll be sketching, you could find a wealth of painting subjects on your doorstep. Without the pressure of having to seek out the 'perfect' picturesque view that will make a super painting, you can start sketching anything you like the look of – it might even be right there in your garden! Your garden furniture, an array of flowerpots, a garden wall with trailing flowers – literally anything that takes your fancy.

Over the years I have travelled to many wonderful destinations at home and abroad and painted them, but in recent times I have taken to painting some of the lovely spots in and around our village.

An often overlooked subject is the lovely network of country lanes which criss-cross the UK and these are an endless supply of exciting and varied scenes for me. I did a series of articles for *The Artist* magazine entitled 'Along a country lane' on this very subject and it brought it home to me just what a super theme it is.

Seek out scenes which excite you in your local area, wherever is home for you.

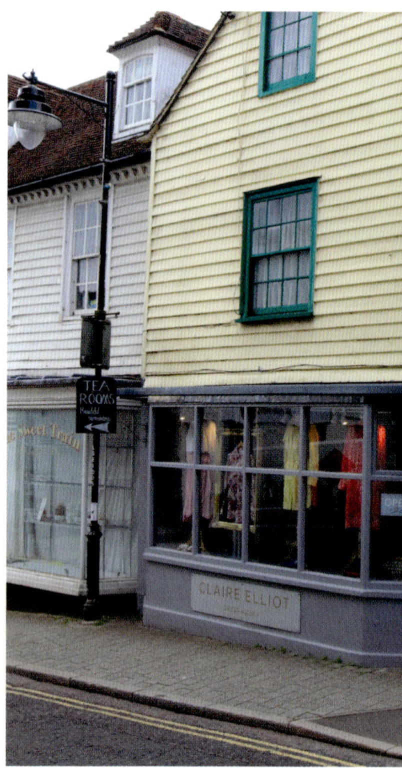

Consider your options before setting out

What types of scene do you really like? Here are a few of the different venues which might be available to you in your local area, and there is a wide variety of scenes within these categories:

- **Countryside and villages**
- **Coast and seaside**
- **Towns and cities**
- **Hills and mountains**

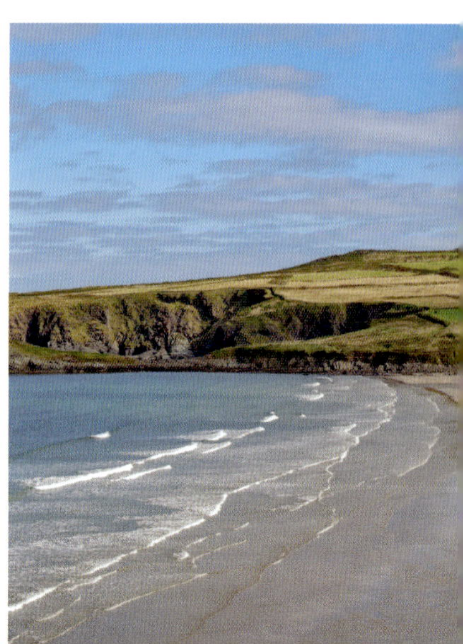

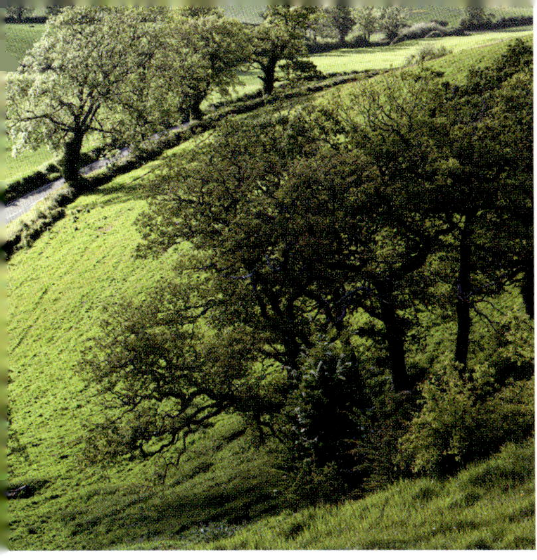
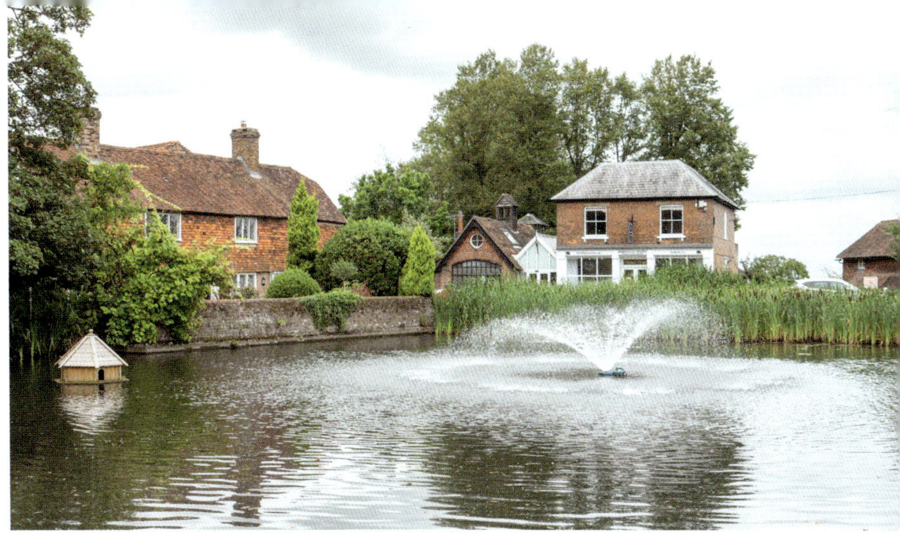
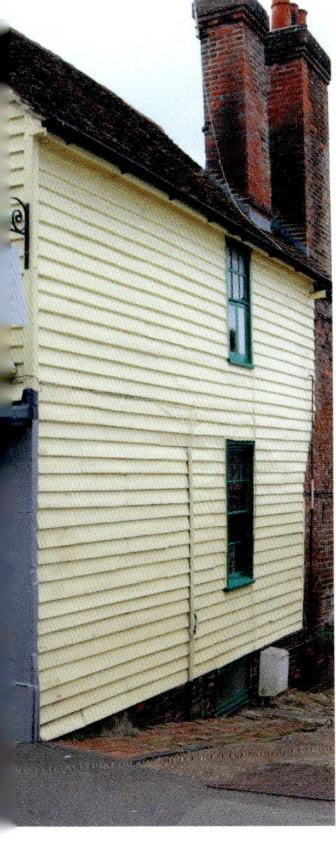
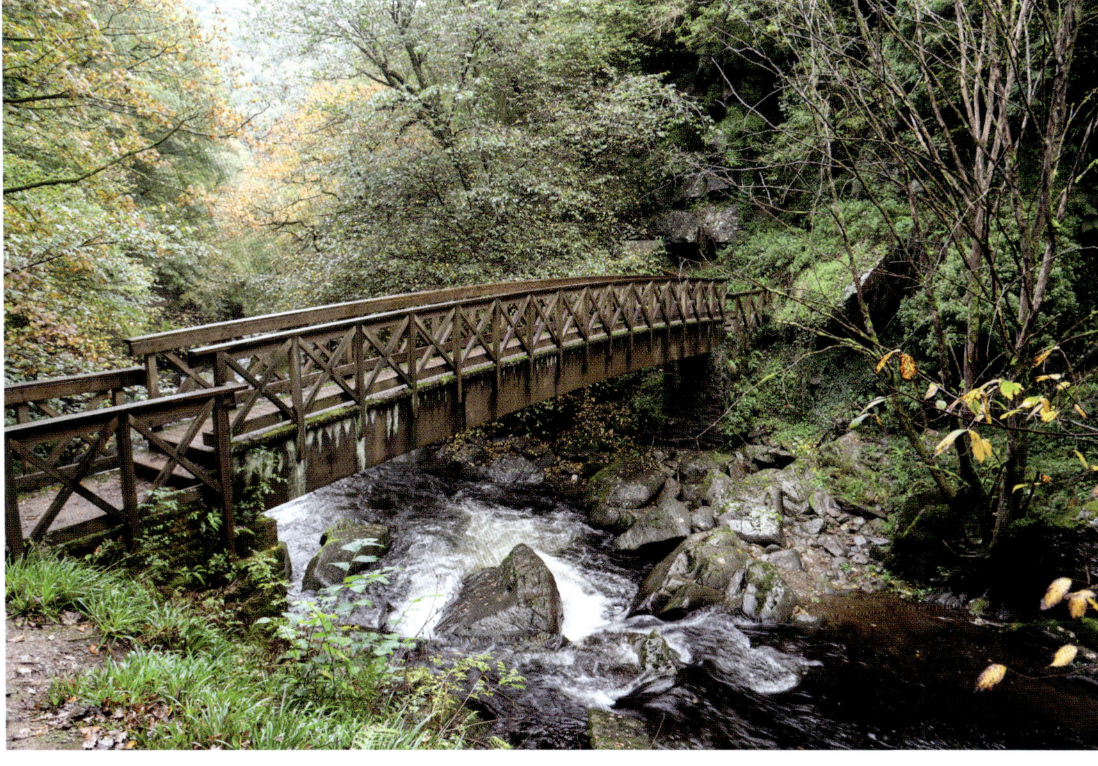
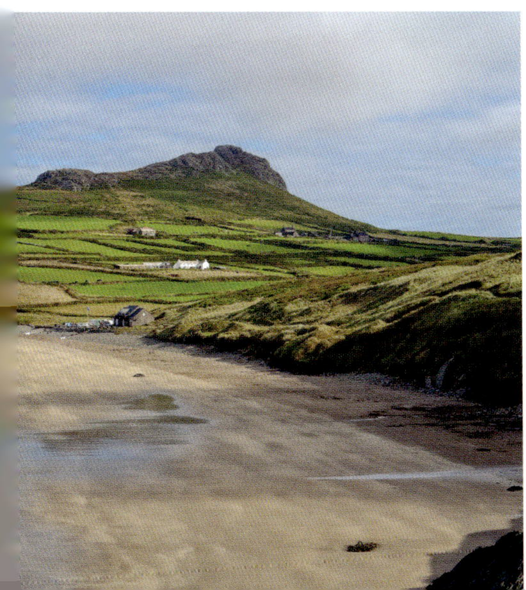
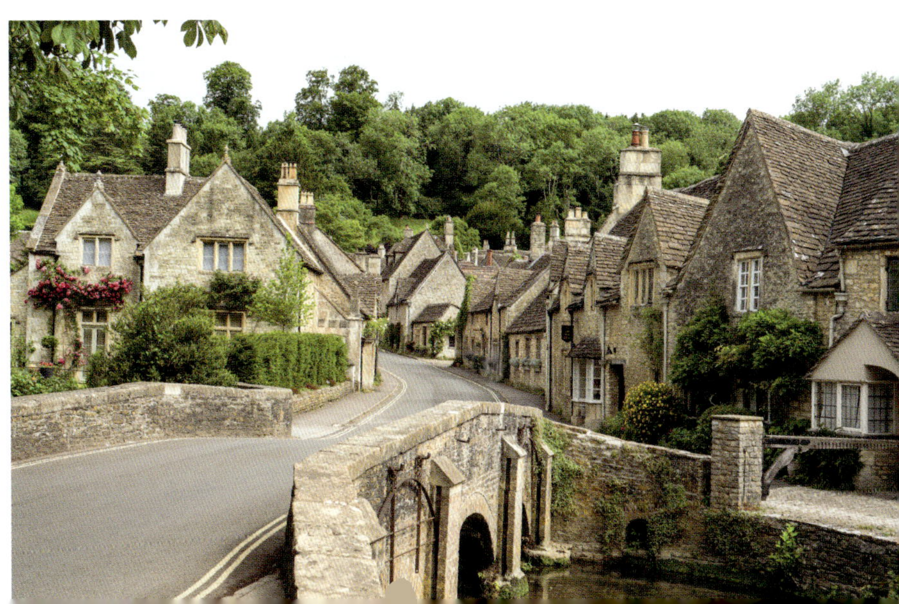

Countryside and villages

Country lanes are all around us in my part of the world and many are eminently paintable. Footpaths, green lanes and bridleways give access to all sorts of lovely countryside views. Small villages with churches, pubs, castles and village greens are an endless source of inspiration for me.

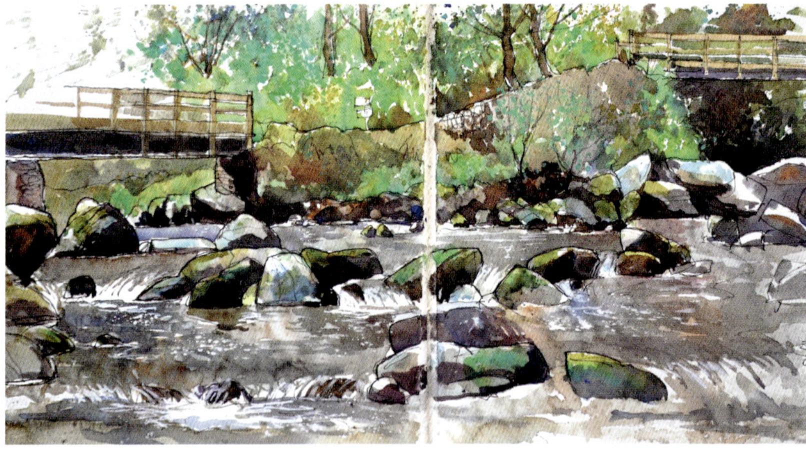

Exmoor has been a favourite haunt for me ever since we had family holidays down there, and Watersmeet was always a magical location. On a walking/painting trip we hiked down from Hillsford Bridge to Watersmeet where we stopped to get some sketching done. I had set up on a few boulders in the middle of the river to do this sketch when the heavens opened and I had to rush for cover. Rain stopped and I resumed, only to be rained off again. After the third time I called it a day but I did manage to get something half decent in my sketchbook (see top). At least you can't fault my perseverance!

On a subsequent trip I wasn't so lucky as the rain never stopped so I had to do some lightning sketches in my small sketchbook. Standing on the bridge I did this quick sketch looking upstream, but it really was too wet so this was all I was able to accomplish.

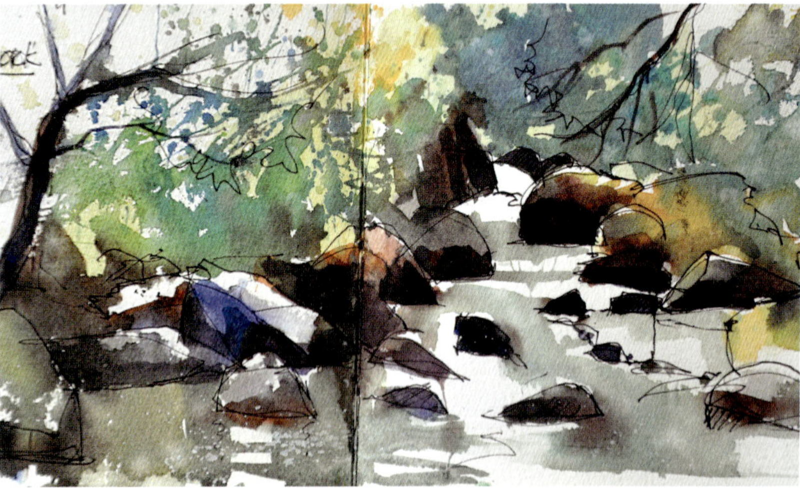

For the sketch below, I took cover under the bridge, only to find that I was being well and truly dripped on, so I might as well have stayed out in the open!

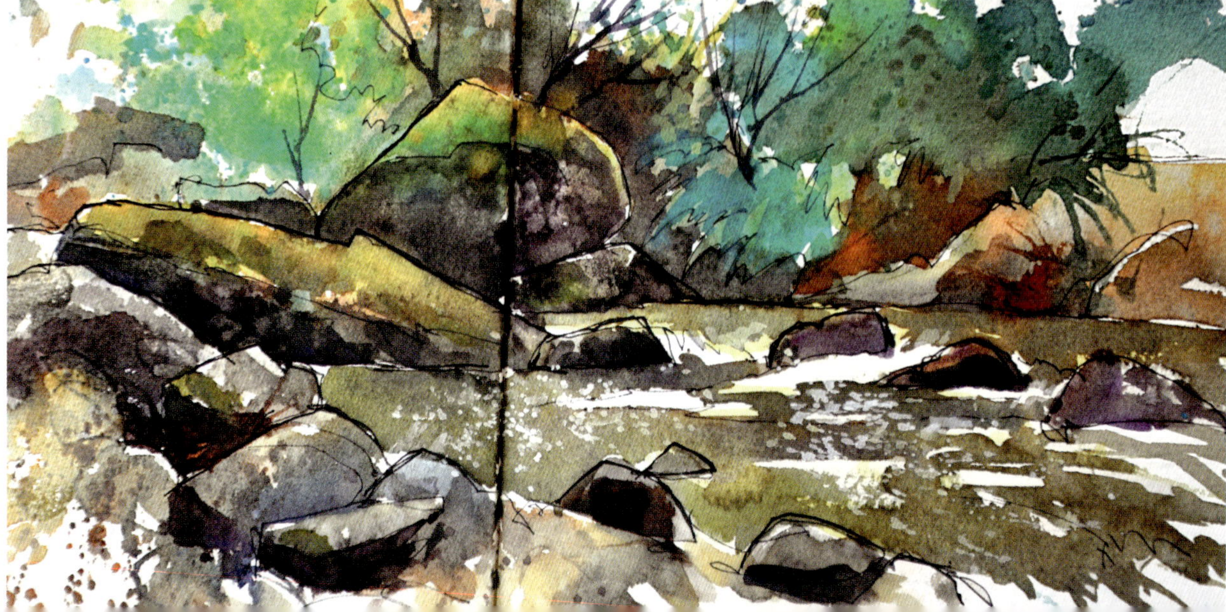

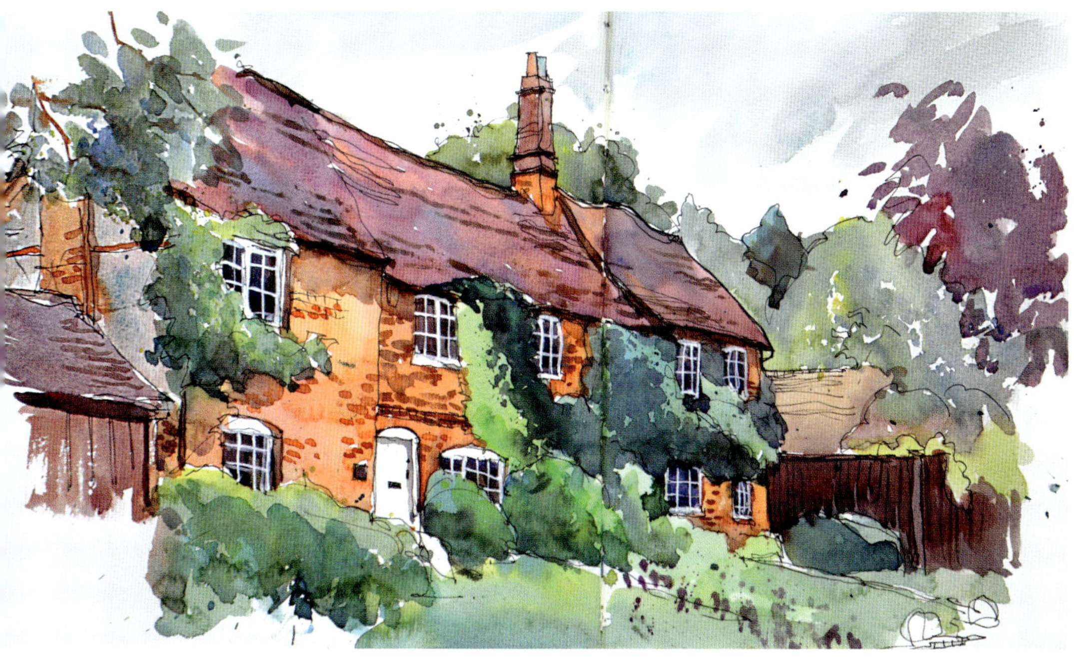

I'm a sucker for a lovely country cottage. I try and shy away from the 'chocolate box' format, instead producing a quick , vibrant and not too overworked rendition. This cottage was in the quiet village of Missenden, Buckinghamshire, down a small lane. This was the first time most of my students had painted en plein air, but they thoroughly enjoyed the outing once they shed their inhibitions.

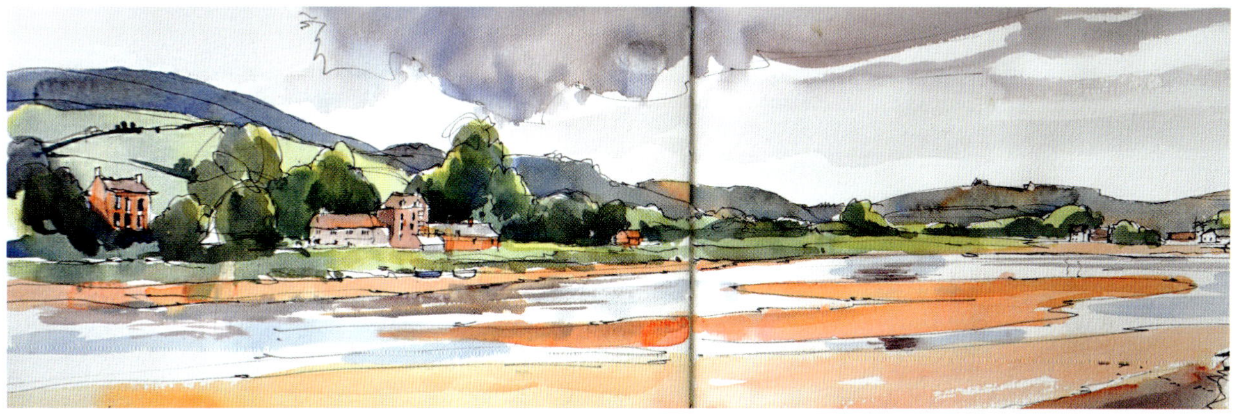

A view across the River Severn, looking towards the village of Newnham on the opposite side at the Arlingham Loop, a huge S-bend in the river.

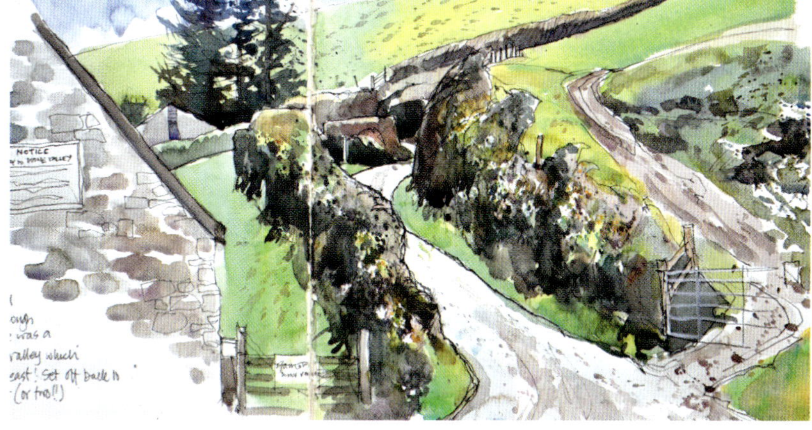

I loved the way this country lane snaked its way up into the moor. We were painting all day at this delightful hamlet of Malmsmead in the heart of the Doone Valley in Exmoor.

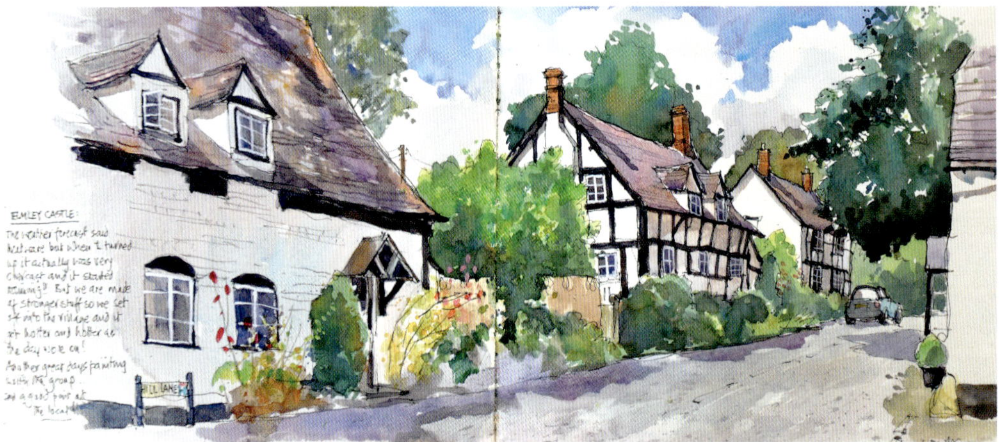

The quiet village of Elmley Castle, Worcestershire, with its array of black-timbered buildings. The weather started off rather unpredictable but once we got started the sun came out and it was a scorcher. The edge of the building on the right is the pub where we had lunch.

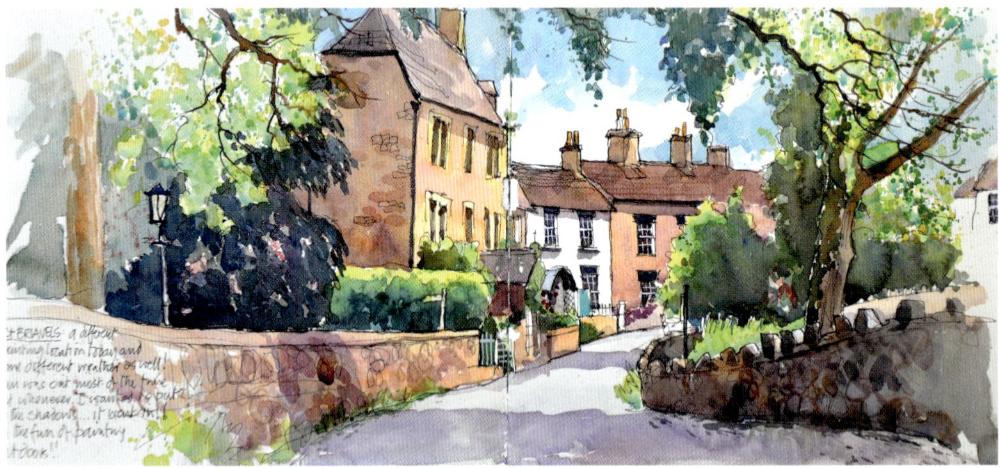

On our trip to the village of St Briavels, Gloucestershire, most people painted the castle which was off to the right of this picture. However I really loved the light catching the buildings and the shadows across the road, so that is what I went for.

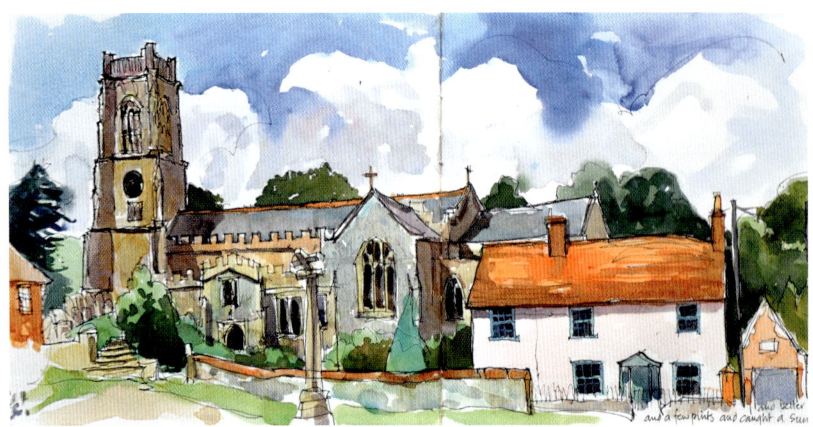

The lovely Church of St Michael stands on a low rise at one end of an elongated village green in Aldbourne, Wiltshire. I had taken groups here a few times and also painted the very colourful Blue Boar pub on the same green. What an idyllic spot.

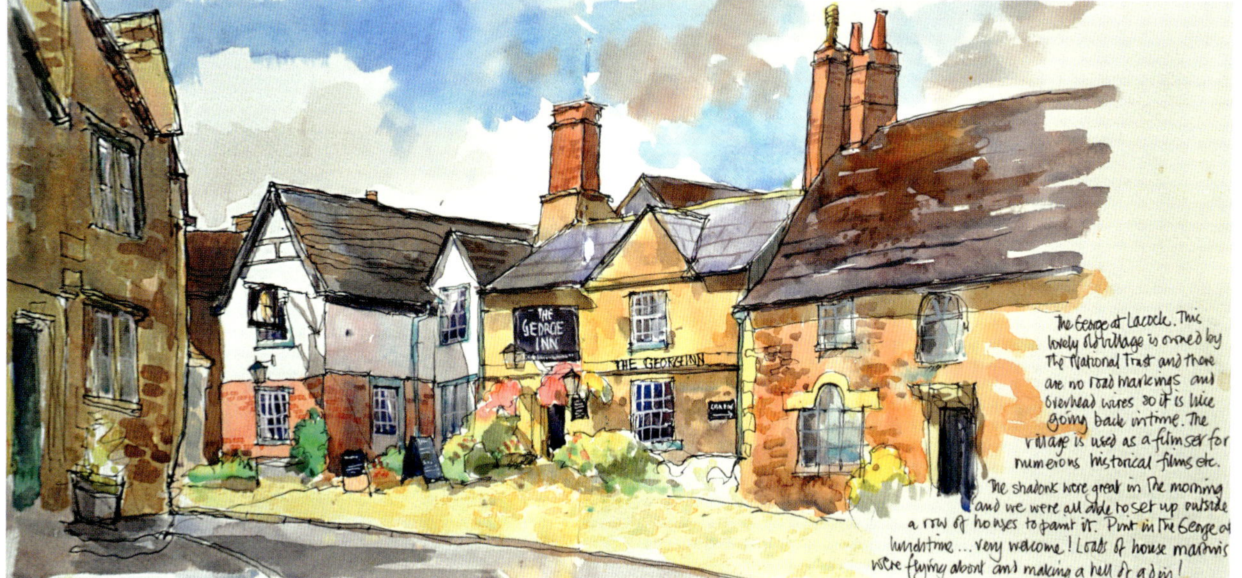

The lovely village of Lacock, Wiltshire, is full of traditional stone houses and looks today much as it did 200 years ago. It's owned by the National Trust and all modern trappings like road markings and overhead cables are absent, which all adds to its unique appeal. We set up across the road from The George Inn to get this sketch and then went inside for a lunchtime pint!

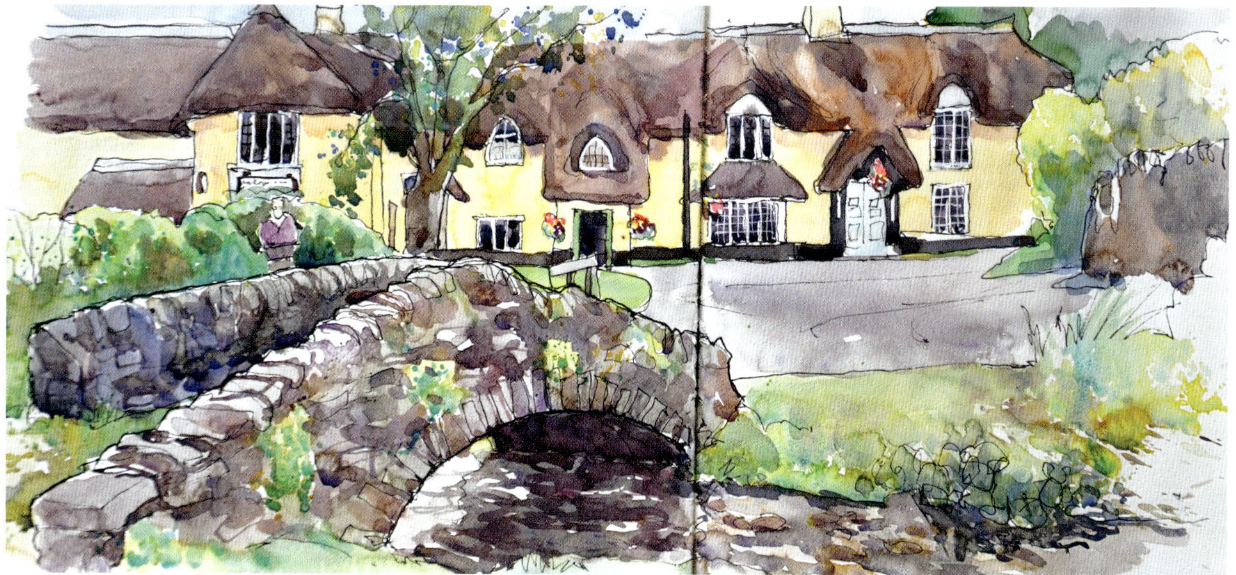

This delightful packhorse bridge is in the middle of the quaint village of Winsford in the heart of Exmoor. My dad was from the area and he would take us on holidays around all the wonderful sights of Exmoor when we were young. It was a treat to revisit this place after all those years.

Coast and seaside

Getting down to the sea is one of my favourite things and the rocky coastline of Pembrokeshire in Wales is hard to beat. The sea with all its moods and atmosphere is a constant challenge and wave studies in your sketchbook can be invaluable. Take a walk around a harbour and experience all the sights and sounds: boats bobbing around at high tide but left high and dry at jaunty angles at low tide; or quaint cottages dotted about the harbour front, criss-crossed with tiny alleyways.

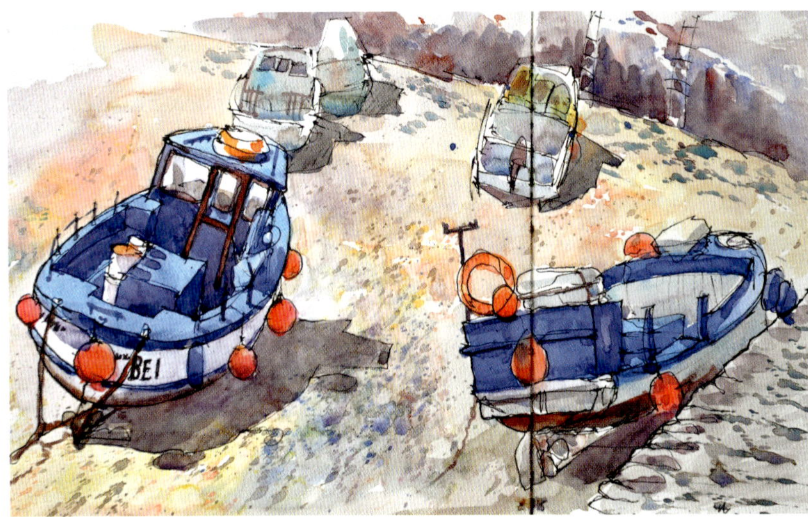

Looking down into Lynmouth Harbour, Devon, with these two lovely blue boats sitting on the sea bed at low tide. A lovely sunny day with strong shadows.

A short walk along the coast of Guernsey in the Channel Islands brought us to this spot with these colourful rock outcrops. It was a really hot day with no sea breeze to cool us down, but a good spot to paint from nonetheless.

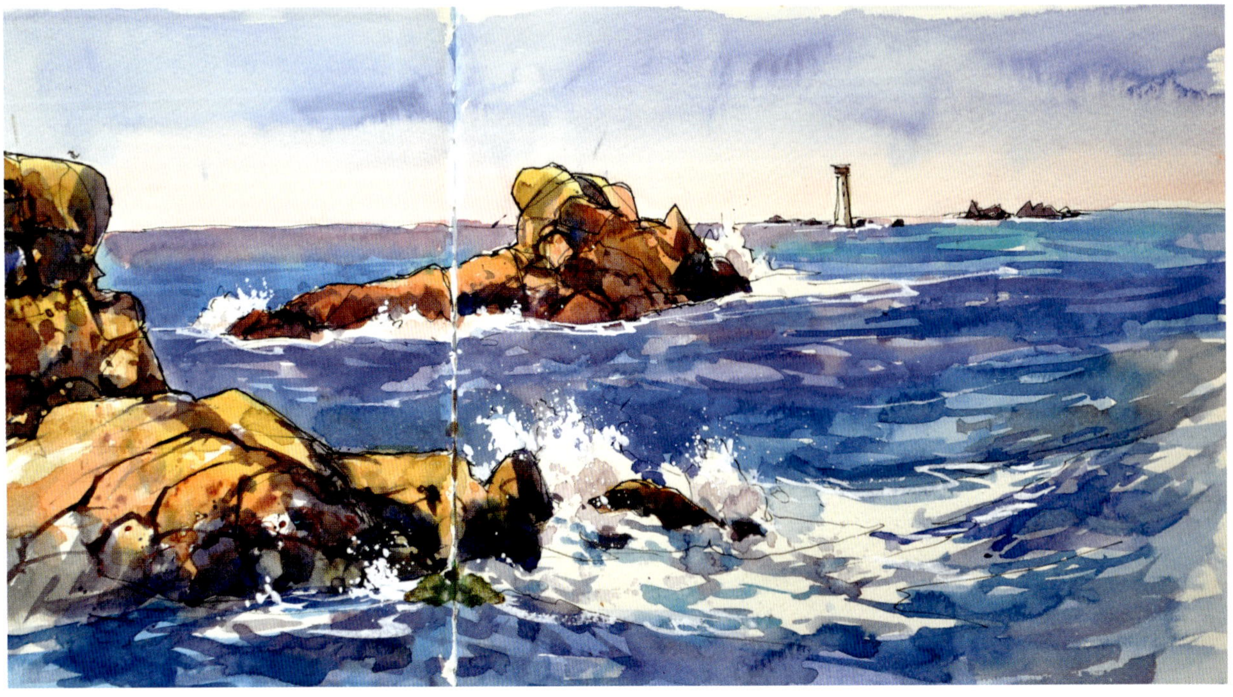

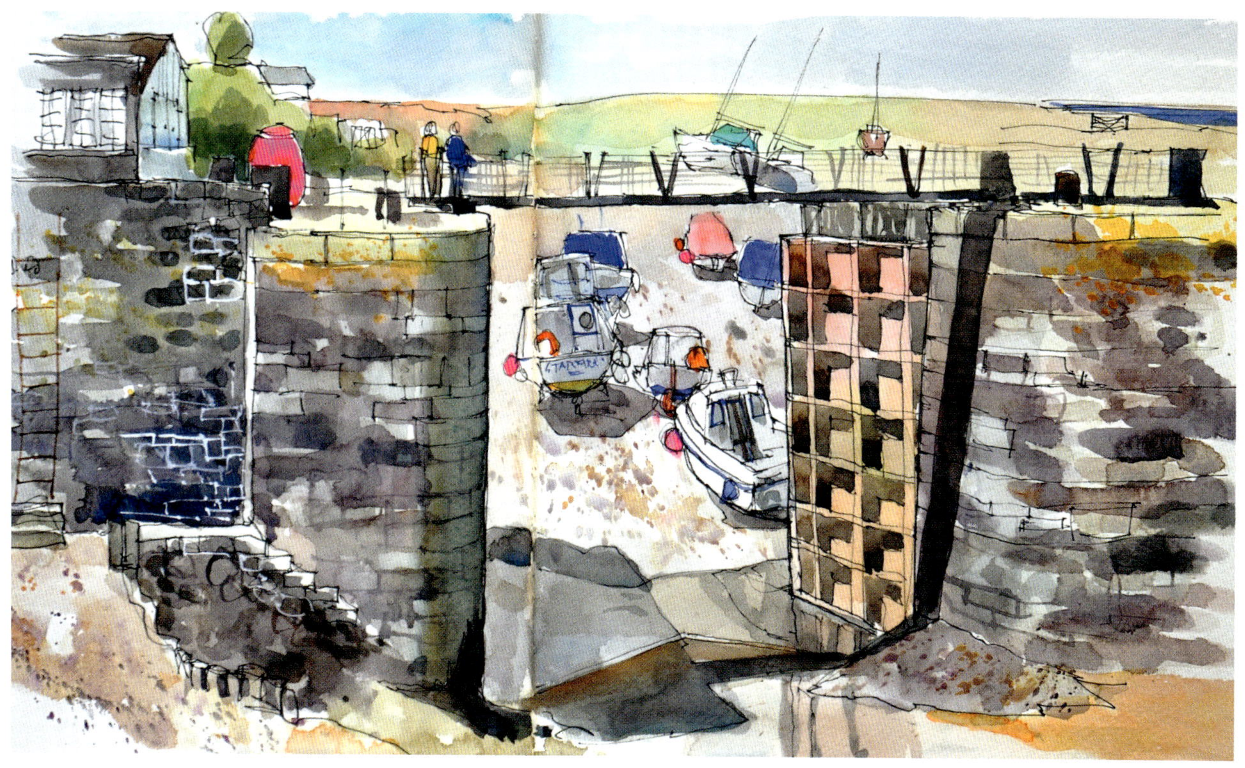

The first things that hit me when we arrived at Porlock Weir, Somerset, were the huge harbour dock gates and the equally impressive harbour walls, so I just had to paint the scene. It all looks totally different at high tide as I discovered on a subsequent trip to the area.

While waiting for the ferry from Sark to take us back to Guernsey, I did this sketch of the Sark Lighthouse perched high up on the cliff. The weather was building up and there were some super cloud formations which I just had to capture.

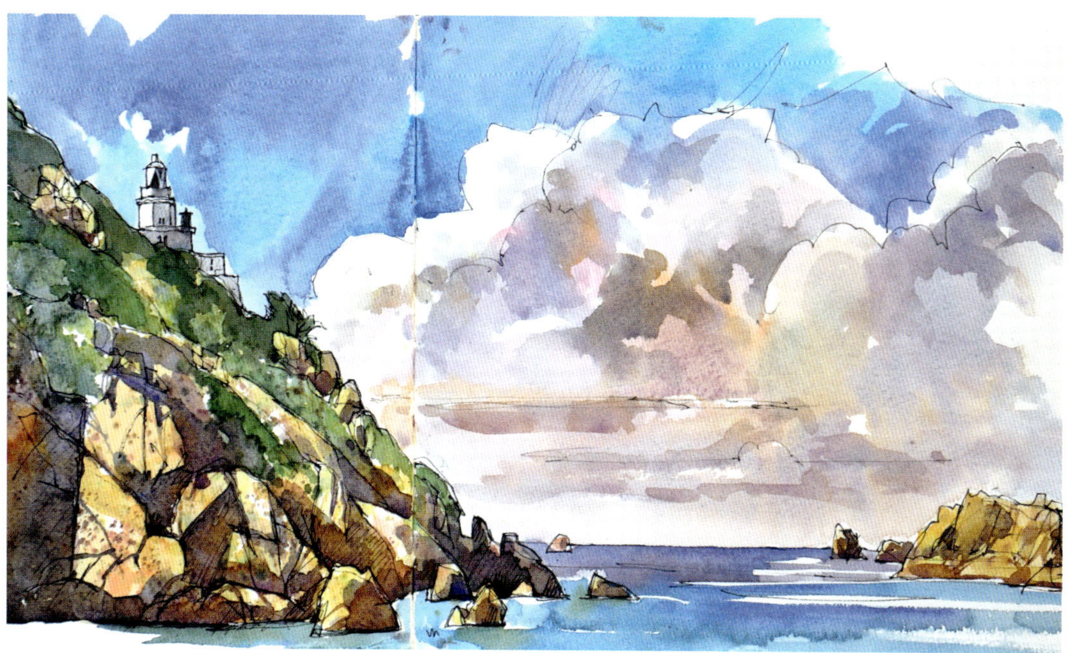

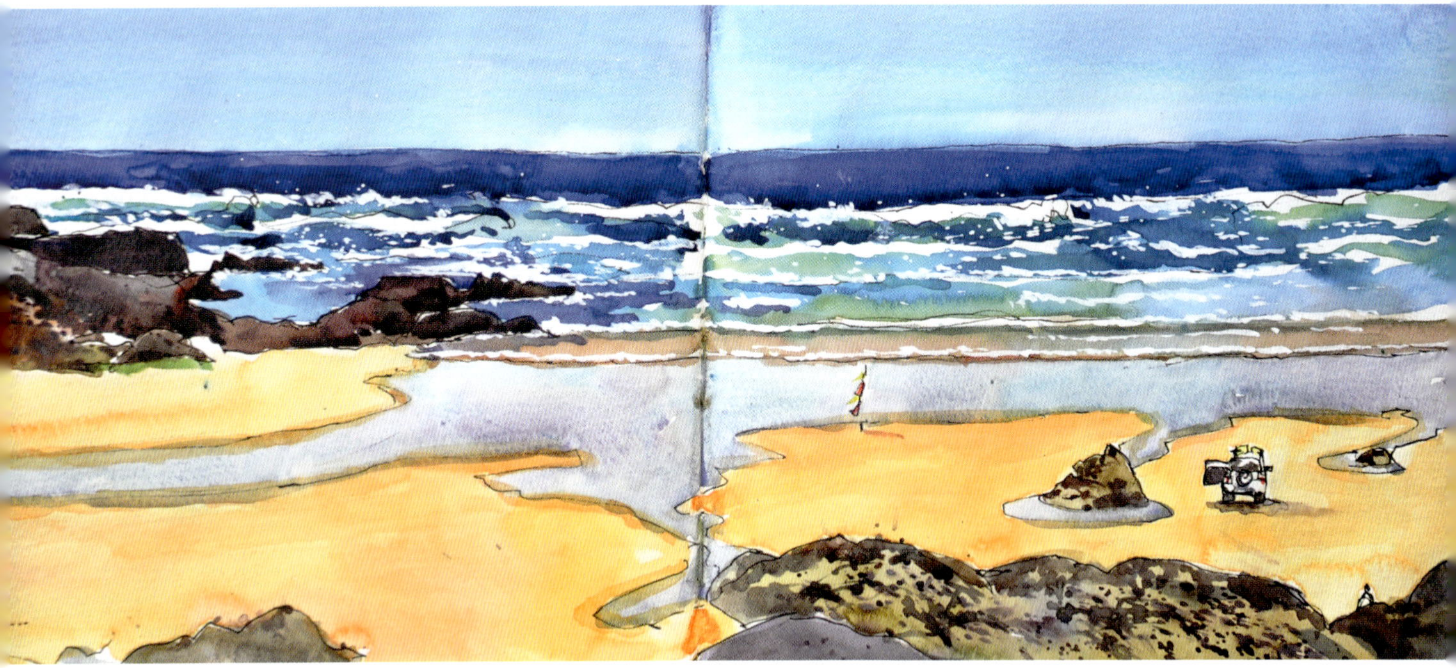

A panorama of a rather wild sea along the Cornish coast. This is when the landscape format of the sketchbook really comes into its own.

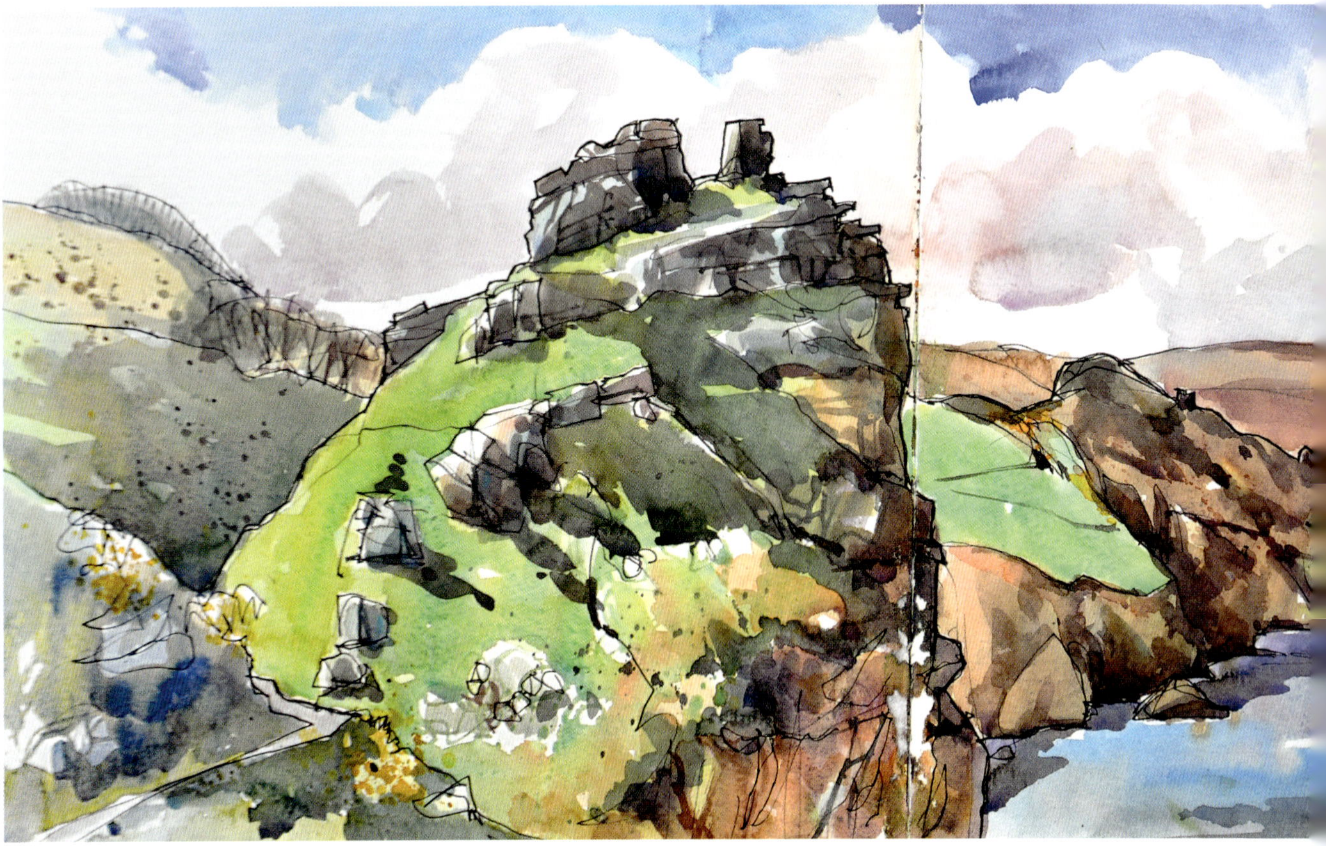

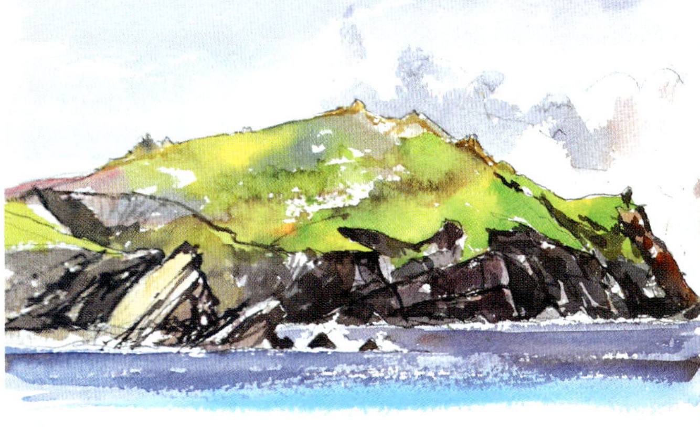

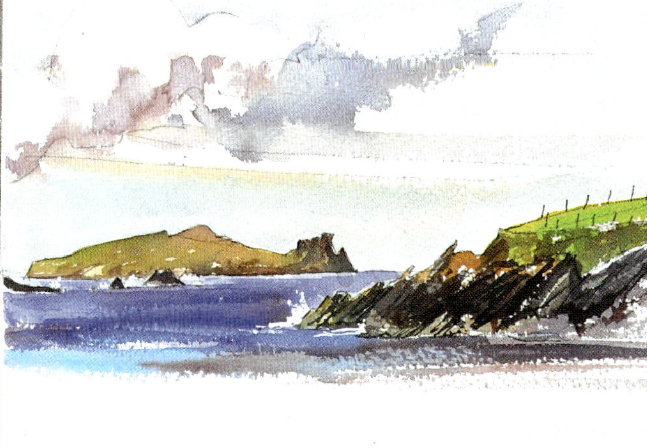

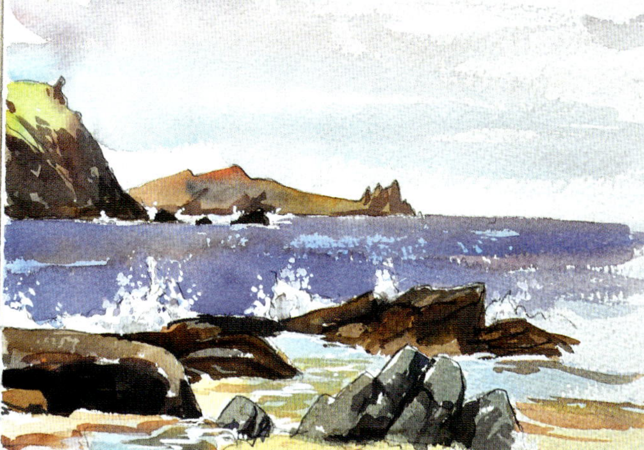

Two sketches looking out from the small semicircular sandy beach of Clogher Strand in Dingle, Ireland, across the Atlantic towards the 'sleeping giant' isle off Inis Tuaisceart. The bottom sketch was done further to the left of the top view towards the rocks to get some shelter from the wind that had picked up.

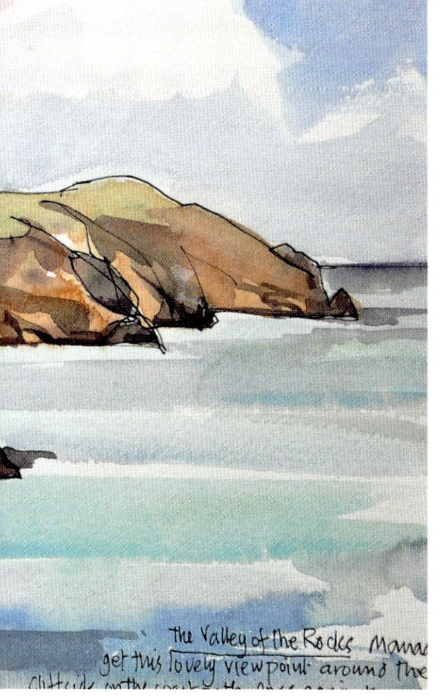

The walk along the coastal footpath from Lynmouth towards the Valley of Rocks is quite breathtaking. Due to its close proximity to the cliff edge, finding a suitable spot to set up and paint was always going to be tricky, and enabling a small group to do likewise was quite a logistical problem. However each artist managed to get their own view with everyone stretched out along the path, so it worked well.

Towns and cities

Don't be put off by the hustle and bustle of a busy town or city as
you might be missing an important trick in your sketching repertoire.
Depending on the venue you choose, there could be all manner of lovely
and quirky buildings, roofscapes, ornate doorways and windows, market
squares, cafés and restaurants with a host of customers dotted about.

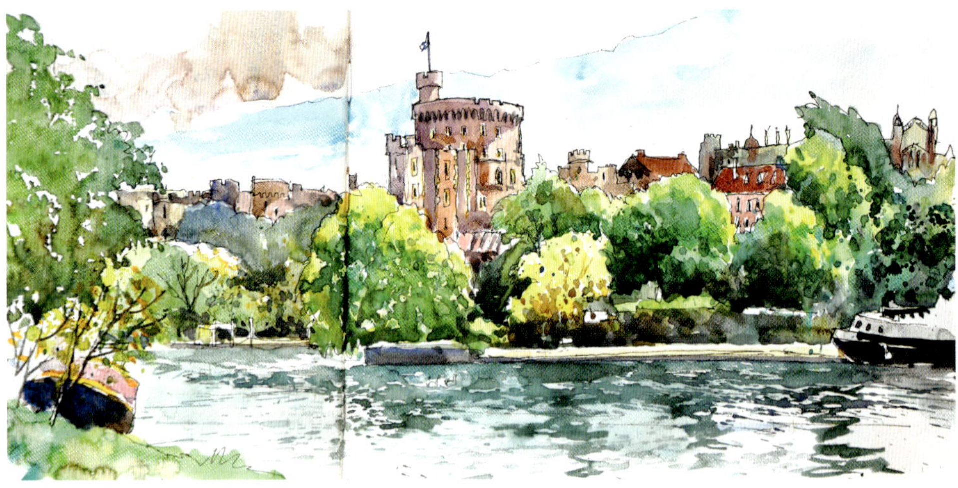

*On a painting excursion to Windsor I had in mind the view I wanted – the castle with the round tower
sitting majestically above the river. We walked all over the place trying to get that view and only found
it when Jean, who lived nearby, pointed us in the right direction across the meadows.*

*Setting up to get this view of the entrance to the Wandsworth Brewery in Devizes, Wiltshire put
me right in the middle of the pavement beside a very busy road! Anyway, I think the result was
worth the effort.*

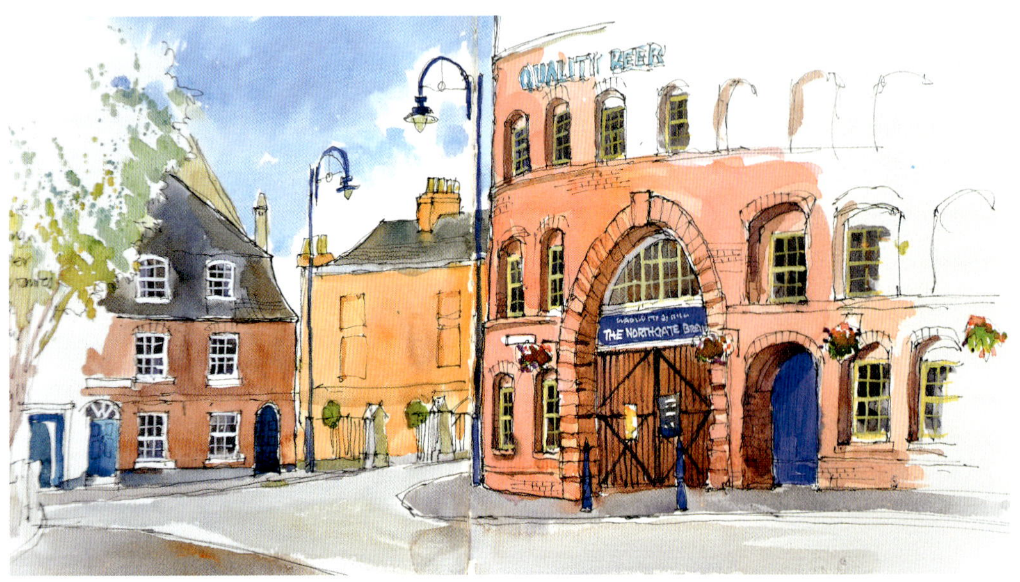

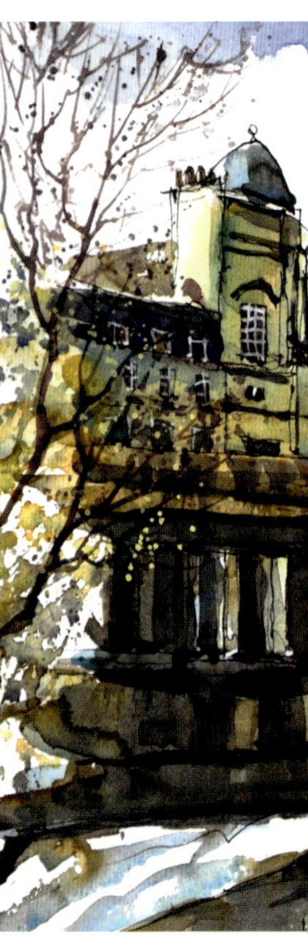

We were supposed to be painting the pubs of
Willshire but the forecast was for torrential rain,
and they didn't get it wrong. So I managed to get
access to the cloisters of Salisbury Cathedral
where we painted the glorious spire under cover.
I had to turn the sketchbook on its end to get
the majority of the building included and it was
certainly a demanding subject.

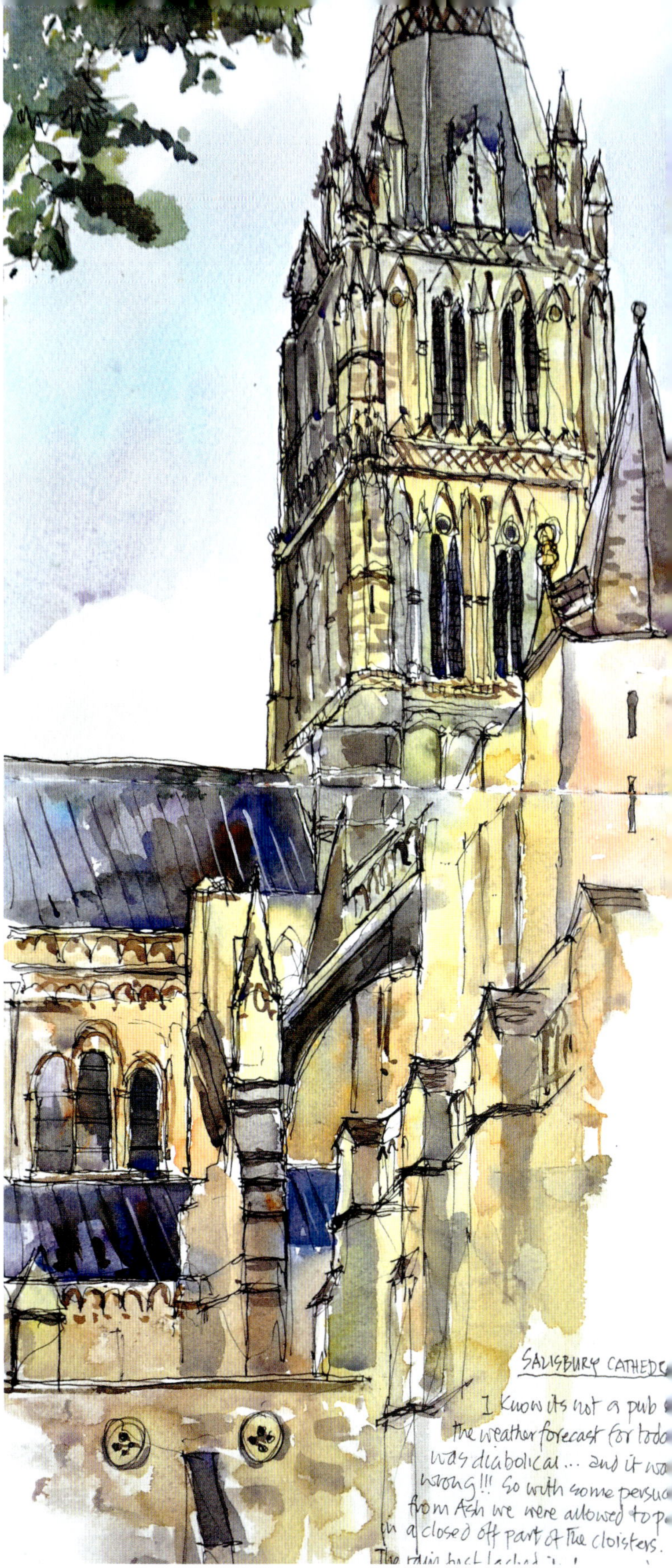

Pulteney Bridge in Bath was styled on the
Ponte Vecchio in Florence, with shops on both sides
of the span. A classical building which is a joy to paint.
This is a pen and wash sketch.

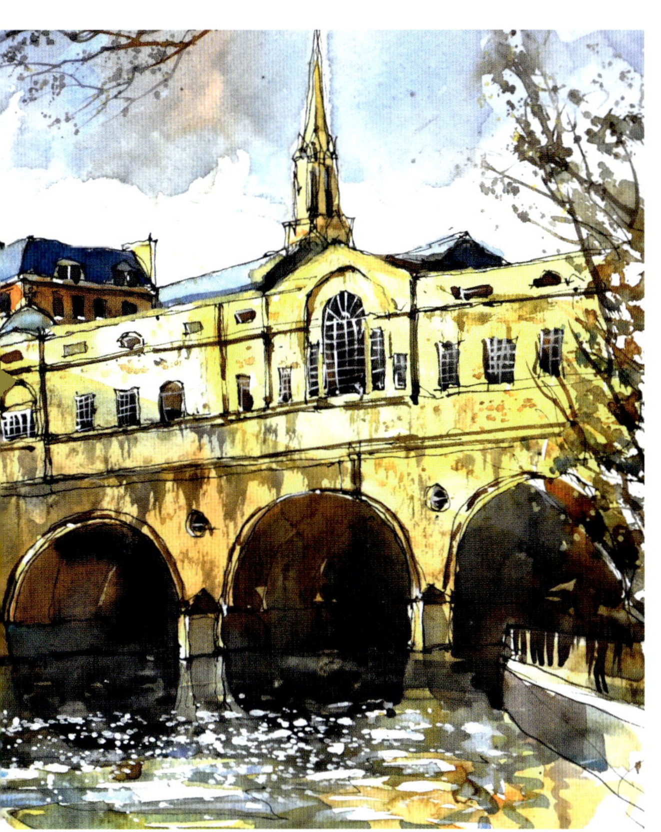

Hills and mountains

From the window of our house in Herefordshire, we can see Garway Hill with its pillbox on the summit, and just discernible on a clear day are the distant outlines of the Black Mountains in Wales. We are never far away from hills and mountains, but I still love my trips up to the Lake District with all their magnificent peaks and lakes, and to the wonderful array of different mountains dotted along the west coast of Ireland.

If you like a bit of solitude and fancy the wider view, then setting off into the hills might be your thing. This is when painting a panorama across two pages really comes into its own to capture the expanse of the view.

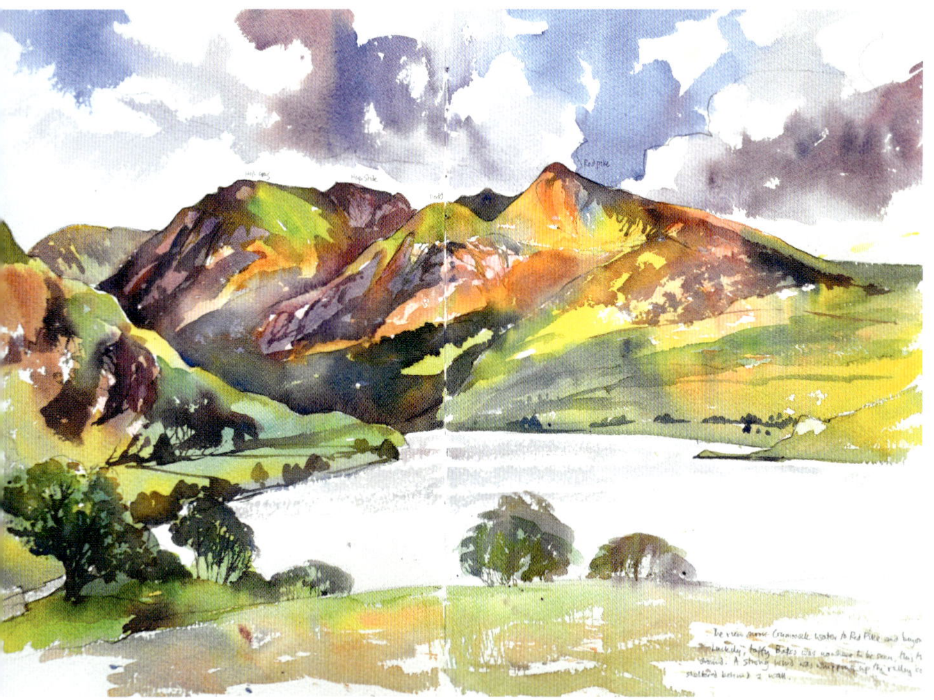

The Lake District was always a very popular destination for painting holidays, but each time we went the dry days became fewer and further between until the last trip was almost solid rain. On the days when it wasn't raining, we managed to do some lively sketches and this is a selection of them. One of the locals who joined us knew the names of all the peaks so I annotated my sketches with them: High Crag, High Stile, Dodd, Red Pike (sketch on left); Herdus, Great Borne, Bowness Knott, Starling Dodd, Red Pike, High Stile, High Crag, Anglers Crag (sketch below). Just another advantage of doing a sketch rather than a more conventional painting – adding all those jottings helps bring back many memories and is so much fun to do!

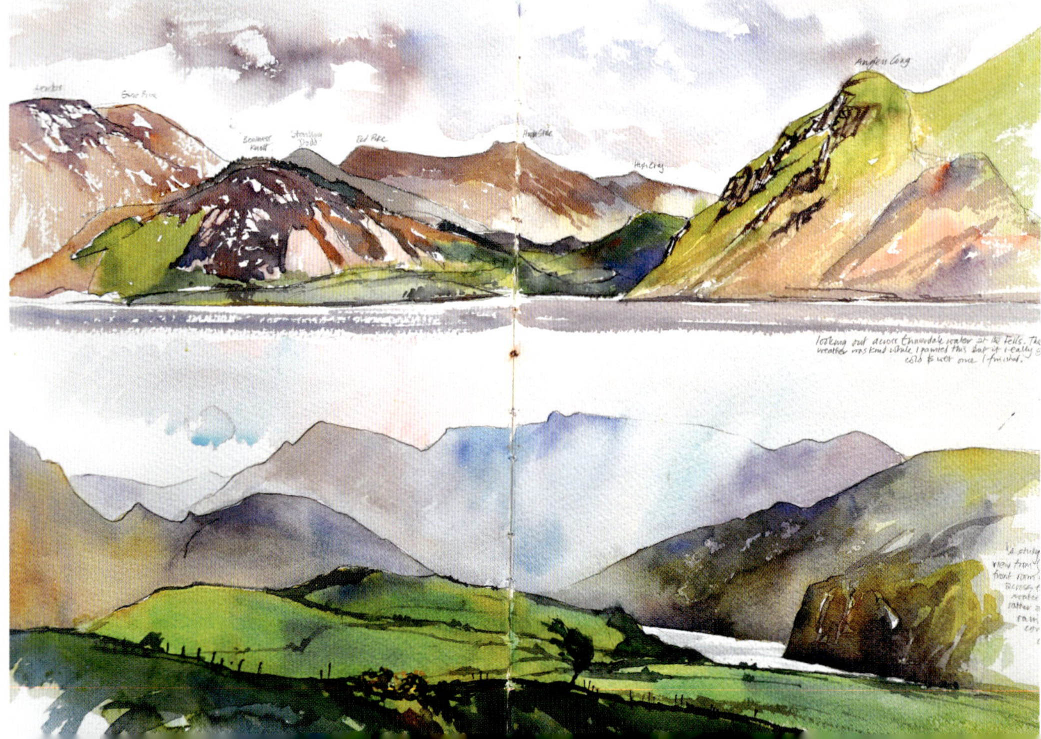

This was a demo I did for the art group at Ashton under Hill,
Worcestershire. There were some lovely clouds that morning so
I set up outside to do an en plein air demo of the scene. This is
the image that features on the front cover of the book.

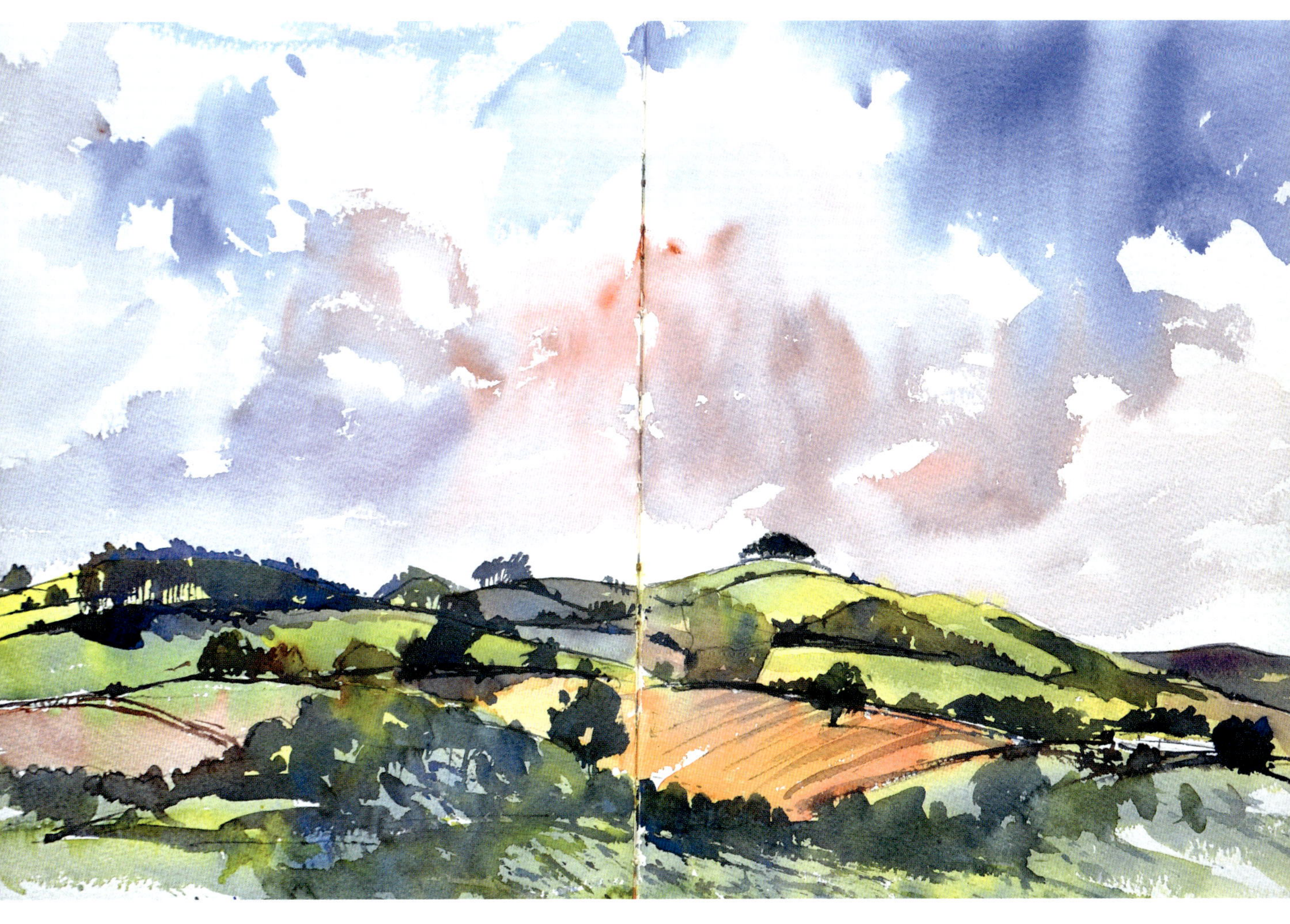

These were morning and afternoon sketches done on the banks of Derwent Water in the Lake District. I painted them in my largest sketchbook which opened out to give me an A2 (420 x 594mm/16½ x 23½in) panorama so I could get lots of detail in there. The afternoon sketch was looking back over where I set up in the morning (you can see the outline arrow on that sketch showing the morning's site), this time towards Skiddaw.

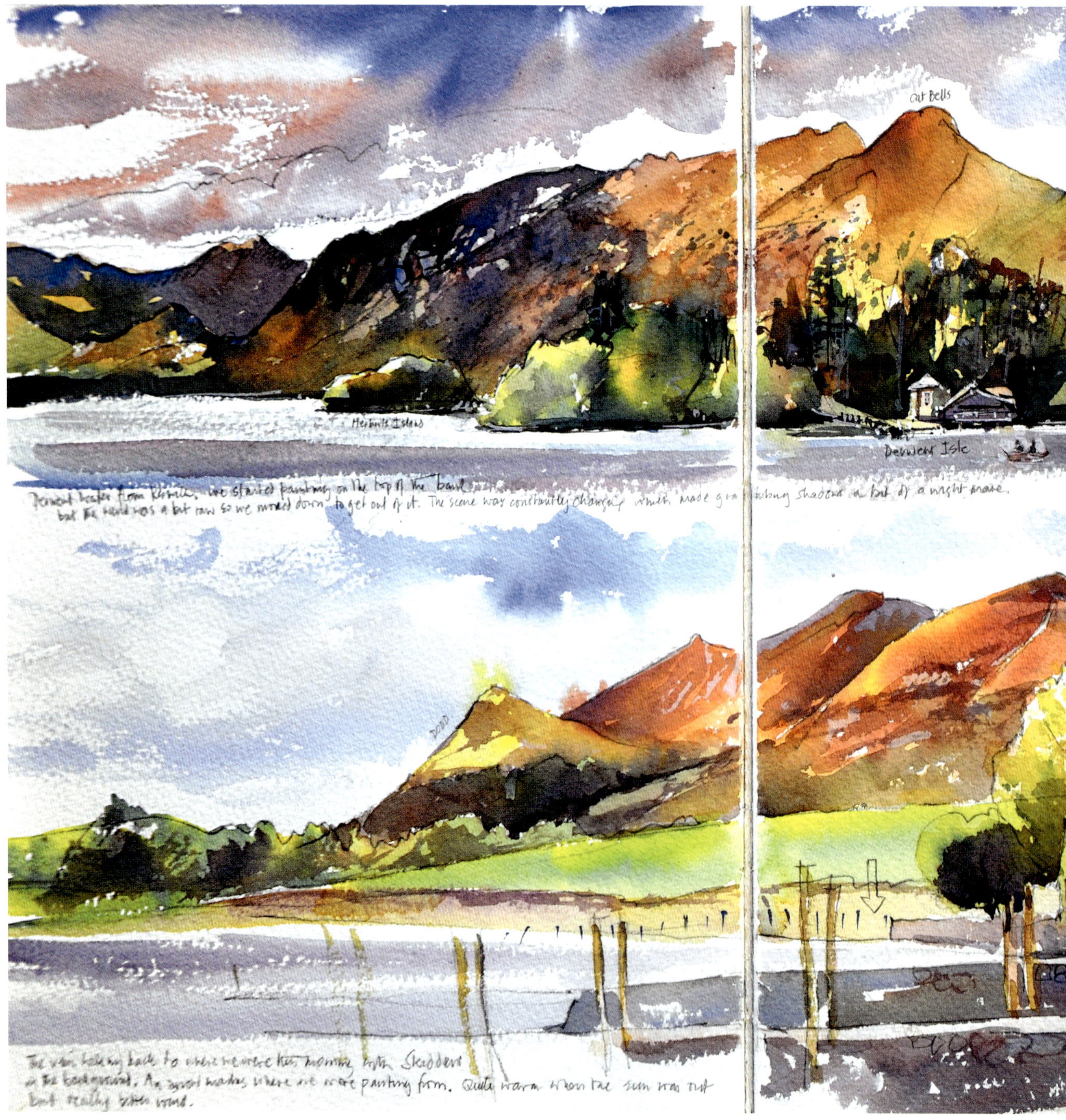

Check conditions

Weather forecast

If you are planning to sketch close to home then it isn't as important, but if you are looking to travel further afield, it's always a good idea to check the weather forecast before you leave. That does sound a bit obvious but if you set off in the sunshine for a day's painting only to be caught out in a deluge, you'll wish you'd had a quick check beforehand, as you'd have known what was ahead!

Coastal areas can be much more changeable and erratic in their weather systems, so always pack a rainproof for those unforeseen elements.

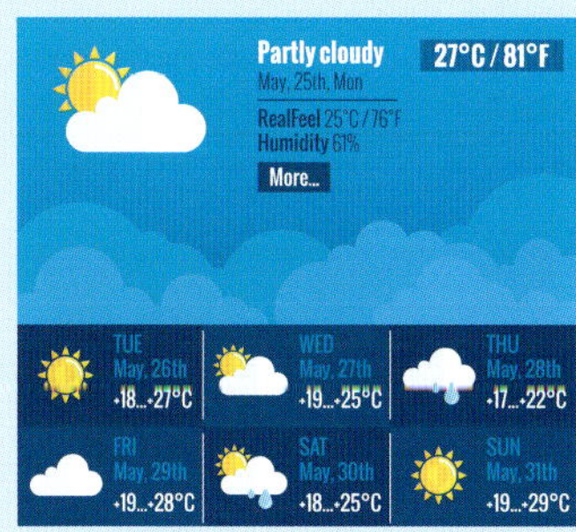

Consult a map

The large scale 1:25K (2½in to 1 mile) Ordnance Survey (OS) maps are a great asset if you are planning a trip, especially if it entails some walking or hiking. The maps cover the whole of the UK and show both rural and urban areas in great detail. For those on foot in rural areas it is most useful as they show public rights of way and a comprehensive contour grid which can give you a good indication of the lie of the land. Find the equivalent of the OS map in your location.

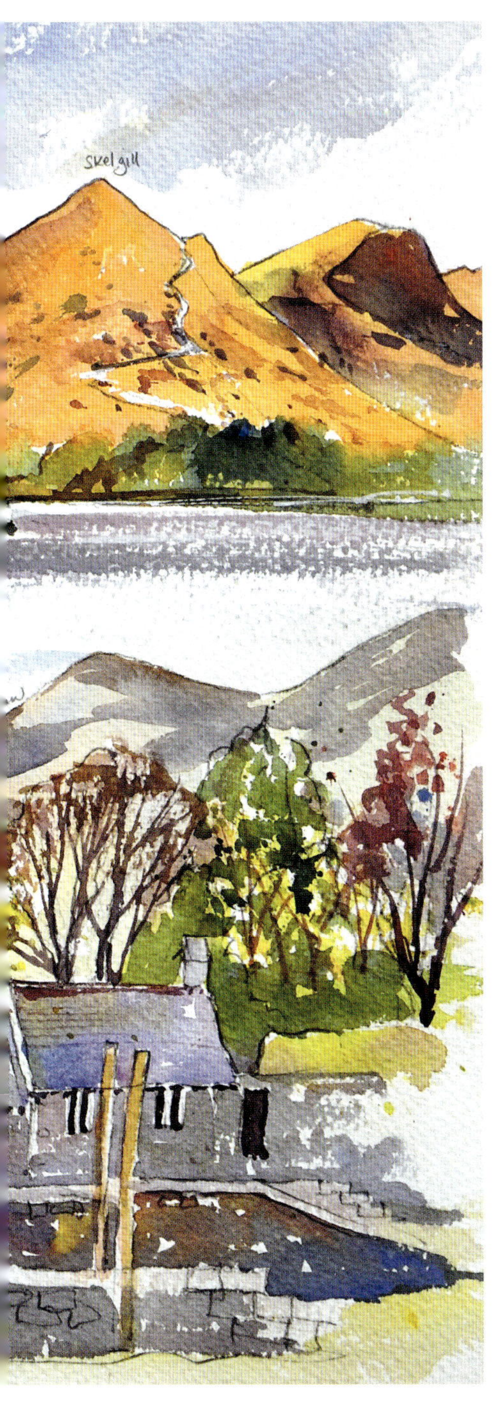

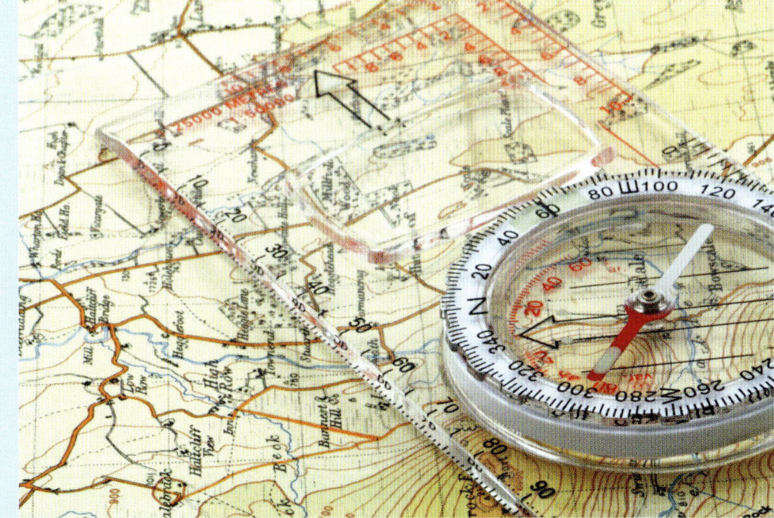

Where should I go further afield?

Packing up all your painting gear ready for a week or two in a foreign country can be an exciting experience. The one downside is having to decide what to take and what to leave behind. In all the years I have been travelling, my kit has been pared down to the minimum without leaving any essential sketching gear at home. I tend to choose hot countries, partly because of the artistic benefits of the glorious sun and light and partly because I prefer sketching in warm conditions! This also helps with what to pack as I don't have to worry about cold weather gear which can be bulky and weighty. So less clothing means more room for painting gear which for me is what it's all about.

Light and shade

One of the first things that hits me when I start to paint abroad is how often the light and shadows differ from those near my home in the UK. Mediterranean scenes, for example, are infused with a strong sense of light and the shadows are imbued with all manner of delightful hues which are a joy to paint.

One important thing to consider when sketching in a hot country is finding some *shade*! This might sound obvious, but it really can make or break an enjoyable sketching session. I have had students painting out in the open sun and ending up with sunstroke: not pleasant!

The day we visited Bocairent, this little gem nestled in the Sierra Mariola mountains in Spain, it was around 45°C and that's hot! We were guided to a flat area on the opposite side of the ravine which was bounded by the huge stone walls of the local cemetery. These walls kept us in the shade for most of the painting session which allowed me to complete this rather intricate panoramic sketch of the town in relative comfort.

I was so taken with the place that I painted up a large acrylic painting back in the Spanish studio (see inset). Having my sketch for reference and not just a photograph really helped me get my original feel of the place into the painting.

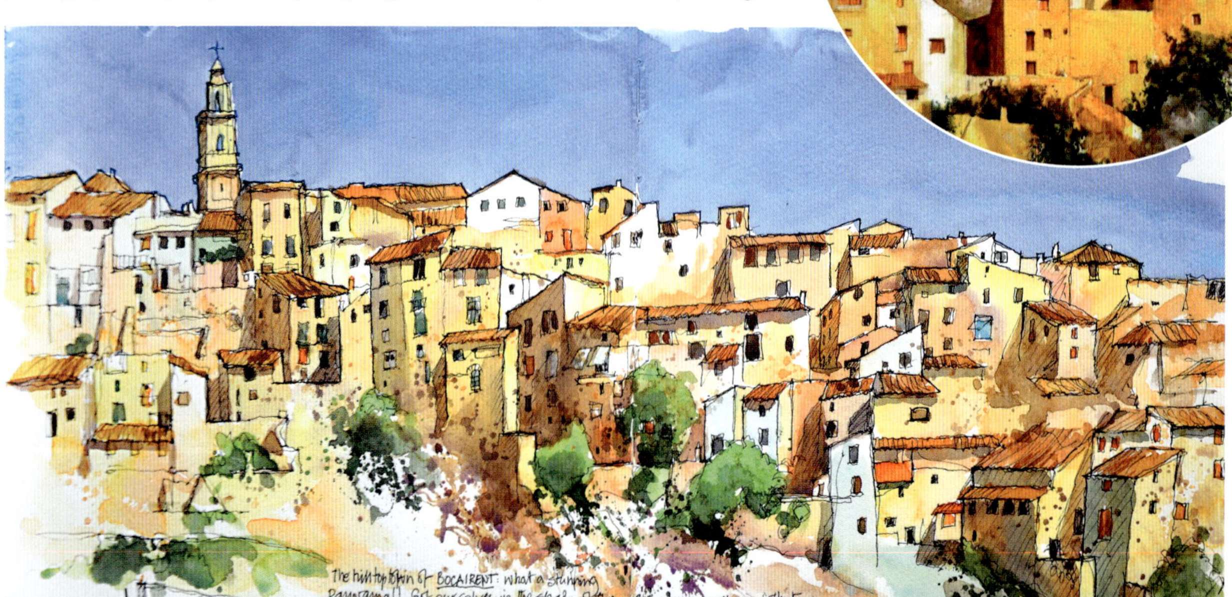

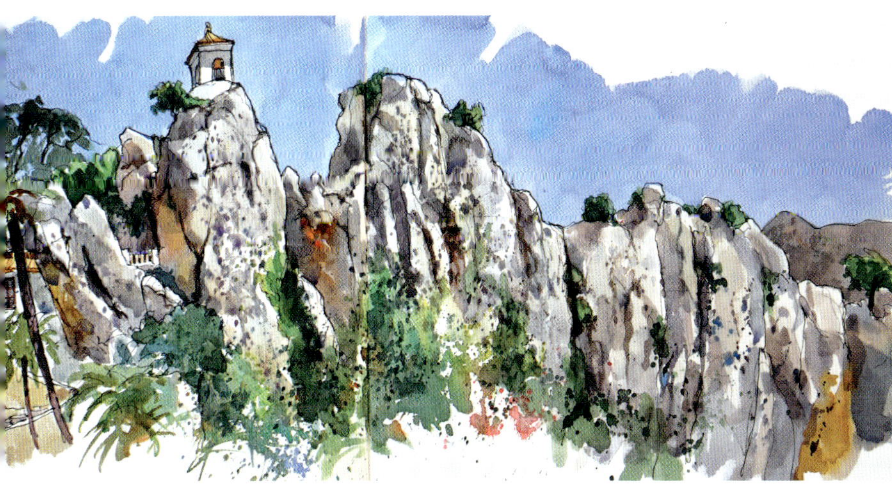

Guadalest was a must-see destination on our Spanish painting holiday and we weren't disappointed. I knew the view I wanted so I managed to talk my way, in my pigeon Spanish, to securing a patio area in a restaurant as long as we had lunch there! It was a great trade-off, as this view is testament to. Using the spattering technique (see page 110) really came into its own to produce all the different textures in the rock surfaces.

This was the view of the mountains from our apartment on the Greek island of Santorini. The shadows were just right so I decided to get a sketch done before the sun rose too high and muted the whole scene. On one energetic morning we walked up to the top of the ridge to the ruins at the top right of the sketch, with most of the journey in full sun – and was it hot! Thankfully we had bottles of cold water with us to drink.

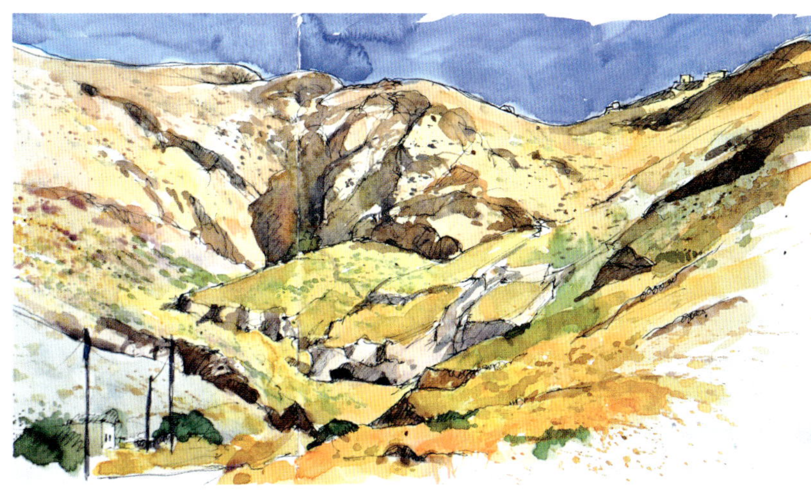

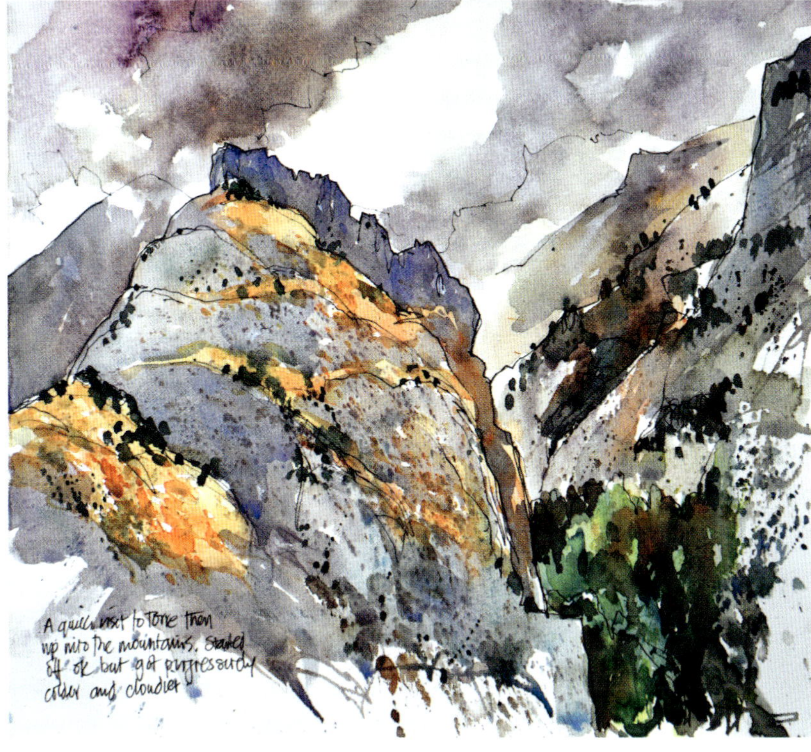

On one of our days out from the Finca, Benajarafe, Spain, we went right up into the mountains to get wild mountainous views. As you can see from the sketch, the weather was rather unpredictable and blustery and it just got worse as the day went on, but I managed to get this quick sketch done. Sometimes the weather conditions dictate the amount of time spent on a sketch, so you just have to go with what you can get!

Colourful shadows!

One of the most common stumbling blocks I find that students come across when painting in a hot country is that they make their shadows a cool grey throughout, without any reference to what is actually there in front of them. Usually light is bouncing off all sorts of surfaces into the shadow areas, which gives them a warmer glow than the grey shadows in colder climes.

In fact shadows, wherever you are, are infused with all manner of colours depending on the surfaces they are covering and the influence of surrounding structures on them. Mixing up a boring, homogeneous grey and covering all shadows with it isn't doing them justice. Leonardo da Vinci wrote that shadows were 'areas of lesser light' and that just about sums it up for me. So please look into your shadows to see all the nuances of colours awaiting you.

I have painted up two identical scenes, one with dull, grey over-mixed shadows (below) and the other with warmer, multi-coloured 'Mediterranean' shadows (opposite) to illustrate my point.

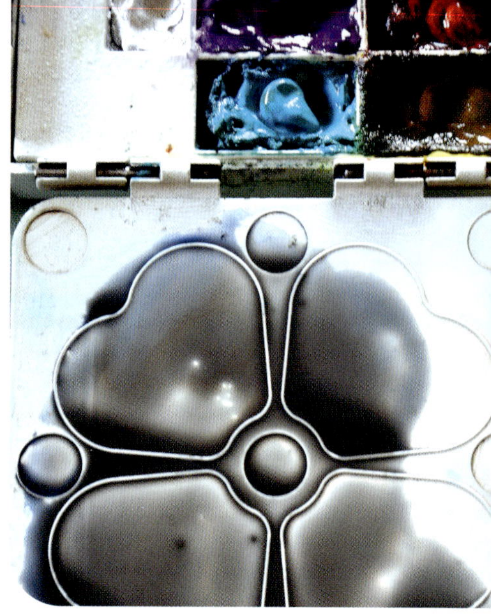

Here is my first dull grey shadow mix of cobalt blue, orange and violet, all blended together in the palette.

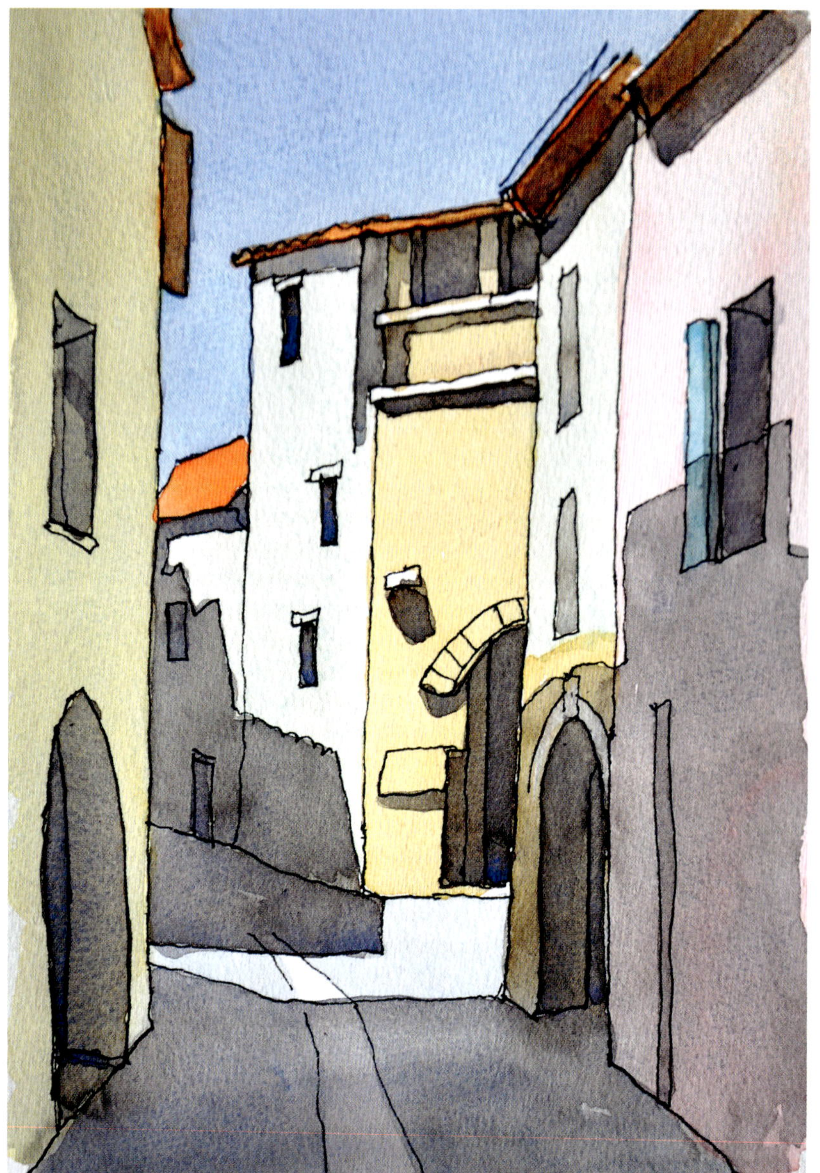

Dull grey shadows
I have now taken a typical sunny Mediterranean scene and overlaid all the shadow areas with this grey mix – and this is what you get. 'Well, what's wrong with that?' you might ask, 'all the tones look fine!' The thing is that there is no warmth in the picture and it doesn't portray that lovely glow of heat you get in these sunny climes.

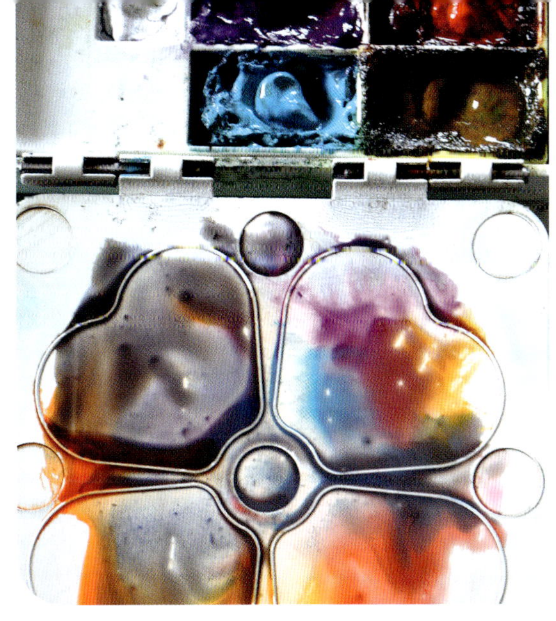

Here I have taken similar colours and made a 'semi' mix for my shadows, but have left them largely unblended so that I can scoop up different mixes for the various shadow areas.

Unblended colour shadows

And this is what the sketch looks like with the shadows painted over the exact same scene as before with the same underlying colours. I think you'll agree that this is a lot more Mediterranean!

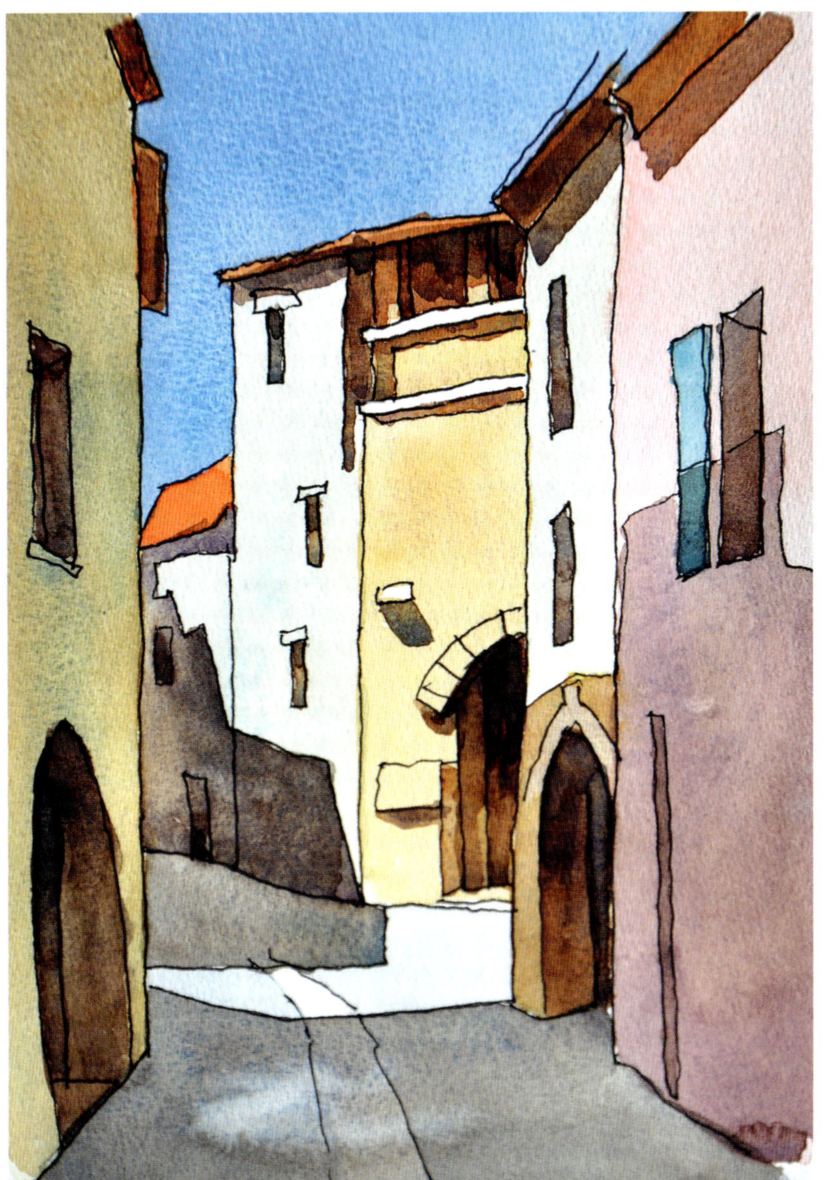

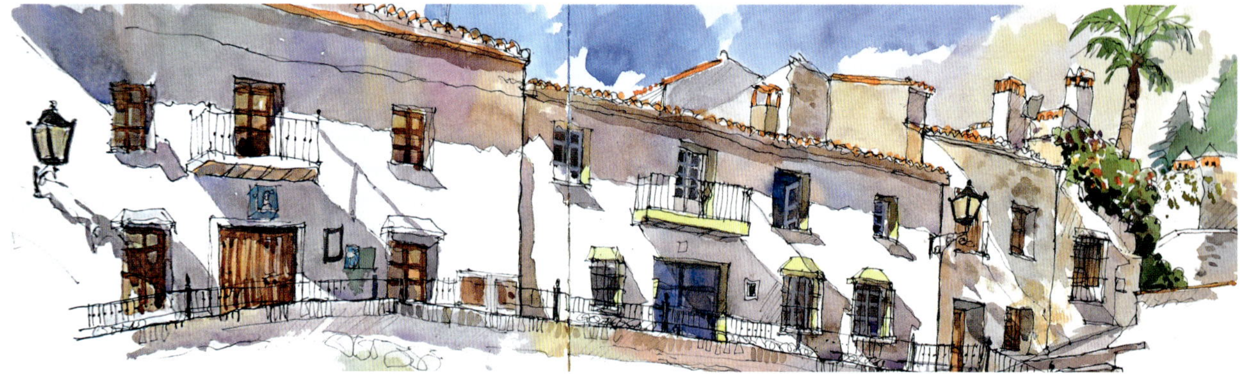

This sketch of the small village of Macharaviaya, Spain, is all about shadows. I needed to work fast as I knew that once the sun got too high in the sky, the scene would change dramatically – we look at this later on in the book. Notice all the different nuances of colour within these shadows.

64

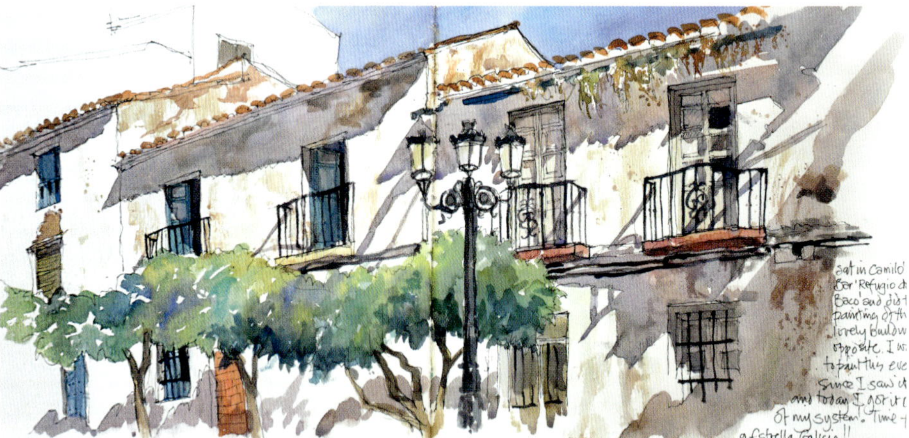

Sitting in the courtyard of a restaurant in Torrox, Spain, I did this sketch of the rather dilapidated buildings across from me, but it was the shadows that really grabbed me.

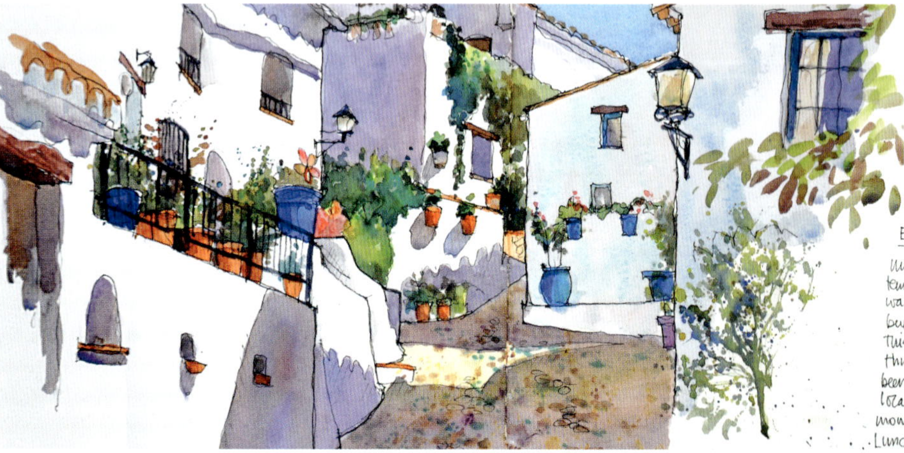

El Acebuchal is rather different. This 'forgotten' village in Spain was evacuated in Franco's time but just lately the old residents are returning. They are renovating the village bit by bit and doing a great job of it. The newly painted white walls reflect light all over the place which makes for a really colourful sketch. Ensure your shadows are invested with colour. Whites are rarely pure white – but in the bright Mediterranean sun, you need the white of the paper to reflect the sun-bleached appearance.

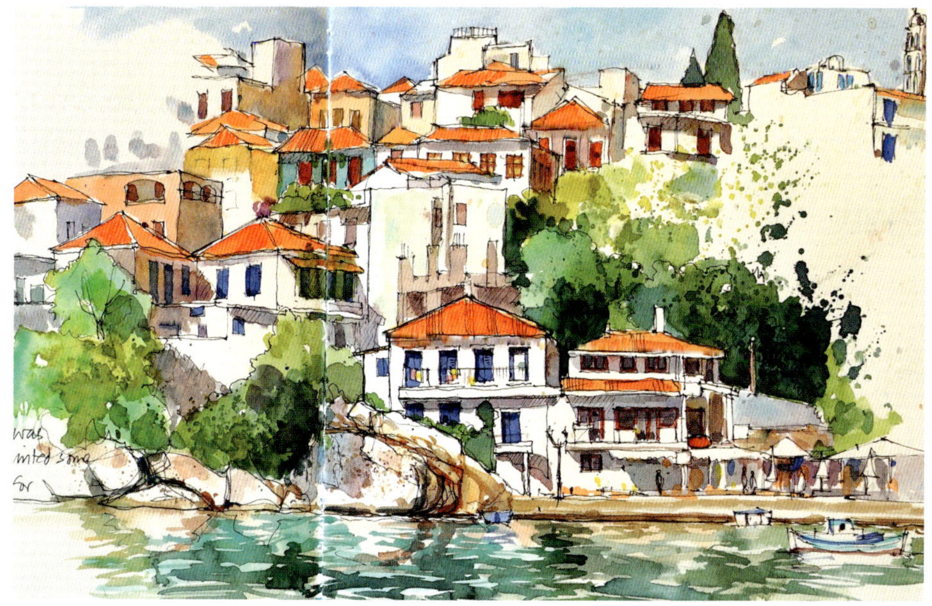

So many times my wife Sally and I had sat on Bourtsi Island looking at this classic view across Skiathos Bay in Greece. It was high time I painted it, so we picked one of the shady benches scattered all along the pathway and I did just that. Even with familiar scenes, it takes close observation to place the shapes accurately – keep checking what's actually in front of you, not what you expect to see.

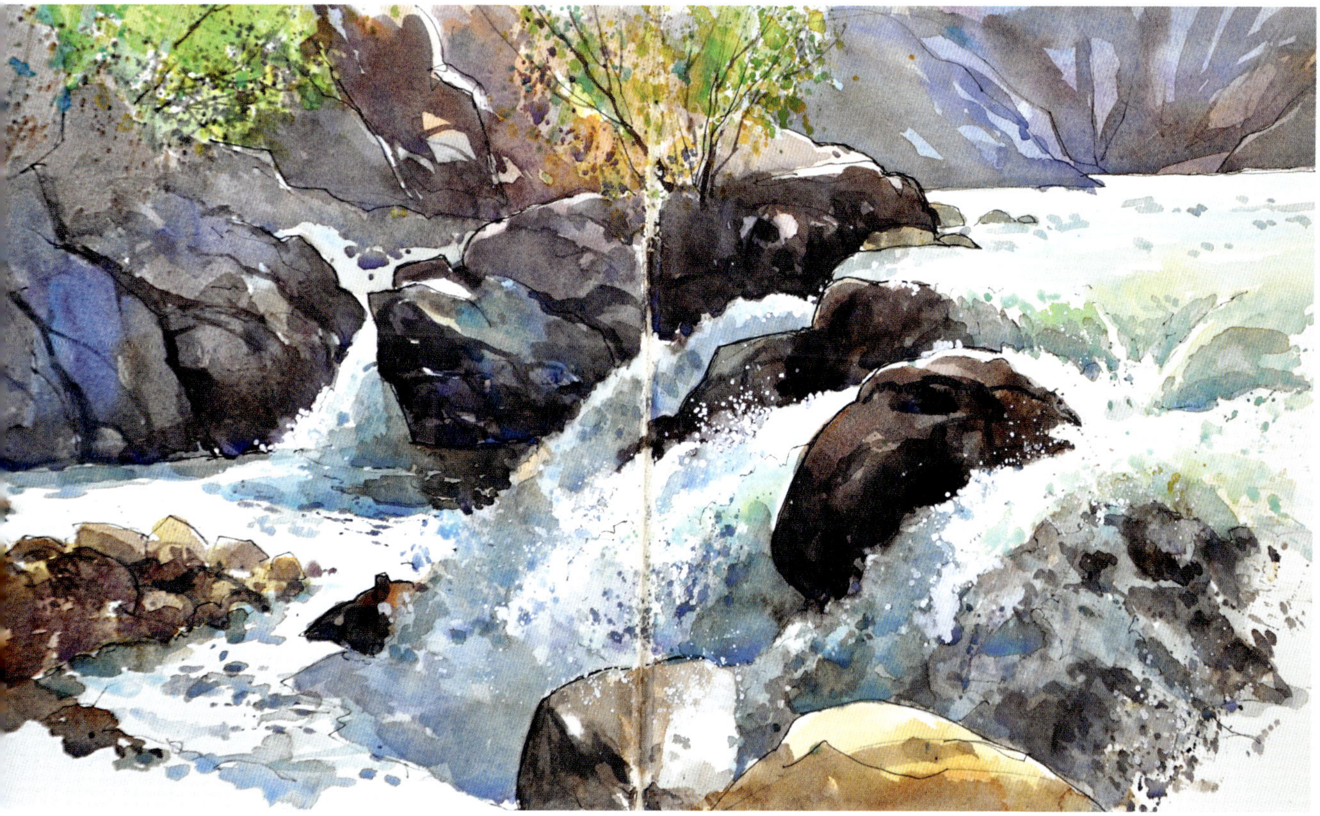

Water is always an emotive subject and this cascade on a small river in Turkey was no exception. We had originally passed this place on our way up the mountain to what we were told was a very paintable village but were very disappointed when we got there. So we all backtracked to this spot and spent the rest of the day here, which turned out to be quite idyllic. Note the vibrant colours of the shadows, both on land and water.

Set on Menorca's South East coast is the magical village of Alcaufar which has been a favourite with my painters ever since we first discovered it. It lies alongside a long, peaceful inlet with a sandy beach at its head. I set up in the only taverna there to do this sketch and spent the whole day taking in the wonderful vibes of the place.

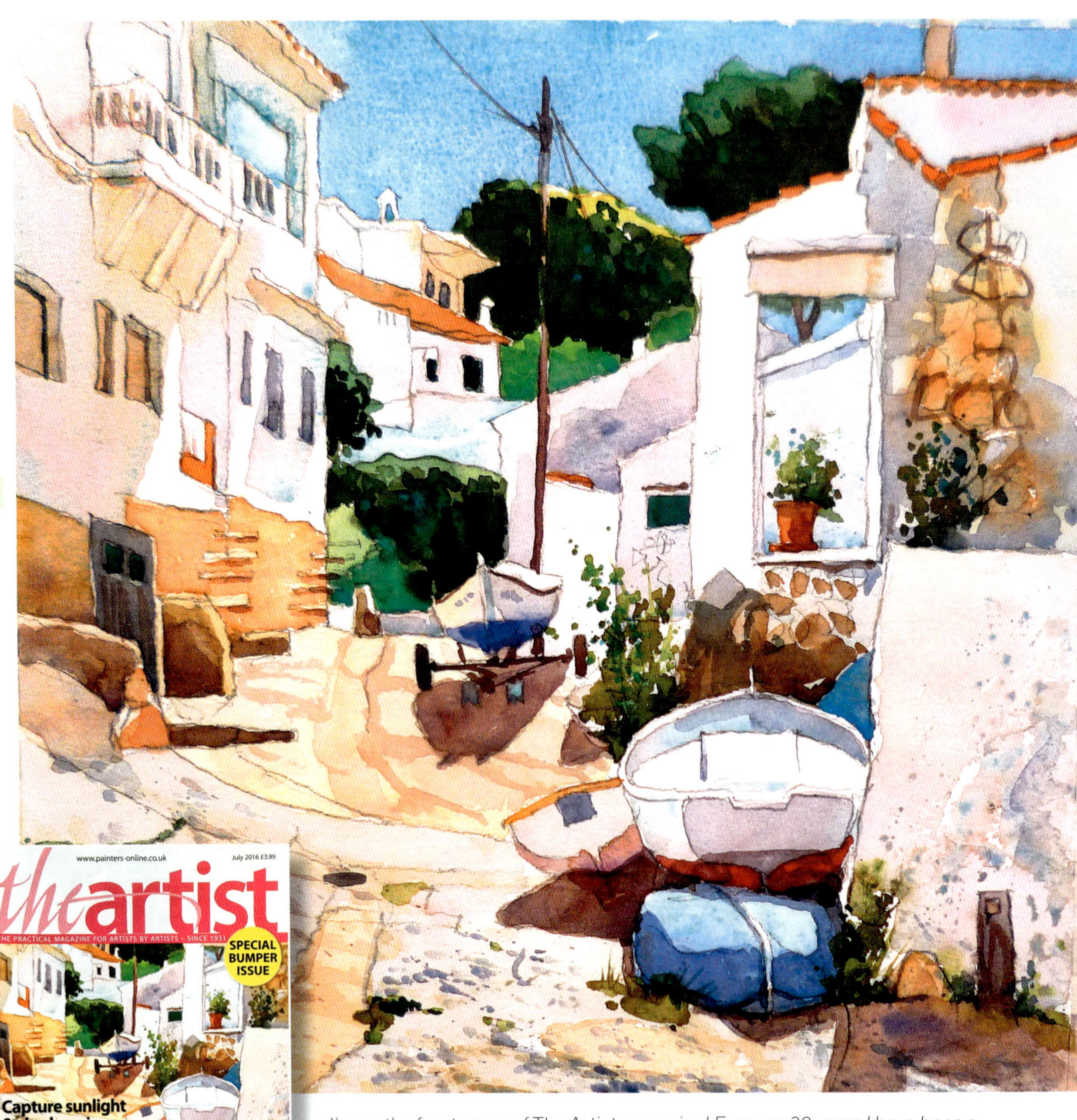

I'm on the front cover of The Artist magazine! For over 20 years I have been a regular contributor to The Artist magazine, so I was thrilled when this painting was featured on the front cover.

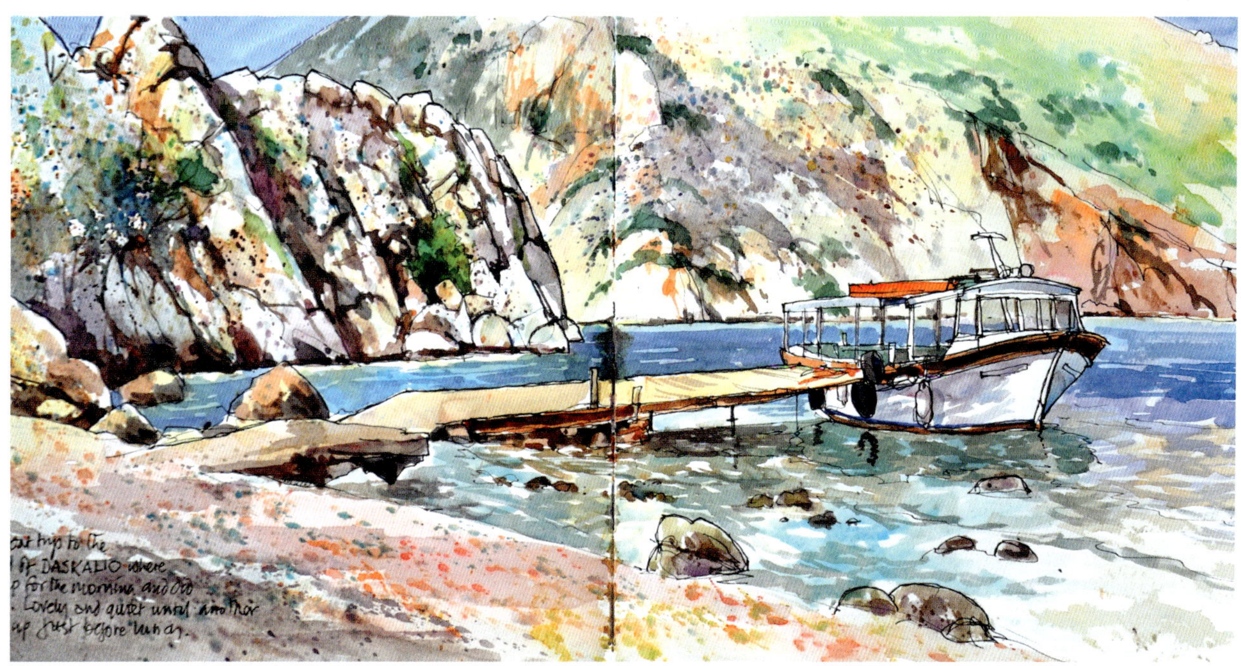

'I know of a small island you would love to visit and paint', said Georgios, the Greek hotel owner, who just happened to have a small boat. So we set off and really did have this island all to ourselves. Lunch and copious cold beers were enjoyed onboard after a stimulating few hours sketching.

Sketching on canvas

I had always wanted to go to Ronda to paint the magnificent Puente Nuevo, Spain, and at last I got to do it. Before I left home I primed a couple of canvas boards with Schmincke watercolour ground to allow me to paint watercolours onto a surface other than paper, which was very exciting. After negotiating with the owner of a lovely old mansion/restaurant on the edge of the ravine with a great view of the bridge, I set up my easel.

The rough surface of the ground produced some really exciting textures; an entirely different way of painting watercolour. I was rather pleased with the final painting so treated myself to a delicious dish of Gambas al Ajillo washed down with a glass (or two) of Estrella Galicia.

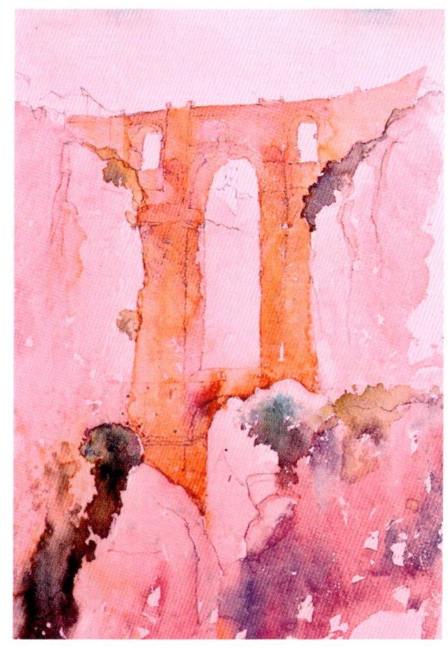

We were shaded by huge dark maroon canopies which cast a red glow over everything, as shown right. You need to consider local colour being bounced onto your painting surface and palette, or it can affect your mixing. I photographed the finished painting back in the studio (far right) which got rid of the reddish cast.

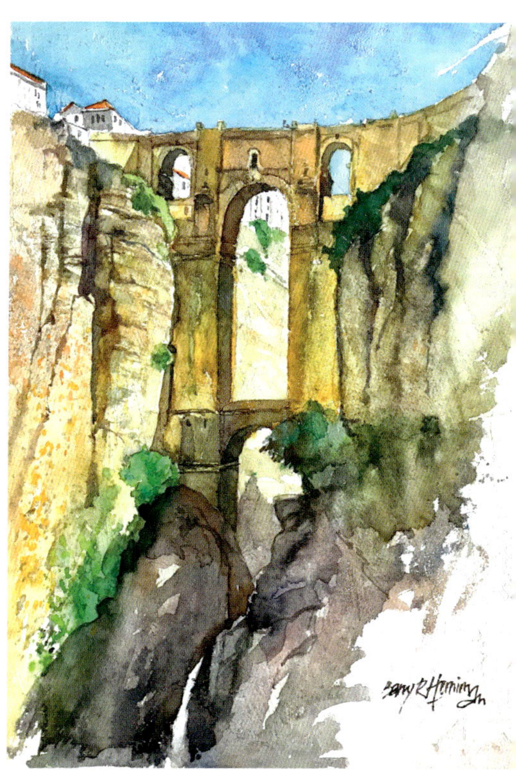

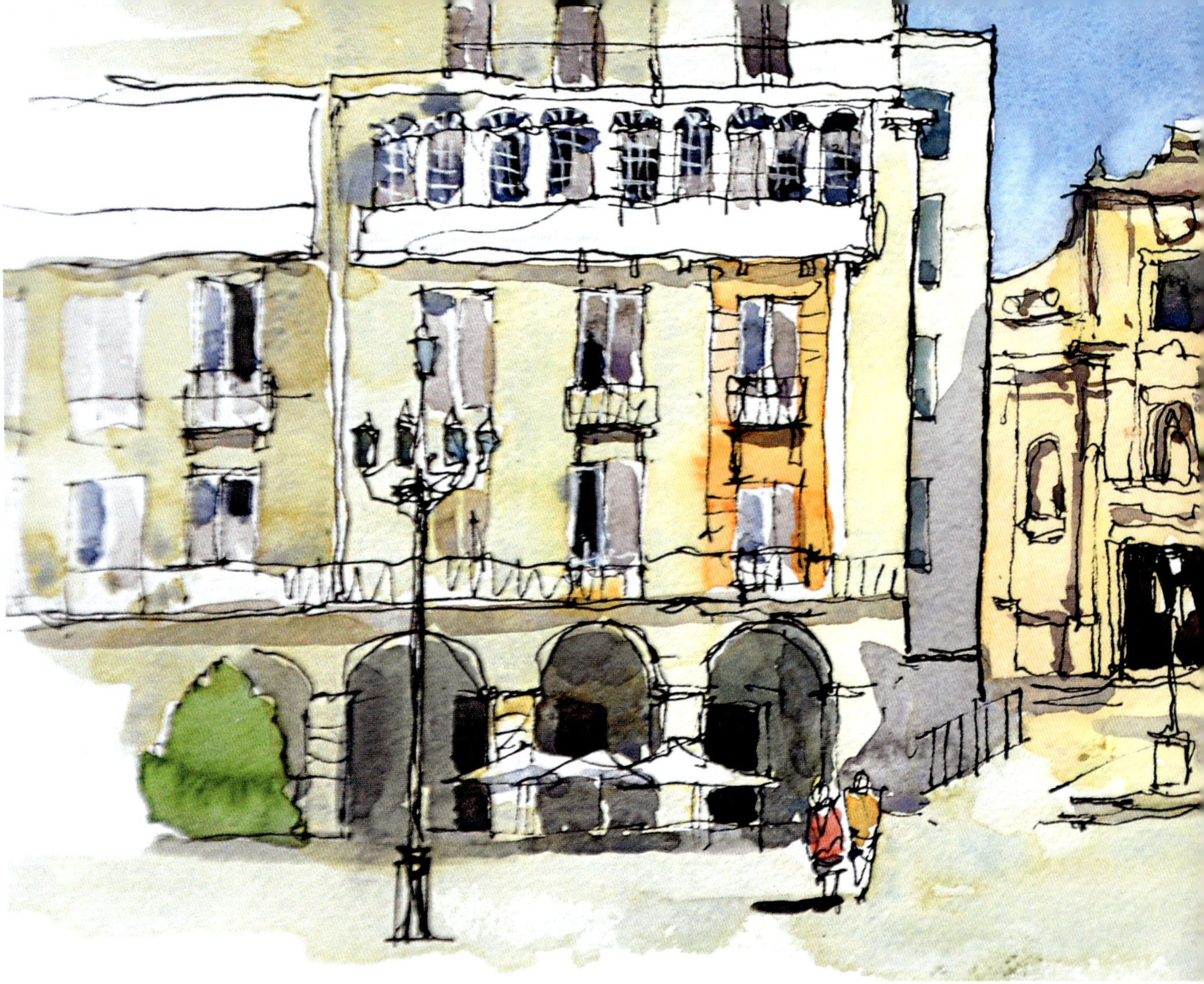

68

The lovely city of La Coruna, Spain, has a wealth of delightful buildings and it was quite difficult to decide where to paint. We came across this imposing square where there was a small café with outside seating in the shade, so I got the owner to ply me with copious café con leche while I painted this scene. The shadows were amazing and that was what I wanted to capture. On this occasion I was lucky to find such an inspired scene, but that is not always the case. If one is not forthcoming, you can always choose something that's less dramatic but equally enjoyable to sketch (see page 96).

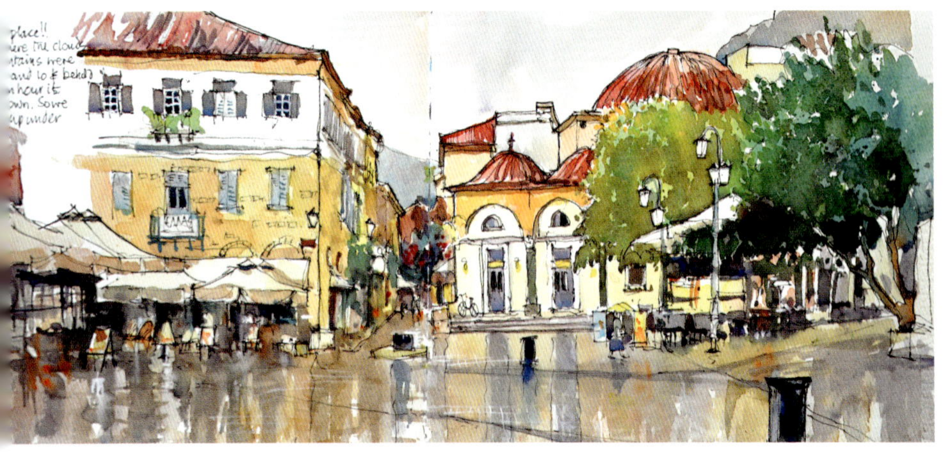

On my first visit to the charming town of Nafplio, Greece, we were beset with a downpour but that soon cleared up and we could get down to the serious job of sketching. The one plus to the rain was that it produced some rather fine reflections across the surface of the square. When painting reflections, use the same colours as what's being reflected.

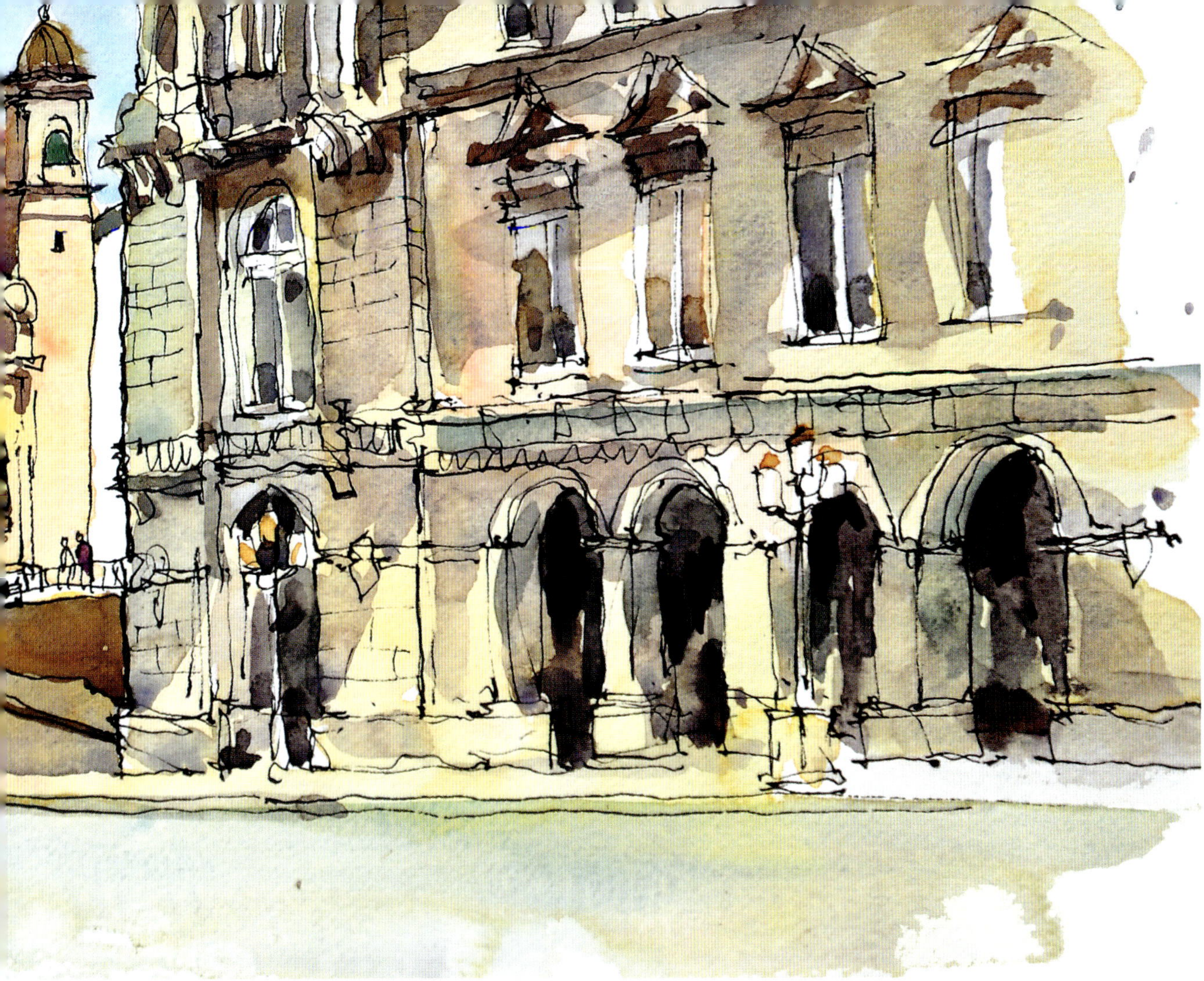

What a difference a day makes! We returned the next day and it couldn't have been more different: wall to wall sunshine. This was the view up one of the side streets where the shadows were out in force.

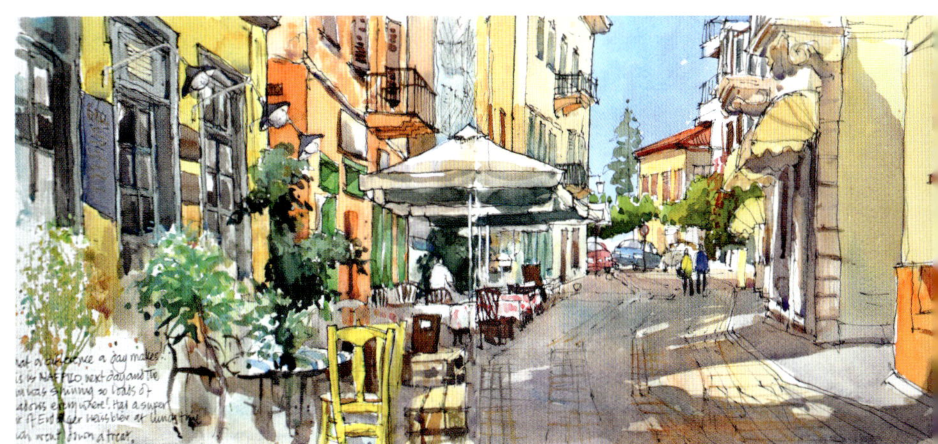

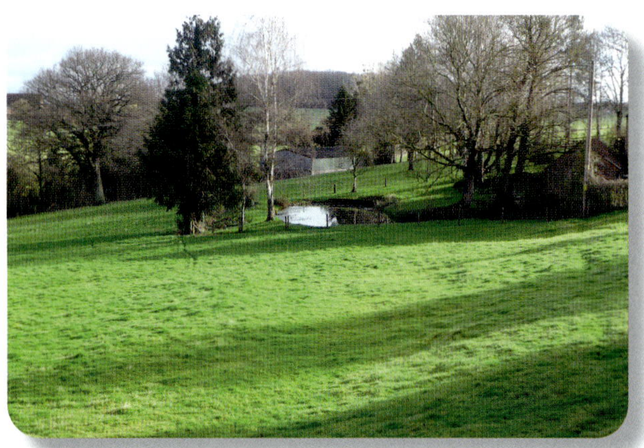

Morning

Lovely strong light and shadows are being cast from the right. Notice how the grass has a sharp green glow and the beech tree next to the pond has a highlighted side. The farm buildings on the right are in shadow and, like the stand of trees, they are casting a shadow right across the pond.

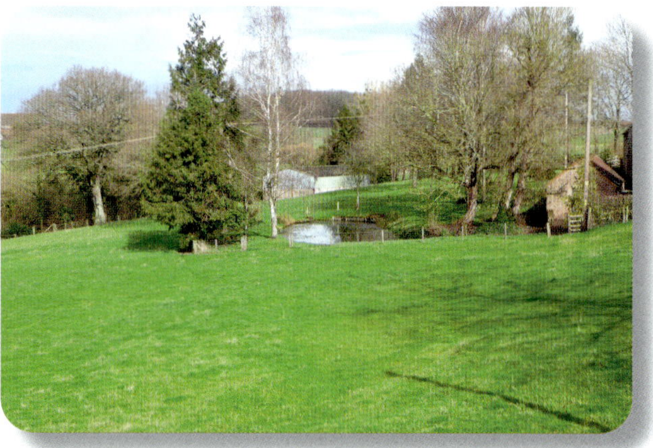

Midday

What a difference a few hours make! The sun is up higher now and lighting the whole scene with sunshine. Everything is infused with a warm glow and shadows are minimal. A pleasant enough scene but not one that would inspire me to get the paints out.

What time of day?

Choosing the time of day to sketch can be very important as light changes dramatically at the beginning and the end of the day and the light and shadows become of prime importance. Once the sun gets up too high, everything tends to flatten out and become rather static but when the sun is rising or dipping it can produce some really striking vistas which you just have to capture. On painting trips to Andalusia in Spain, I have taken groups up into the hills where the morning shadows play over the interlocking valleys, clearly defining the undulations within the range, but once the sun gets up, the scene becomes flatter and looks almost two-dimensional.

I am often asked, 'when is the best time of day to paint?' I love the early morning or early evening as the light is more intense and the shadows are usually long and strong.

The mid-morning sun was just catching the side of Gorey Castle, Jersey, and the tops of the trees. I had to work quickly to capture that moment before the whole scene was bathed in sunlight and went rather flat. Once the castle was painted, I went in and sorted out the houses in my own time.

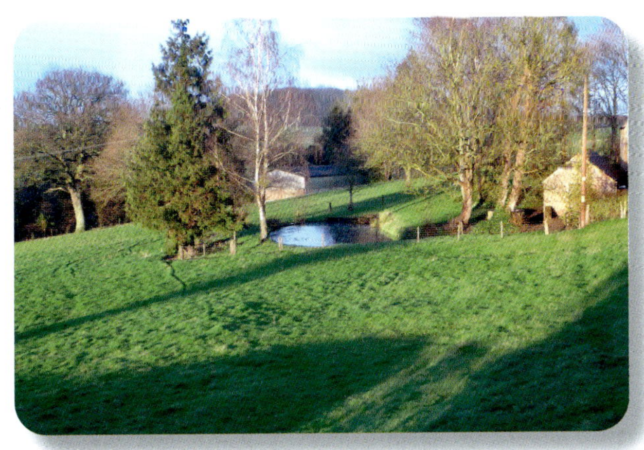

Here I have taken a view across the fields of our neighbouring farm to give you an idea of how the view changes throughout the day.

Evening

Another very different view, this time with the light and shadows coming across from the left. Notice how all the trees and buildings are lit up with an early evening glow, a completely different view from the morning shot.

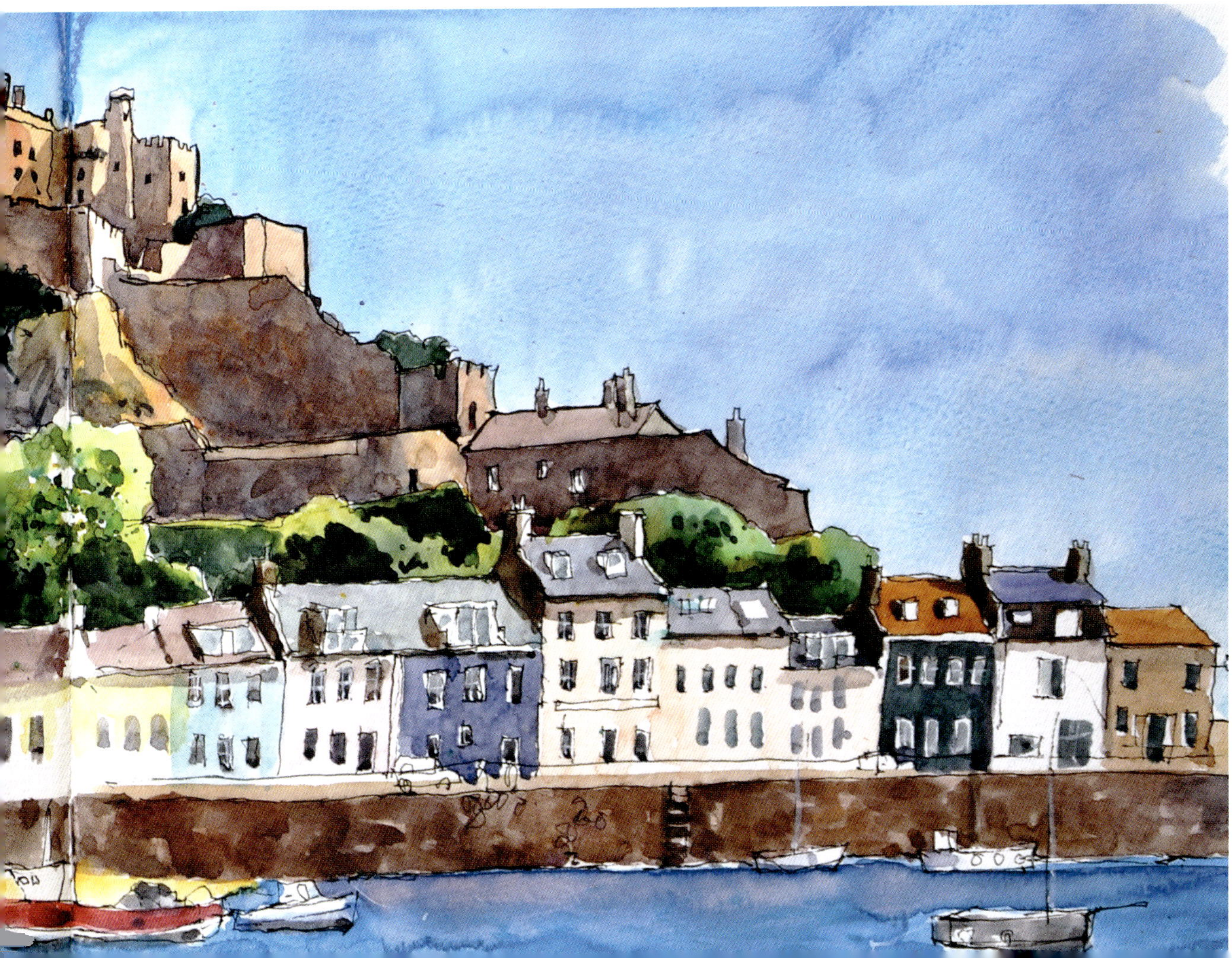

How the light changes during a session

One thing that becomes really noticeable when painting outside is how the light changes. This can throw up all sorts of problems if you don't take it into account.

Before setting up for a lengthy session, take time to assess the possibilities of changing light and weather; highlights and shadows; and anything else that may hamper or readjust your view.

One of the best ways of focusing the mind is to do a quick, postcard-sized tonal study (in your sketchbook of course). This can help you to establish the main tonal structure of the subject, eliminating any fussy detail from the outset. Here I have done a quick ink study of the view looking up one of the lanes near my house.

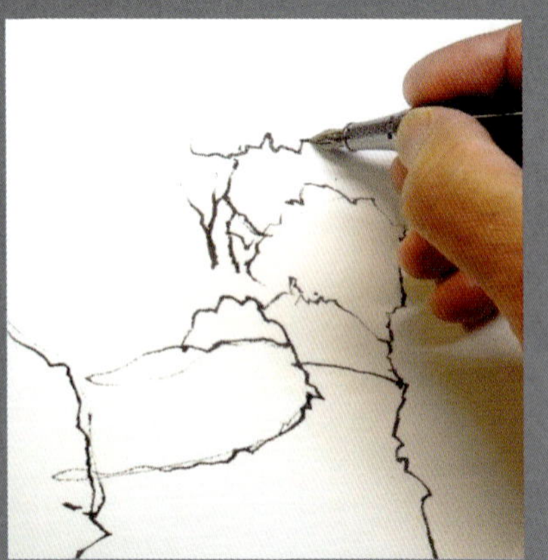 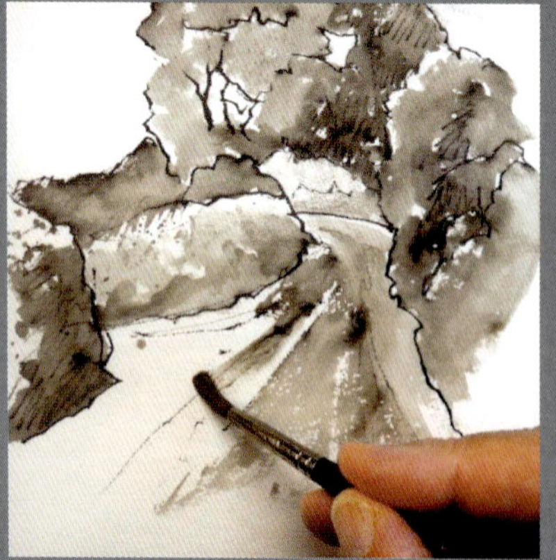 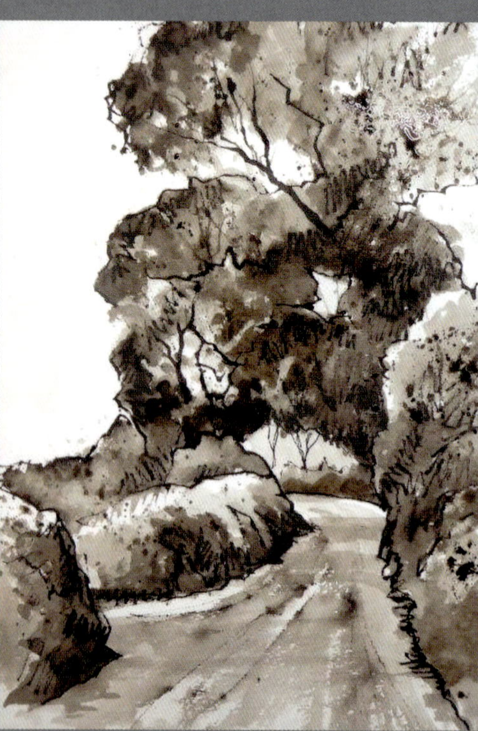

Tonal study
I use my Fude bent nib drawing pen to draw in the main elements of my subject. Using a brush and water, I then wash over the wet ink to produce various tones within the scene. Lastly I press down onto my nib to produce my darkest darks. There you have it, a quick tonal study.

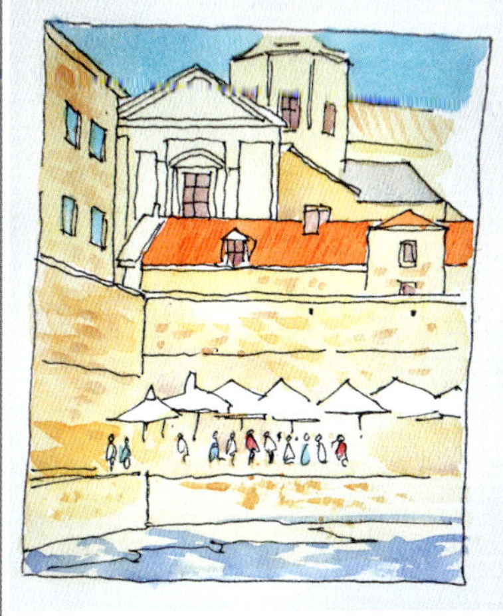
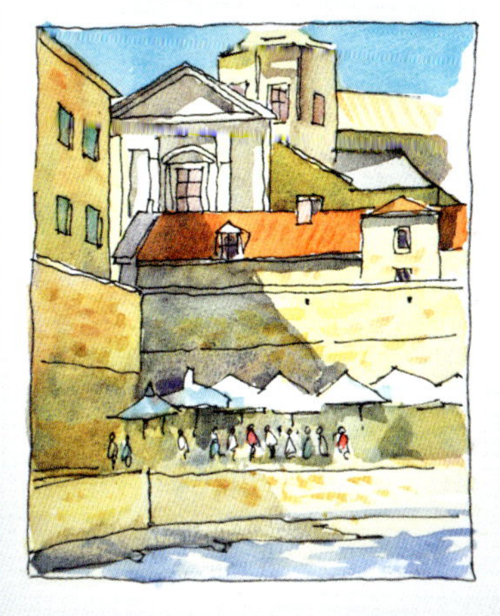

Tackling shadows on site

These two sketches show where I have added shadows to a basic underpainting. First I established all the local colours (the *actual* colours of the different elements), then I overlaid the shadows.

If you arrive at your painting spot and the shadows are at their best, it's a good idea to 'grab' them first, then overlay all the local colours afterwards. This works well either way as I am using transparent colours so each layer does not obliterate the previous one.

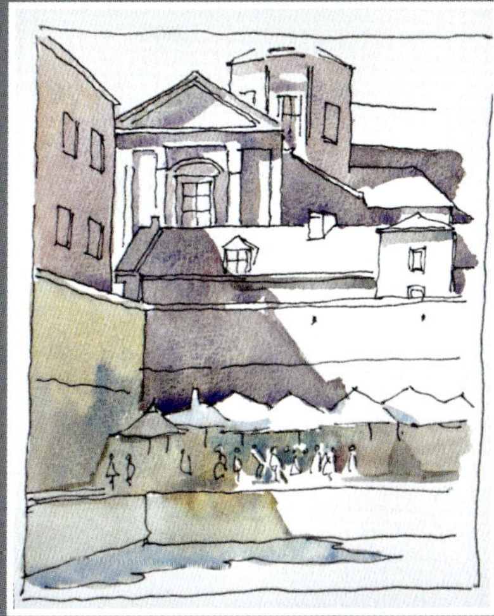
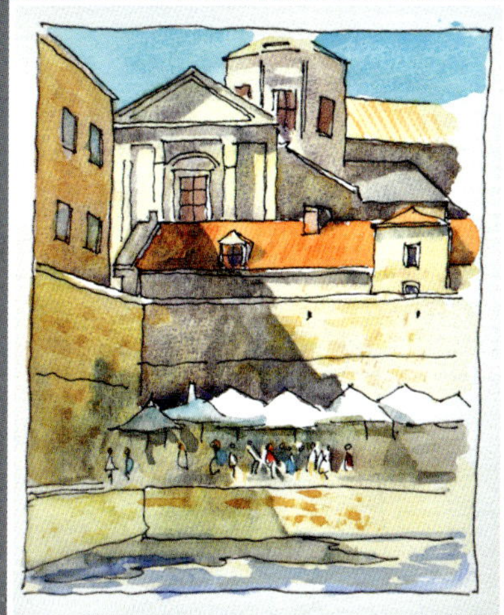

If time is really short, why not go for a tonal sketch? Here I have done the line drawing and then established the shadows in tone only. You can always overlay a few colour washes later on if you desire, but you will have the basic building blocks of the scene in seconds.

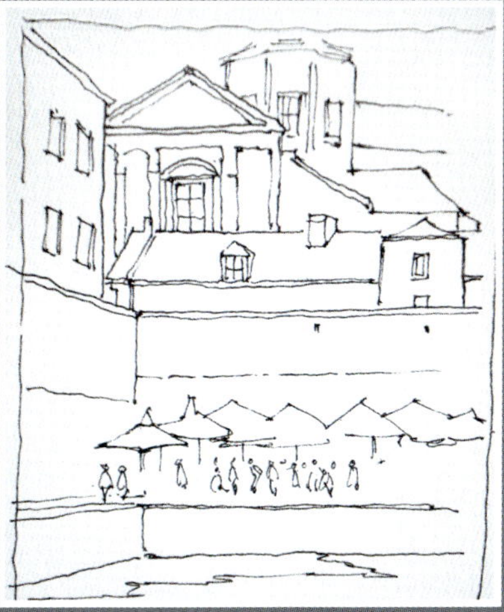
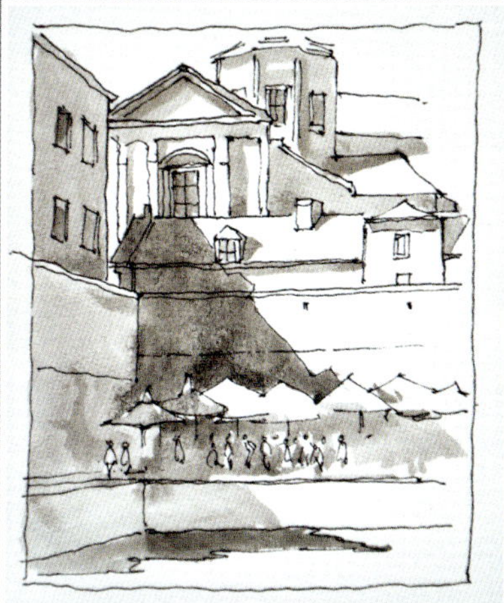

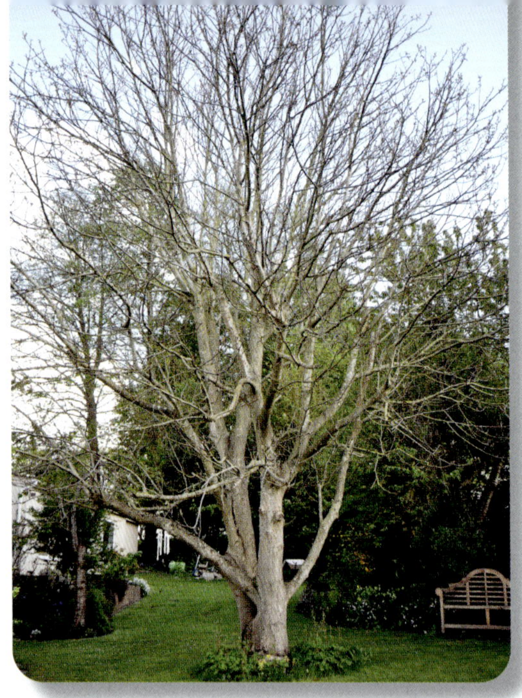

Counterchange

For me one of the most important aspects I am always on the lookout for in a scene is that of counterchange. This is the play of light against dark and dark against light and it can turn a fairly ordinary scene into an *extra*ordinary one! Trees can be prime examples: where the lower trunk emerges from the dark undergrowth, it is viewed as being lighter but once the branches move upwards they look darker against the light sky.

I have taken a photograph of our walnut tree on a dull day to give you an idea of how counterchange works.

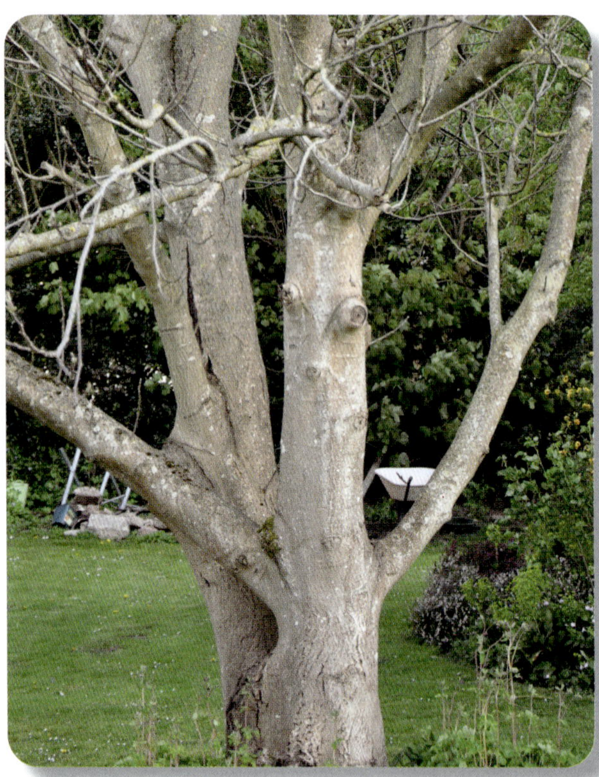

Light against dark
You'll notice how the main trunk and branches stand out as light against the dark foliage behind.

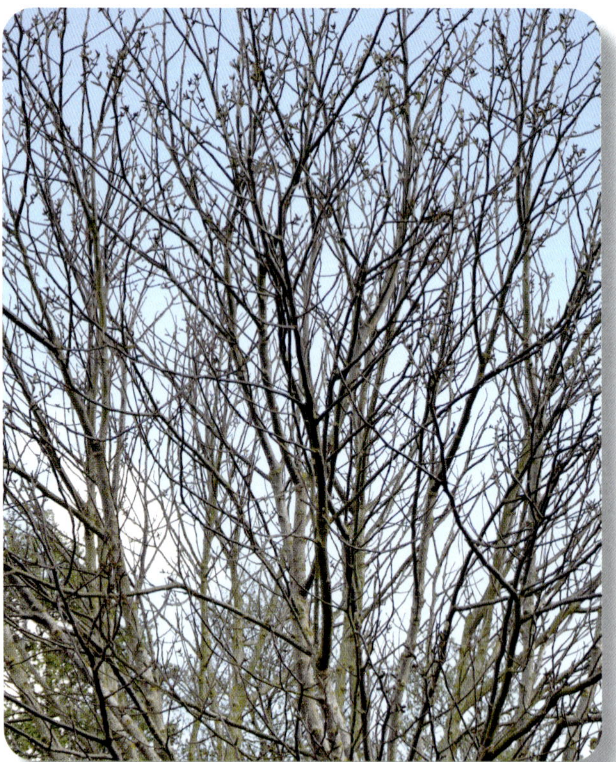

Dark against light
But once you move up into the light sky, see how the branches are now quite dark against it.

Keep a look out for counterchange. It can be used to great advantage to bring to life a subject that might otherwise have been lost to view, a bit like the black cat on the black mat! This sketch was done in Tenby Harbour in Wales, where the white boat contrasted beautifully with the dark harbour wall.

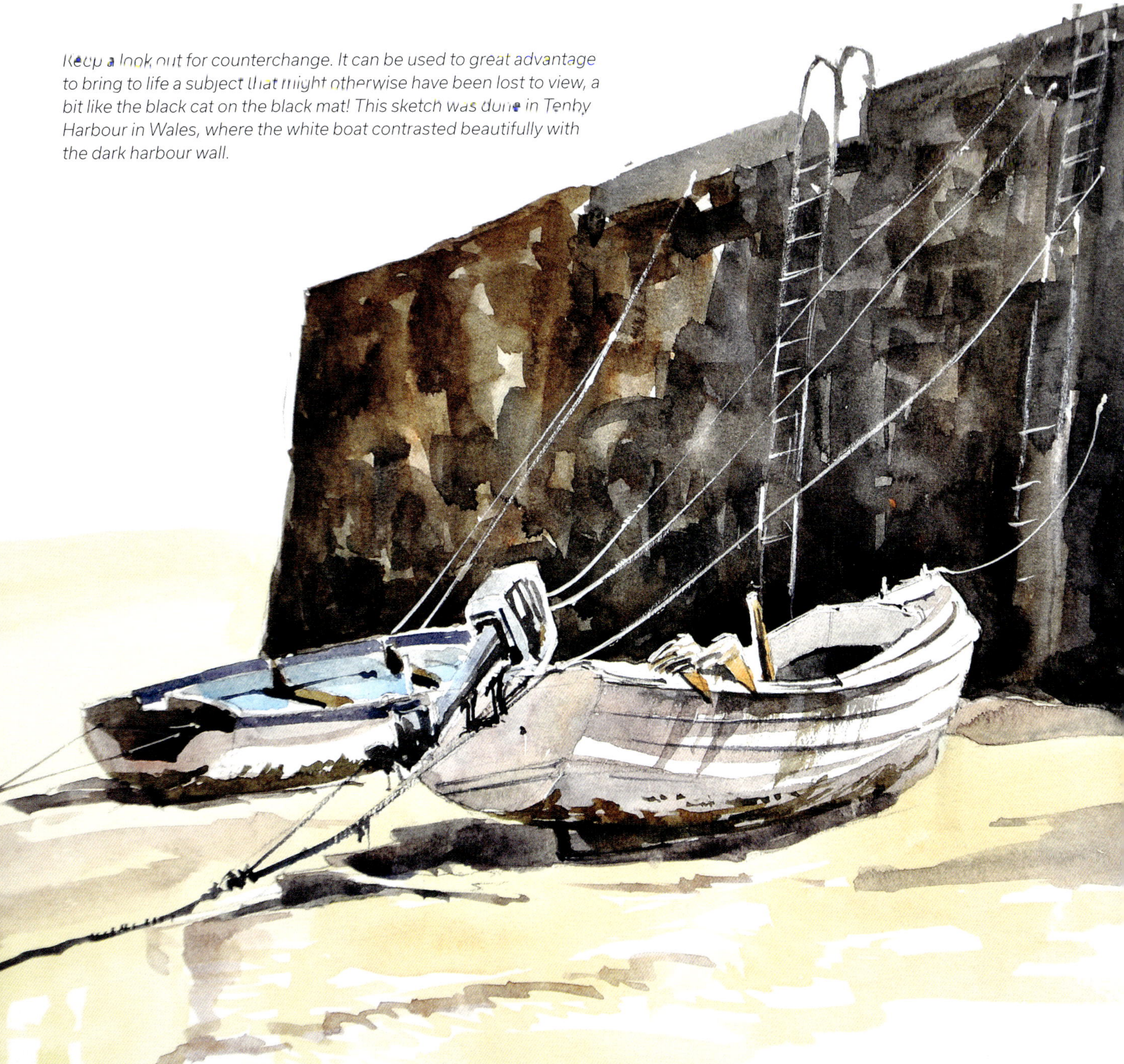

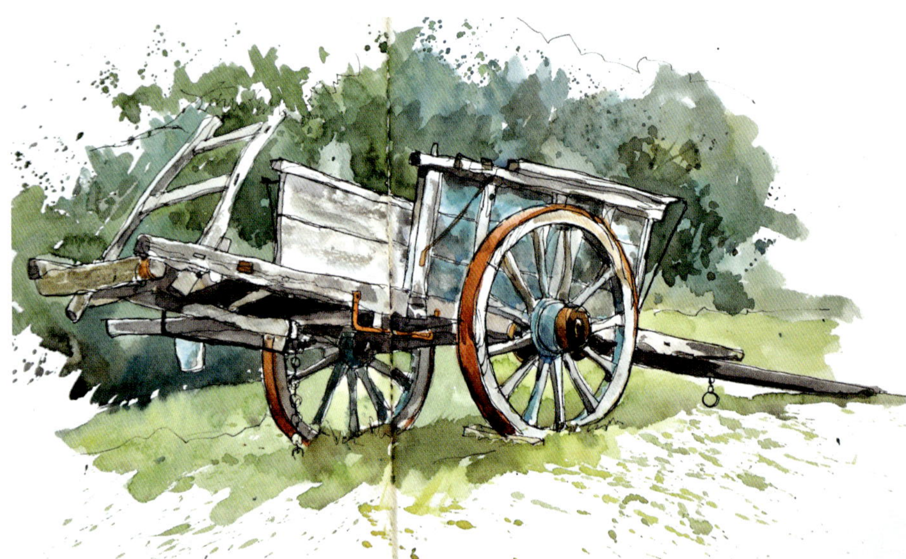

Notice how the lovely darks of the background foliage accentuate the lit edges of this old French cart, plus the contrast with the lighter sides and the attachments.

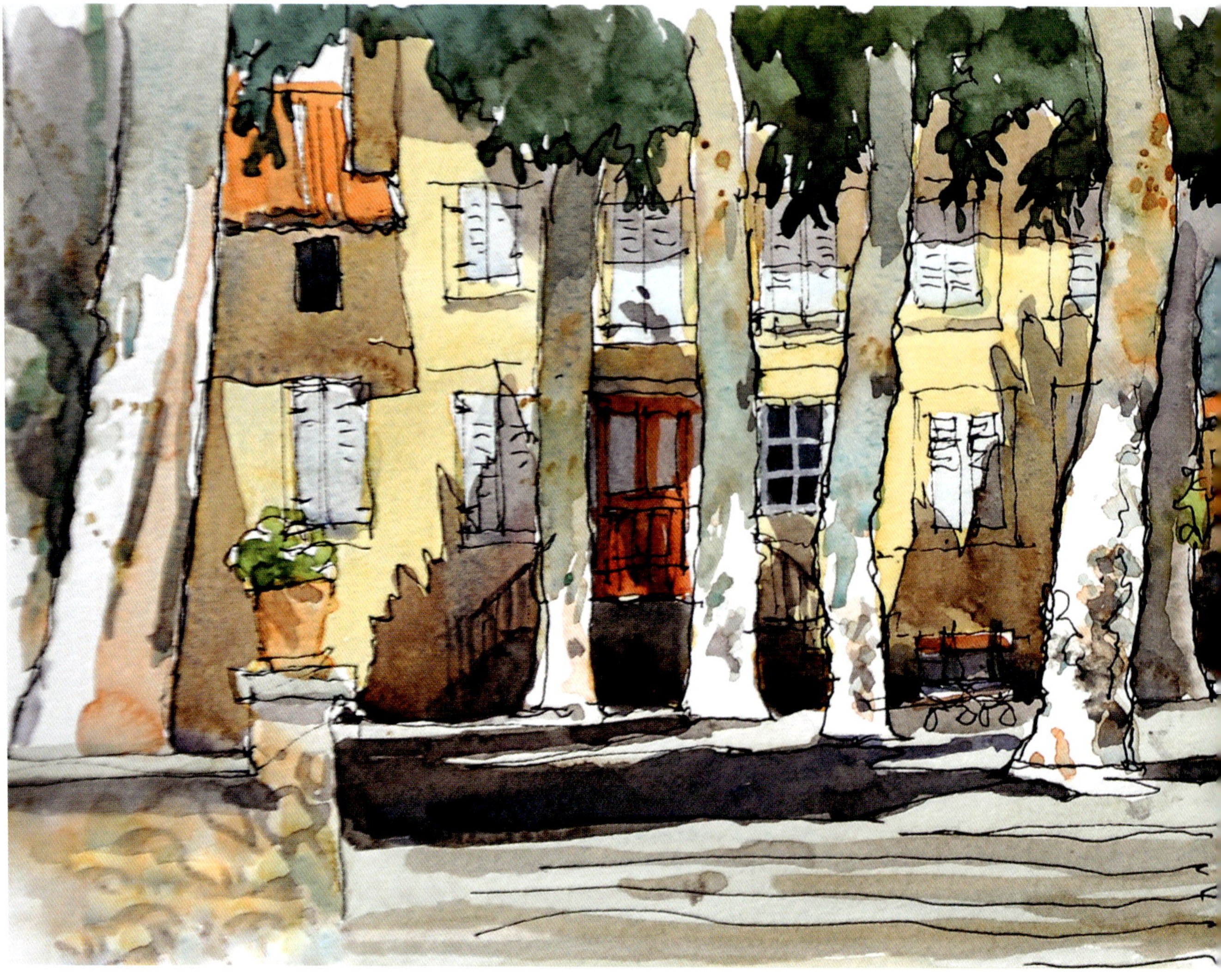

To finish off a day's painting in France, I set up in the shade to capture the late afternoon sun on these lovely plane trees in a small square. Flicking paint into both wet and dry surfaces is a fabulous way to add natural texture to tree bark. Notice how the lower trunks contrast beautifully with the darker background shadows. A great example of counterchange as well as being a super subject.

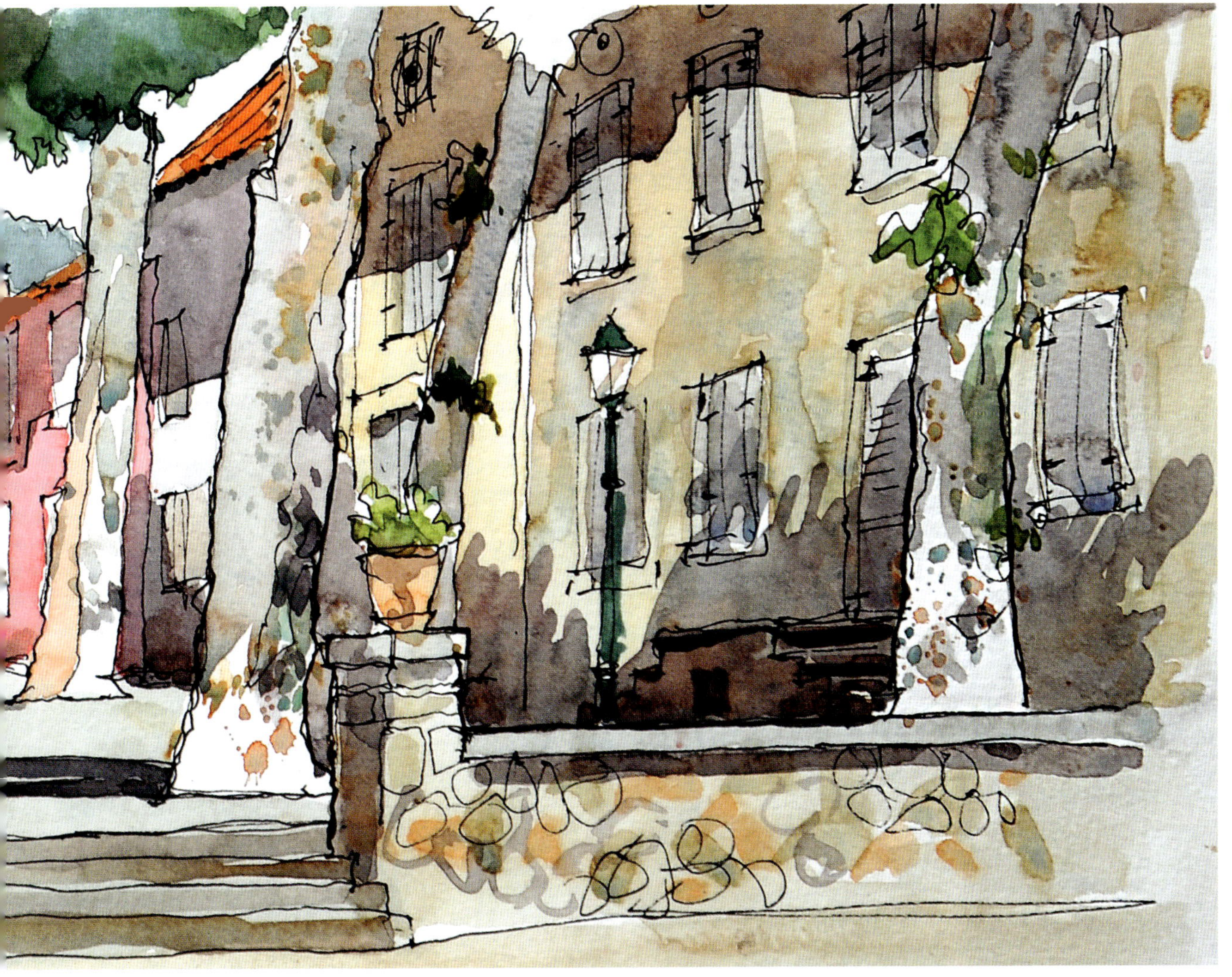

Sketching at night

Obviously trying to do a painting while all around you is dark can be difficult, but the effects can be rather exciting. Knowing where all your colours are in the palette really helps when it comes to choosing the right one for the job. If you have a torch and a kind person to hold it over you while you paint, it does make the whole process a lot easier. Note, however, that this skews your perception of the colours, something that is not evident until they are seen in the daylight, when you can see how they turned out.

On a painting holiday river cruise along the Rhine and Moselle in Germany, we moored up at the lovely town of Berncastle. However, we arrived too late for me to do a demo, so we took a tour of the town and arrived back for dinner. I then set up on the front of the boat and did this sketch of the town at night.

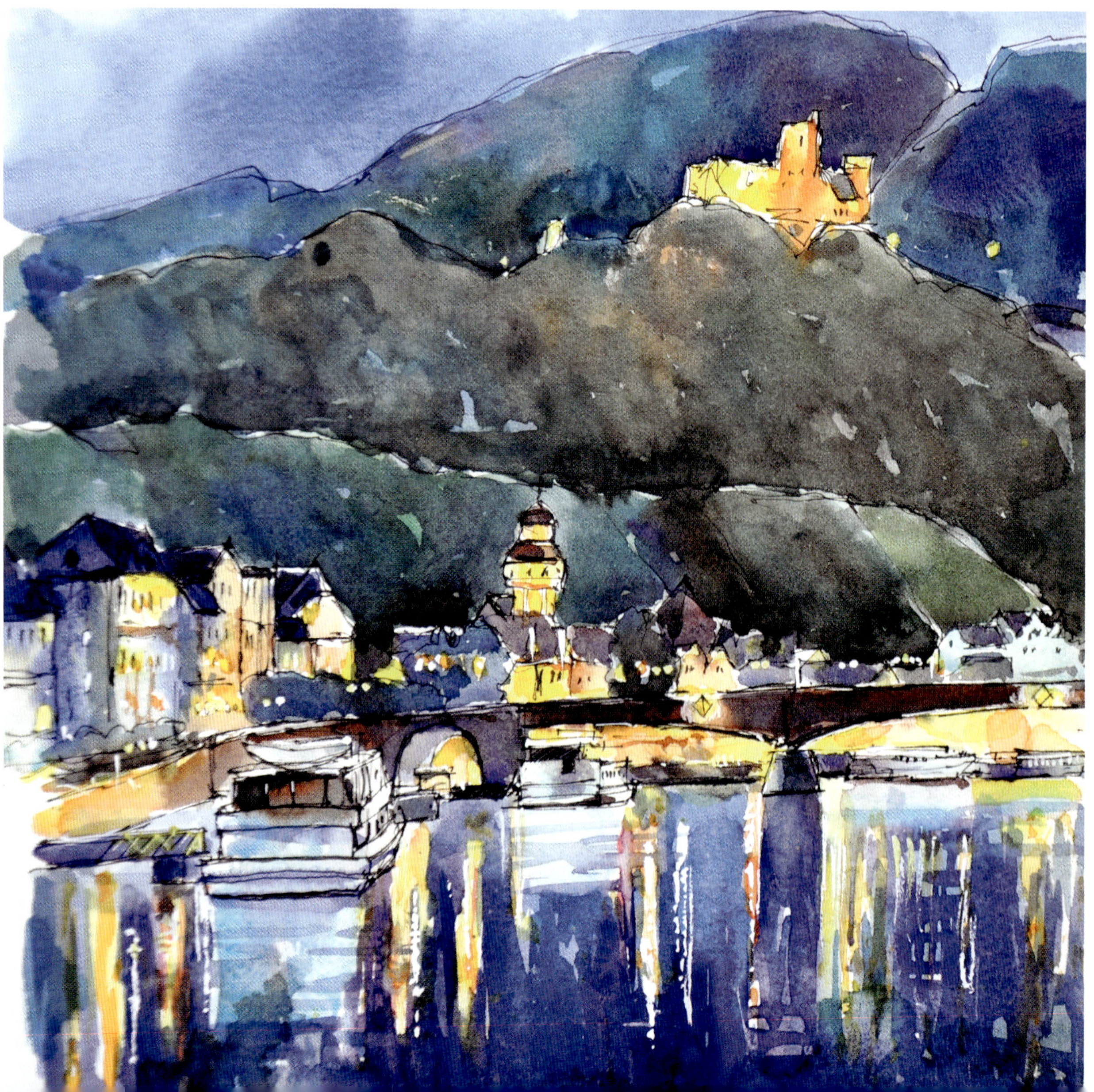

On a painting holiday to Sardinia I spied this scene across the road from our hotel and one night I decided to gather the troops and do an on-site demo. So I set up in almost complete darkness in the hotel courtyard and painted this watercolour which turned out rather well, all things considered. So much so that Sue and Mike bought the painting and it is hanging on their wall.

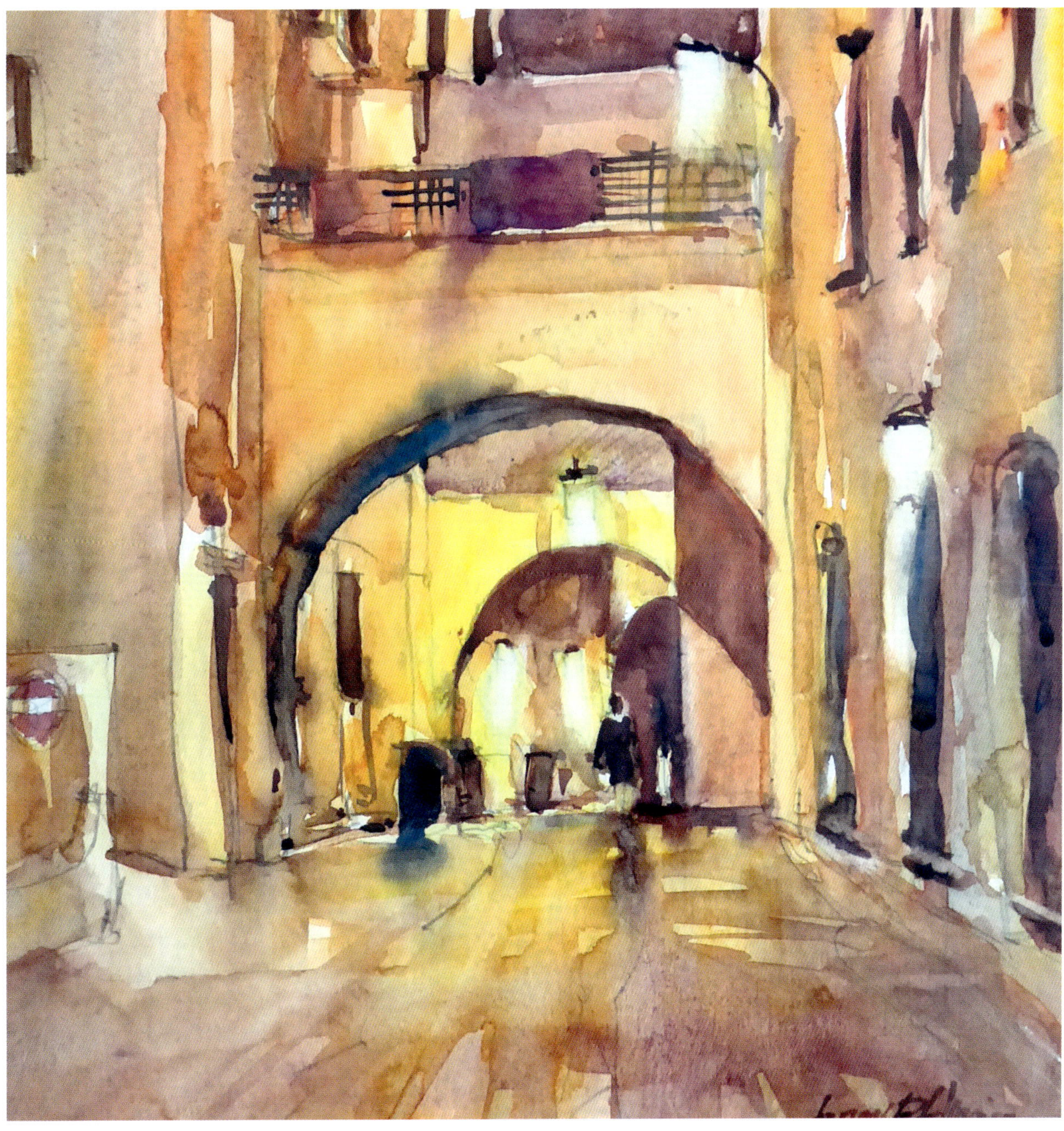

What time of year?

Each of the seasons presents the outdoor sketcher with an array of different vistas and each season has its own advantages and colour systems. In this section I want to take you along with me as I explore some of the wonderful sketching possibilities that each of the seasons affords and the different ways to capture them.

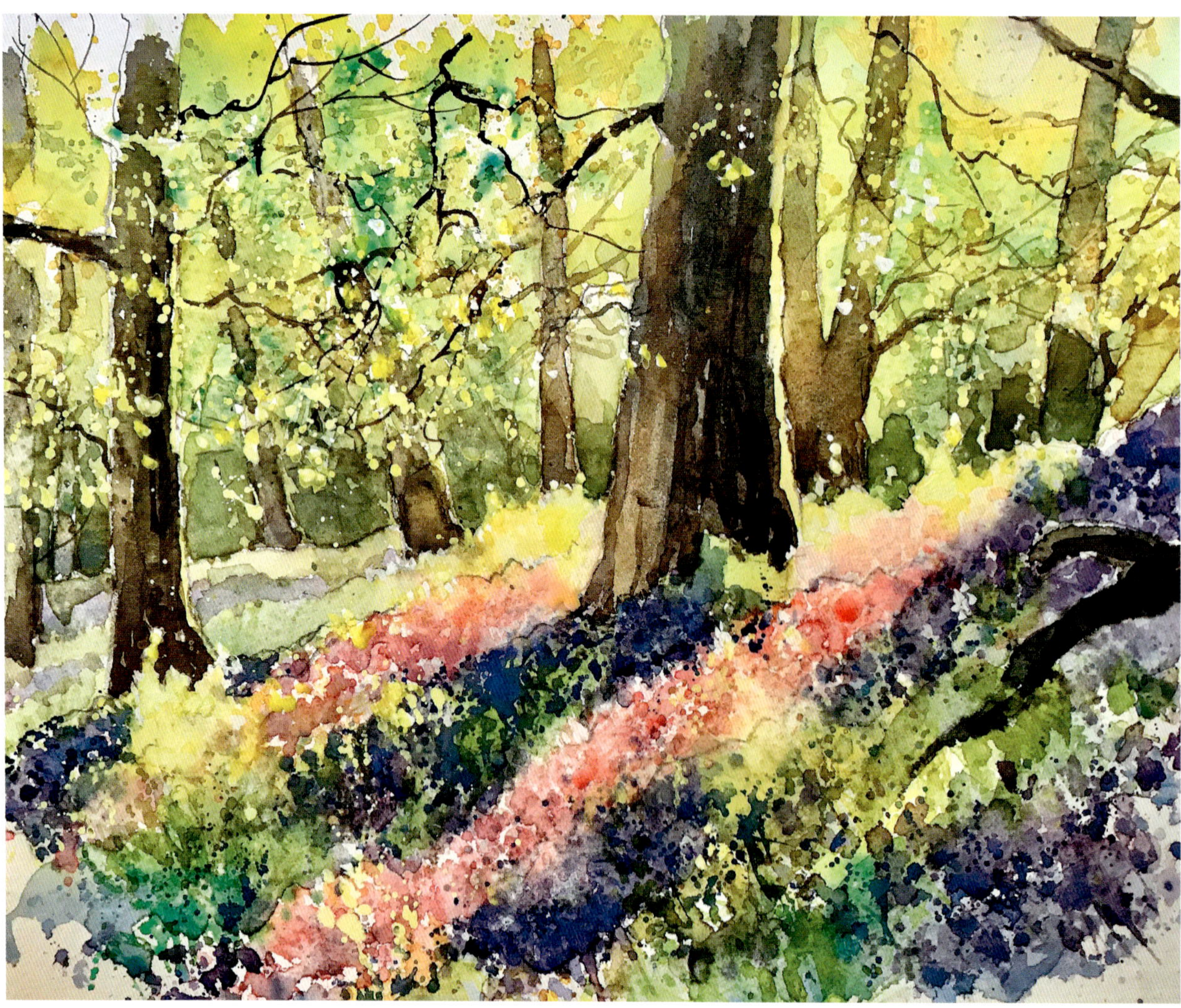

Bluebell woods are always a harbinger of spring with all its new, vibrant growth.

The new growth of spring

It is a sight to behold when walking along a forest track with the sun pouring through the new shoots and casting a golden glow over the whole scene. How to capture that moment in sketch is quite another thing. I keep all my colours very loose and light to replicate as best I can the ethereal glow that permeates the scene. My yellows are predominantly pure yellow and aureolin mixed with cobalt turquoise and a touch of cobalt blue for the shadowy areas. I also leave quite a lot of areas pure white to convey the intense light.

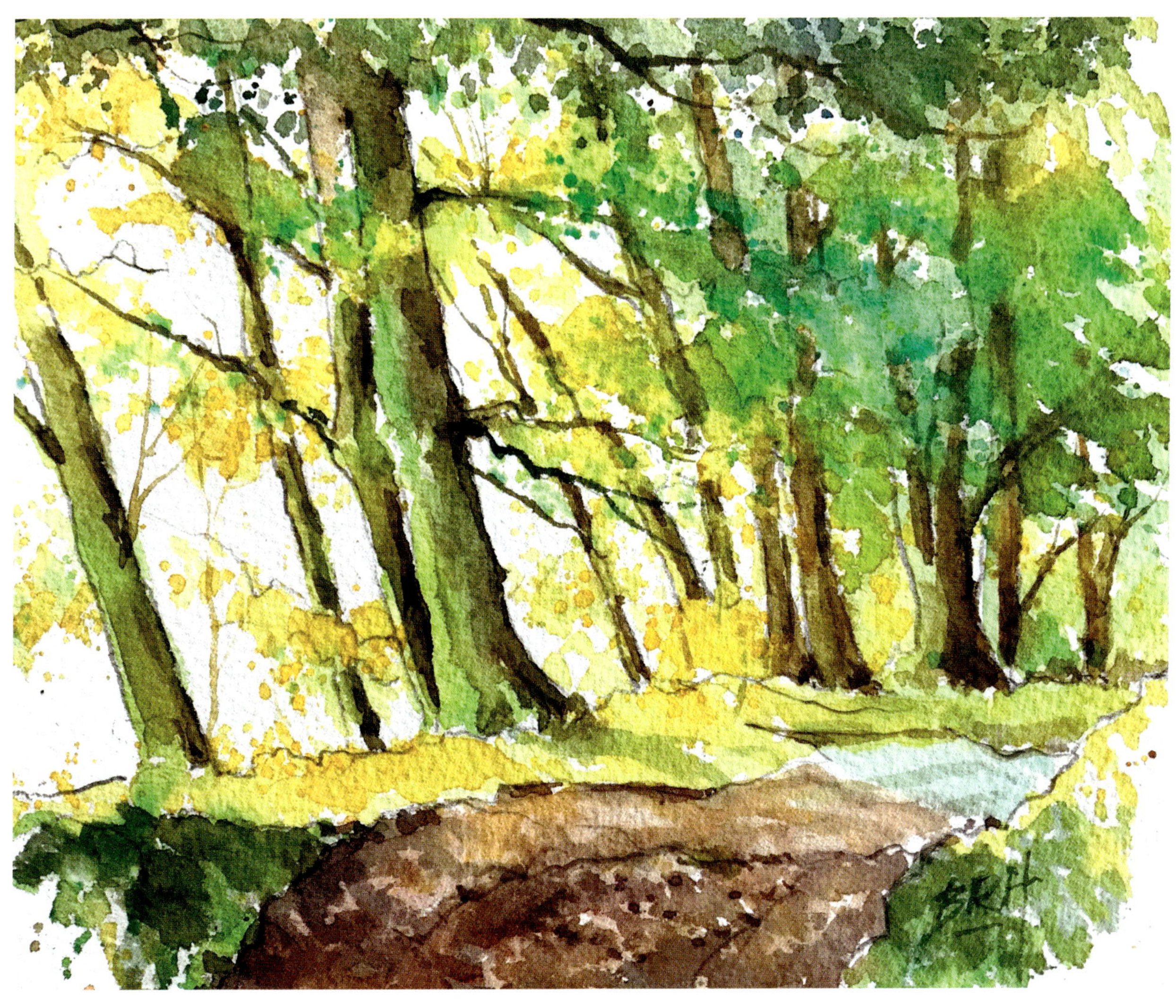

The myriad greens of summer

I used to shy away from full-on summer views with all that luxuriant green foliage, but have recently realized what I have been missing all these years. I have also held workshops under the heading 'Greens without green' in which I have got students to paint views in full summer foliage without using a single green pigment – and the results were super.

Here are a few sketches I did in summer:

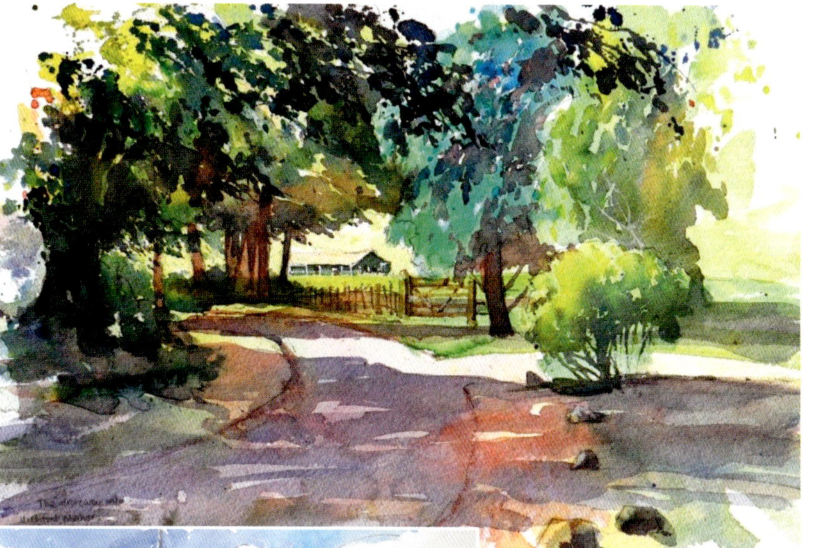

The drive into Urchfront, Wiltshire

It was a really hot afternoon and my students asked how I would tackle this scene with all its shadows and greens. I sat down and did this quick sketch to show them. As I have no greens in my repertoire, all my greens were produced with a variety of my different blues and yellows together with the odd addition of orange and violet in the darks.

Urchfront Manor

Sadly, the manor has since closed down, but I had been going there for many years while taking students out and about to a multitude of varied locations around the Wiltshire countryside. We sketched everything from villages, canals, hills and even pubs plus the buildings and the grounds around the Manor, which were eminently paintable.

Down into Edge

Perched up on the side of the valley looking down into the village of Edge in Gloucestershire, I sketched this scene. Note the almost purple trees that sing out against the green. Look for contrast in the scene before you.

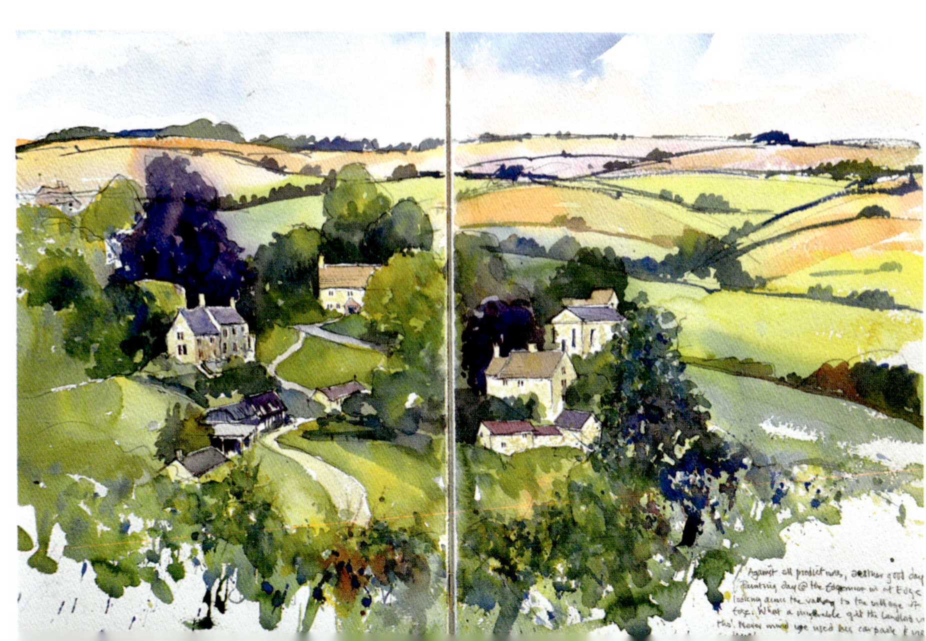

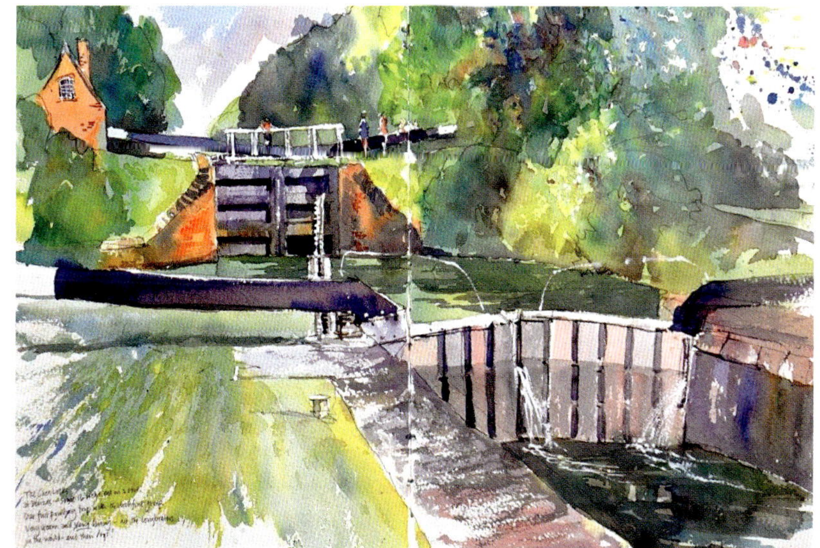

The Caen Hill locks

We set up at the bottom of the magnificent Caen Hill Lock system on the Kennet and Avon Canal, Wiltshire, to do this sketch. There are sixteen locks in total on this stretch going straight up the hillside into Devizes.

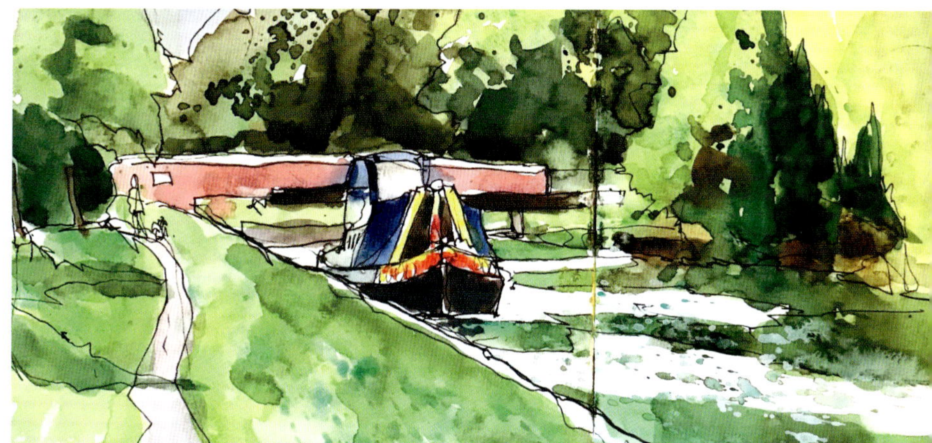

Messing about on the river!

Our trip along the Kennet and Avon Canal was a rather wet affair but there were breaks in the weather when I could grab the odd sketch. Lots of summer greens everywhere.

A delightful stopover

On our way to Ronda in Spain to paint the wonderful bridge (see page 67), we stayed over in this delightful village just a few miles distant and got to do some sketching into the bargain. I sat up on the wall surrounding the cottage to get this view of the small river that meandered through the undergrowth among all the different greens.

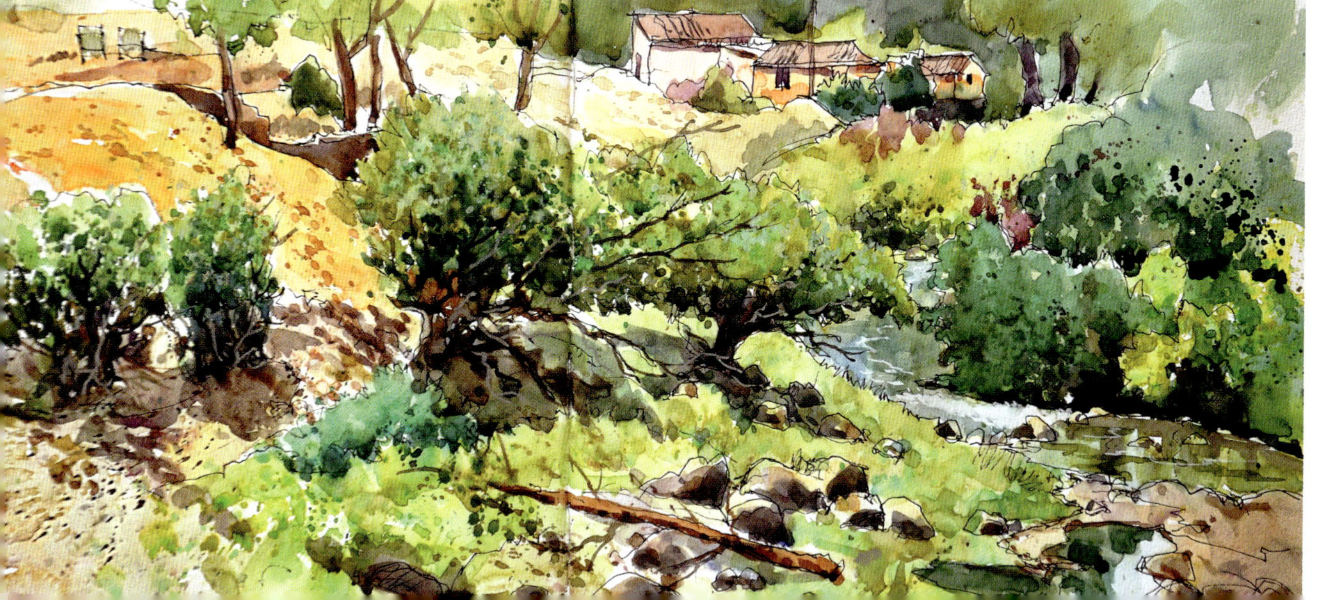

The bright colours of autumn

Autumm is always a time of an abundance of striking colours, and never more so than in the midst of a New England fall. Our painting trips to Vermont were absolutely blinding with a bright array of yellows, reds and golds that were everywhere. I found that by using pure pigments like aureolin, Indian yellow, orange and rose madder I was able to get somewhere close to those colours.

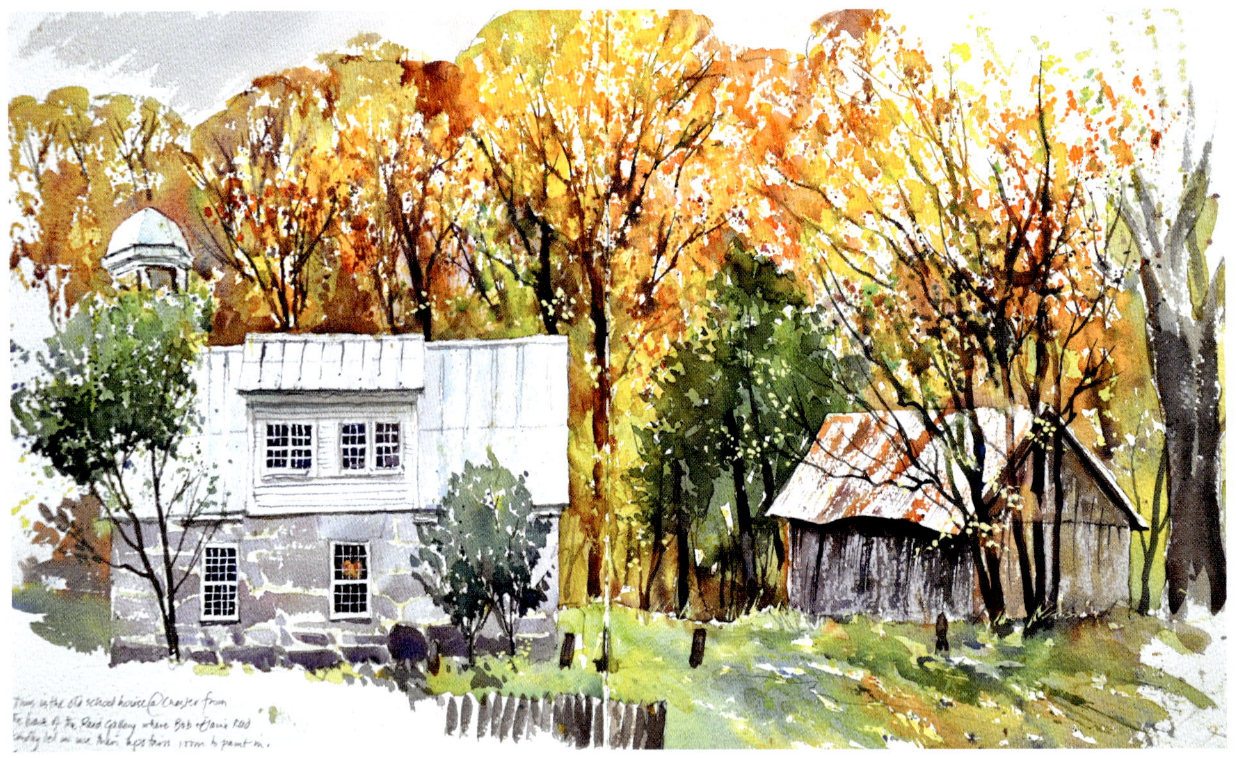

Painting the old schoolhouse
The day we came to paint this lovely New England village of Chester, it started to rain, but as luck would have it the owners of the nearby Reed Gallery let us sit in their upstairs room to paint this scene of the old schoolhouse. Such was the hospitality we found in this part of Vermont, USA.

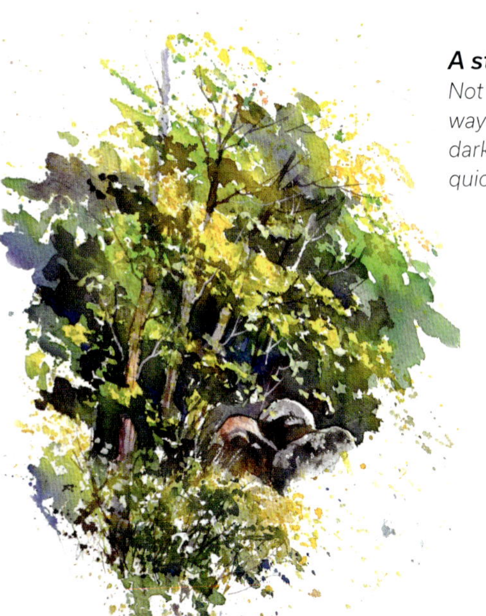

A study of yellows and greens
Not all the colours change during fall and I loved the way the bright yellow leaves counterchanged with the dark greens behind them. These small studies can be quick and thoroughly enjoyable to paint.

Opposite
A study of fall colours
Sometimes it's just nice to zone in on a small area and concentrate on getting the colours down that captivated you in the first place. This was done in my largest sketchbook so it wasn't exactly a compact sketch but I did do it rather quickly to get that vibrancy of the fall colours that abounded in New England, USA.

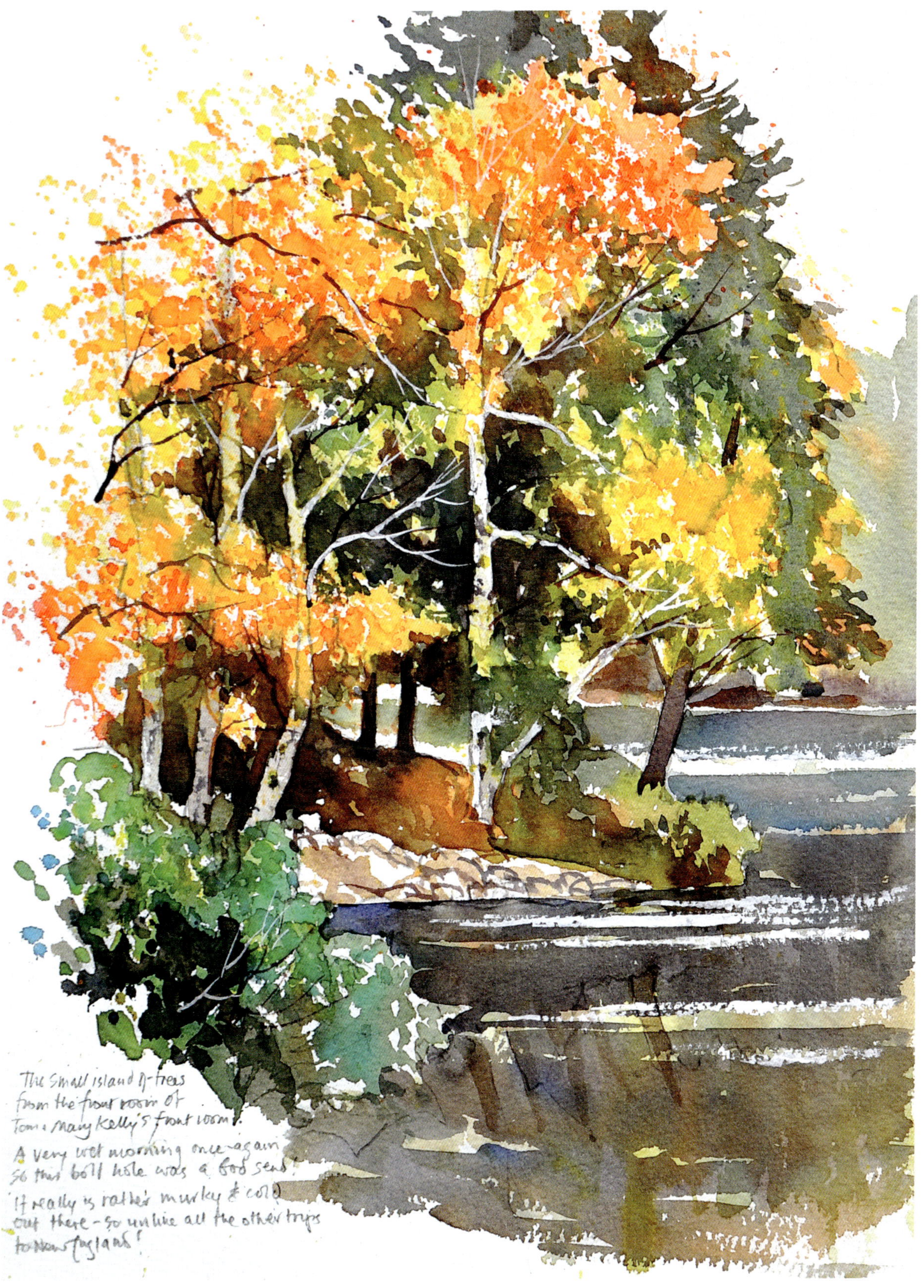

The small island of trees
from the front room of
Tom & Mary Kelly's front room.

A very wet morning once again
so this bolt hole was a God send!

It really is rather murky & cold
out there - so unlike all the other trips
to New England!

The stark outlines of winter

As I have mentioned, I am rather a fair-weather painter and that extends to not relishing painting in cold weather either. As a result, most of my winter scenes are studio-bound. While winter might reduce the sketching you do, it also provides all the excuse you need to use your sketchbook. I have included a few of my local scenes in the grip of a wintery snow shower or an early morning frost. Don't be put off by my reticence about cold weather sketching as you may really fancy it and produce some lively winter sketches which could be worked up as a studio painting or two with a hot drink.

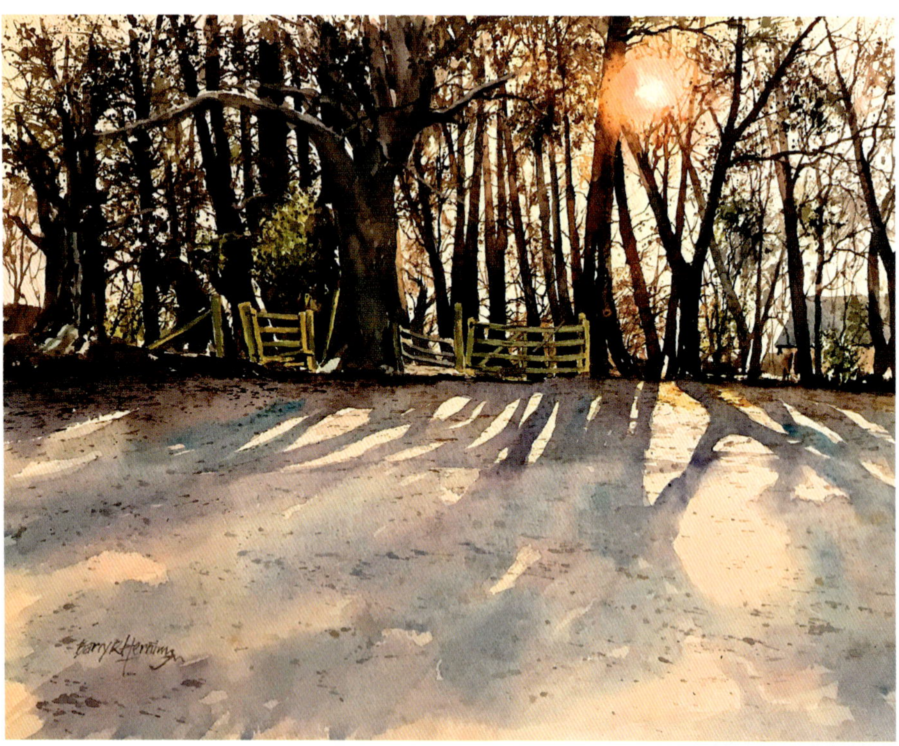

'Way Go Through'
One view I have painted many times is the gate in the small wood behind Way Go Through Cottage on one of our favourite walks. I had painted it in all seasons, always from the same viewpoint. Early on this particular frosty morning, we walked on down the field but something made me look back...and I got this striking view of the low sun glimmering through the trees and casting these long shadows over the frosty foreground. It was worth the cold to be rewarded with drama like this.

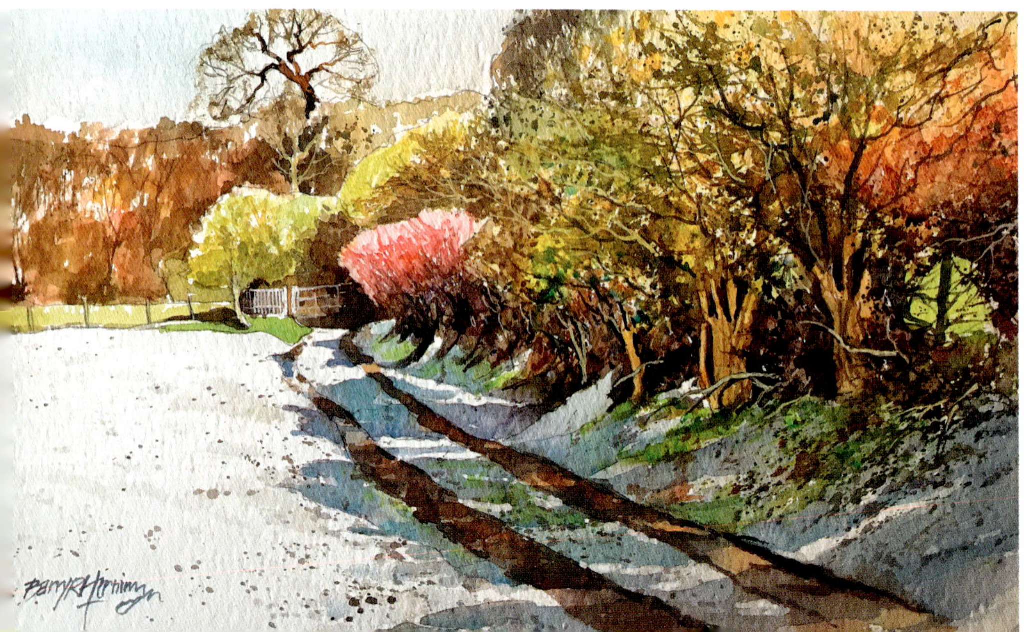

The track to 'Way Go Through'
Another early morning stroll to get the shadows across the track. Loads of textures in the hedgerow bushes and some nice shafts of light creeping between them over the track.

Early morning light

A little closer to home, in fact the adjacent field to our cottage, is this view looking towards the village church. We had a decent snowfall overnight and this was the scene that greeted me early next morning.

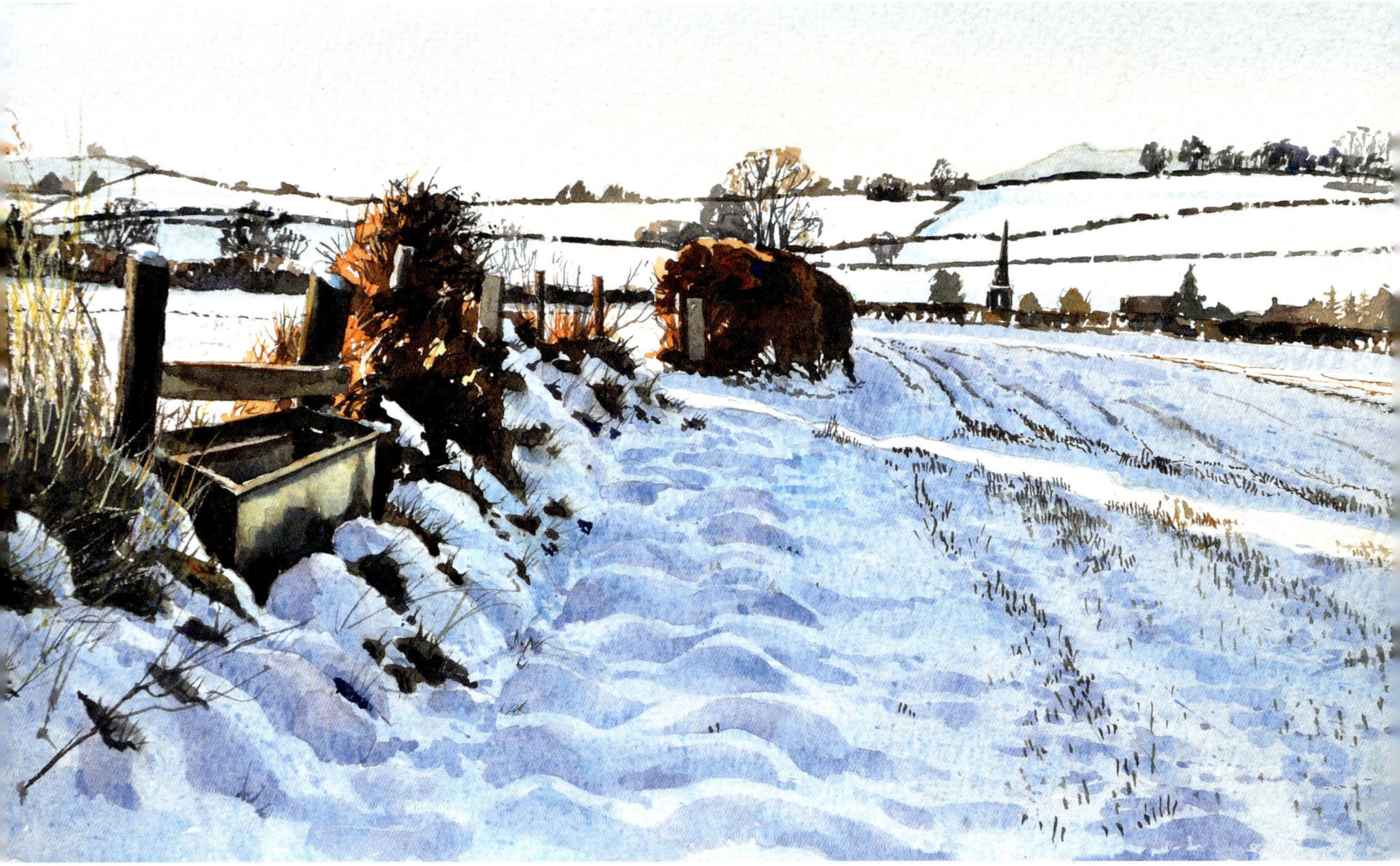

Colourful snow shadows

It's all too easy to think of snow pictures as 'black and white' but if you look closely at this section of another of my snow paintings you'll see that is very far from the truth. Obviously the sunshine plays an important part in lightening the scene, giving high contrast to the view. I used a variety of different blues with a touch of orange and manganese violet here and there in the shadows across the snow and the hedge.

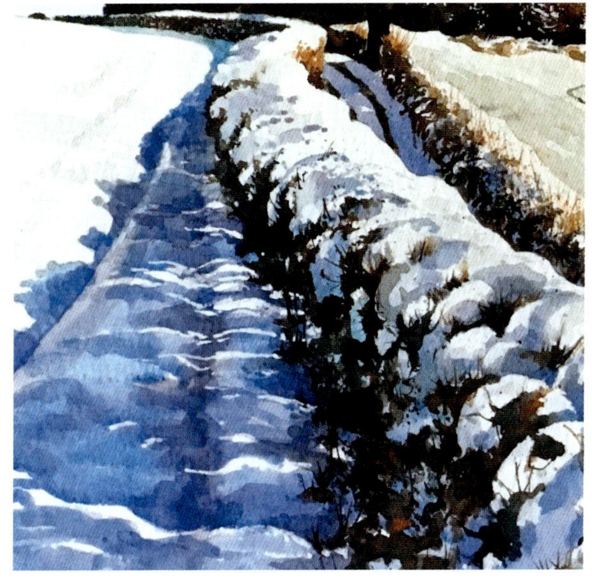

Developing the artist's eye

This quiet lane runs along the eastern boundary of our farmer's fields and is part of our circular walk around our village in Herefordshire. We have seen it in all weathers and all seasons but when we actually get a decent snowfall, the scene becomes magical. Keeping an eye out for such serendipitous moments relies on you developing an 'artist's eye' for that distinctive scene. Light obviously plays a great part in producing an exceptional scene and you need to be aware of all the impacts it has on the setting. The following pages show some examples of the scenes that 'grabbed' me – and give me a chance to show off one of my favourite haunts under different conditions!

Here are a few paintings I did around Ruxton Lane with all that lovely snow. I took countless photographs and then painted these up back in the warm studio.

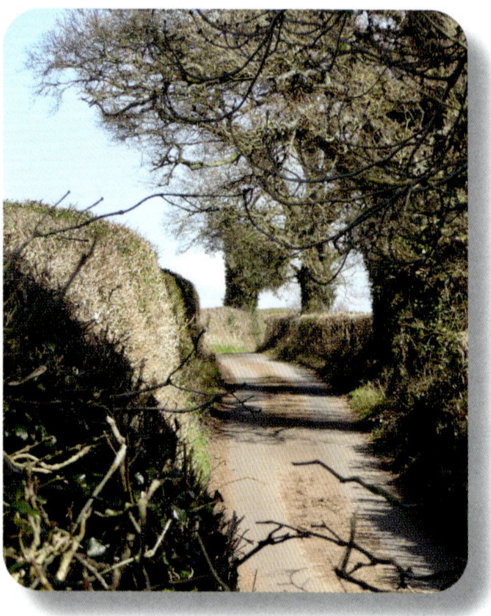

Here is one of my photos of Ruxton Lane – I have many!

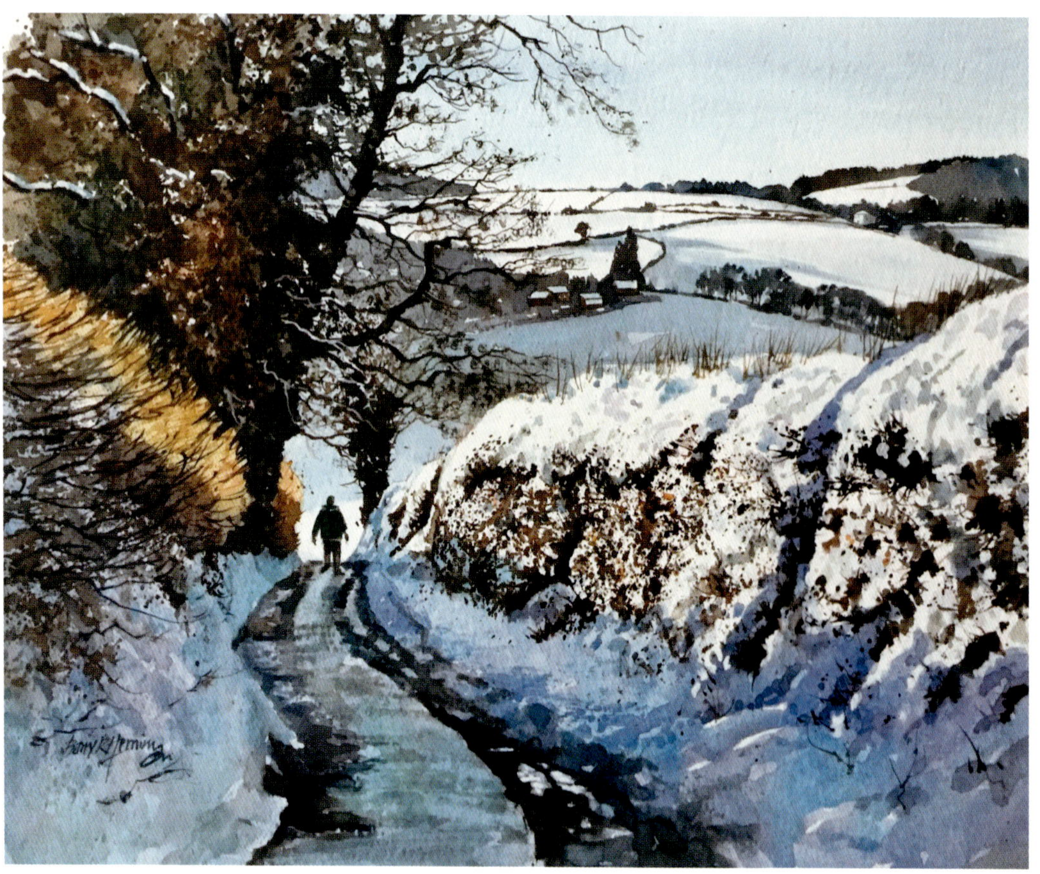

An effect called counterchange, which we looked at on page 74, often figures strongly in my paintings, especially on the sunlit tops of the hedges. Here's a good example in Ruxton Lane.

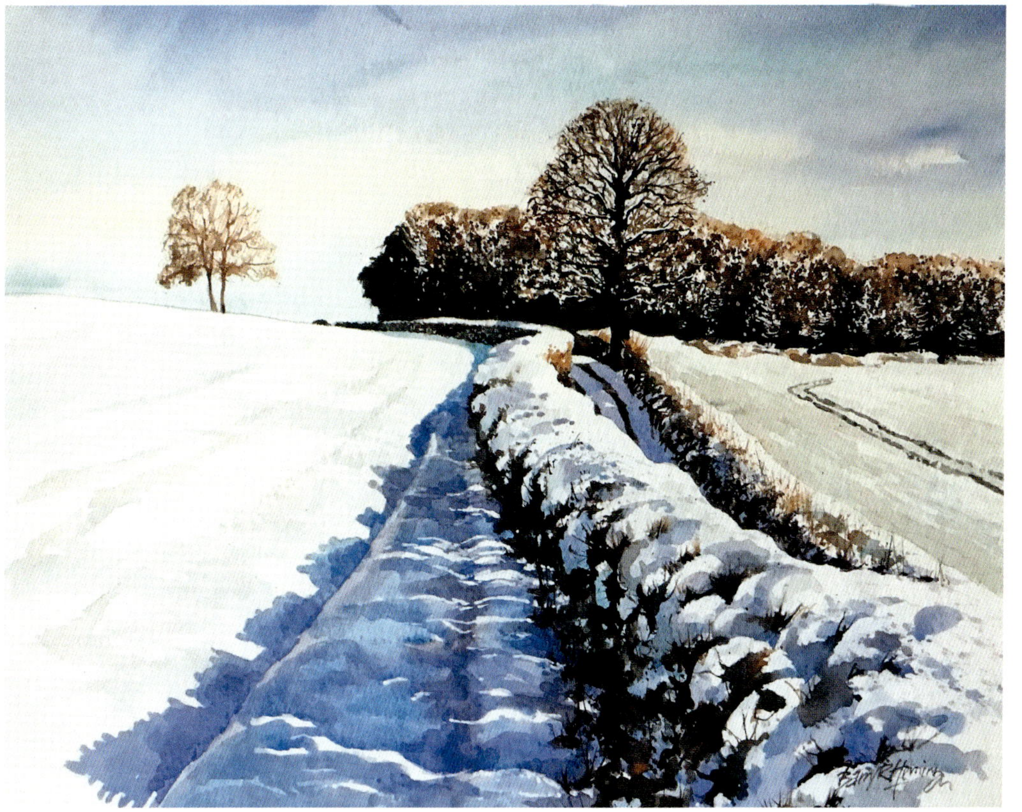

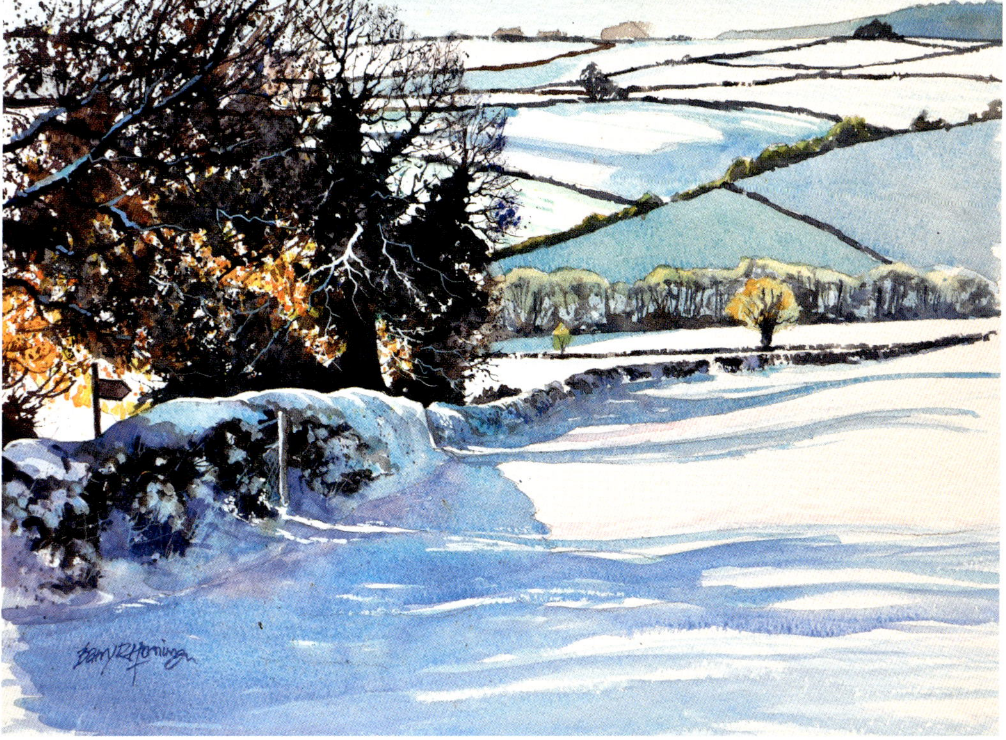

Two views of the hedge boundary with Ruxton Lane. In the bottom one, you can just see a small shaft of light between the hedge where the footpath decends to the lane.

Contra jour

When looking for a scene to sketch, the most obvious choice is the beautifully sunlit view with lovely sharp details and colours. But take a moment and look behind you *into* the sun (*contra jour*) and you'll get a totally different view with a whole new set of contrasts. If there's a strongly lit, full-colour scene in front of you, there might be a much more subtle one behind you. The colour tends to get bleached out but the backlit scene produces wonderful highlights around edges and dramatic, forward-facing shadows.

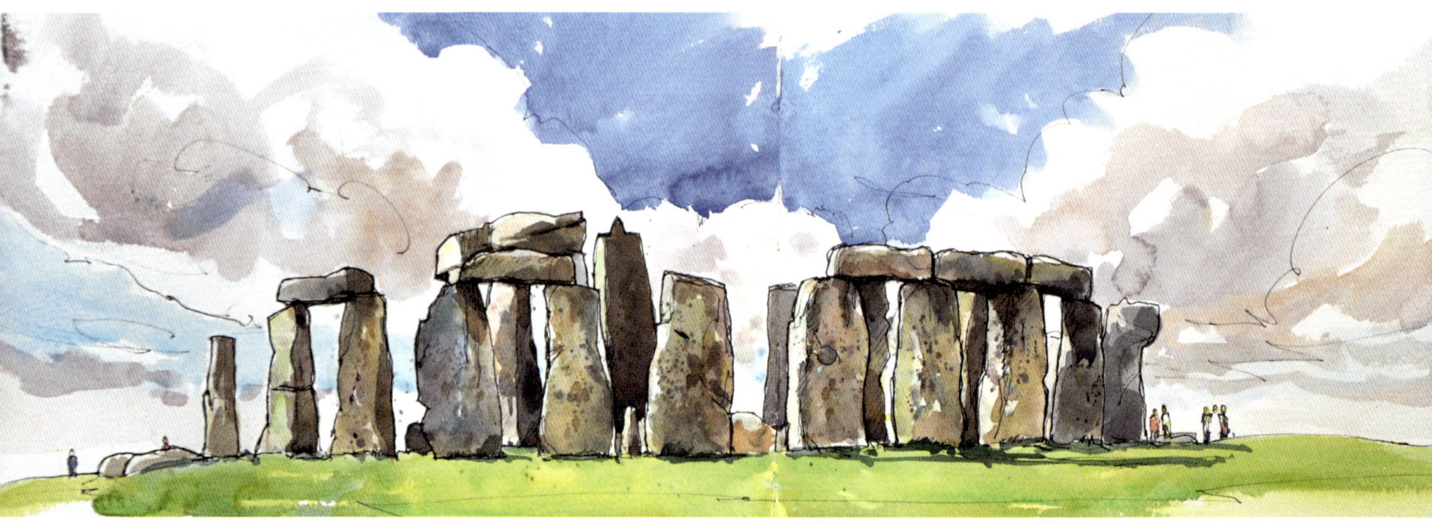

Sunshine and shadows

It's always exciting visiting the magnificent stone circle of Stonehenge and painting it! Of course it all depends on the weather because it is extremely exposed on the Downs but when the sun shines it's really magical. On one of our first visits, the weather was against us, so sketching was cut short. But when we returned it was a really hot day with some very strong light so I decided to do the view of the stones looking into the sun, with them silhouetted against the light sky, as shown above.

On another occasion I sketched the stones in full sun as it was such a beautiful day (see below). You can see how weather and choosing a different viewpoint of the same subject can produce very different paintings.

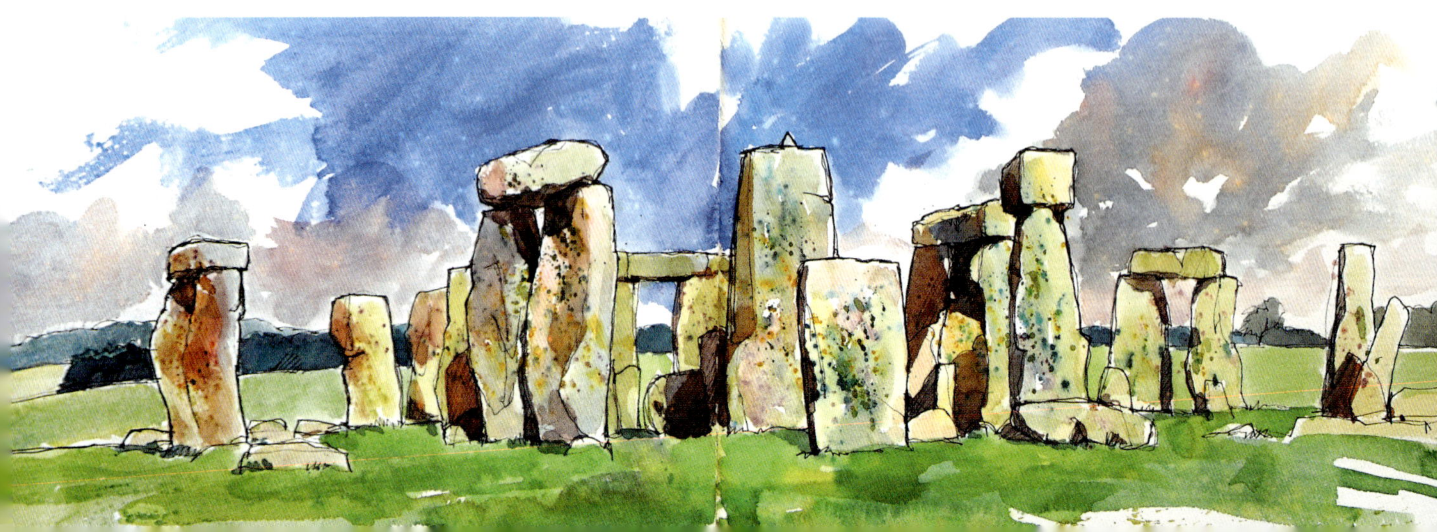

Using a viewfinder

When looking at a scene, the eye scans a wide panoramic view and sometimes this can be daunting for you as an artist, especially if you haven't done much or any painting outdoors. For this reason it is a good idea to take along a viewfinder so you can zone in on a subject and frame it up to see how it looks as a prospective sketch. When painting from photographs, you don't have this problem as the camera has already cropped the view for you. Not so when outside! Originally I used to take a blank slide mount and hold it up to my eye, framing different areas of the view to see if anything grabbed me. A piece of stiff card/mount board roughly postcard size with a rectangular window cut out of it also provides a good viewfinder. And if you want to go further, you can always stick a piece of clear plastic over the aperture and draw some grid lines on it to give you even more possibilities, such as panorama, square, portrait or landscape.

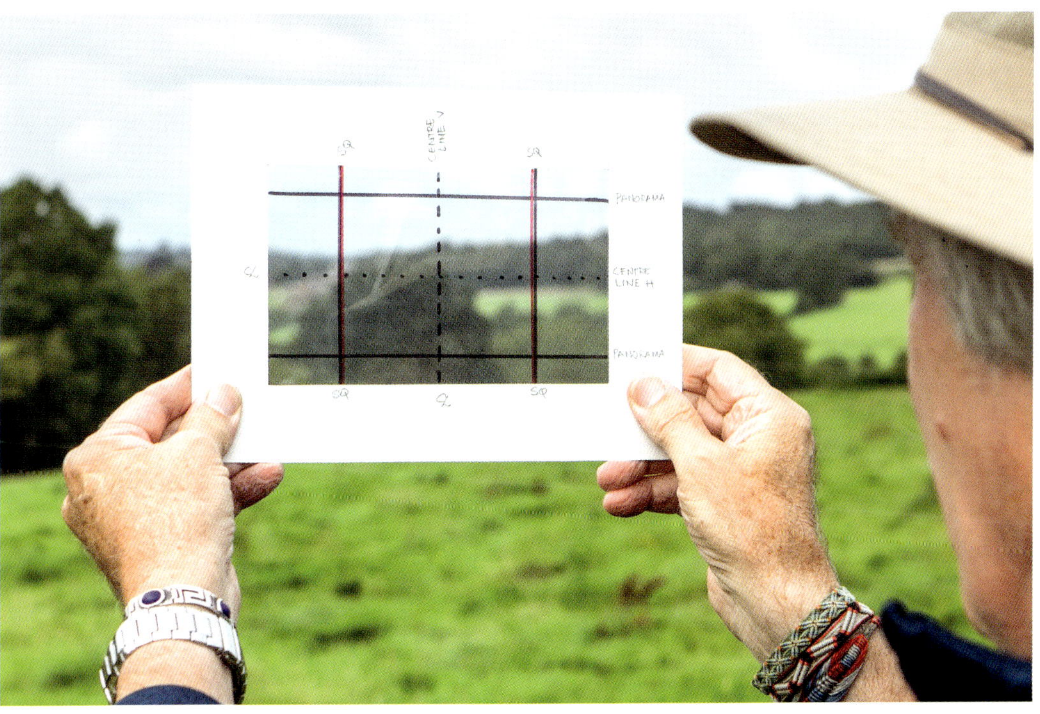

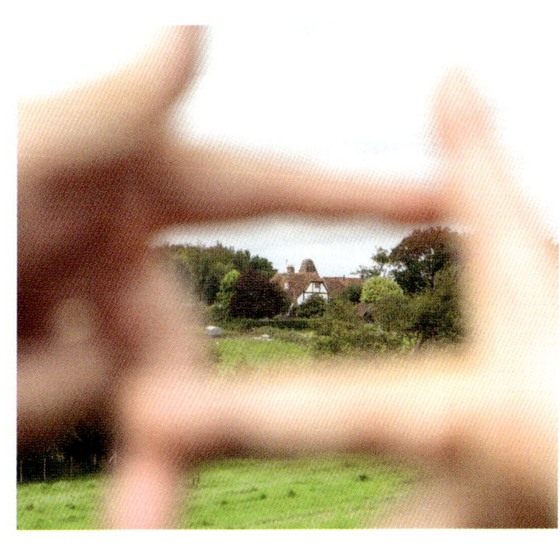

Fingers work too!
I tend to use the middle and index finger of each hand in an L shape as my viewfinder, which I can move about to get the view I want.

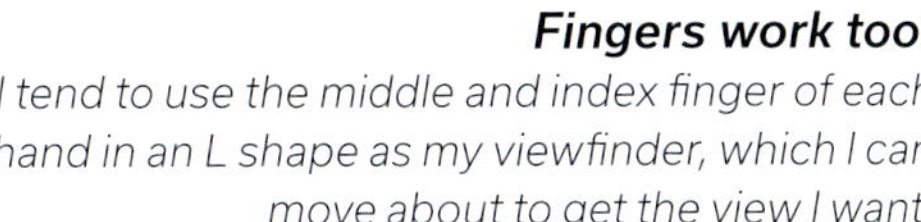

"

Zone in

When you have a busy townscape in front of you with all those buildings jostling for attention, take your viewfinder and zone in on a detail like an ornate doorway, an elegant window, a distinctive pub sign or an intricate roofline.

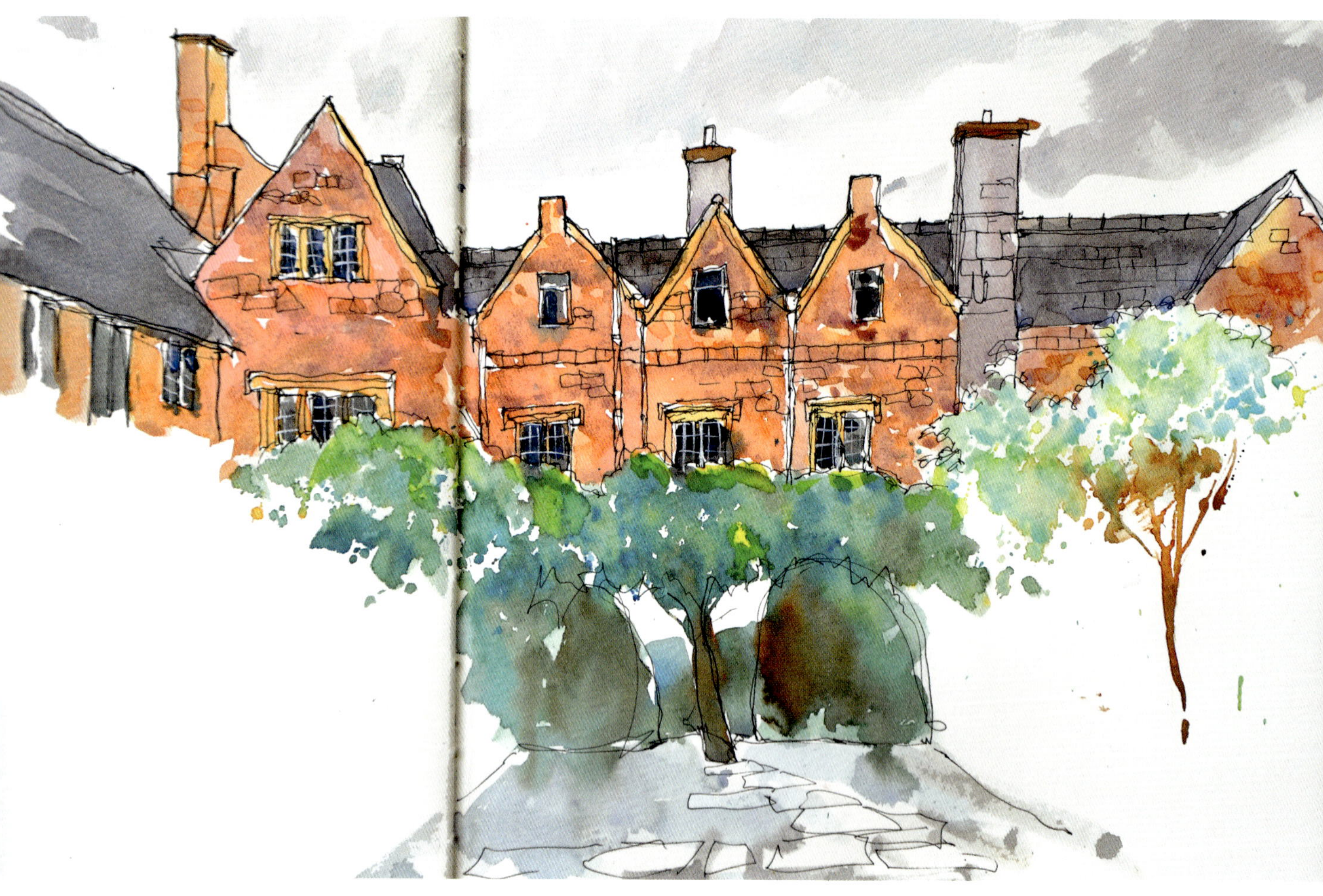

I set up in the afternoon to do a demo of rooflines of the back of the Old Court Hotel where we were staying in Symonds Yat East, Herefordshire. I just managed to get the rooflines ticked in and painted plus the beginnings of the foliage before the sky opened up and down came the rain. That's the beauty of a sketchbook: a half finished sketch can be as satisfying as a completed painting.

Zone out

Getting in the whole scene (or at least a goodly part of it) is my preferred format, so I tend to sketch across the two pages of my sketchbook to get the peripheral view as well as what's directly in front of me. It is eminently satisfying to be able to record that far-reaching view as I see it, especially as a photograph of the same view invariably ends up rather compressed and disappointing.

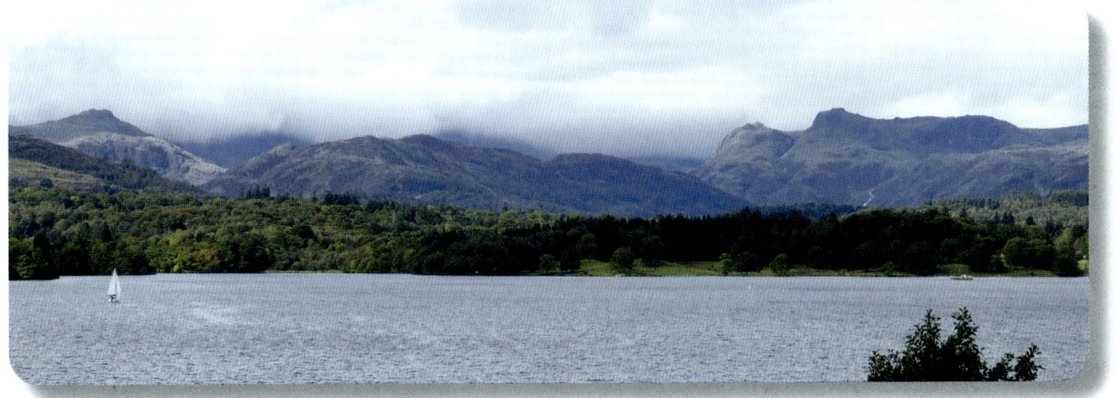

The view of the mountain range across Windermere in the Lake District had the potential to be quite striking but for the most part it was rather dull and featureless, until one day the sun came out in fits and starts and lit up areas of the range. Once again I took a photograph then set about sketching the scene in front of me. Here is the result of the photograph I took and it is underwhelming to say the least.

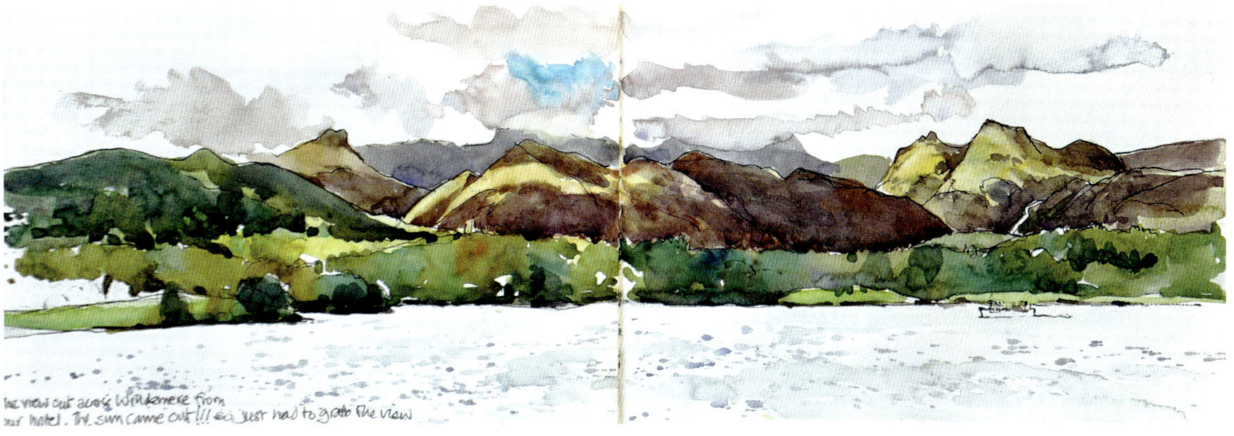

Even though the light was moving about all over the scene, I managed to capture the essence of view in the sketch. Unlike the photograph which was predominantly bluish grey, the actual colours I saw were completely different. The foreground hills were an array of bright and vibrant yellows, browns and greens which were not picked up in the photograph.

Same place, different aspect

On a walk down Ruxton Lane (see page 88), we were greeted by this lovely sunlit view (below) of the lane as it weaved its way through the countryside. Then when we turned round, we saw the view (shown opposite) from the same spot but now looking into the sun to get this altogether different scene with muted colours and highlighted edges.

I have done these two quick sketches to show how I would tackle these elements.

Using my Fude bent nib drawing pen I establish all the lights and shadow areas with different strengths of tone. This gives me a nice tonal study of the view of the lane in bright sunlight.

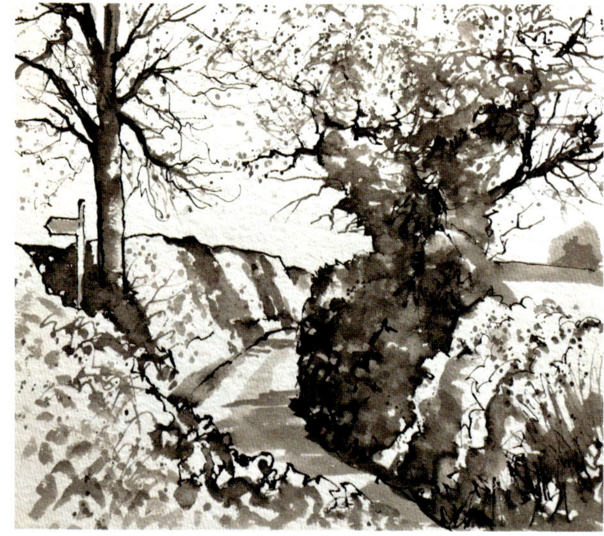

Then by adding some simple colour washes, I can really bring the scene to life. Because I have already established all the tonal areas with the ink, applying the colour washes is a quick and simple process.

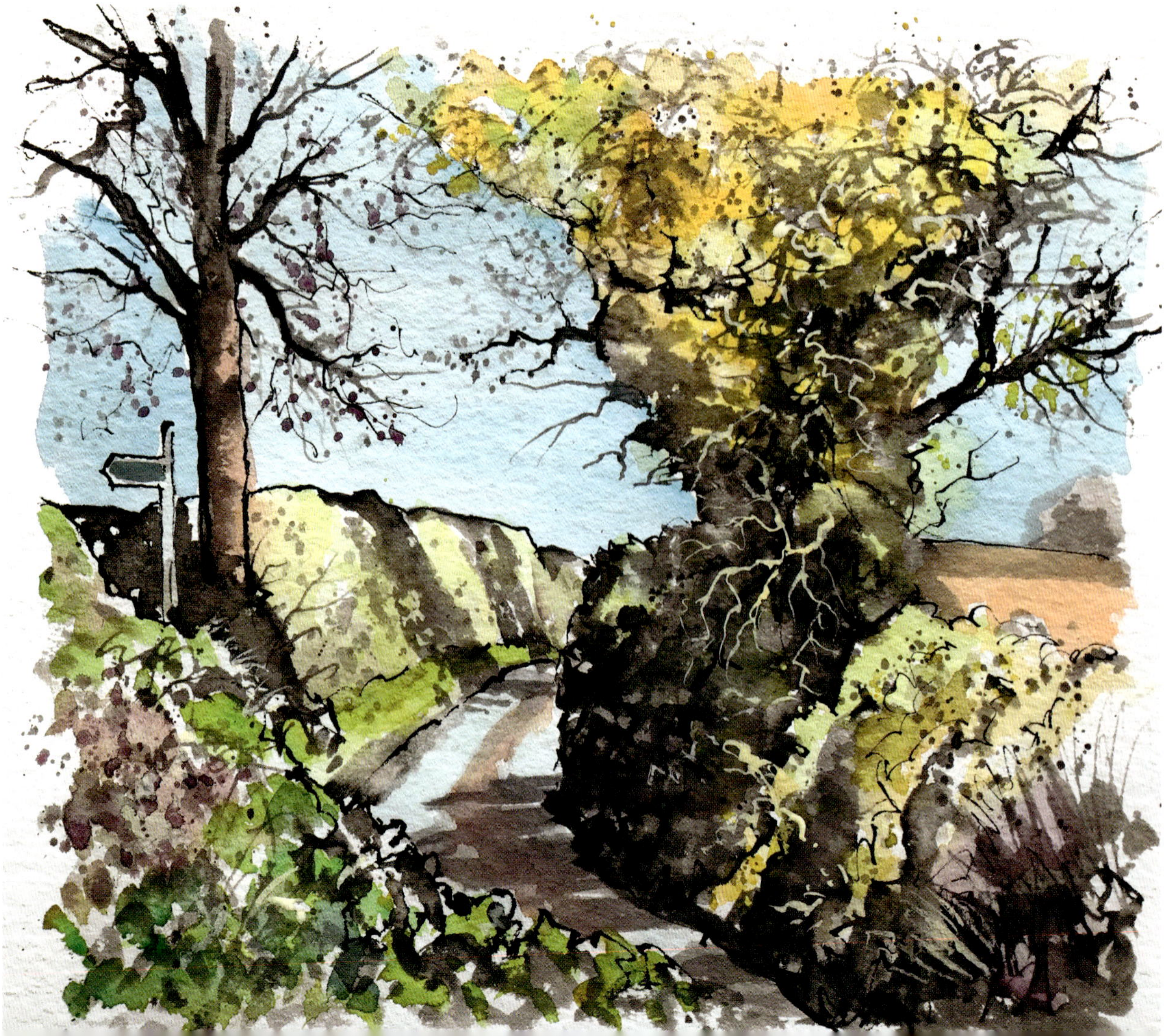

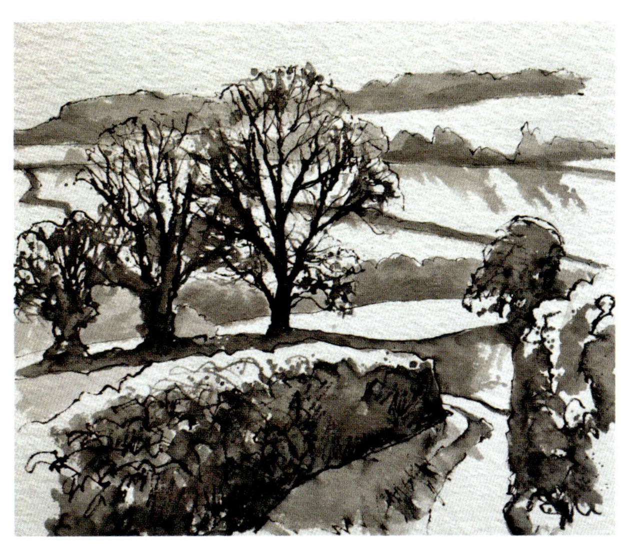

*By adding the colour washes, you can really
see the difference between the two scenes.
Because I was looking into the sun, all the
colours are bleached out and the outlines of the
trees and hedges are in sharp relief.*

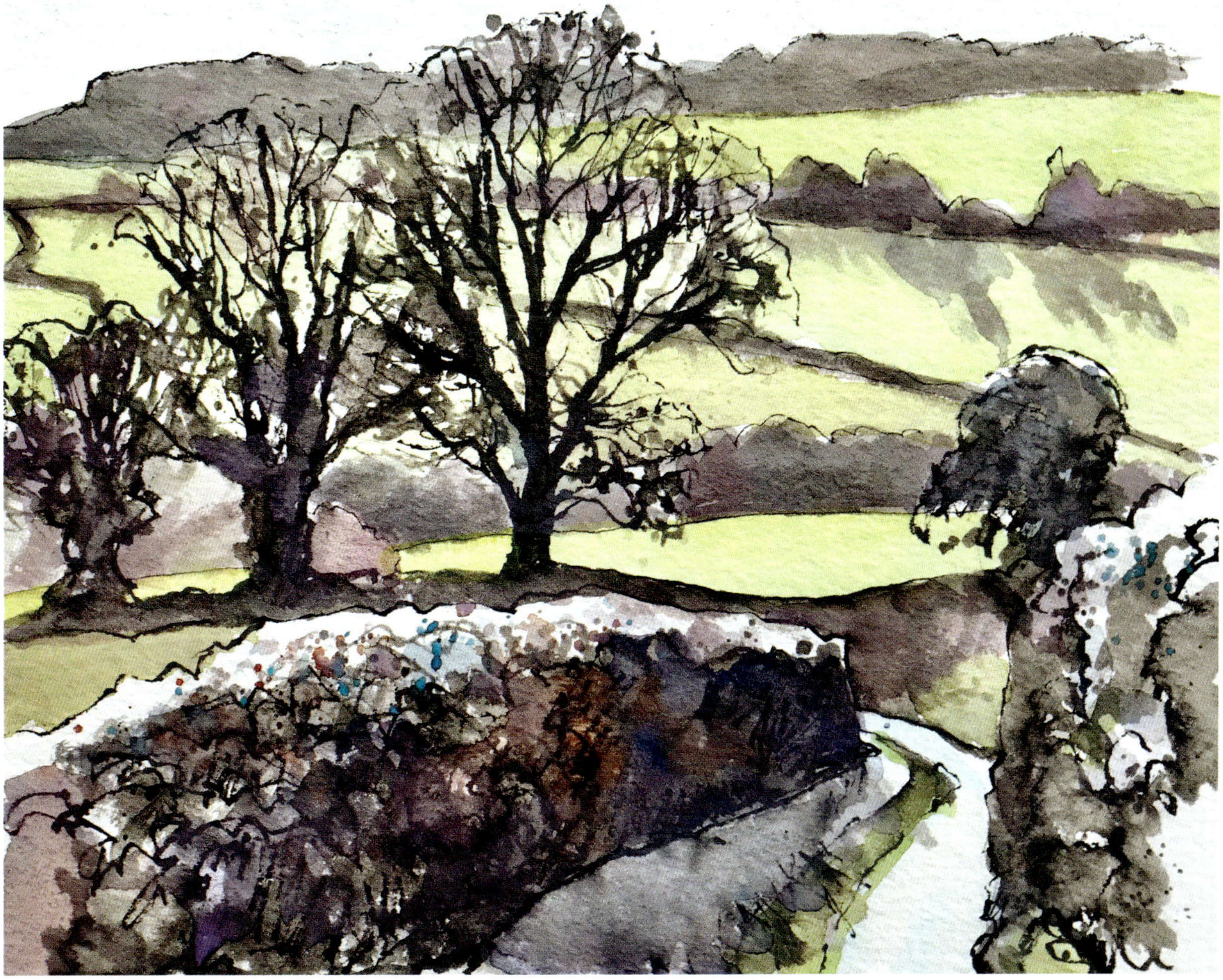

What to sketch

Sketching is a bit like doing a jigsaw puzzle. You see the overall scene, but one piece in particular might interest you the most. What is eyecatching and grabs your attention? As well as what is in front of you, look up, look behind you and look at the ground. Sometimes retracing your steps can provide you with the subject that holds your interest, and it doesn't need to be something of epic proportions, as I demonstrate in the sketches that follow.

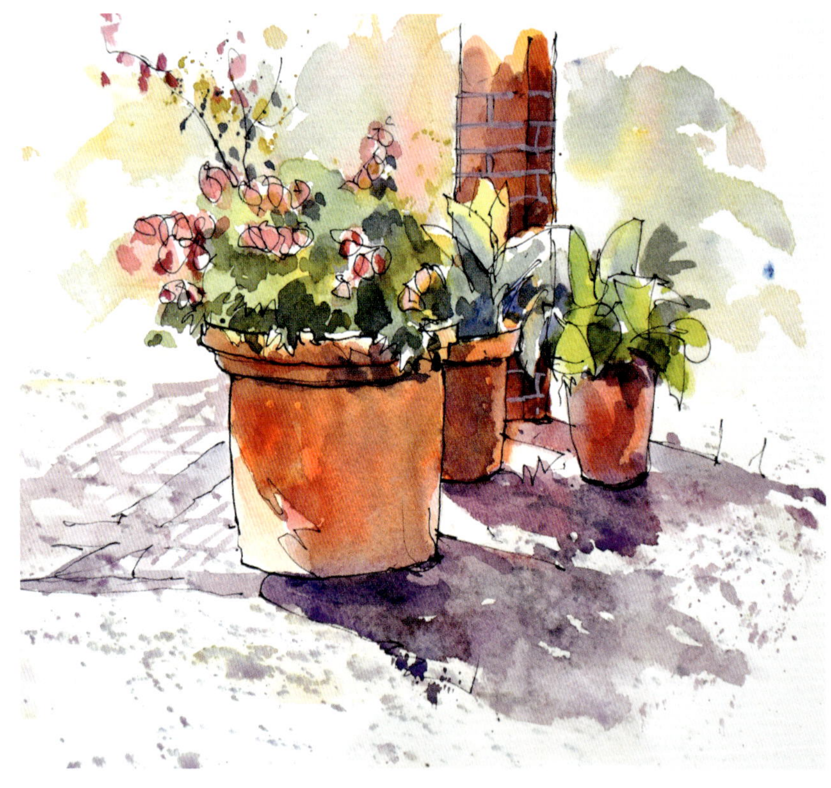

Flowerpots
When I am teaching, I like to get everyone into the swing of painting loosely and mixing all their colours on the paper rather than in the palette. What better subject to sketch than the lovely terracotta pots that adorn the Finca patio, with vibrant washes in both the pots and their cast shadows.

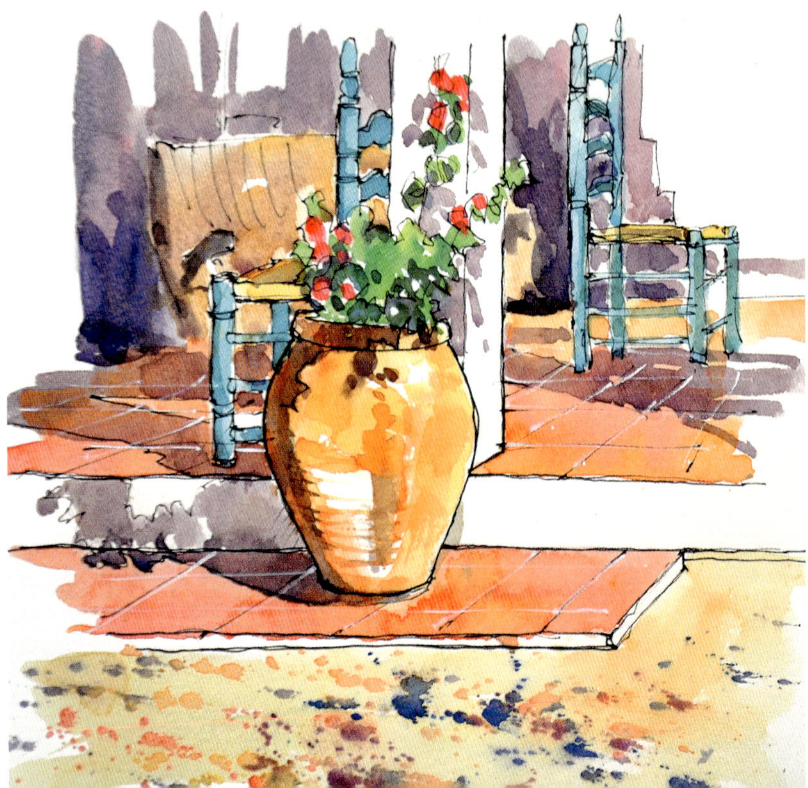

Blue chairs

This Greek scene with its ubiquitous blue chairs just had to be sketched! The tiny waterside taverna seemed to be set up just for us to paint. After we had finished the sketch, we sat on those very chairs and partook of some Greek cuisine and a few ice-cold beers from the friendly owners.

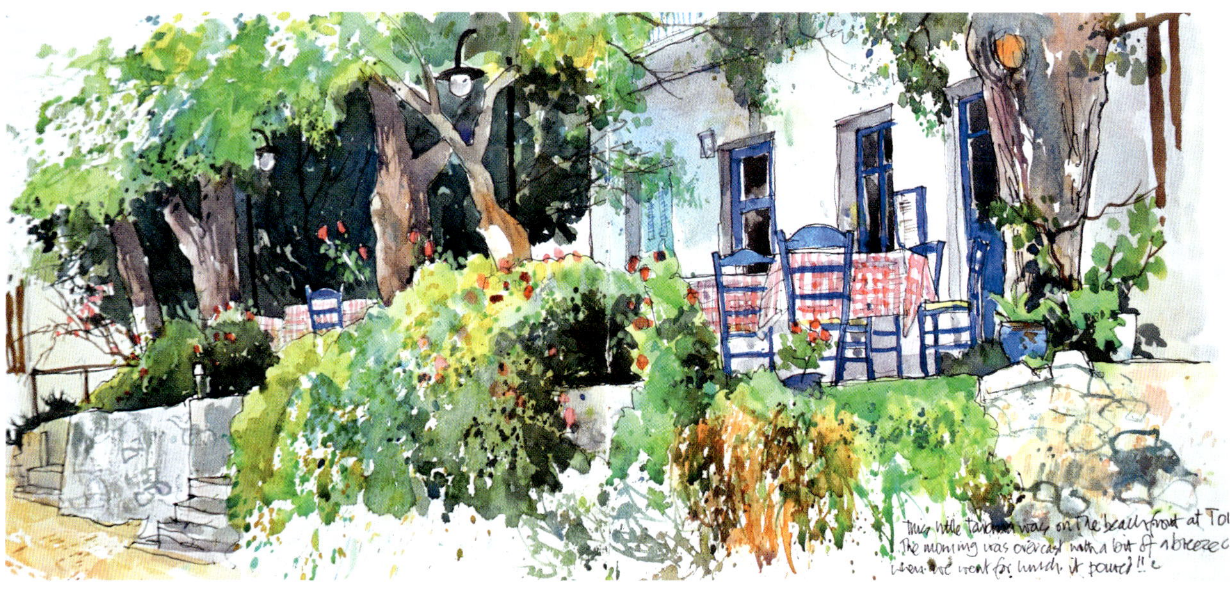

Herbs for sale

Driving around the roads of Kent looking out for some oast houses to paint, we came across this jumble of buildings which took my eye. It was a real hotchpotch of fairly run-down buildings but was a great subject to sketch with all the different textures and facades.

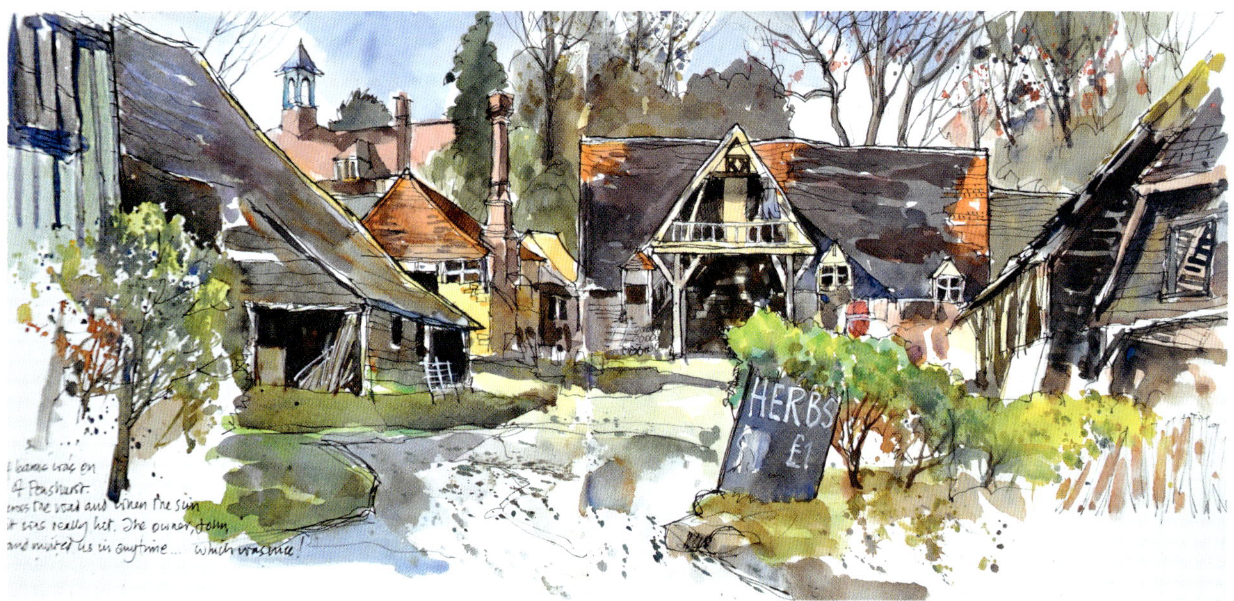

Sketching people

Quite often I have found myself in a quiet bar or café where I can people-watch…and paint! Be careful you don't offend anyone as some people may not want to be sketched. Pick a quiet table where you can observe without being overly noticed. Of course it is usually much safer if you can use some of your friends or painting group as models, as I have done here.

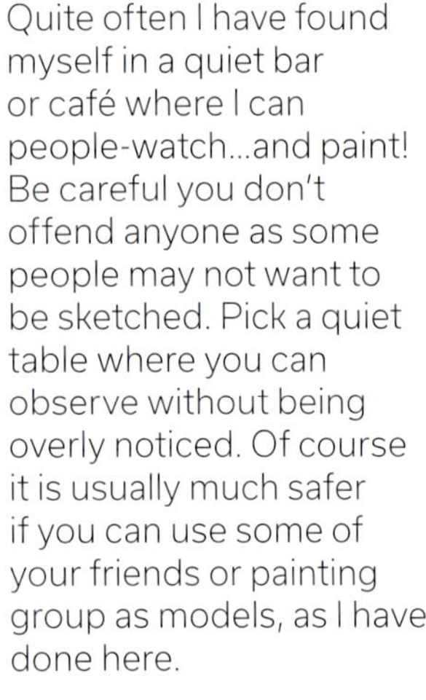

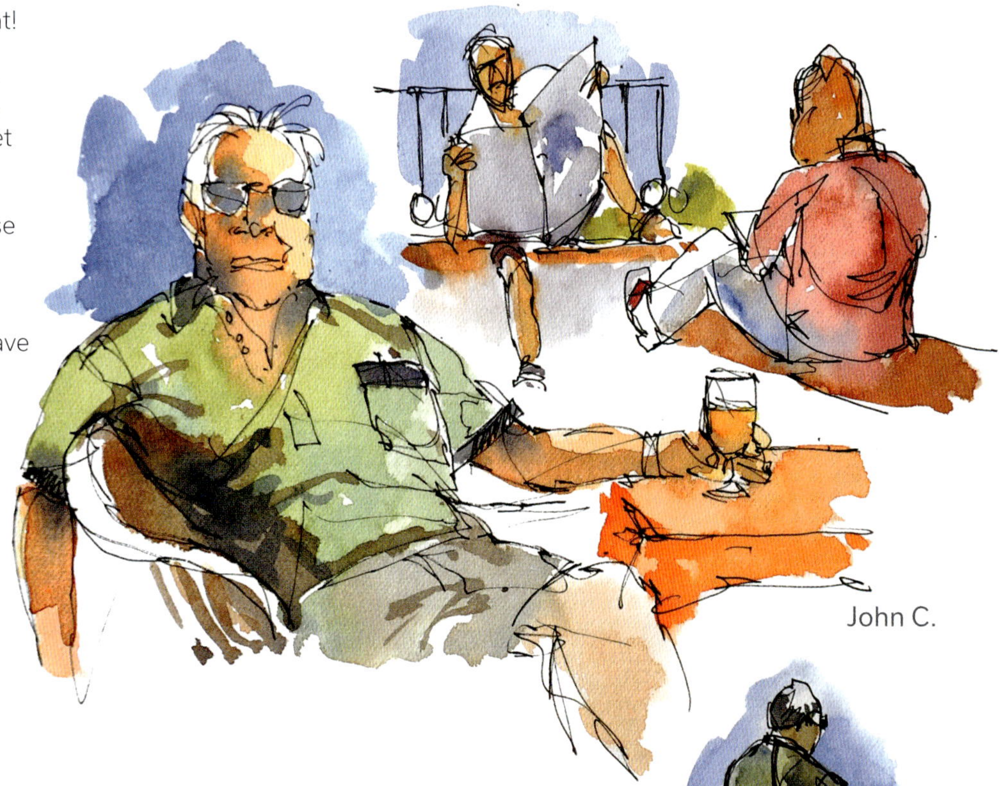

John C.

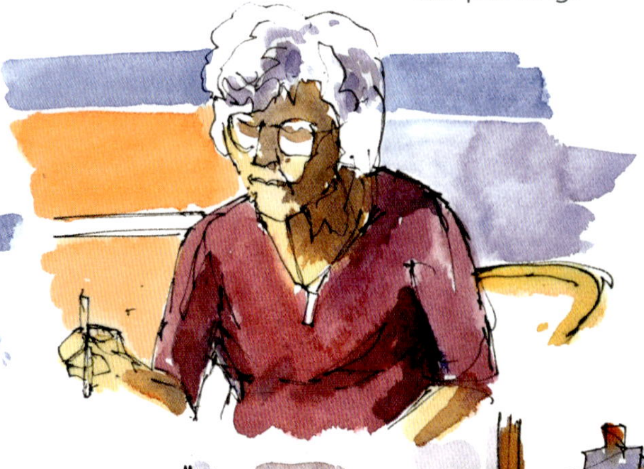

Ann concentrating on her painting.

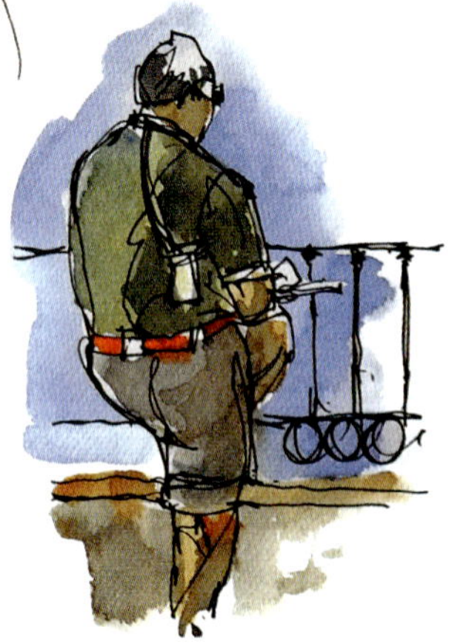

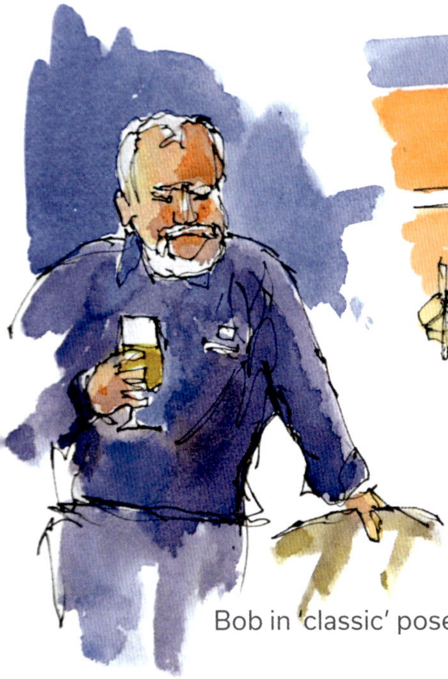

Bob in 'classic' pose.

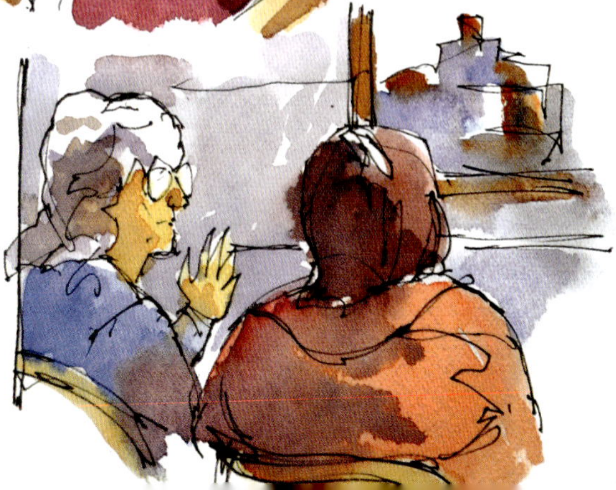

Corralie and Peta in conversation.

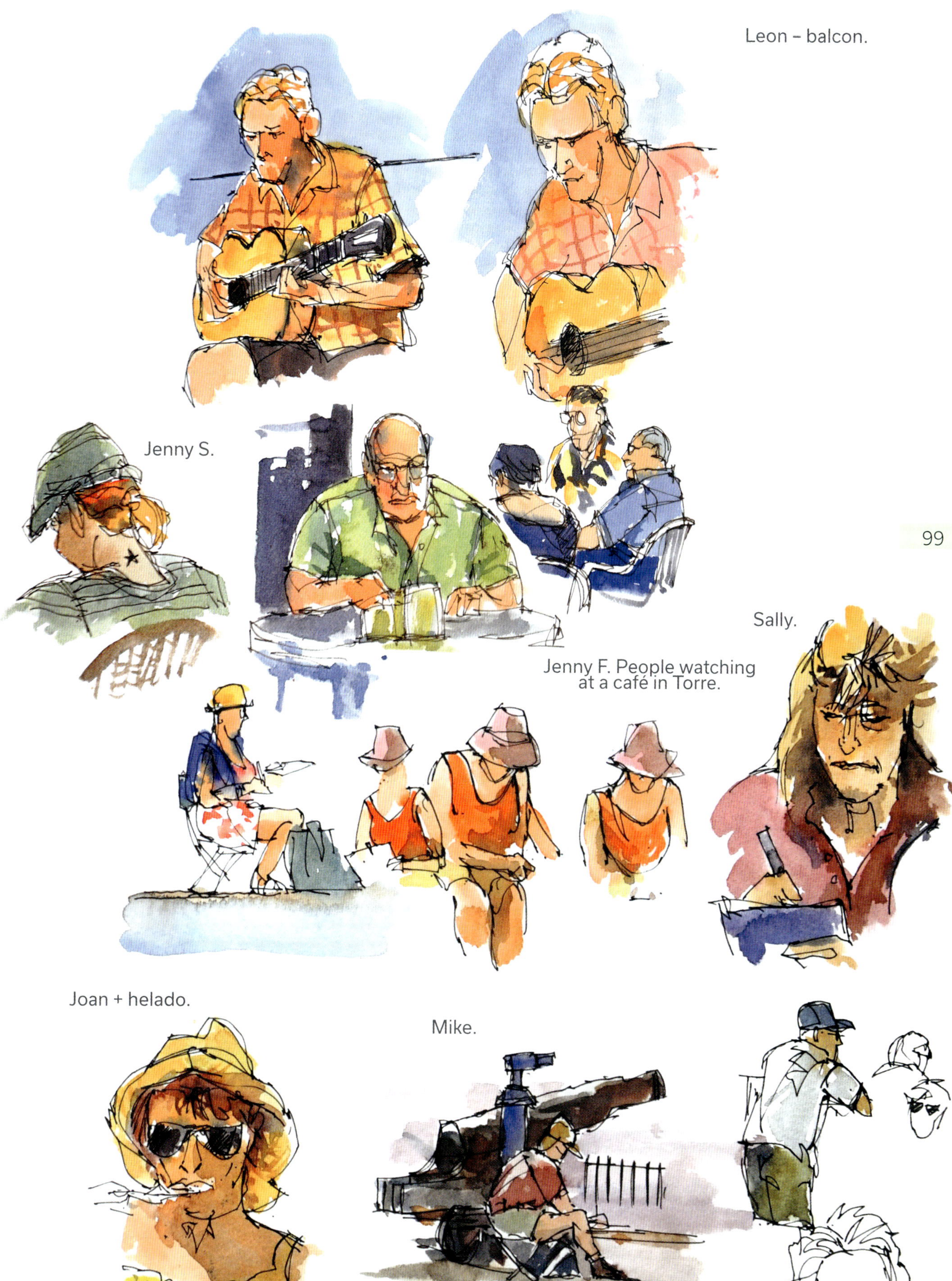

Leon – balcon.
Jenny S.
Sally.
Jenny F. People watching
at a café in Torre.
Joan + helado.
Mike.

What to include and exclude

'Because it's there!'

I'm sure you will have come across a time when that wonderful view you want to paint has something that either partly obscures it or is an unsightly element. If you are a photographer, then you are rather stymied unless you can get an alternative viewpoint, but not so us artists! We can literally move mountains and I have done so if the mountains I wanted were not where I wanted them.

Deciding what to put into and leave out of your painting is also a consideration to keep in mind. I always recall a time I was in Gloucester, Massachusetts painting a super view of the boatyard from my friend's house on a large sheet of watercolour paper. When I finished, I realized that a third of the way into the painting, I had painted in the whole trunk of a palm in his front garden. When I was asked why I had put it in my painting I said, 'Because it was there!'

Now, however, if there is any element I don't like and want to remove or move around then I jolly well do it!

Here are a few examples of scenes where I have used my 'artist's license' to produce what I want (well Turner did it a lot in his landscapes).

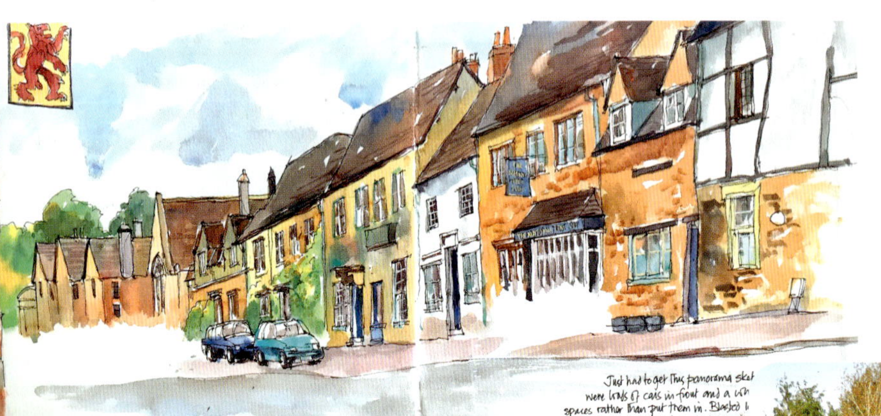

This lovely village of Lacock, Wiltshire has been beautifully preserved and unchanged over the years. However, modernity was ever present in the long line of cars and white vans parked right in front of these lovely houses. I sketched in a couple and left out the others, leaving a white space. If I had the time or inclination I could have walked around the vehicles and ticked in the details, but that's the beauty of a sketch: you don't have to put everything in.

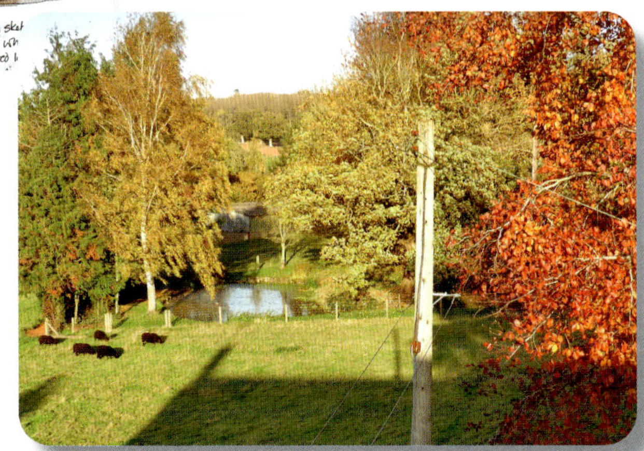

This view across the fields towards the pond is a prime example of an unwanted element with an electricity pole smack bang in the middle of it. So just get your chainsaw out (figuratively speaking of course) and hey presto, problem solved.

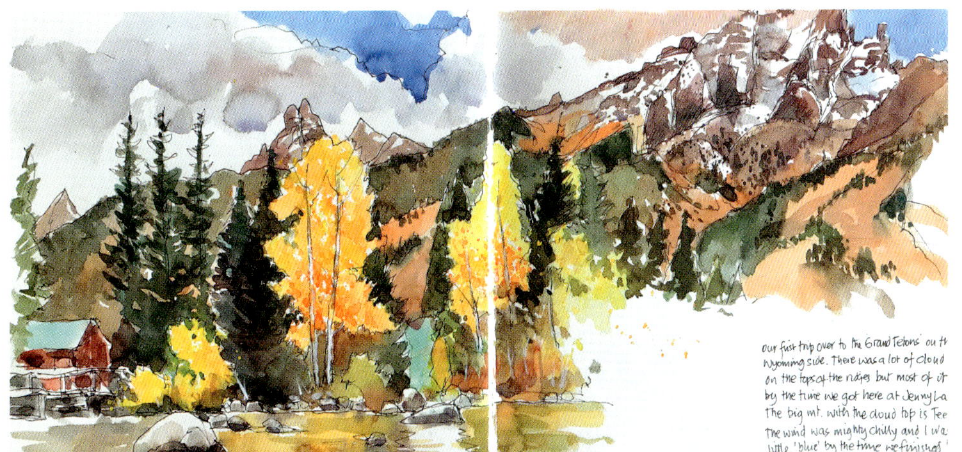

On our first day out to the Grand Tetons, Wyoming USA, we came across this view that took in the mountains and the river. The downside was a large black building which partly obscured the view to our right. I just painted all the bits I wanted and left a white space where the building was. As it turned out it was a useful area for my handwritten notes.

How long should I spend on a sketch?

This is ultimately down to each artist and the view in front of them, the complexity and also whether it is inspirational enough to spend much time on.

Obviously, when sketching outdoors you are at the mercy of the elements and therefore you might have to tailor your painting time to the weather. Often you could find yourself sketching away in the sunshine only to be brought up short by a downpour or failing light or both so you may have to abandon your session with what you were able to capture in the time you had.

The reverse is also a consideration as you may start out on a dull, overcast day only to find as the day wears on that you are in bright sunshine. As you start sketching, the scene is rather flat with the absence of shadows but when the sun appears the whole scene changes: all the colours become more vibrant and there are shadows everywhere.

Before I set out I had it in mind that I wanted a double-page panorama so needed a view that would fit the bill. Here you can see the finished sketch in front of the scene I was painting.

This sketch took roughly an hour actual painting time, as I had to wait for the initial washes to dry before overpainting them.

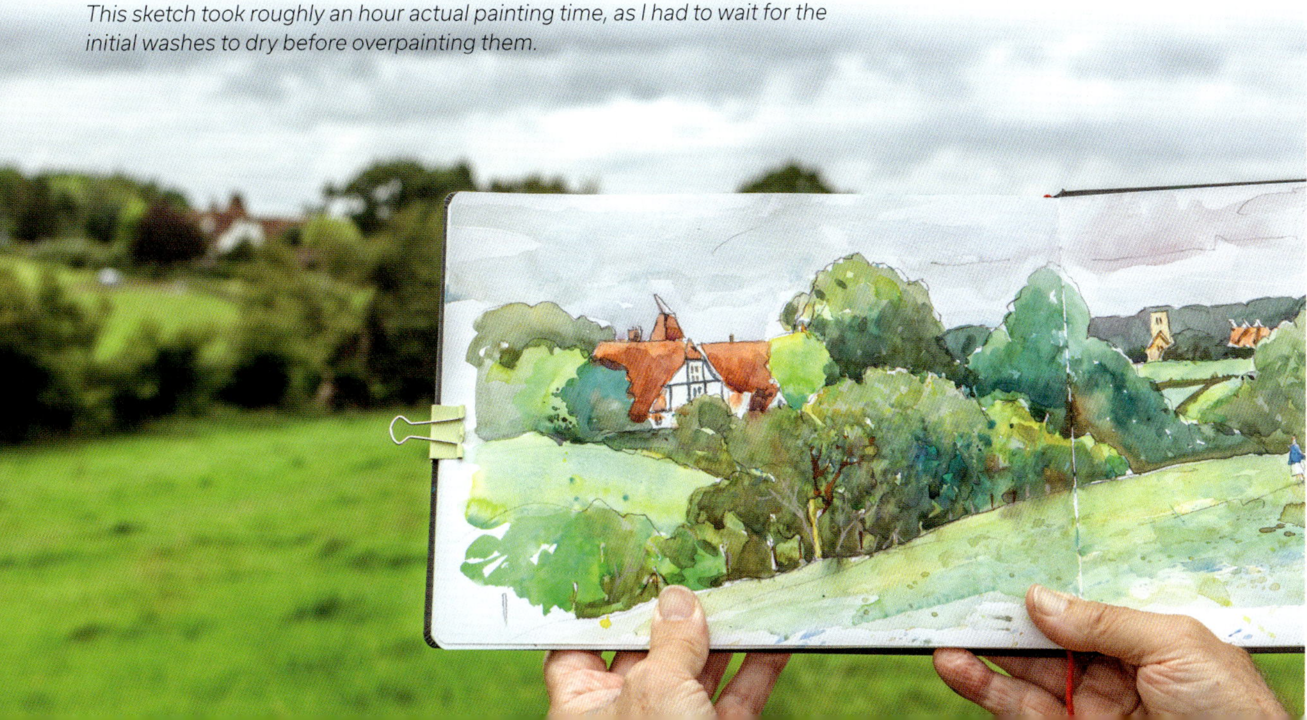

The 10-minute sketch

Just to give you some idea of what is possible to capture in 10 minutes I have produced a few sketches, in different media and I hope you'll have a go yourself.

I have found that the 10-minute sketch is a great way to focus the mind on getting to grips with a quick sketch, rather than a more considered and time-consuming piece of art. Telling yourself at the outset that you're only going to spend 10 minutes sketching helps you look beyond the panoramic view and concentrate on zoning into those specific detailed areas that inspire you. That way you can really get into the whole mindset of sketching and thoroughly enjoying the experience without all the angst of having to produce a finished masterpiece every time.

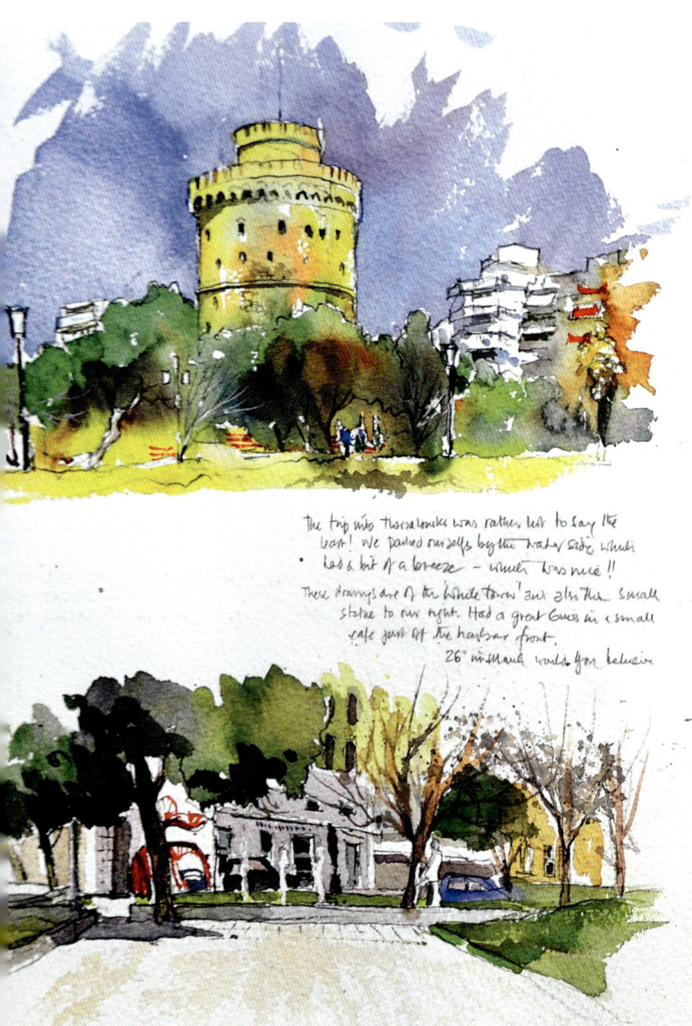

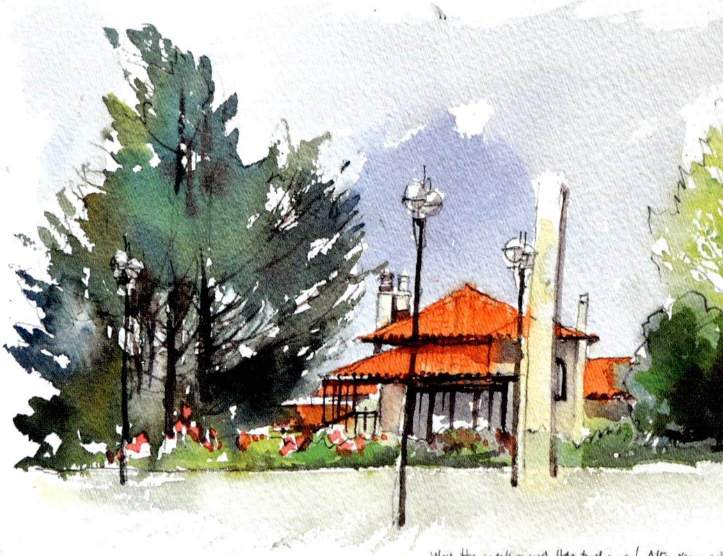

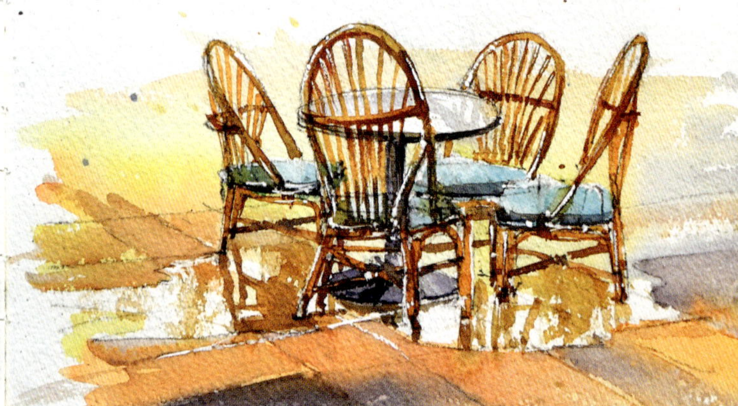

Watercolour vignettes

On a painting holiday to Greece, I did this series of four quick sketches in my A3 sketchbook which contained 300gsm (140lb) Saunders Waterford Rough paper. I used a 2B pencil for all the preliminary drawings. The paper was great for producing all those lovely textures.

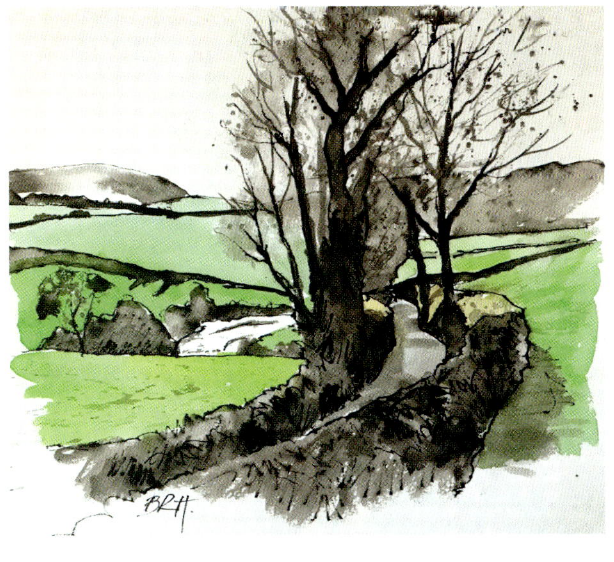

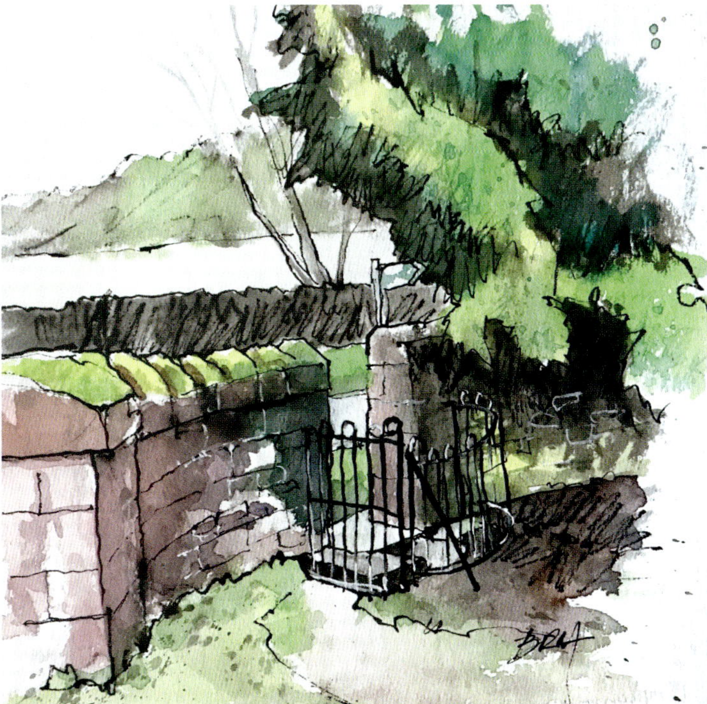

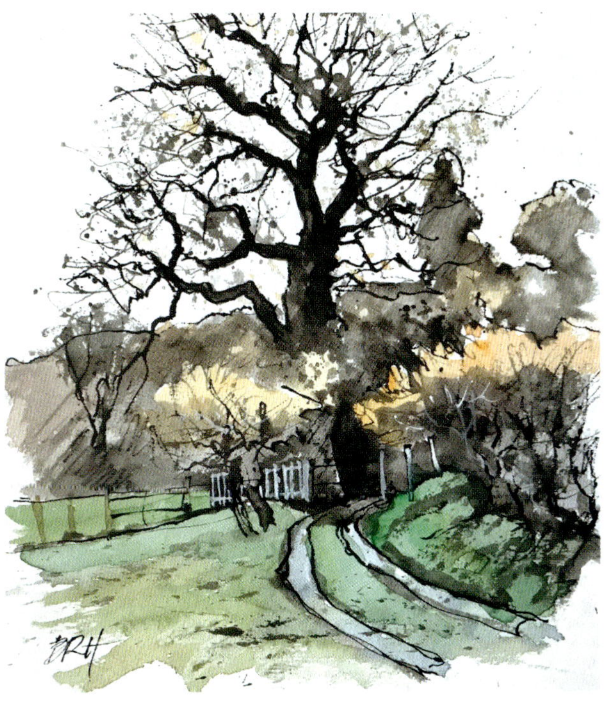

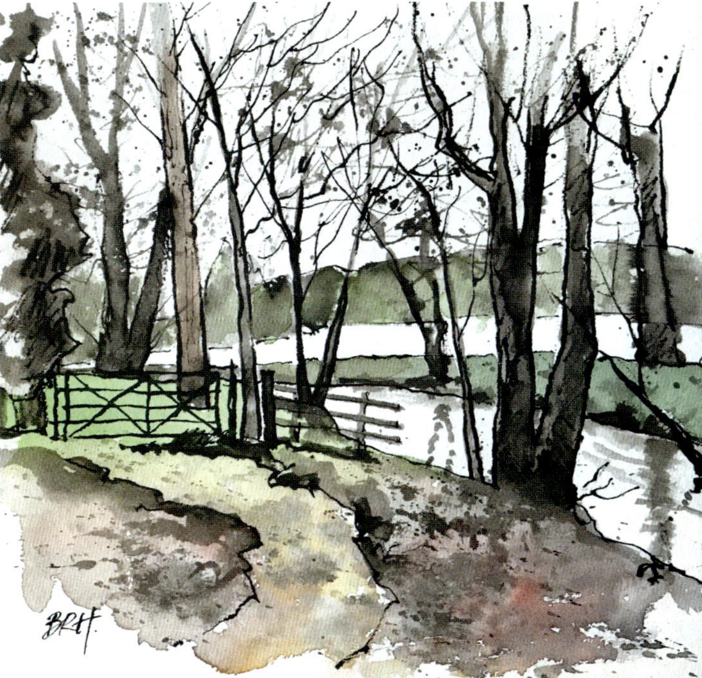

Pen sketches with watercolour washes

This series of quick pen sketches with some basic watercolour washes was great fun to do and it's surprising how much you can achieve in so little time. These are all taken from one of our favourite walks around the village and many a time I have gone on and done a full-blown studio painting from some of these viewpoints. Using my Fude bent nib drawing pen I went straight in with the ink drawing, using water over the wet ink to produce all the tonal areas. Then when all the ink work was dry and waterproof I went in with some simple watercolour washes to give them a bit of sparkle.

From quick to slow

Here I have gone literally from a quick doodle to a more involved piece to show what you can achieve within any time constraint.

Quick pencil sketch: 10–15 minutes

When time is limited, a pencil sketch is a great way to capture a scene 'on the hoof' so to speak. A pencil and a piece of paper and away you go. As long as you use a soft pencil such as a 2B, you can also smudge areas to create and blend tonal passages, as you can see within the wooded areas here.

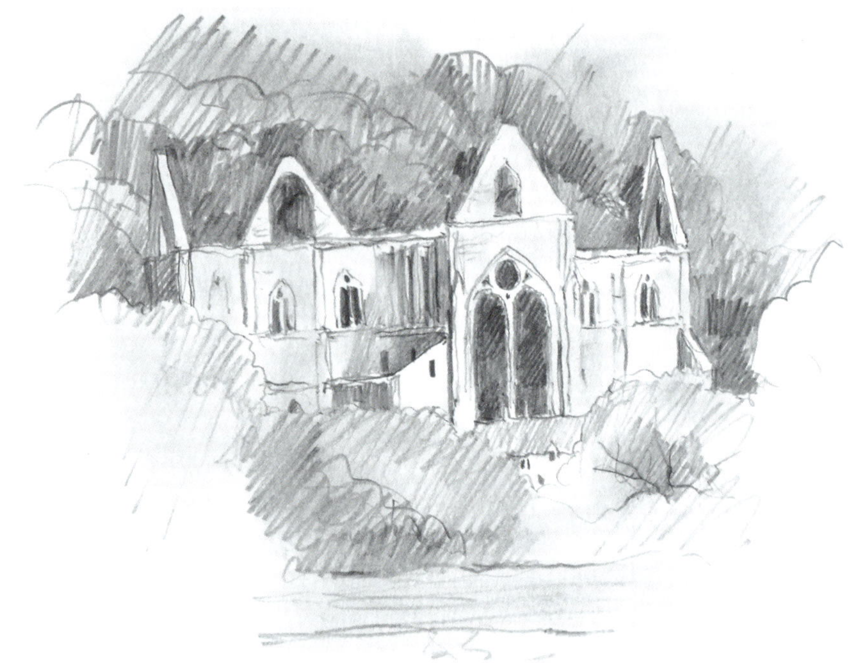

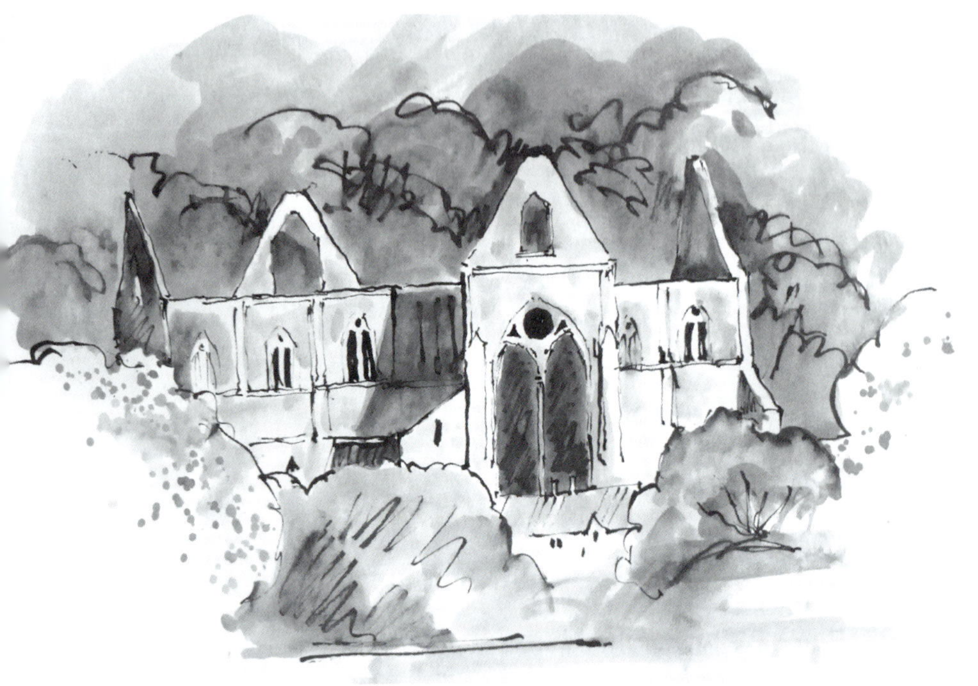

Slightly slower ink sketch: 15 minutes

Using ink for your sketches might take a little more time as one has to take more care in getting it right, or thereabouts, because you cannot rub out ink lines! You can, however, very quickly produce some lovely graded washes with the wet ink which is a definite plus for speed. And while you're here, just look at all that lovely counterchange within this sketch...it's everywhere!

Adding watercolour: 20–25 minutes

So you've done your ink sketch and you still have time on your hands then you can always overlay some simple watercolour washes. You don't have to worry about tone and shadows as that has already been established in the ink sketch; just overpaint the different areas with their local colours.

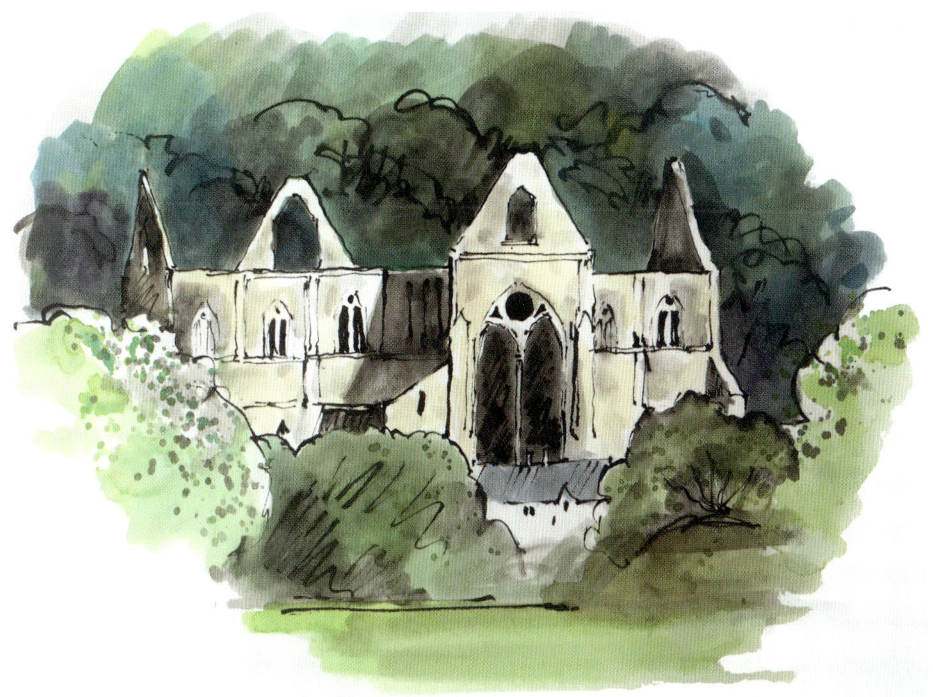

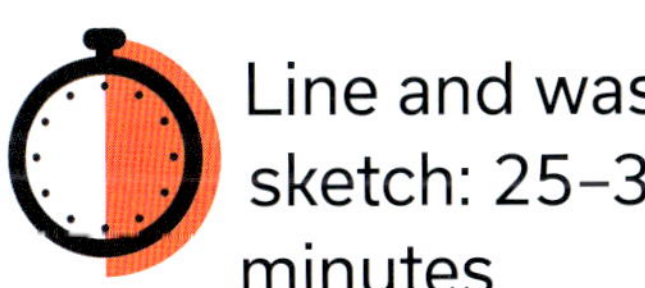

Line and wash sketch: 25–30 minutes

If you have time it's great to settle down, get out your sketchbook and paints and do a more considered sketch. This can be a very rewarding pursuit but please don't bypass the quick sketches as they have their rightful place in your painting repertoire and in the pursuit of your own sketching 'shorthand'.

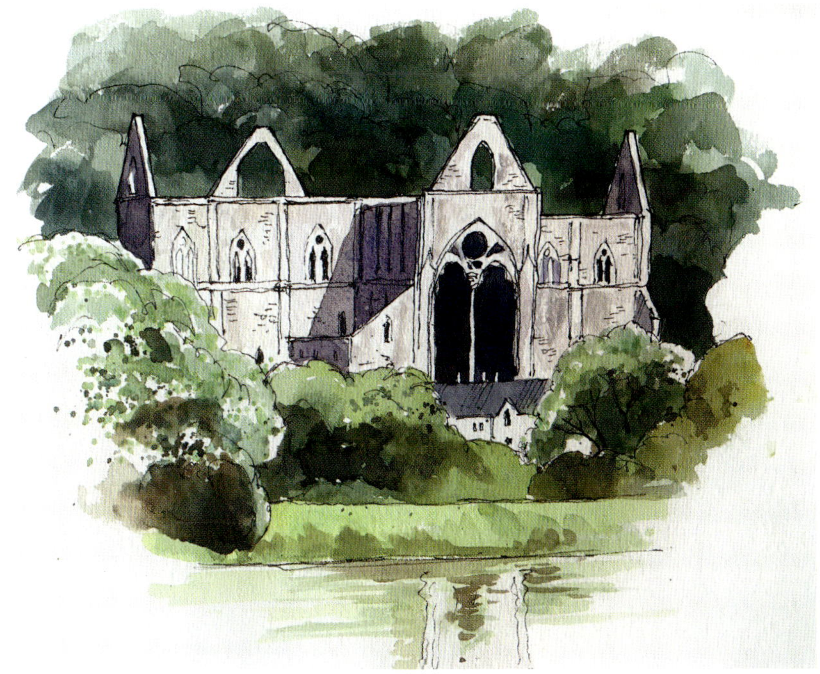

Straight in with the brush

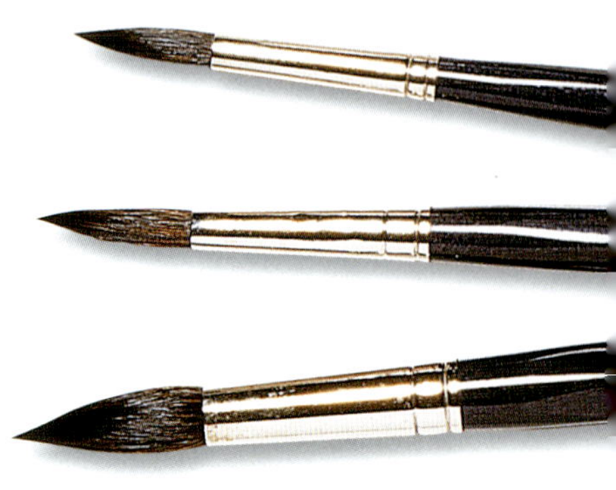

You will notice that I have always started off my sketching session with some sort of preliminary drawing, be it ink or pencil, but going straight in with the brush and paint is an exciting alternative.

   Here is a quick demo I did of a steam locomotive, going straight in with the brushwork without any preliminary drawing beforehand. When 'drawing' with the brush, I favour a Kolinsky sable as the point is great for getting all that detail. This sketch took me about 20 minutes.

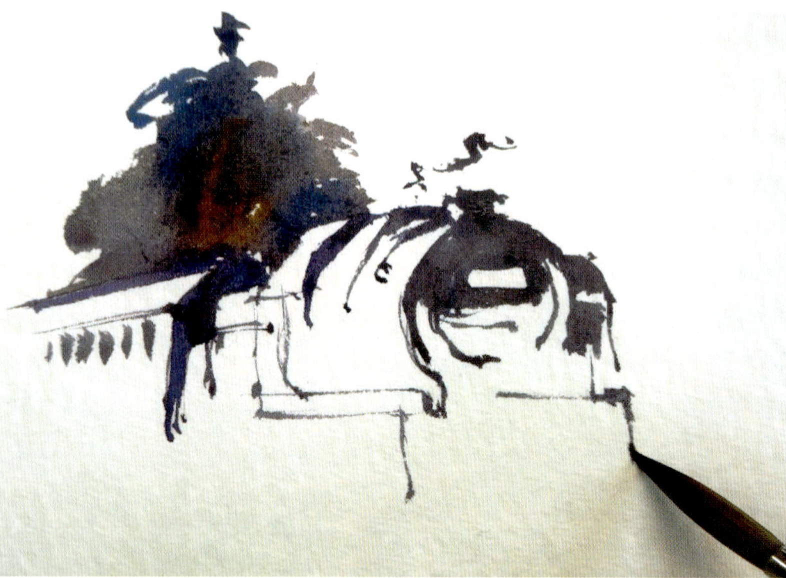

These are the first few marks I made of the front of the locomotive as a starting point.

Then it was a case of carefully observing the lights and darks and filling in with loose washes between them.

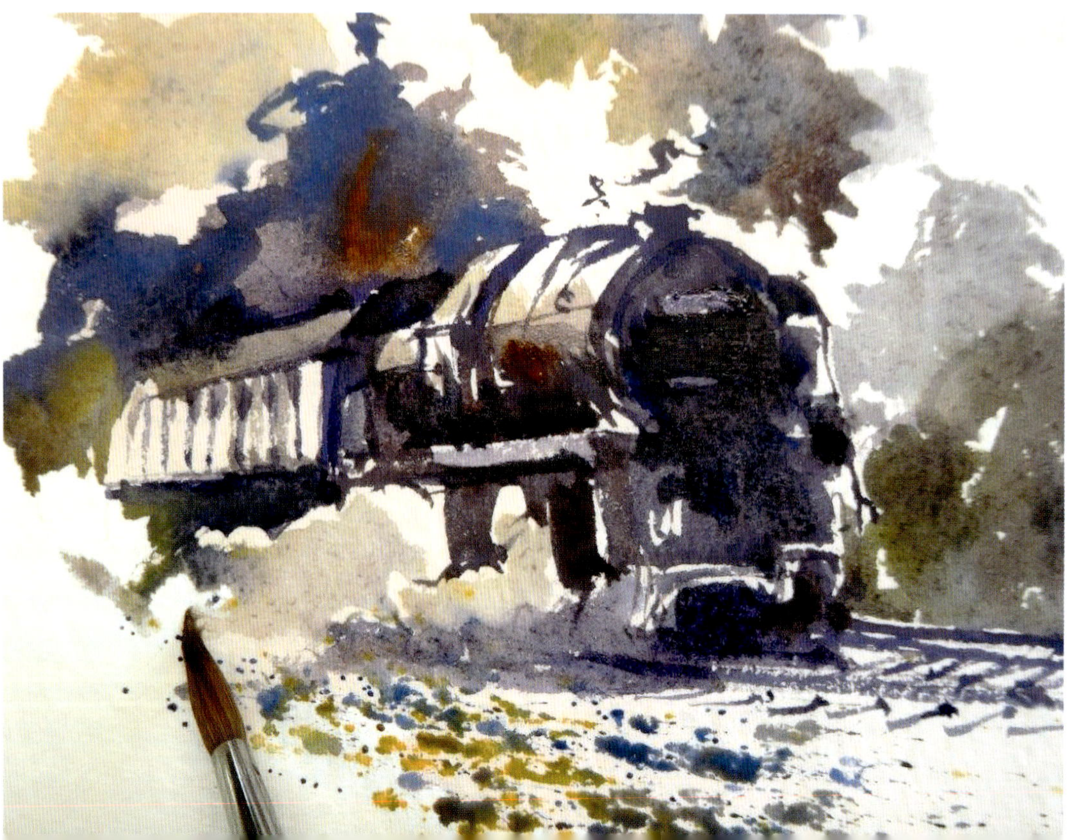

The final sketch has a bit more detail but not so much that it detracts from the immediacy of the piece.

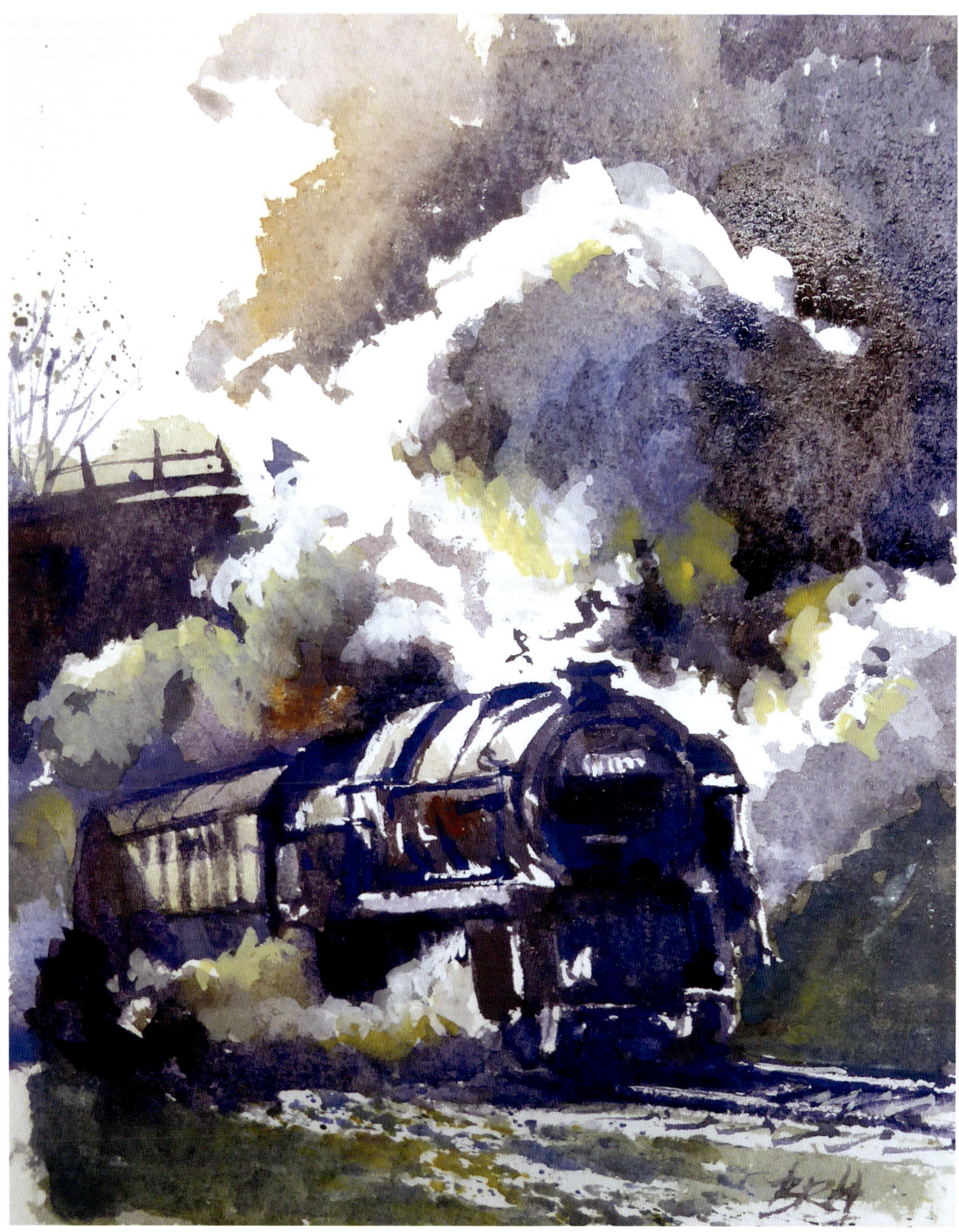

Countryside panorama in watercolour

Finding the view you want

For this sketch I wanted a fairly far-reaching countryside view with the possibility of a church or another building of interest nestling within it. I liaised with Lyndsey who lives in the area and gave me a few possibilities which I researched online to get an idea of the surrounding views. I found a view of Horsmonden church, Kent, which looked spot on. The next step was to find out from where this view was taken so we could set up for sketching there. Time to hit the Ordnance Survey map!

Studying the map, I couldn't find a church with a tower in Horsmonden itself, but further south there was one near Church Farm. I found images of the four quintessential Kentish oast houses, so knew this was the right spot.

Trial and error

Although I had in mind the exact spot on the map where I wanted to set up and sketch, we drove slightly further up the road until we found a break in the trees. Happily, we stumbled upon an even better view, which included an oast in the foreground as well as oasts in the background. We hopped over the stile on the High Weald Landscape Trail, which gave us a great view across the valley to St Margaret's Church and surrounds.

> **My advice**
> Although it's important to do your research before you set out, it's also wise to be flexible in altering the landscape you had in mind and not spending ages trying to find the 'perfect' spot.

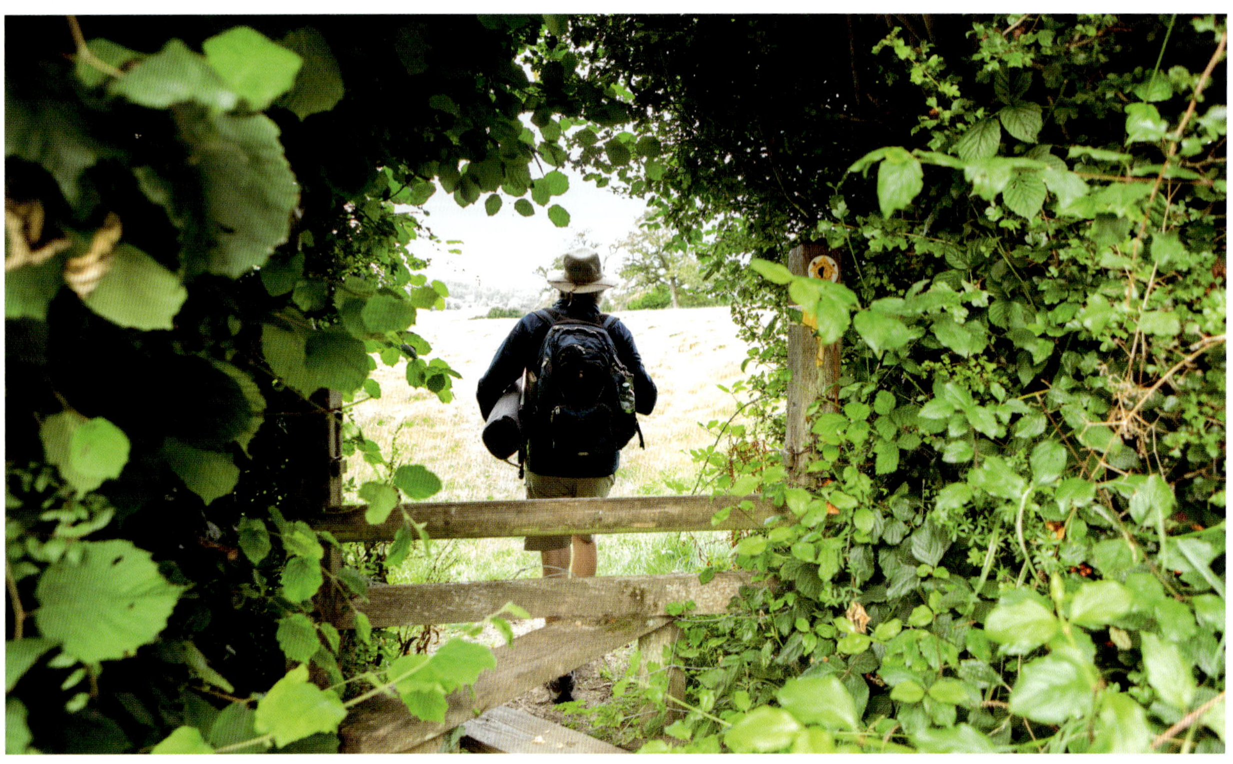

Setting up

The first part of setting up was pacing around the field, assessing the best spot. I asked myself a series of questions such as 'What is the weather doing?', 'Which direction is the light coming from?' and 'What are my senses aware of in this scene?' I find talking to myself and thinking aloud helps... After all, there were no passers-by to hear!

Using a viewfinder

I used both a viewfinder (see page 91) and my fingers to determine where the boundaries of my sketch would be. I experimented with lots of different crops until I settled on one I was happy with.

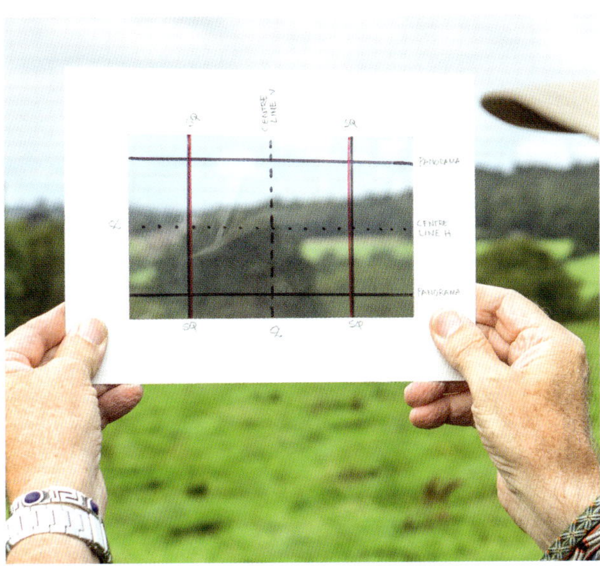

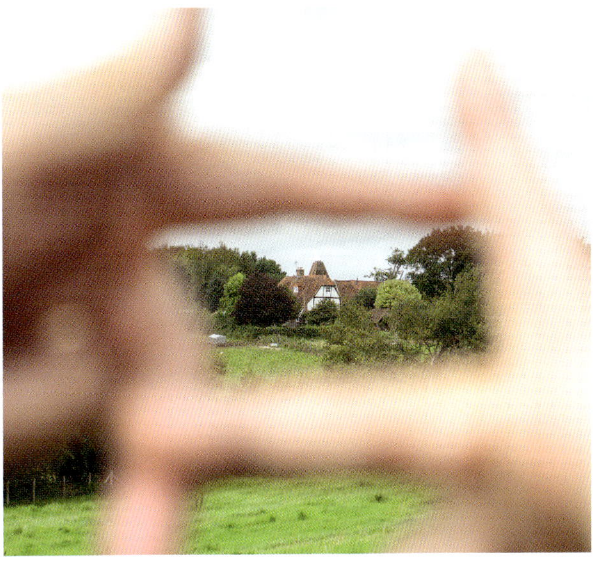

Starting off

Using my sketchbook of HP paper and a retractable clutch pencil (2B), I started to sketch the farmhouses and the oast in the foreground. Without adding too much detail, I added in the church and the distant oasts. I don't worry about drawing straight lines for buildings because that level of accuracy isn't important. This sketching stage should be quick and you almost sweep across the sketchbook as you draw in the outlines.

I decided at this point to reduce the trees in the foreground. Always feel free to use artistic licence when you're sketching.

Adding paint

Once the sketch was in place, I started to add artists' quality paint from my palette, spraying the paint with water to reactivate it. Painting wet onto dry, I used spattering to emulate the broken feel of foliage. This is very quick to do and serves as the undercoat which can be painted over. I made sure I maintained a sharp edge for the contours of the landscape.

Next I added an overcast sky, with intermittent sunshine. Keeping an eye on those grey clouds that were looming, I painted fluently, without hesitating, knowing that we might have to suddenly pack up at any moment.

For the rough meadow, spattering added texture. The scene is very green, so I needed to add lights and darks, as well as counterchange.

Next, I painted the roofs and the church. This meant all the main parts of colour were in place. Now it was time to fill in the rest.

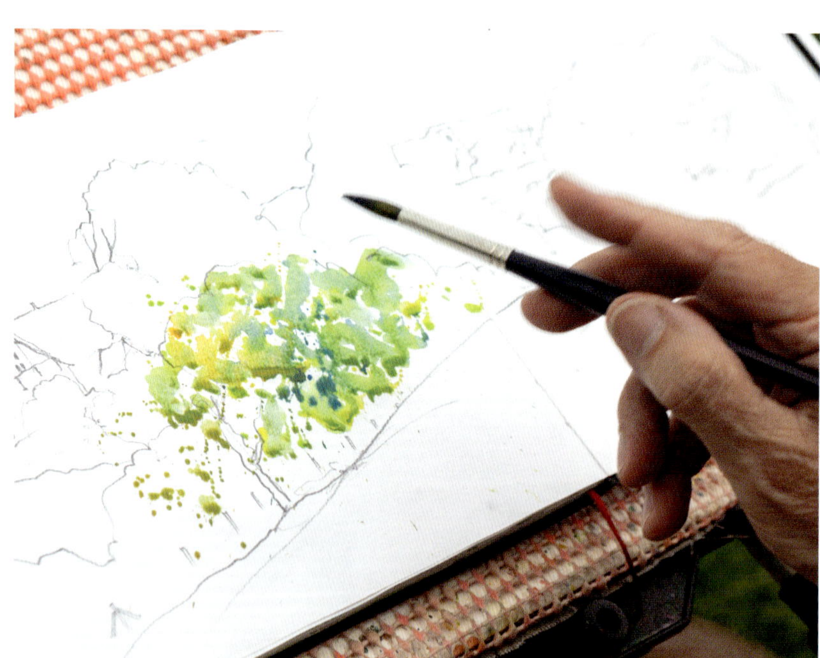

Spattering
I load the brush with paint, then flick it onto the paper by tapping the end of the brush sharply downwards.

My advice
Introduce a bit of colour everywhere. If you get the basic colours down, then if you are rained off you have the essentials in place.

The colours used for this summer scene were Indian yellow, aureolin, Schmincke orange, cobalt blue, cobalt turquoise and helio turquoise.

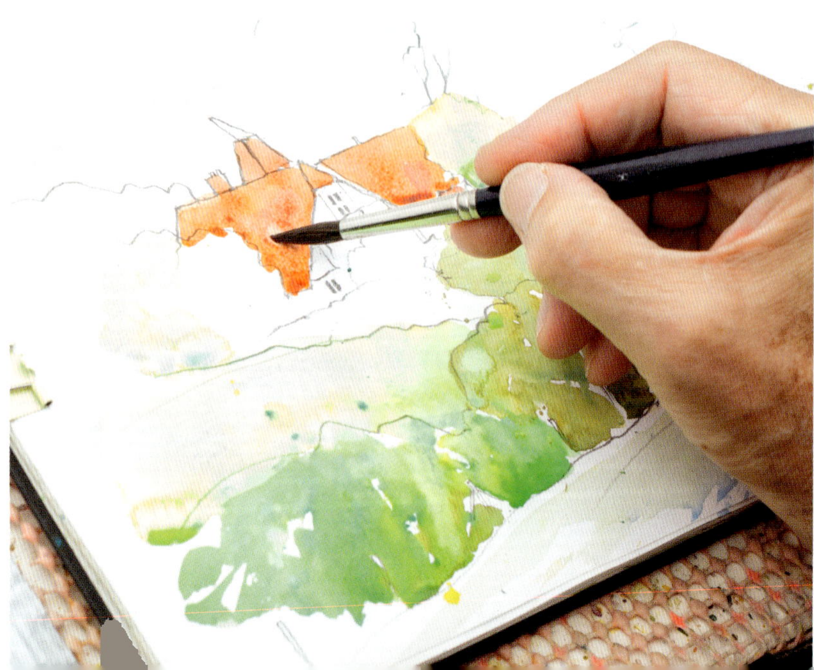

Finishing off

The background is painted, rather than flicked, whereas the foreground has spattering. Add the final 'calligraphy' to increase interest, but don't be tempted to overwork it.

When I paint in my sketchbook, I tend to add a note to remind me of the event, in this case how we came across the view by accident and managed to capture it before the weather changed its mind.

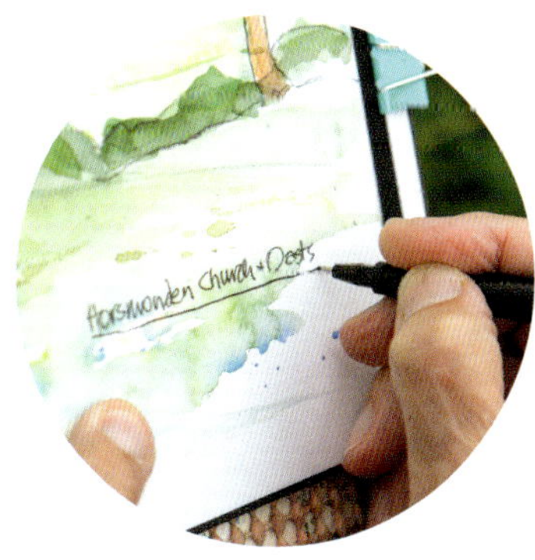
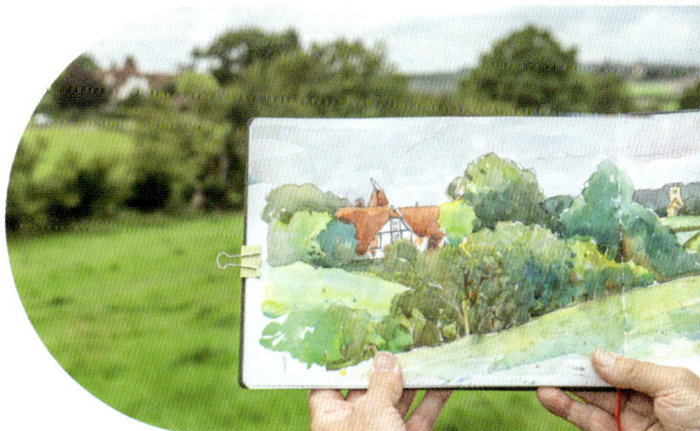

Horsmonden Church and oasts.

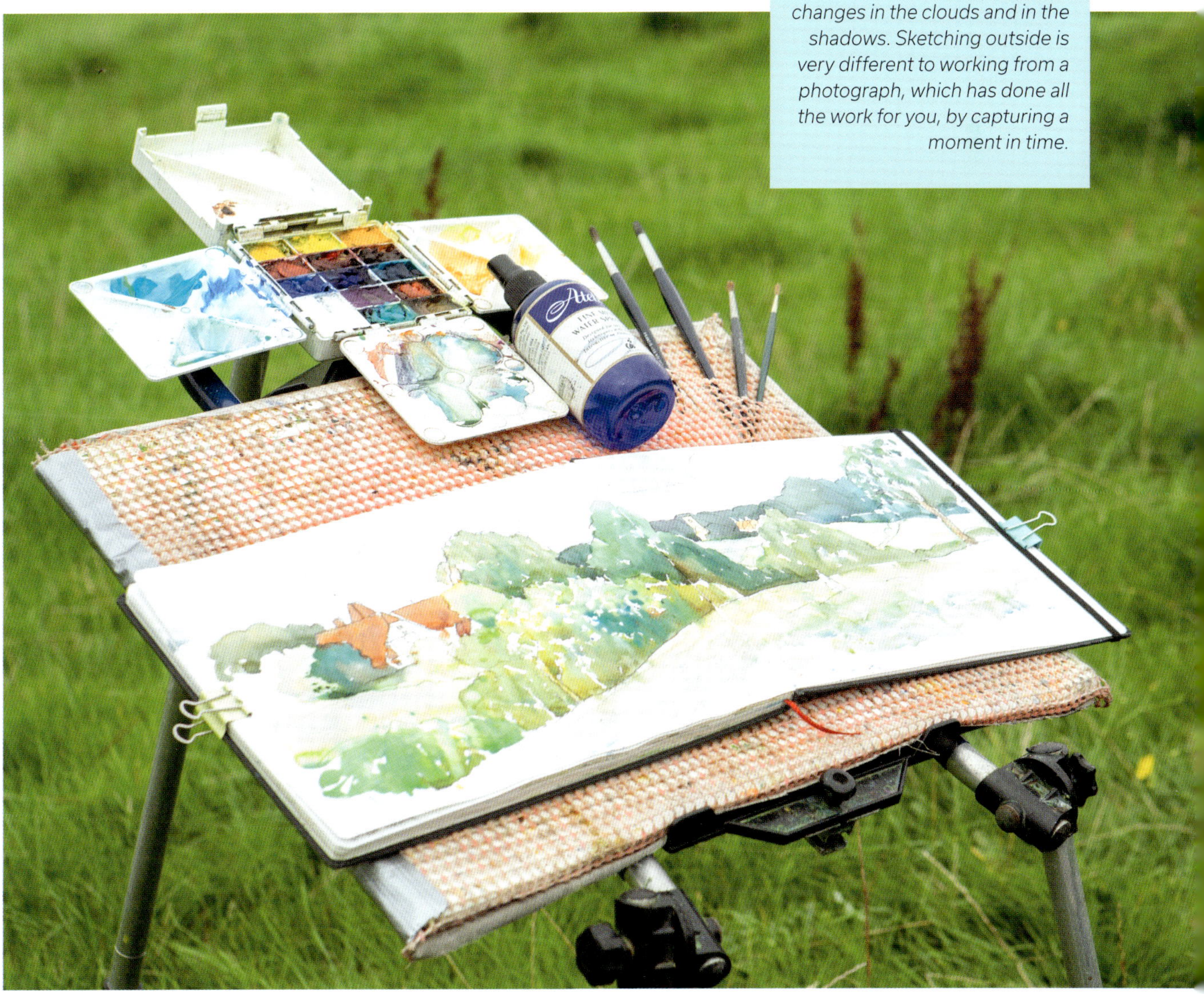

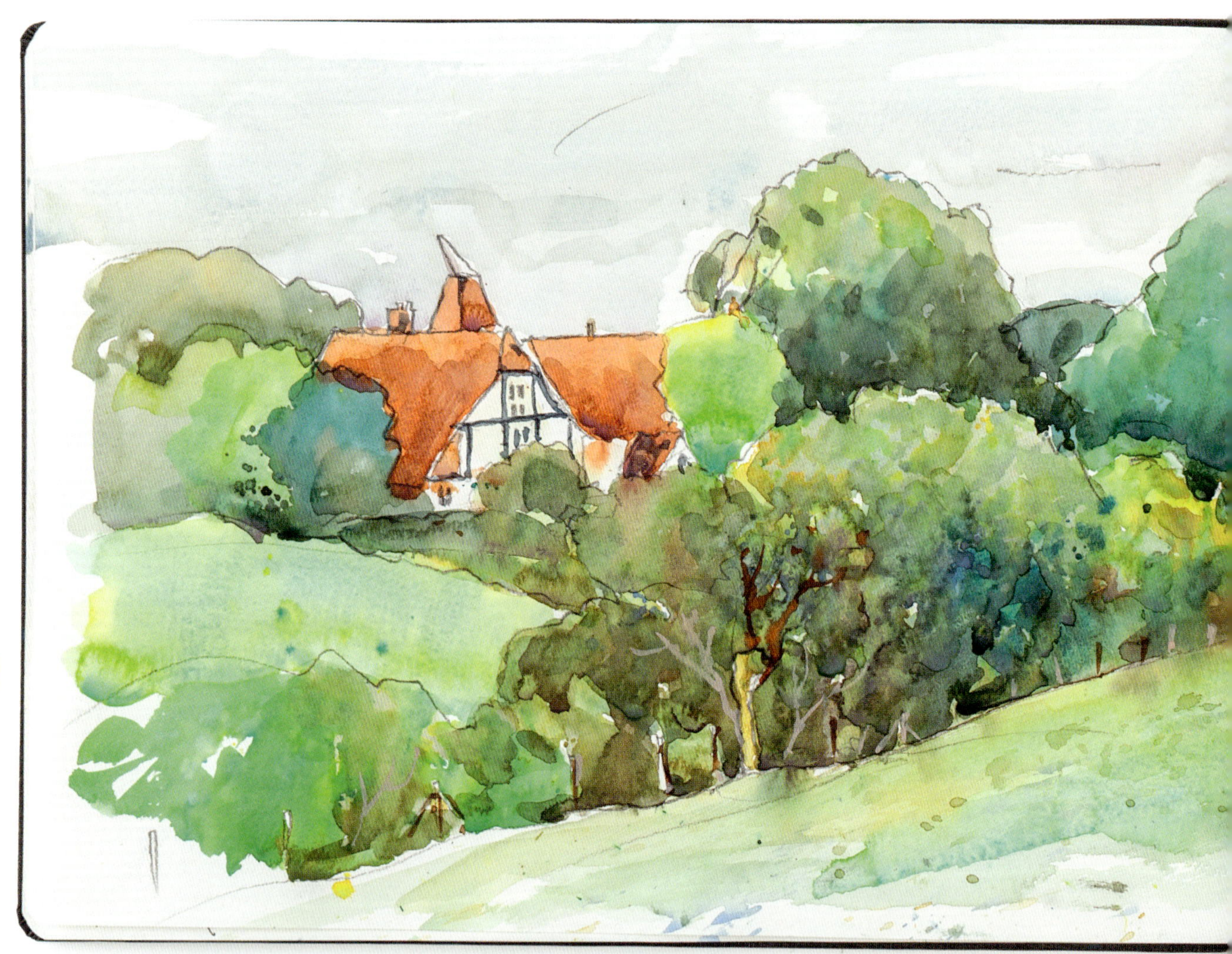

My advice

One thing I have observed in my students is that if they paint in their sketchbook as I have here, it relaxes them because they feel it is only a sketch. Otherwise, there is a tendency to feel intimidated by a clean sheet of loose watercolour paper.

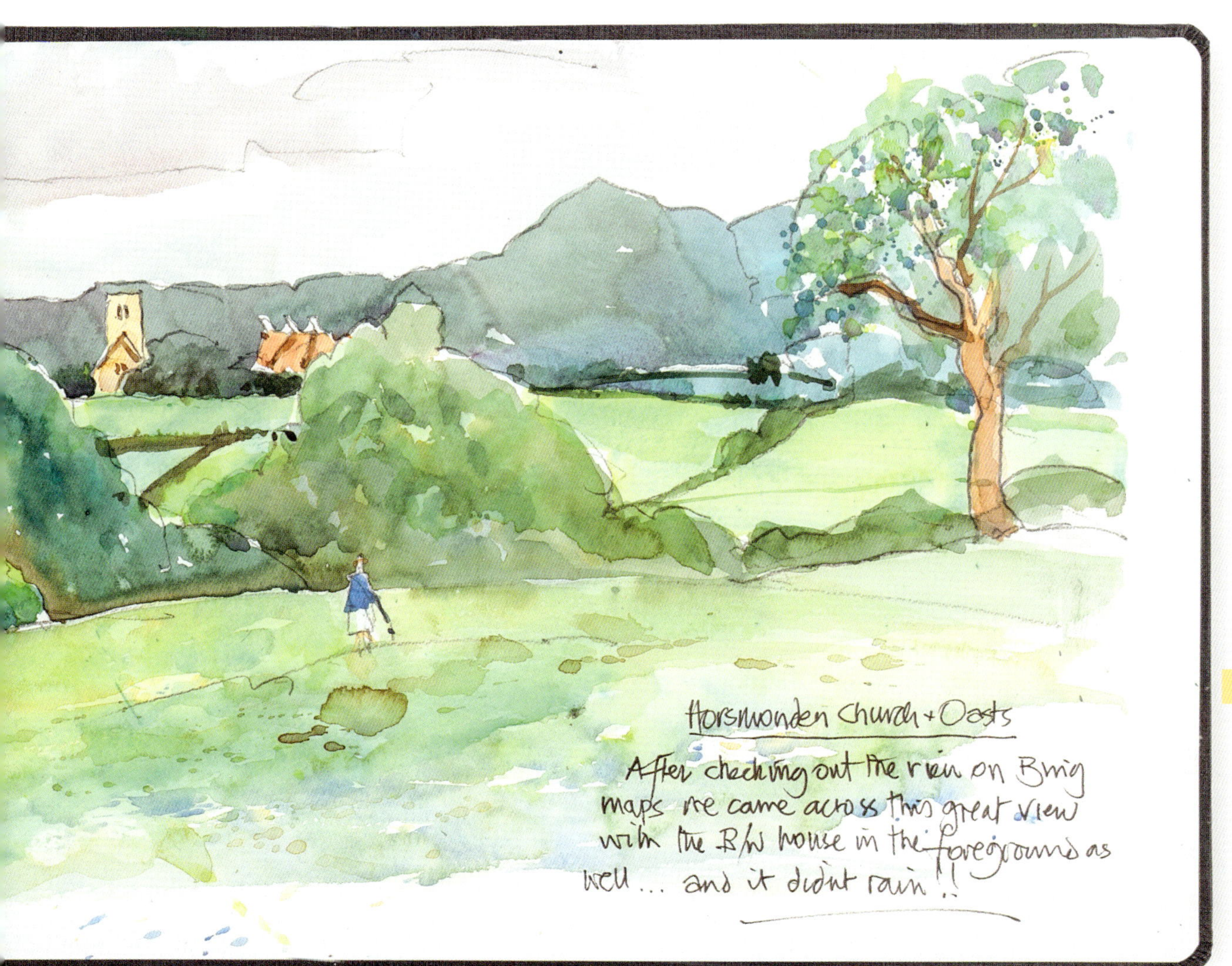

The finished sketch

The joy of this demo was in the remote, undisturbed setting.
The rural tranquility was idyllic.

Coastal scene in pen and ink

What could be more emotive than a captivating coastal scene? The sea in all its different moods presents the painter with a whole host of exciting possibilities, from a storm-battered coast to a calm and gentle vista. For this demo I have chosen a peaceful view of the Irish coast to sketch in the studio.

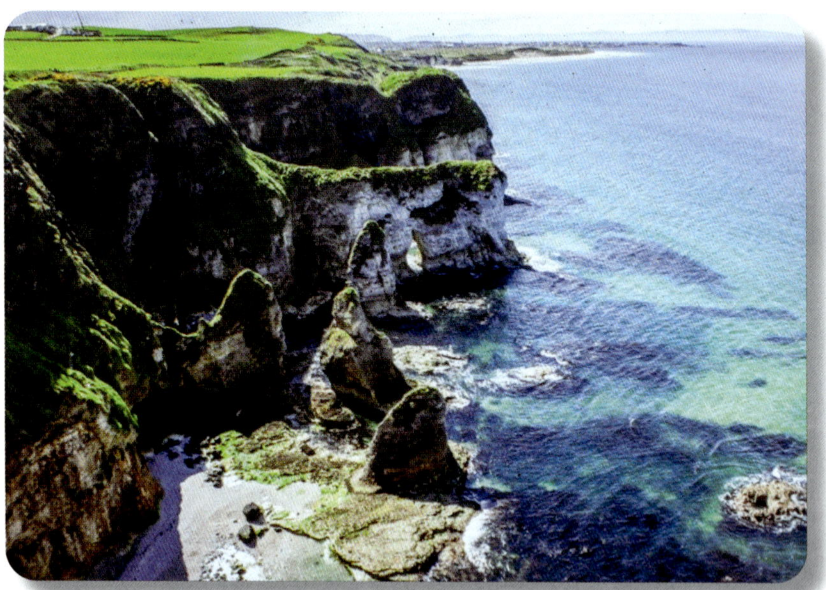

Reference photograph

Here is a photograph along the coast in County Antrim, Northern Ireland, just up the road from Giant's Causeway. I decided it would be great to draw in pen and ink because of the lovely light catching the tops of the coastline and the sea stacks.

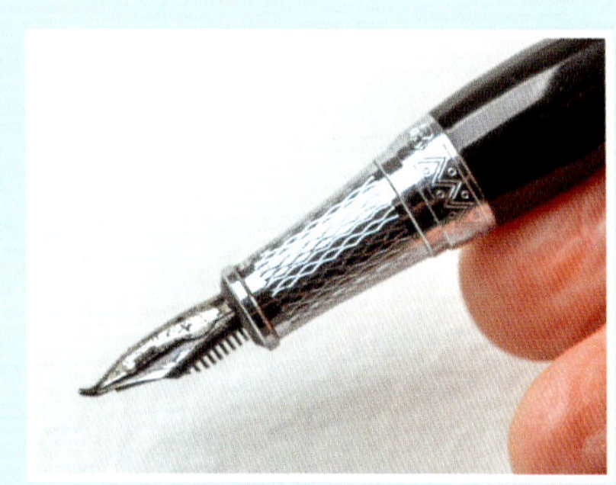

My pen

I use my trusty Fude bent nib drawing pen which contains carbon black ink. Unlike other pens I've tried, the ink doesn't dry in the pen; it is always ready to use. However, it does dry waterproof on the page.

I use the tip to create very thin lines, but if you use the edge of the pen you can achieve thick lines for contrast.

A quick tonal sketch

Using my Fude bent nib drawing pen, I start off drawing the shadow areas first. I keep the promontory in the background simple. Next I add water, using a size 4 brush. I repeat this process to create the rocks in the foreground. At this point, I am working fast, adding light washes over the top of the ink.

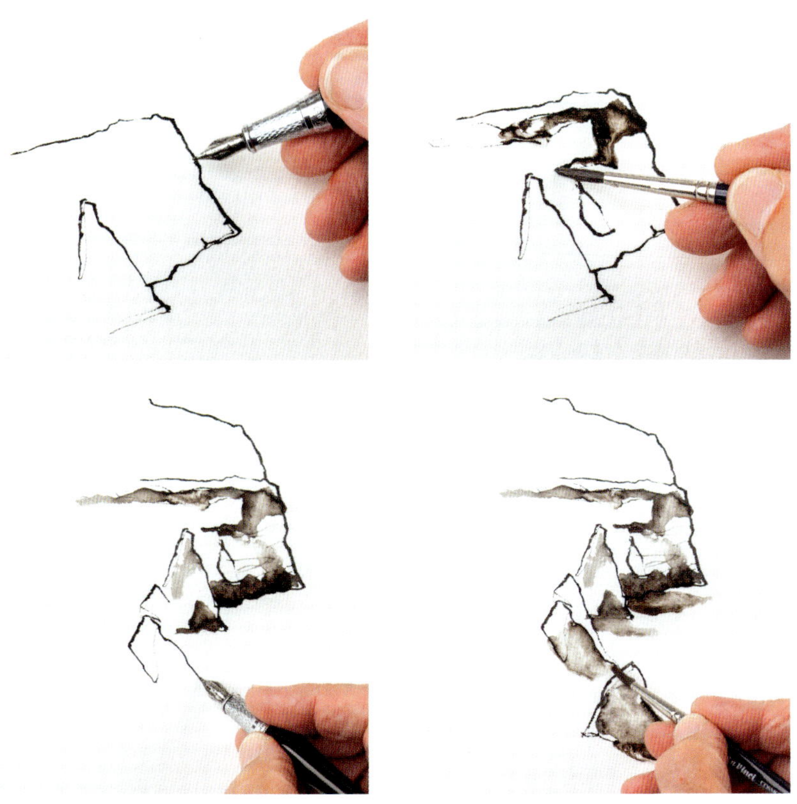

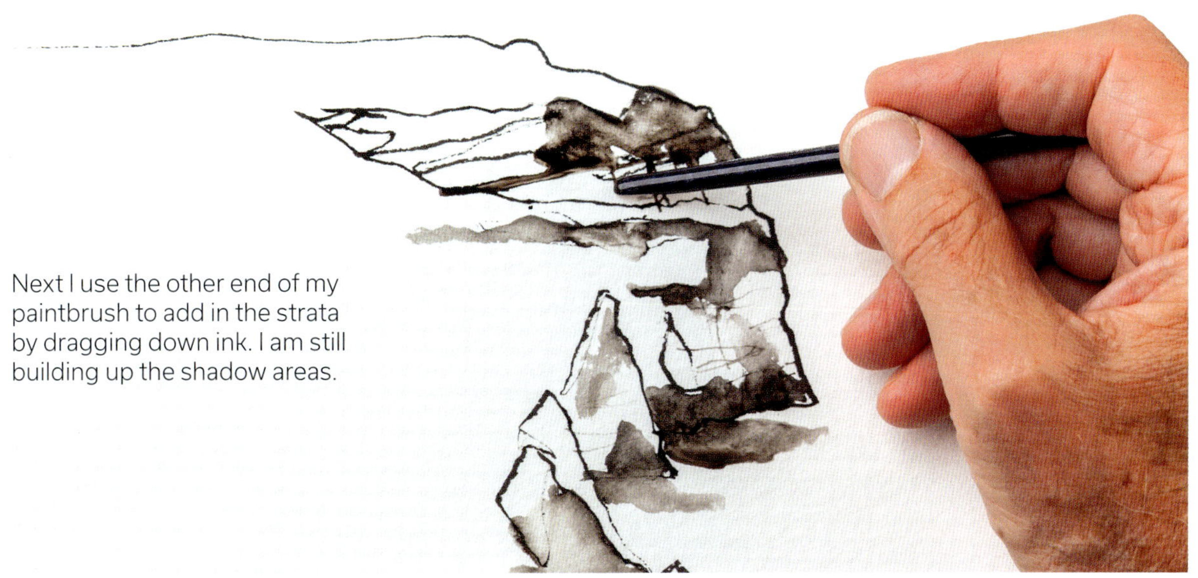

Next I use the other end of my paintbrush to add in the strata by dragging down ink. I am still building up the shadow areas.

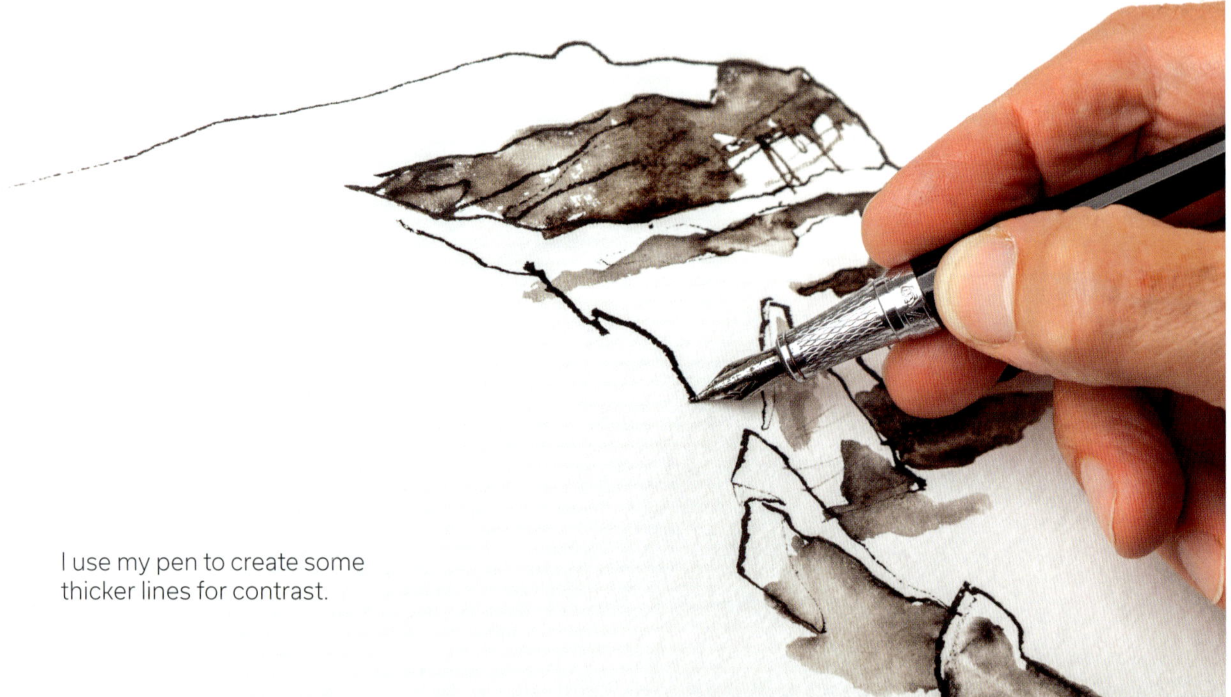

I use my pen to create some thicker lines for contrast.

> **My advice**
> *Tip your watercolour block so that water runs down the page. This allows the water to pool at the bottom of the rocks, giving a shadow effect.*

Counterchange

I add counterchange by introducing shadows next to the lightest areas with my paintbrush and water. This creates a striking contrast and draws the eye towards the darker points. If you let the ink partly dry before adding water (and remember the ink dries waterproof), you can still retain the lovely linework underneath.

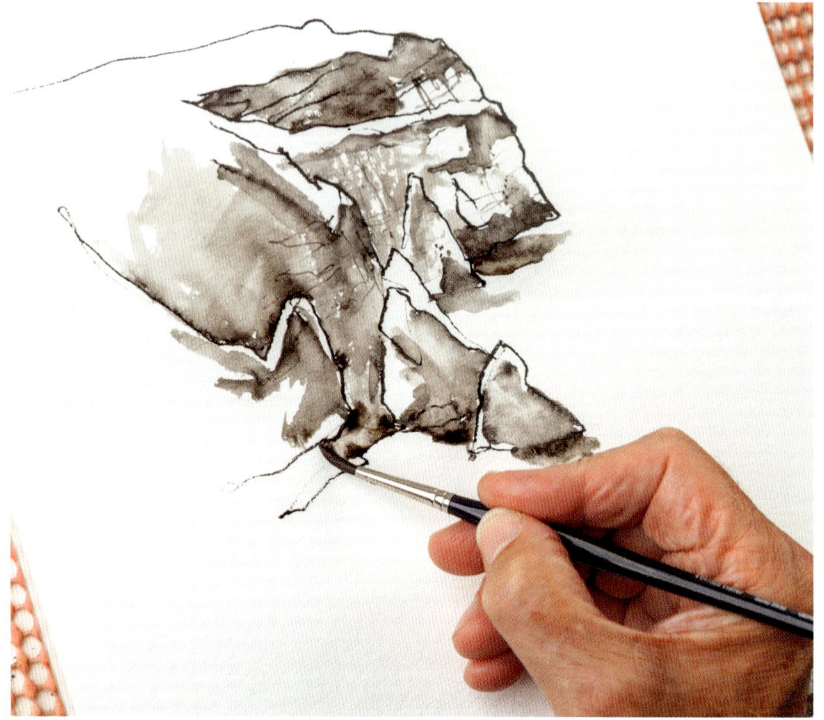

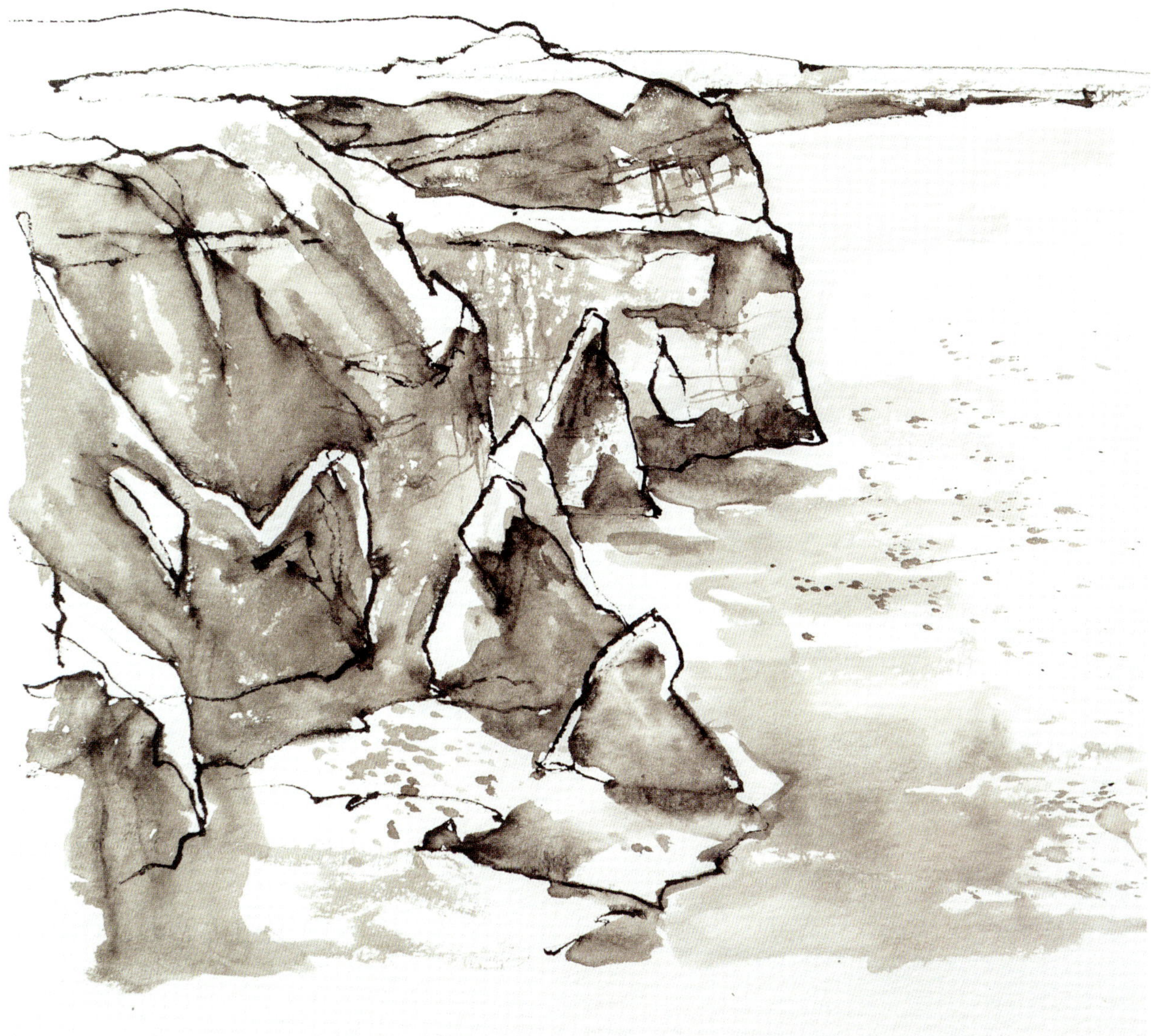

The finished tonal sketch

Now your quick ink sketch is finished and all the tones are in place. For speed, I will add simple watercolour washes which really lift the artwork. It starts out as a tonal sketch, then you add colour and it becomes a watercolour sketch.

My advice
Once you have got this far you will need to make sure that the ink work is bone dry and therefore waterproof before adding any watercolour.

Watercolour sketch

The next stage is to quickly lay down the vibrant watercolours. If you have the luxury of more time, you can slow down. However, sketching should be done rapidly, especially if you're relying on the weather in Northern Ireland!

Using size 8 and size 4 brushes, I added aureolin, Indian yellow and cobalt turquoise to my tonal sketch. Watch the colours zing!

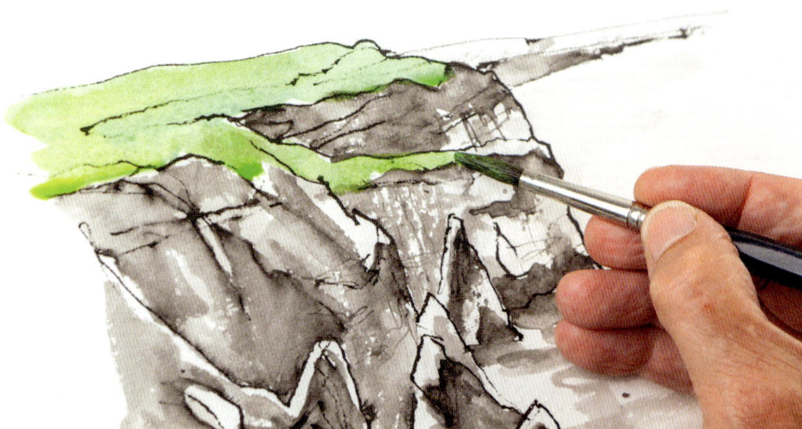

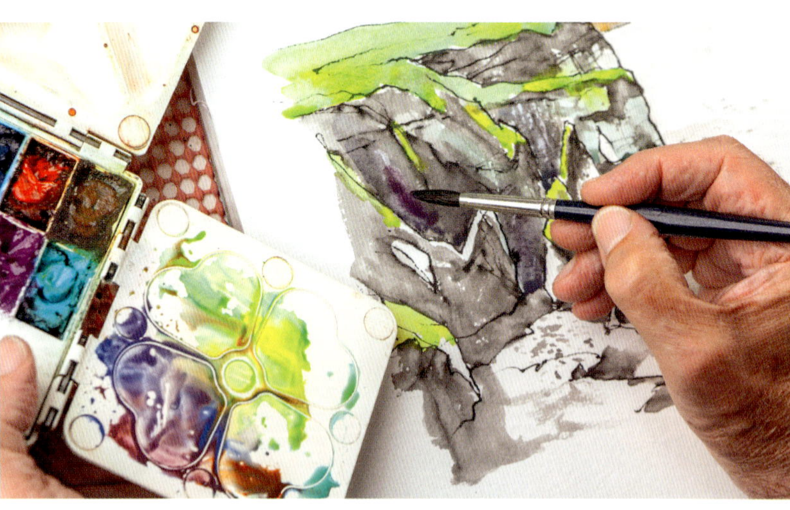

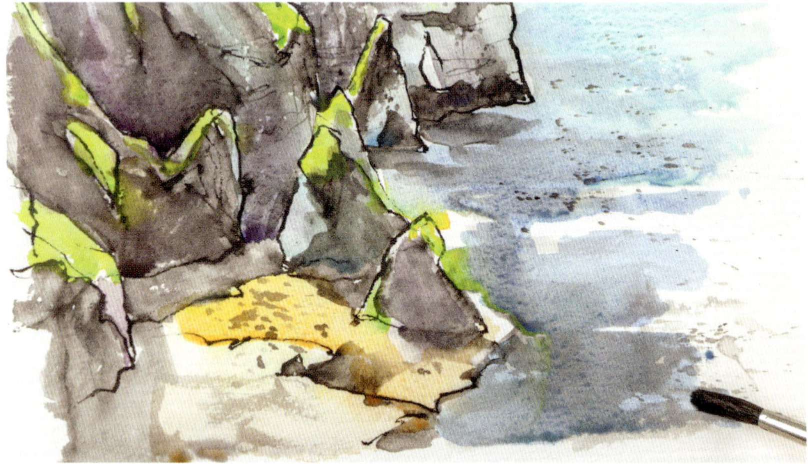

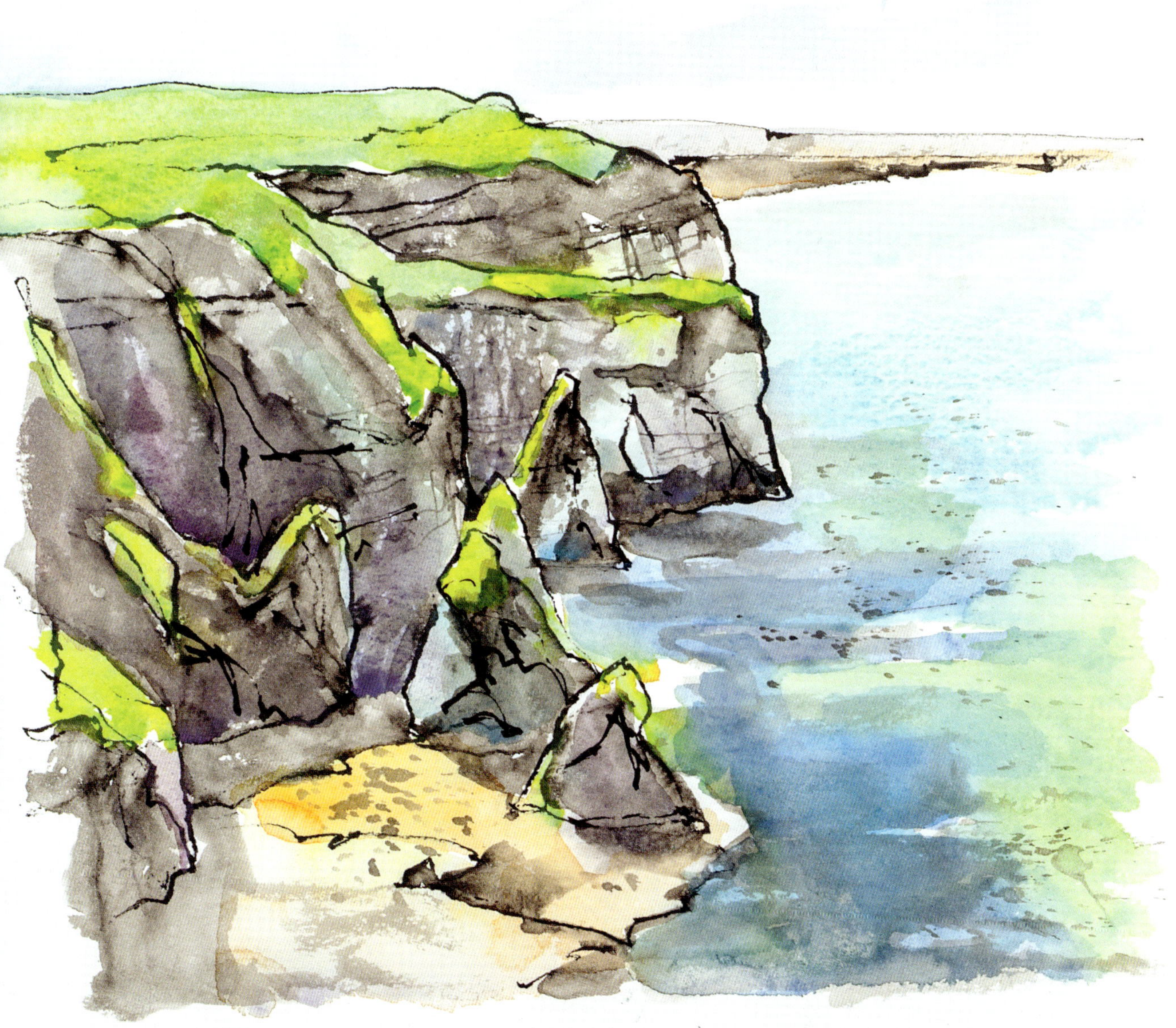

Finishing touches

Finally I added the darker waters in the foreground and the
greener waters to the right of the painting.

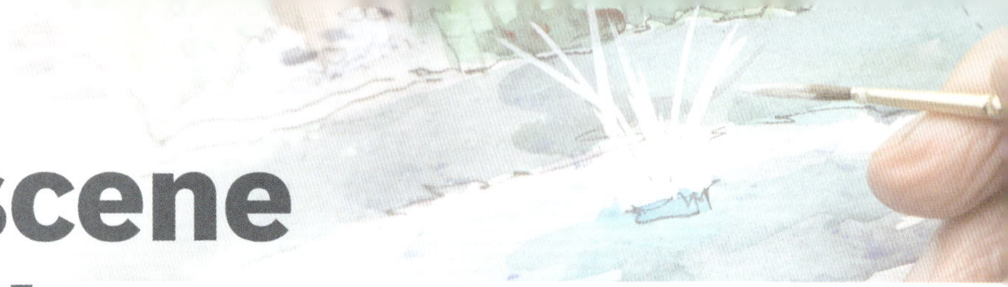

Village scene in gouache

Choosing the right medium

Goudhurst village, Kent, with its pond – wow! I decided to use gouache to capture this lively scene outside. If you like working with oils, you are bound to like gouache. The beauty of it is that you paint in the darks, then overpaint the lights. My favourite brand of gouache is Schmincke and it comes in small, portable tubes. Beware, though, gouache dries quickly in windy conditions!

Reading the scene

The first thing I do once I'm set up is to read the scene in front of me and jot it down as a simple sketch. As well as the visual impact of the water fountain in the middle of the pond, I was aware of the sound of the water. The traffic on the road behind the pond was typical of a busy weekday lunchtime and we met many passers-by, out walking near the village hall. We had to move out the way for some builders a couple of times, but this all added to my enjoyment of the bustle in this picturesque Kentish village. My senses had plenty to take in.

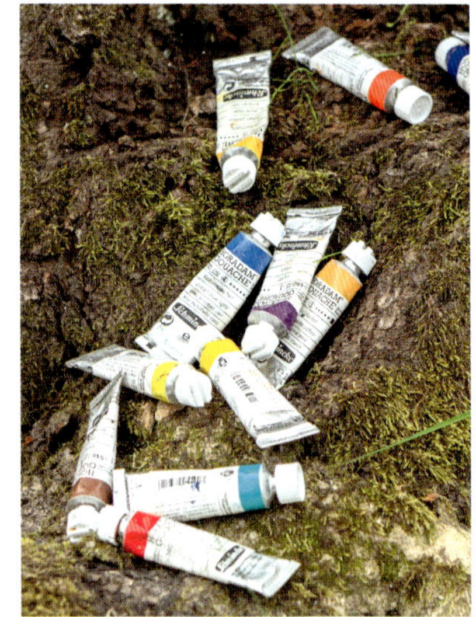

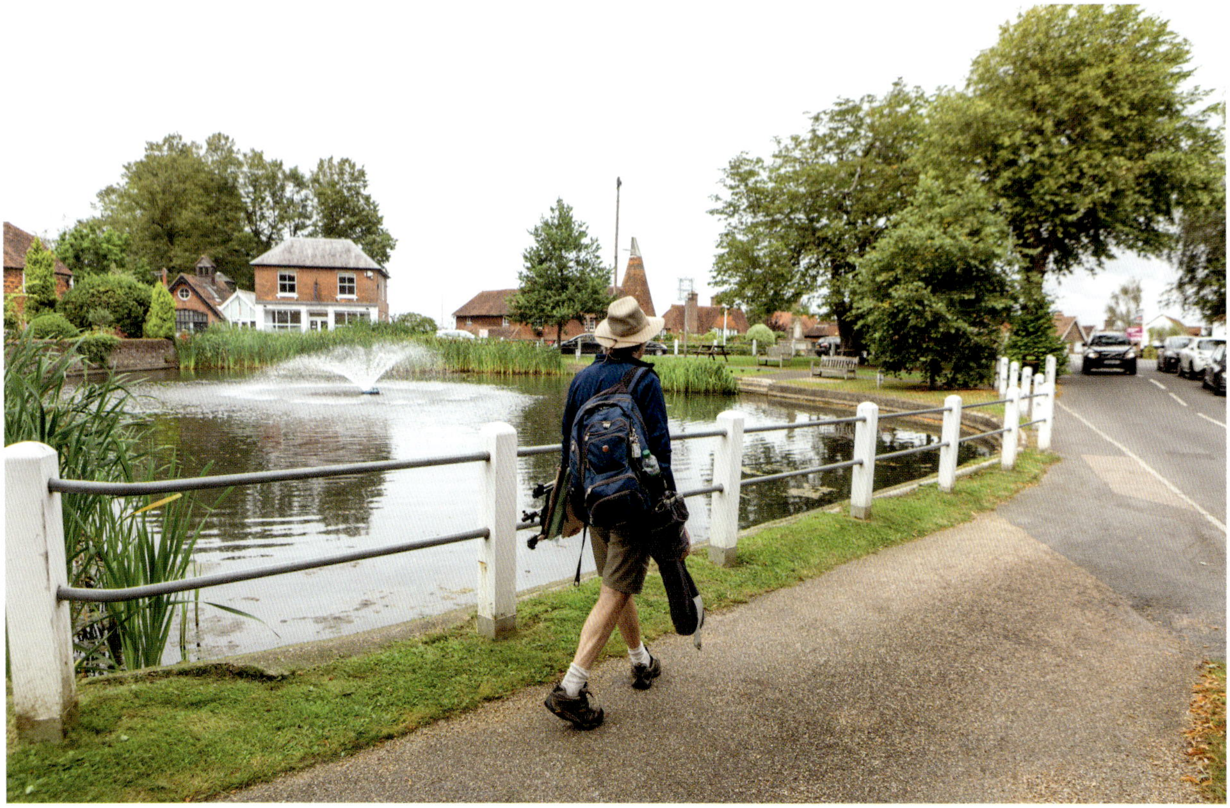

Improvising

When we arrived on site I realized I had forgotten to pack my paint palette, so I used what I had to hand: a lunchbox lid. It's important to be able to improvise if you forget some of your kit. I decided to fill up my water jug from the pond – well, why not?

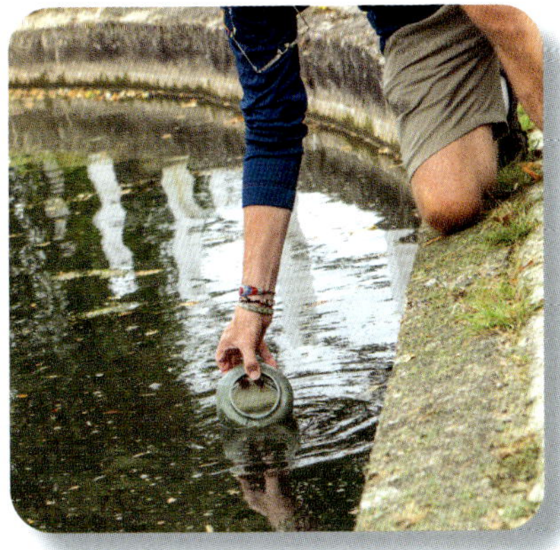

Drawing the scene

I aim to draw as much as possible with as little effort as possible. If I'm going to paint my drawings, then they can be really simple. With my Faber-Castell PITT artist pen and a watercolour block, I took down the main outlines. I chose the buildings I liked the look of, and decided to exclude an oast house from the right of the scene.

Although my markings at this stage are uncomplicated, I did spend time observing and taking down a few details which serve as an *aide-memoir*. For example, I added a few bricks, knowing that if I needed to rush off due to inclement weather, I would remember that the rest of the chimney stack was brick. I also indicated the reflections in the water.

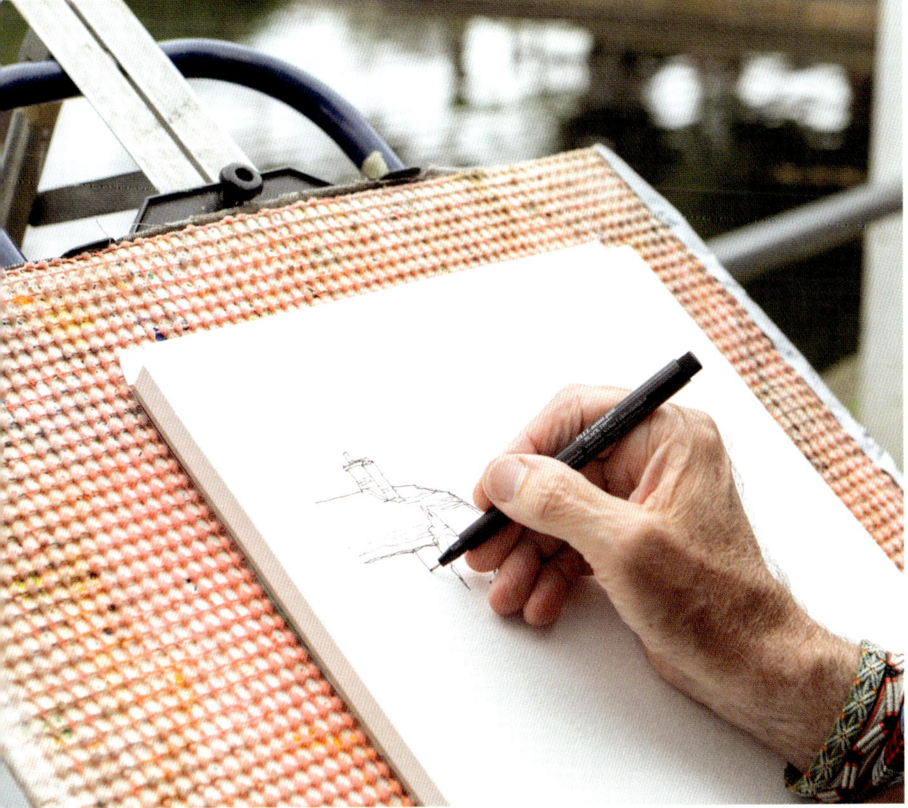

My advice
If you find that your lines are wobbly, you're in good company! It is perfectly acceptable to have wobbly lines when sketching.

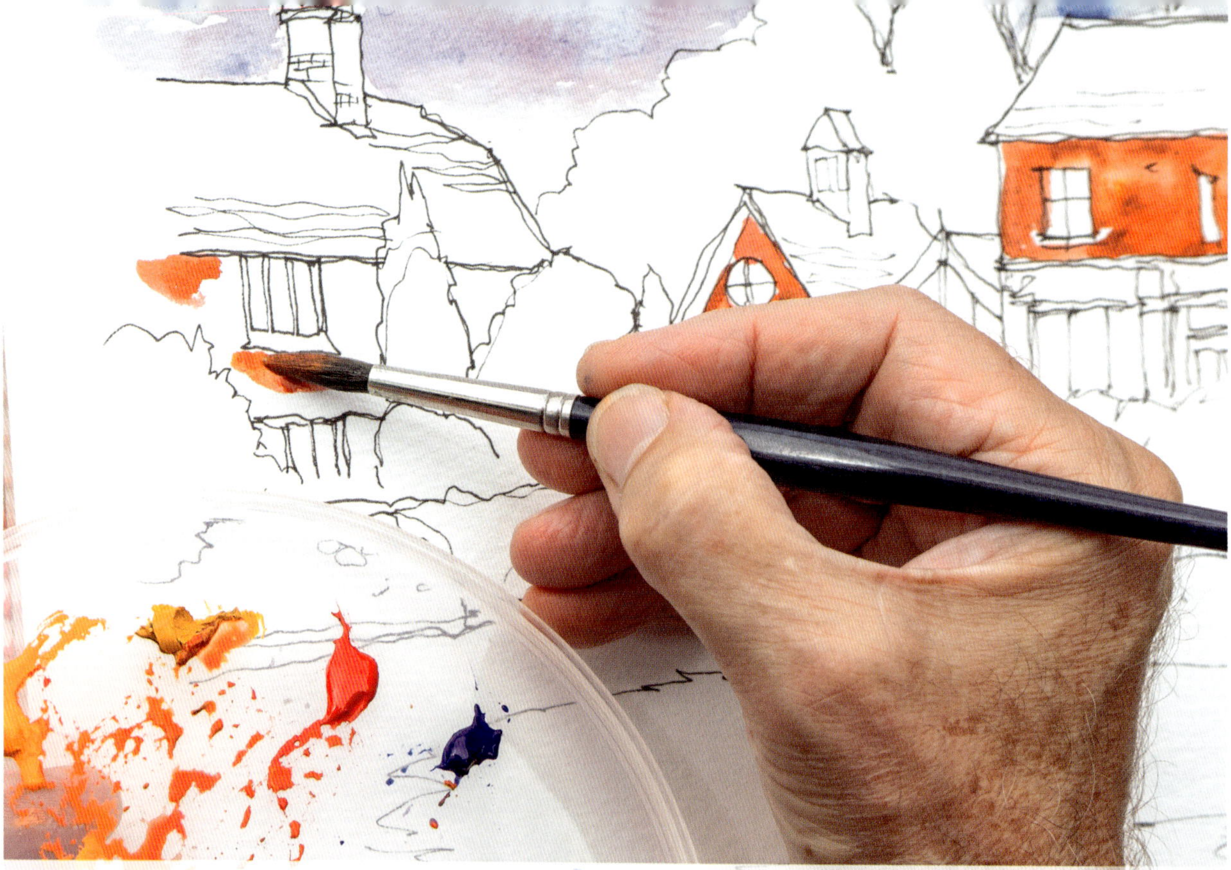

Adding paint

Once I was happy with the sketch, I started to add paint to the sky with my size 8 brush. I semi-mixed orange, carmine and Indian yellow for the buildings. I always avoid overmixing the colours, as they have a habit of mixing themselves perfectly well.

One tip: by first painting the interiors behind the window frames you get the effect of looking *into* the house rather than just *at* it. You also avoid the fussy process of trying to paint all the individual window panes.

I used the other end of my brush to drag down the paint to avoid hard edges where the buildings meet the bulrushes. I rotated my board 180° to add in the shadow at the base of the bulrushes where they meet the water's surface. That is the undercoat finished and a lot of the white paper covered already.

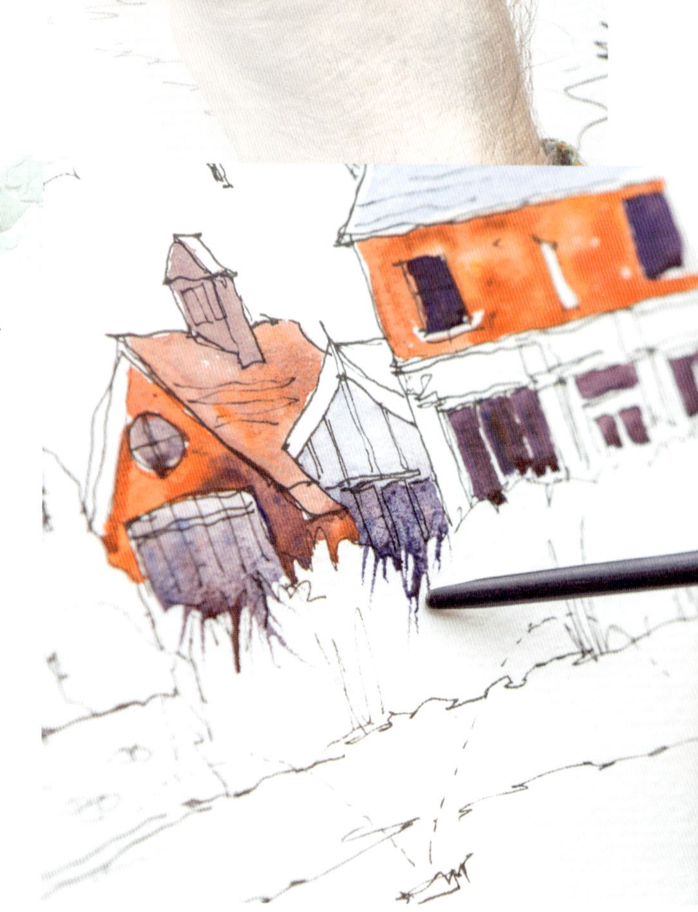

Next steps

I added reflections in the water. Then I added the impression of bricks and hung tiles to the buildings, without overworking the detail. This adds texture. At this stage, the painting may still look flat, but adding more layers later will help. The beauty of gouache is that you can add layer after layer, painting light over dark as well as dark over light.

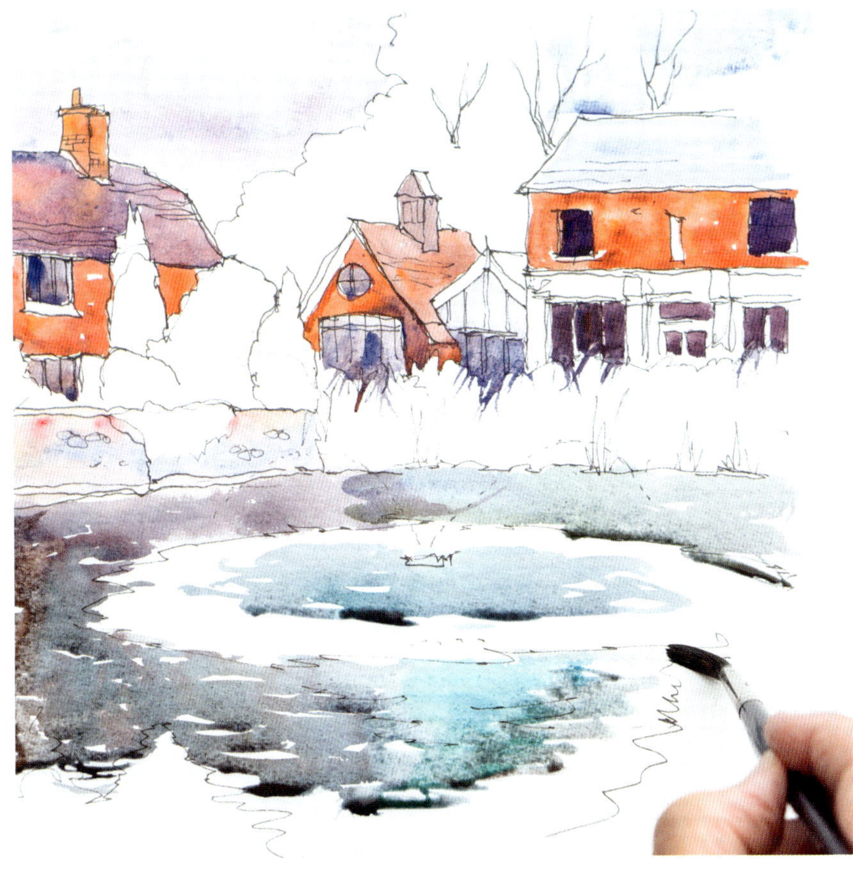

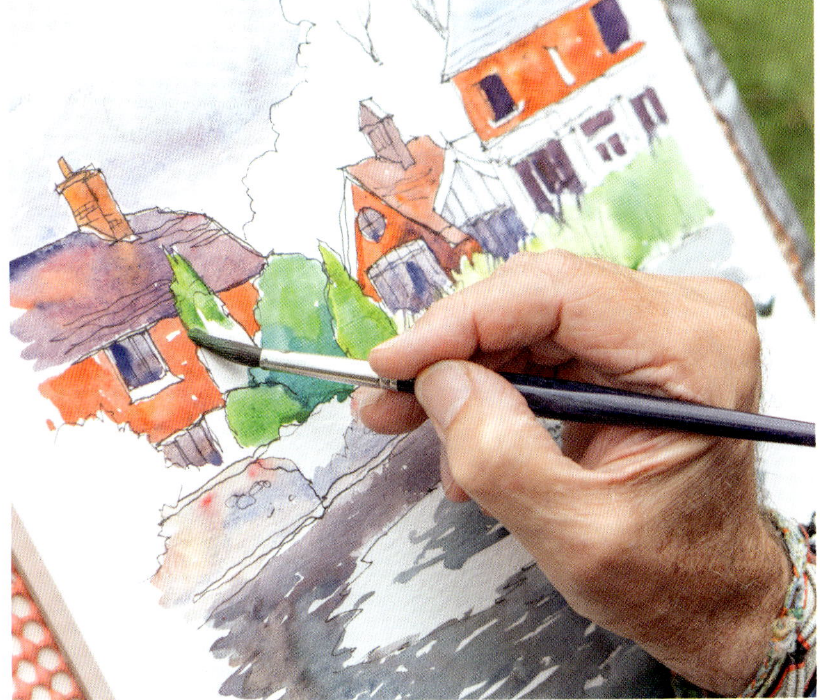

My advice

If you accidentally spatter or flick paint somewhere on the page that you didn't intend, just wipe it off with your finger.

Adding in the trees at this point gives a real splash of colour to what is becoming a very lively scene.

Finishing off

For the finest tweaks, like the writing on the front of the shop and the tree branches, I find the rigger brush works best.

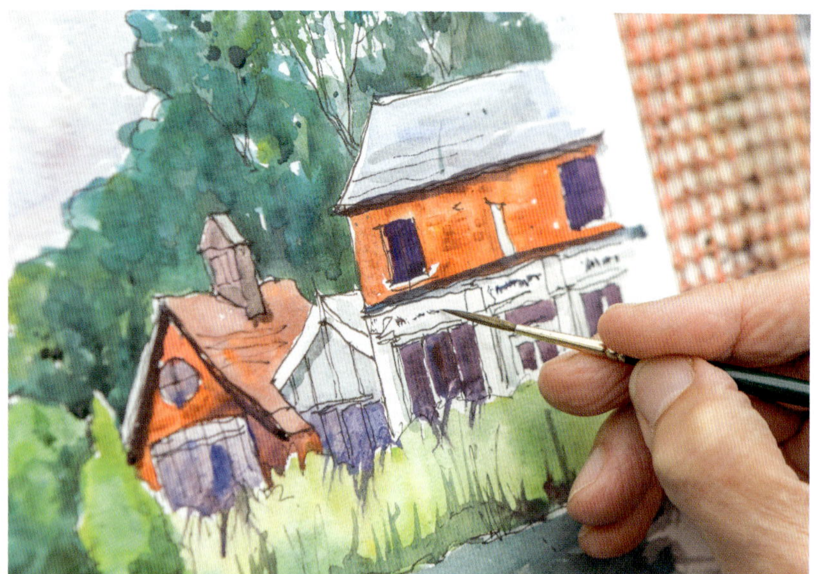

My advice
Be prepared for the odd fly or spider on your work! That's all part and parcel of working outside.

The rigger brush is also perfect for painting the window frames and sills. If you use white gouache, your painting will zing! As all the window apertures have already been established, it's just a simple exercise to paint in the window frames.

Finally, for the fountain, apply your gouache thickly to ensure the white colour shows.

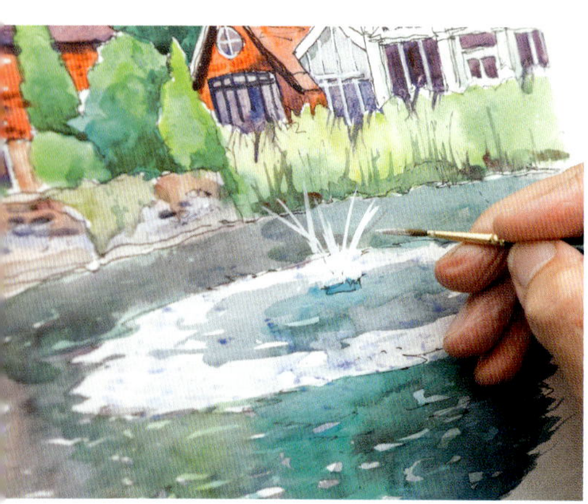

Goudhurst pond
Great little village and a super bakery...flapjack!

I enjoyed that – I should paint outside with gouache more often! Now, where did you say the village bakery was?

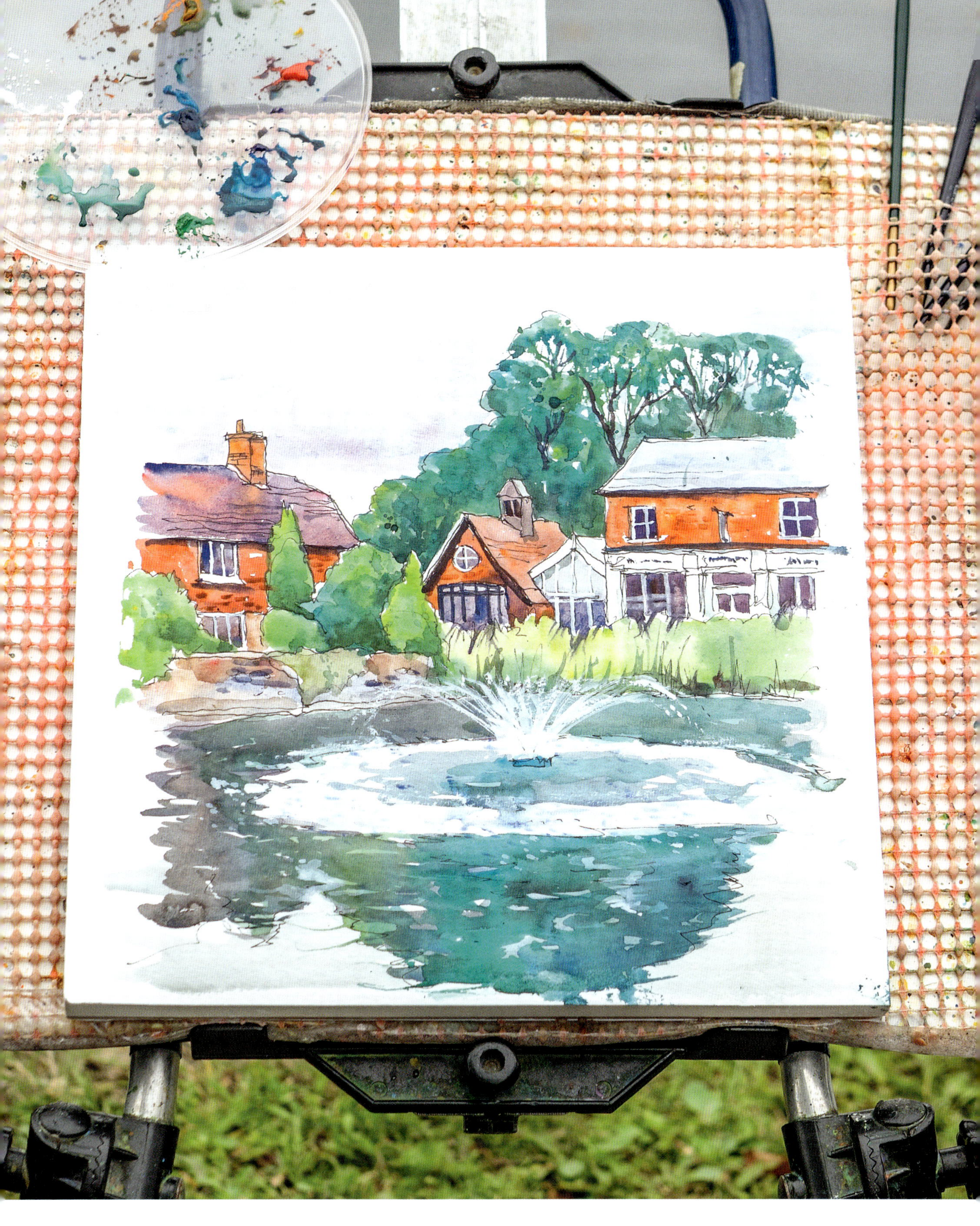

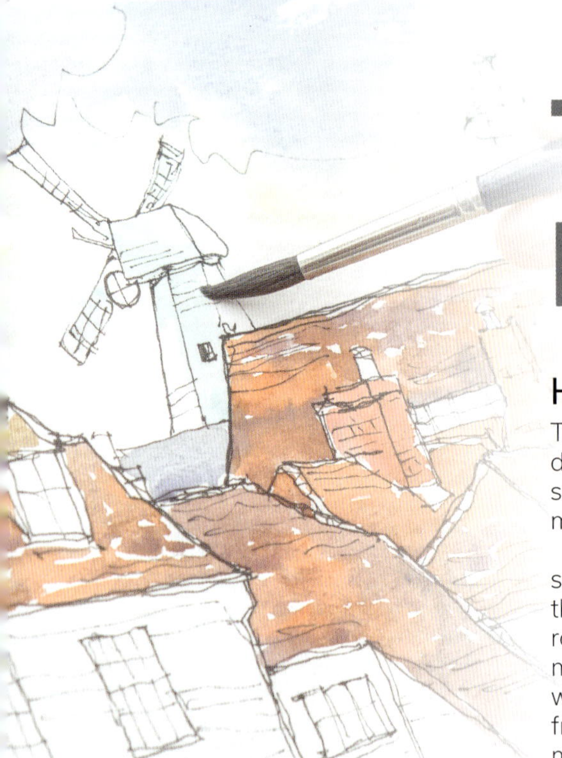

Townscape in line and wash

Hustle and bustle

Townscapes are, by their very nature, busy places. We arrived on the last day of the summer holidays and there was a queue outside the barber shop – lots of people leaving their haircut at the last minute. I had to crane my neck around the queue of people in order to see my view.

The joy of this sketch was in interacting with the pedestrians. One lady said she'd like to buy my sketch. A child came to tell me that he lived in the house I was painting. A lady who owned the sweet shop across the road brought her son out to see my work, and she later gave me a jar of my favourite penny sweets. As well as the sounds and smells I remember when I look at my finished painting, above all else I certainly got my fix of friendly people that day. The cars, noise and comments from passers-by made me buzz.

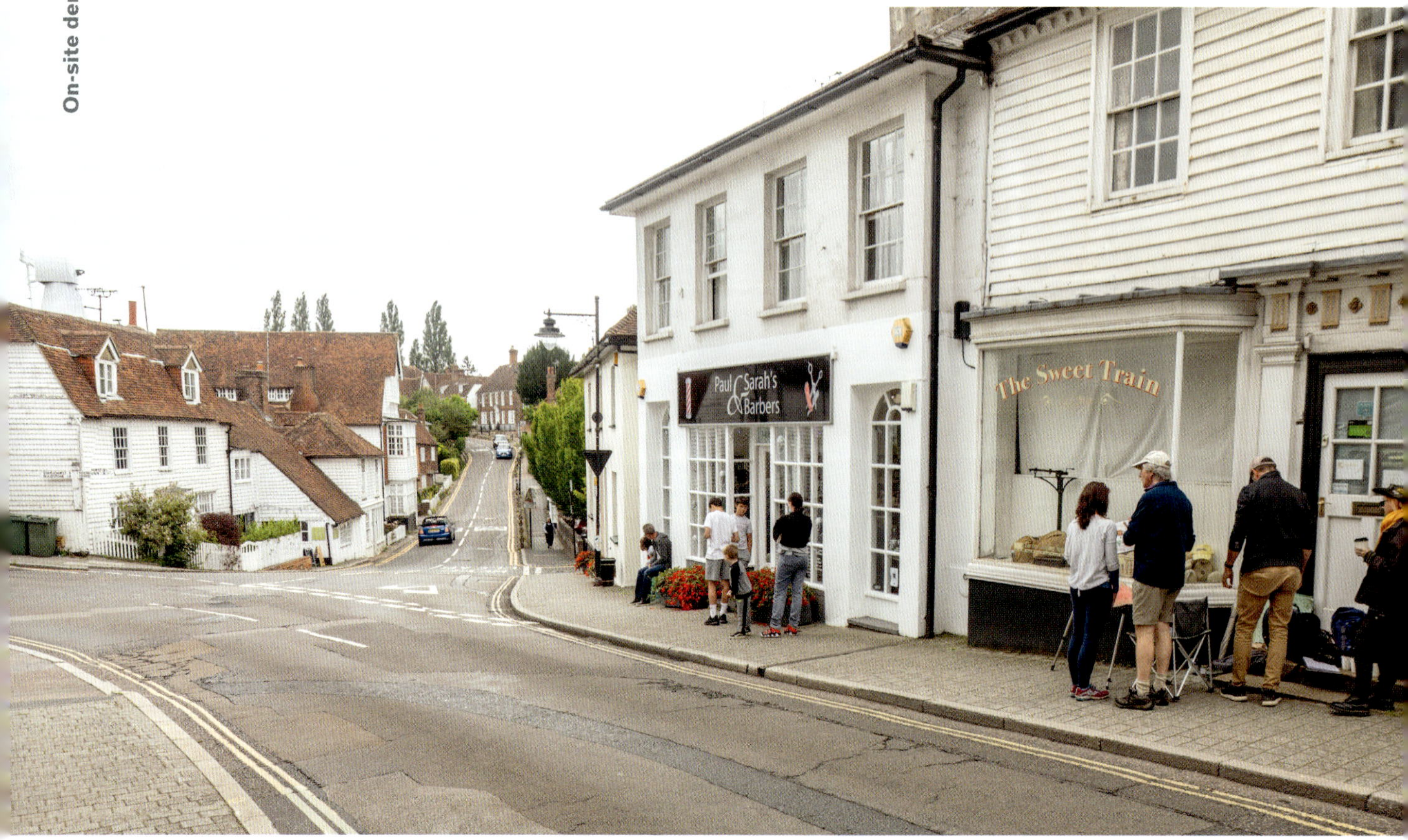

Artistic licence

The first thing that struck me when we set up was that the sweeps were missing from the windmill! There was also scaffolding surrounding it. Oops! The locals told us that the windmill was being renovated from the top down, so the sweeps had been removed for painting. I certainly hadn't bargained for that, but did we up and leave? No, I used my phone to find a picture to refer to for where to add the sweeps instead.

A kindly passer-by informed us that the term 'sweeps' is preferred to 'sails' in Kent and Sussex.

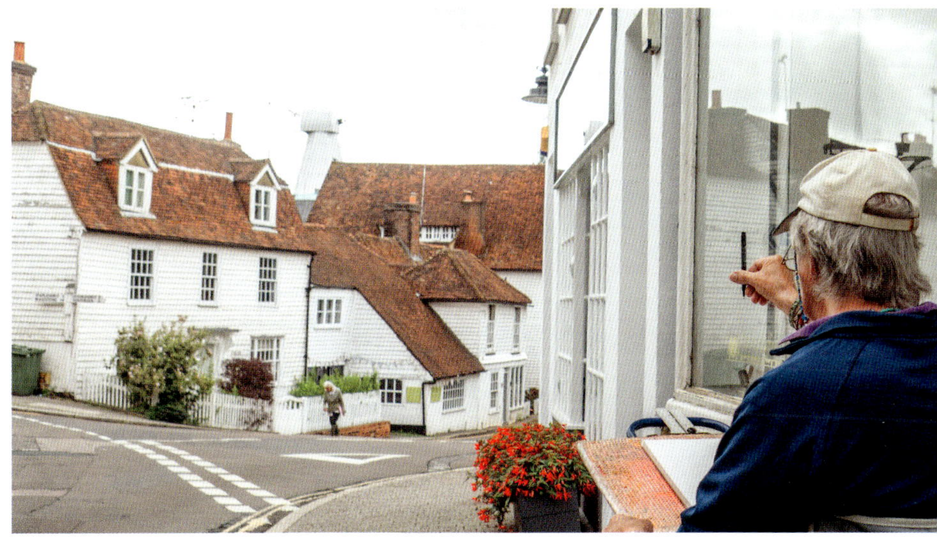

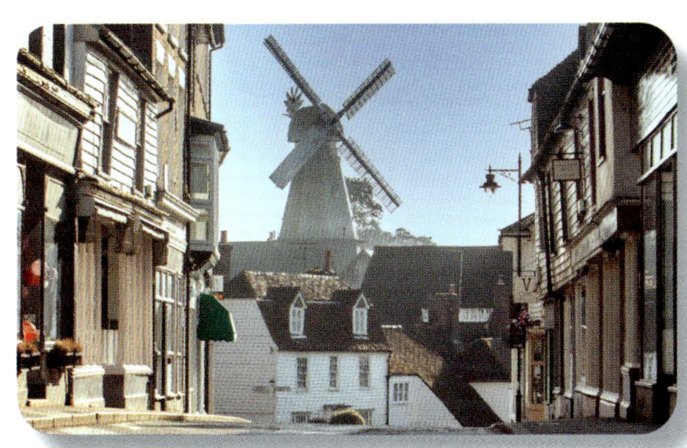

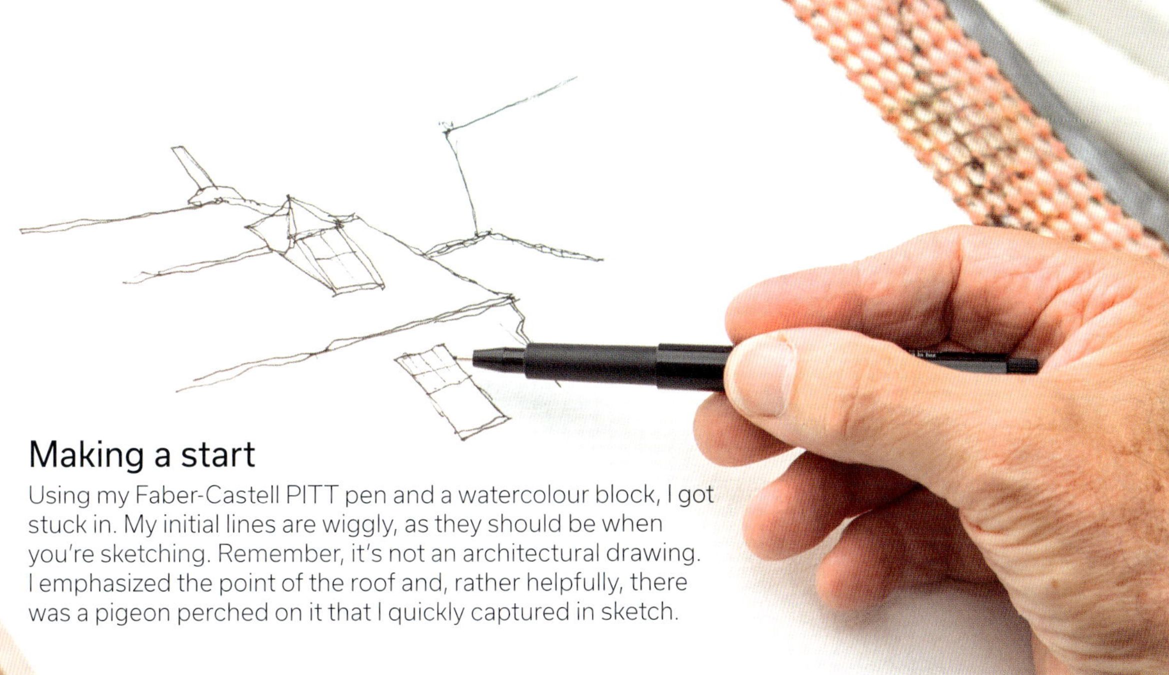

Making a start

Using my Faber-Castell PITT pen and a watercolour block, I got stuck in. My initial lines are wiggly, as they should be when you're sketching. Remember, it's not an architectural drawing. I emphasized the point of the roof and, rather helpfully, there was a pigeon perched on it that I quickly captured in sketch.

Drawing buildings

For the main house, I started with the corner of the roof, then added the windows. I then drew the rest of the house around the windows. This helped to keep everything in proportion.

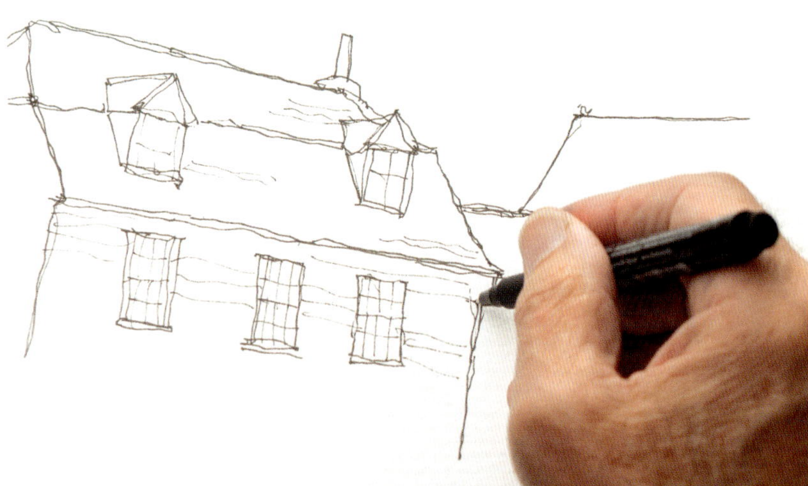

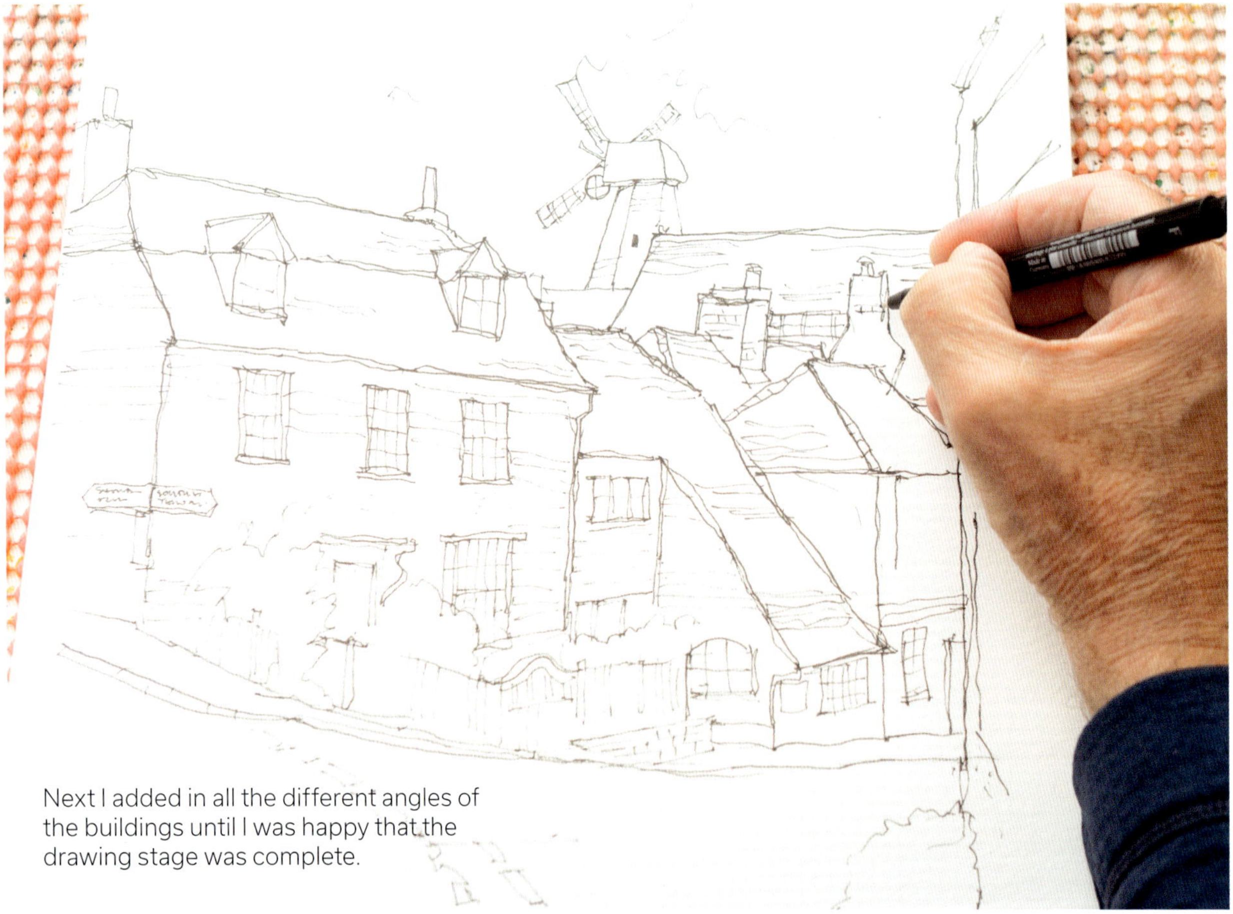

Next I added in all the different angles of the buildings until I was happy that the drawing stage was complete.

Adding paint

I semi-mixed the colours for the roof. This gentle mixing produced the different tones for the roof tiles. I used a size 8 brush and orange, manganese violet, cobalt blue and brown madder.

Next I added in the shadows to bring the different shapes to life. Carving out the roofs made them appear three-dimensional.

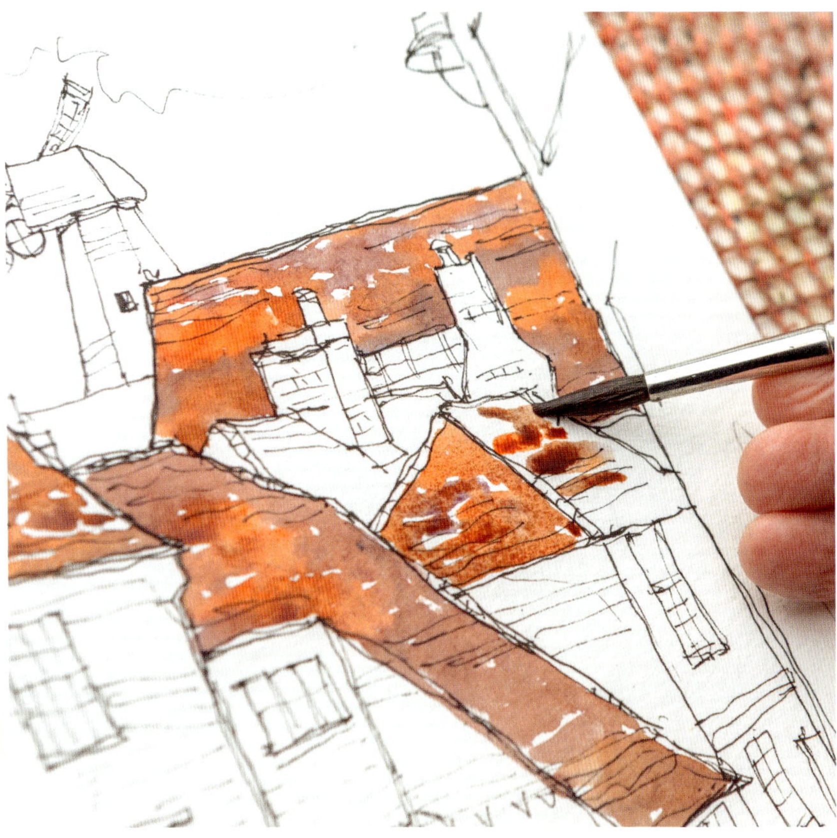

From here on, the colour picked up pace. I added the sky with those heavy clouds, the windmill itself and the tarmac on the road.

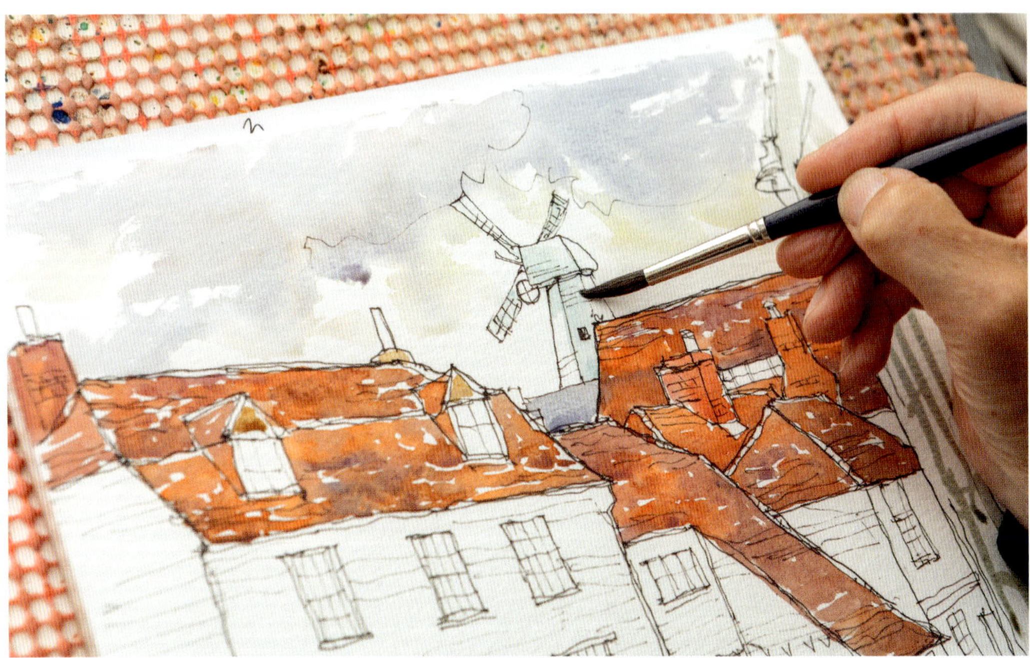

Adding colour

I added details that gave splashes of colour, such as the bushes and flowers at the front of the house. I used aureolin and cobalt turquoise for the bright green bushes and a dash of madder red dark for the colourful red bush.

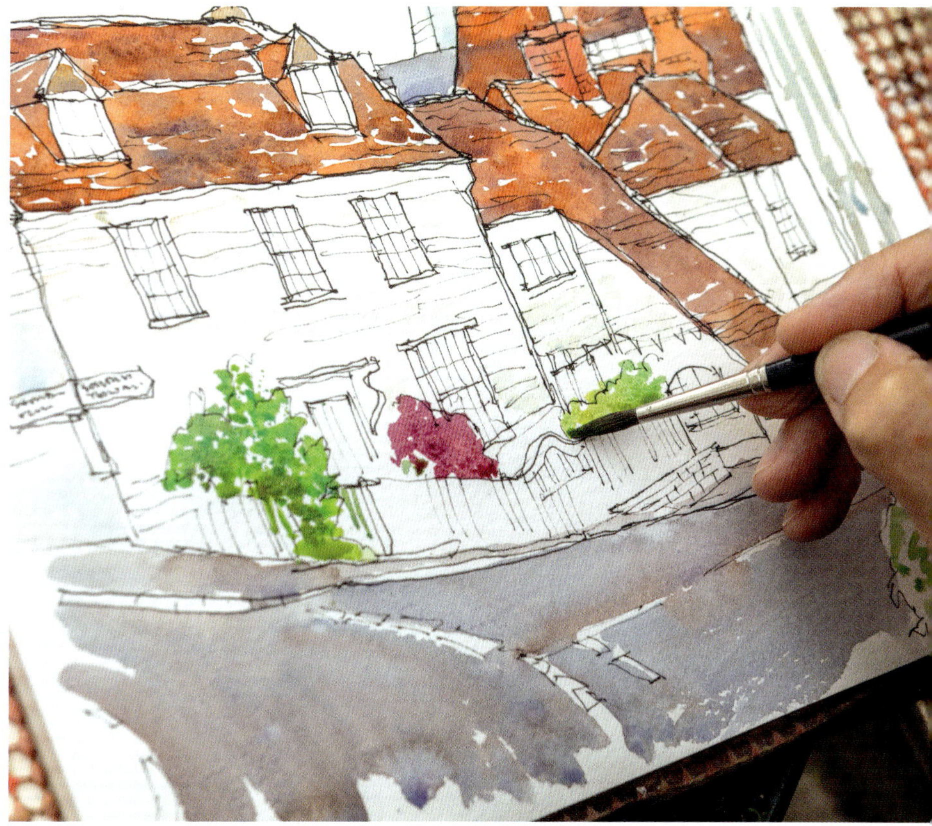

I introduced the shadow inside each window. The colourful front door and the side wall of the house were the next things to put in.

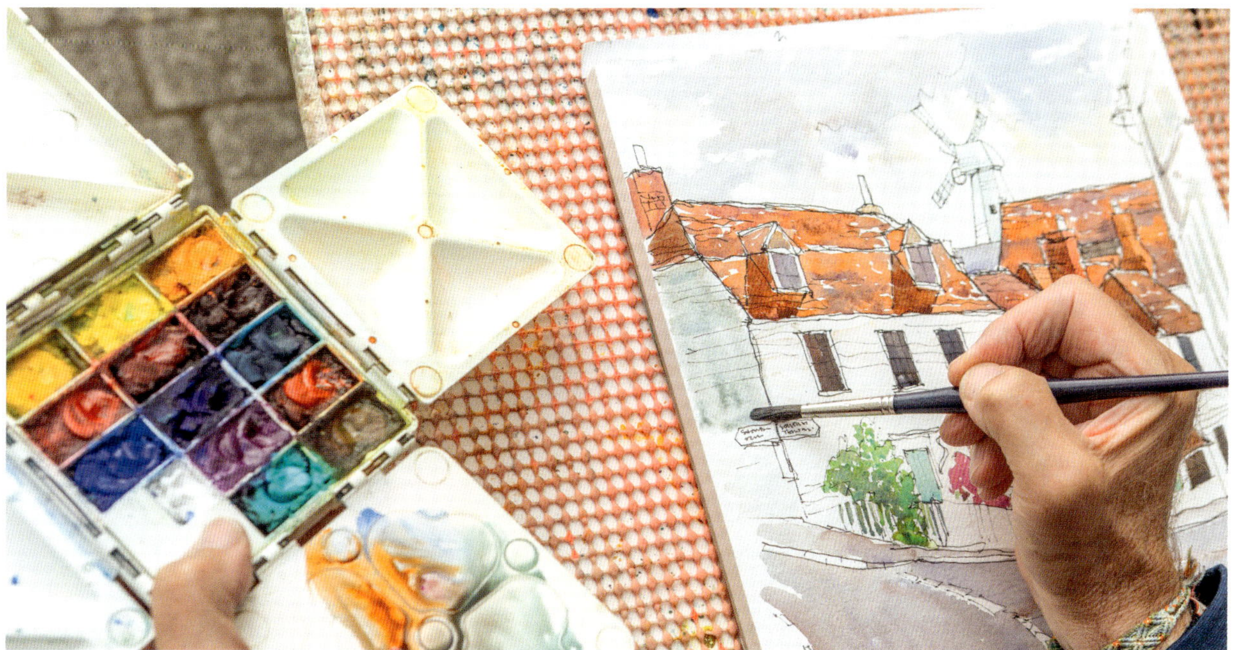

Finishing touches

Finally, I added in the guttering, downpipe, fence and brick wall in front of the house. I brought the windows to life by adding white frames, using one stroke only. I like to keep these details painterly and spending too much time trying to get them exact can work against you, plus it's so much quicker.

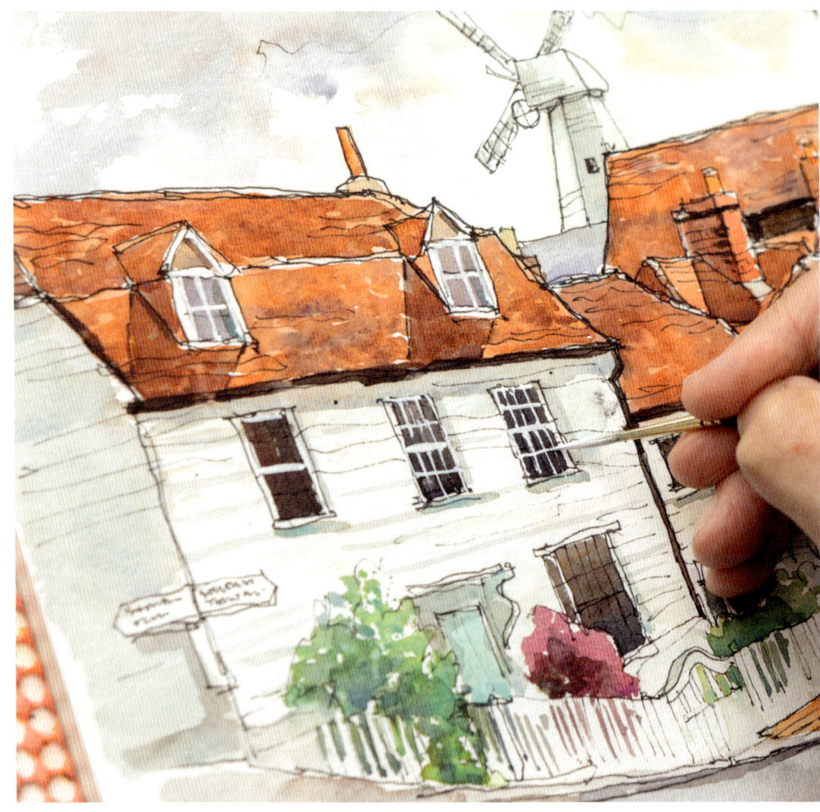

Here are my materials, shown in situ.

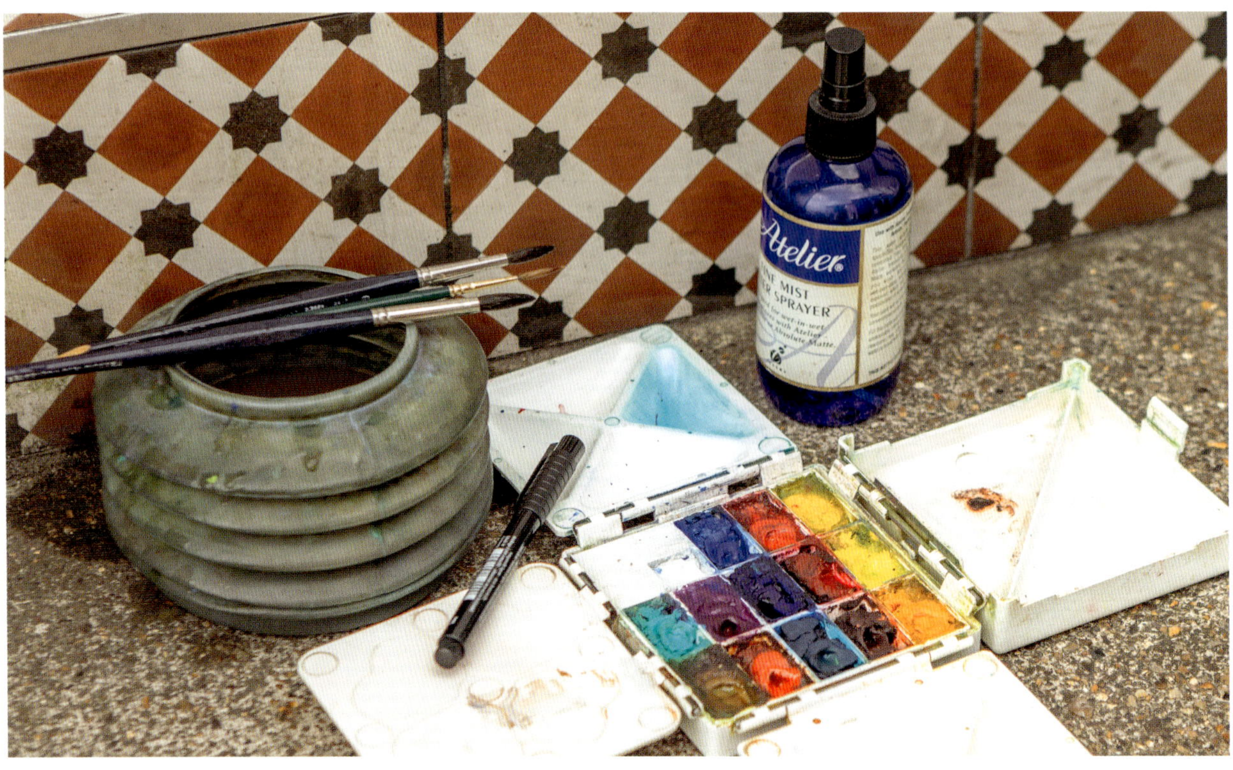

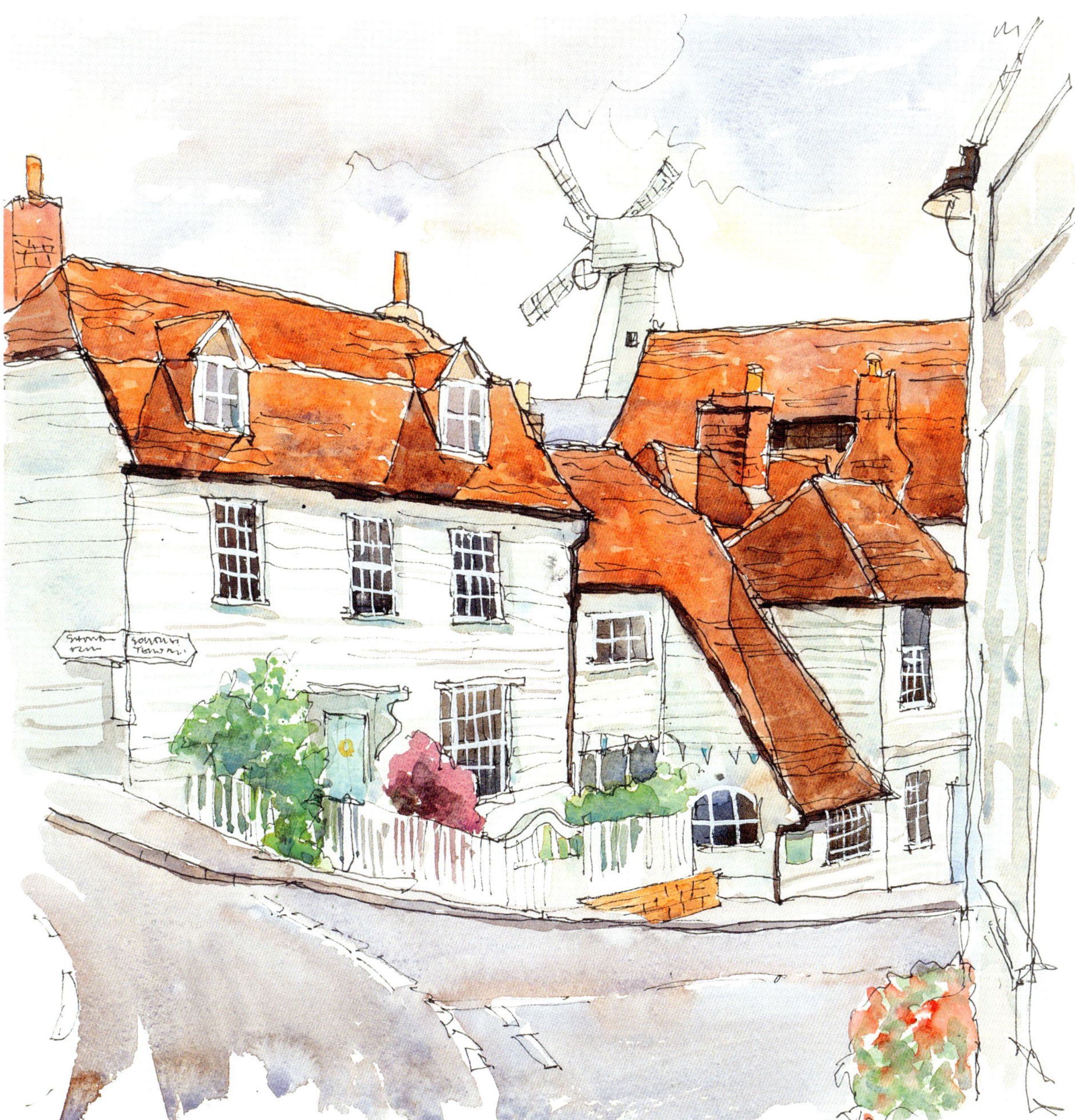

The finished sketch

When I look at this sketch I am reminded of the traffic coming round the corner, the chatty pedestrians passing by or waiting outside the hairdresser's and the fun we had capturing the townscape scene.

Watercolour pencil woodland

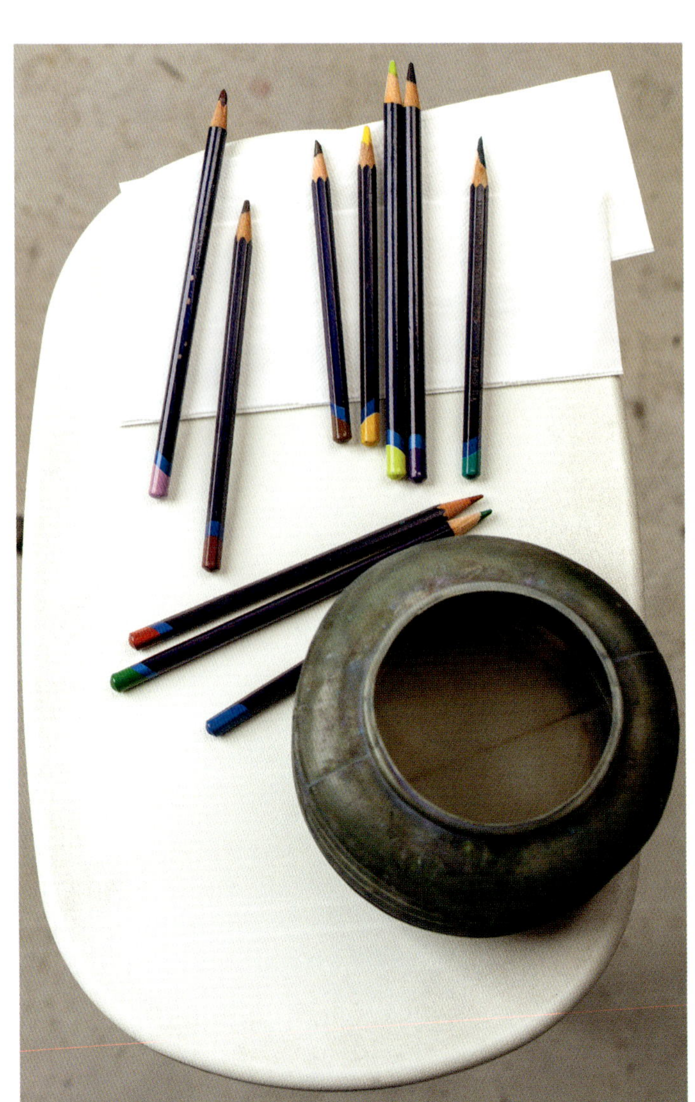

Working in the studio

This was a 10–15 minute lightning sketch that I did in the studio, using Derwent Inktense watercolour pencils. I have a box of 72 pencils, but I tend to use only a dozen, making them a very portable medium. For this sketch, I worked from a photograph I took in Exmoor, on a painting holiday. When painting from a photograph, you work in the same loose style as when working outdoors. The difference is that you have already decided on and photographed the subject that you want to paint. The fact that I took the photograph myself meant I had already benefitted from the experience of 'being there'.

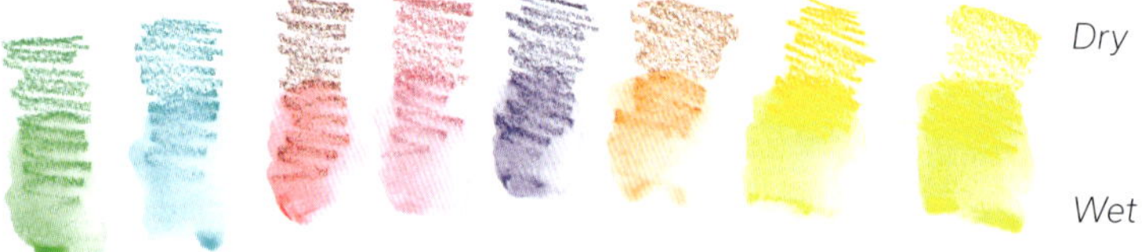

My advice
Always keep your colour swatch for future reference.

Colour swatches

When working with watercolour pencils, first make yourself a colour swatch of the pencils dry, and then wet, so you know what colours to expect. My students are always amazed how much the colours change once water is added.

Here are my materials. As you can see, there are very few. The names of the Inktense pencil colours bear no relation to watercolours, with such exotic labels as sherbert lemon, poppy red, fuchsia and my favourite: shiraz! If you look at my swatch chart above it will give you fair idea of the actual colours I used.

Making a start

I like to draw my preliminary lines in the actual coloured pencil required. Other people prefer to draw it in graphite pencil or pen first, and then colour it in. However, working with the actual colours is much quicker, and enables you to get down your initial impressions on paper immediately.

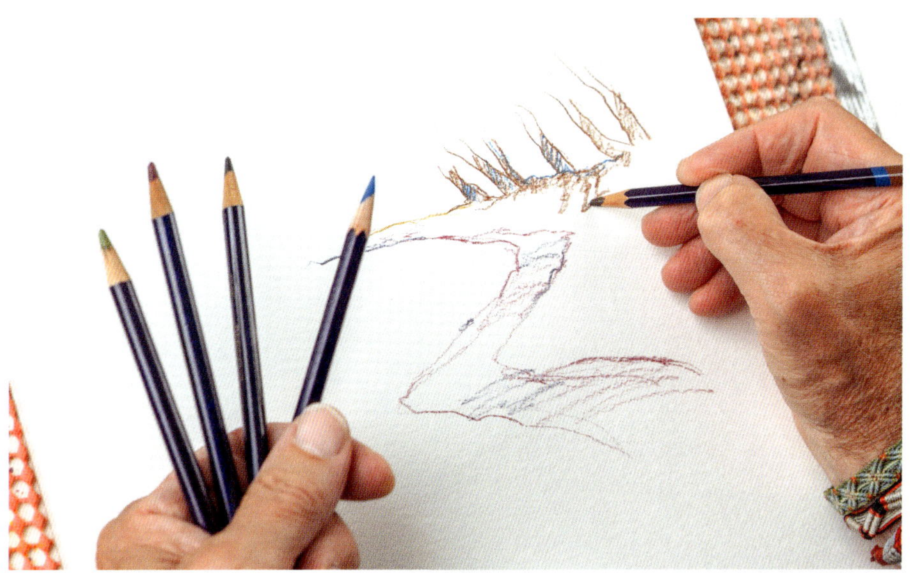

Misconceptions

A misconception you might have is that you draw the whole thing first and then apply water. I much prefer to draw a bit, add water, then draw a bit more. This enables you to build up the basic underlying colours. Once the paint is dry, it is waterproof, so you can add layers. This is useful to bear in mind when sketching outdoors with Inktense – you can work in a natural, organic way, bit by bit, rather than being strict and inflexible.

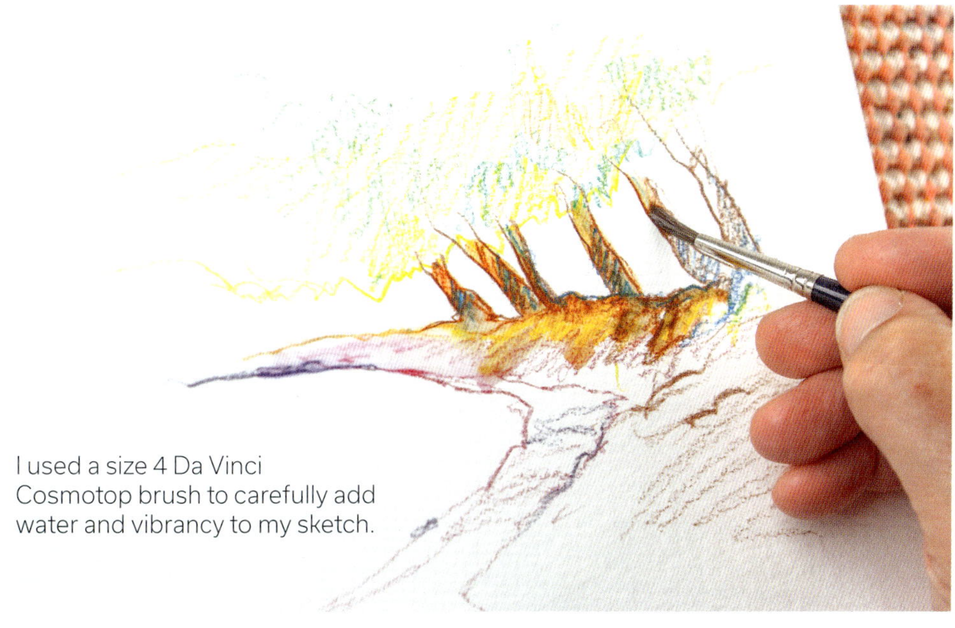

I used a size 4 Da Vinci Cosmotop brush to carefully add water and vibrancy to my sketch.

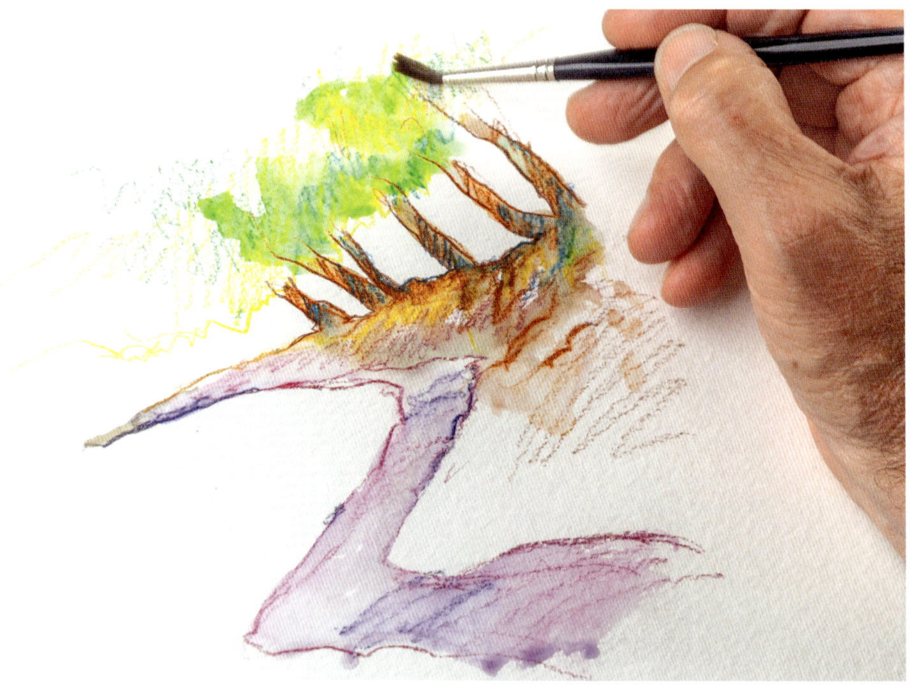

Notice how all the pencil marks merge together once I add water to them.

I continued with my paintbrush until all the pencil marks had water over the top of them. Then I returned to my watercolour pencils again to add more to my sketch.

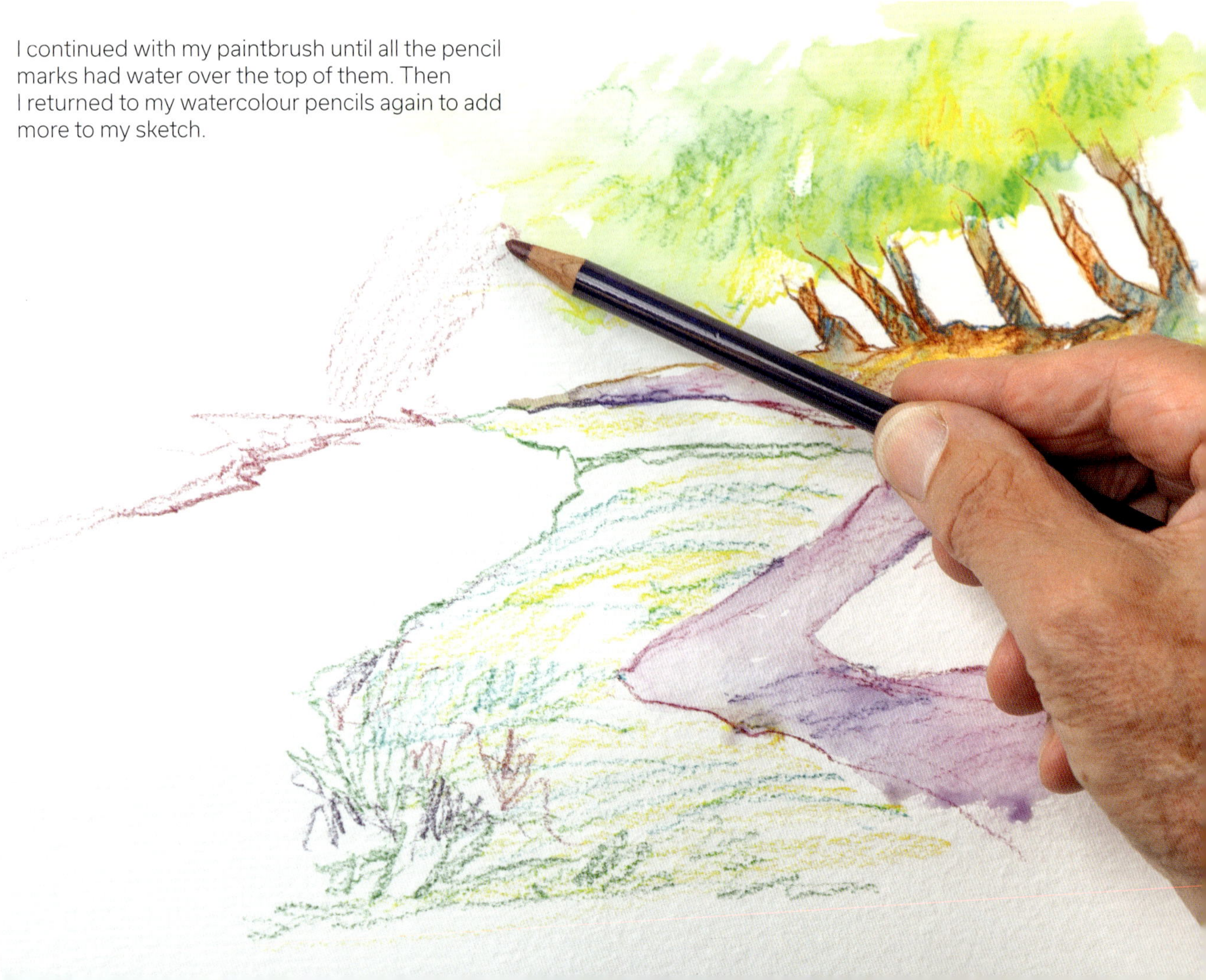

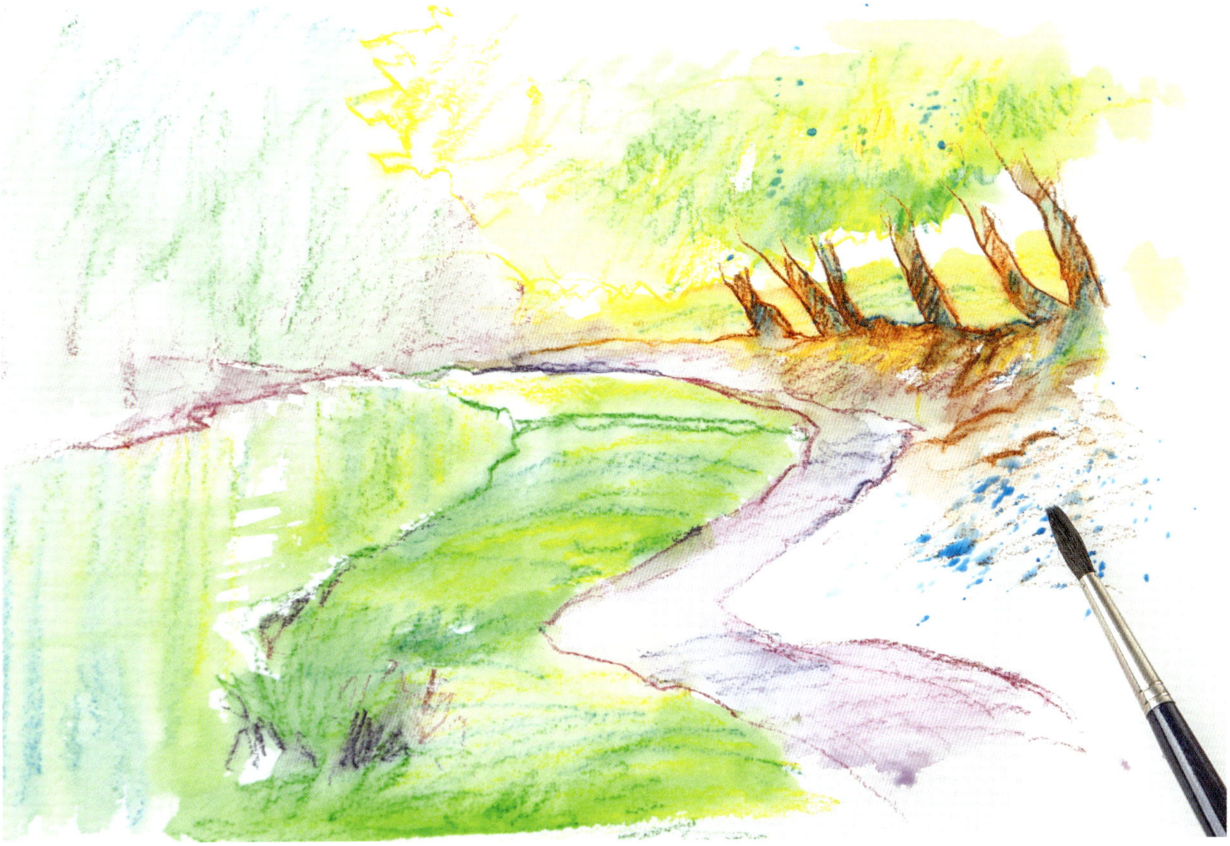

Once I was happy that the next set of pencil lines were in, I once again added water to the sketch to make the colours pop. Loading my brush with some wet colour I started to flick some paint into the right-hand bank.

Using your pencil in the semi-wet

After adding water to a particular area, you can use your pencil in the semi-wet to give the effect of the drawing showing through. This is useful for tree roots or branches that you want to emphasize.

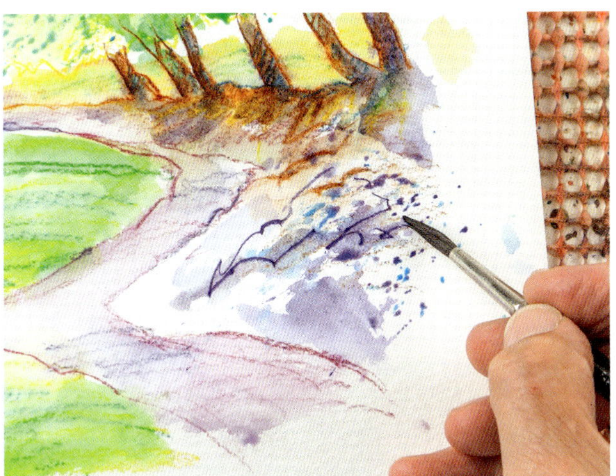

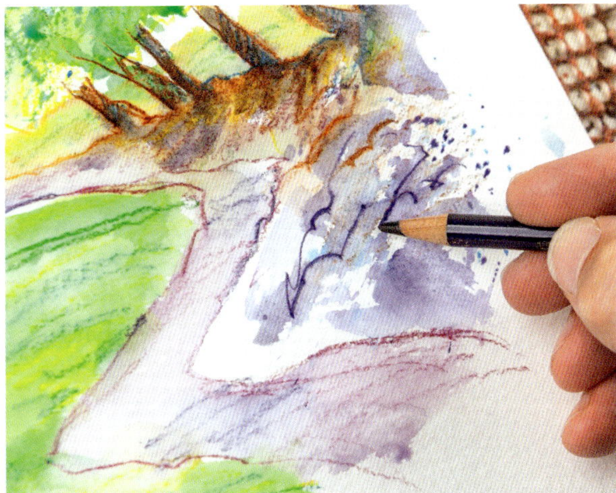

Building up layers

Once I had finished adding the main details in pencil and then going over them in water, it was time for the finishing touches. Using my pencil on the semi-wet page again, I carefully added dark horizontal branches to the foreground trees and paler trunks to the trees that lean towards the water.

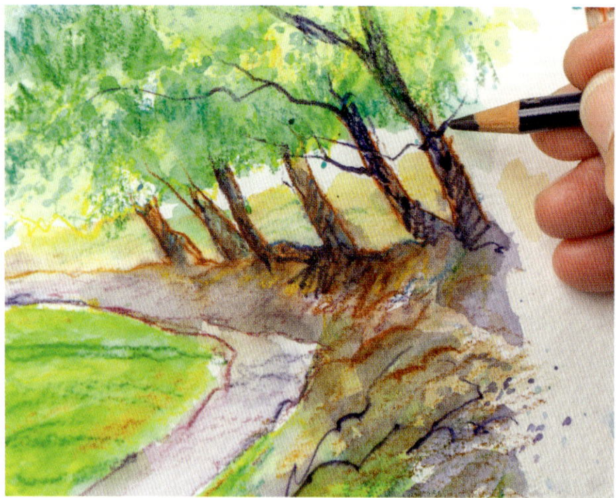

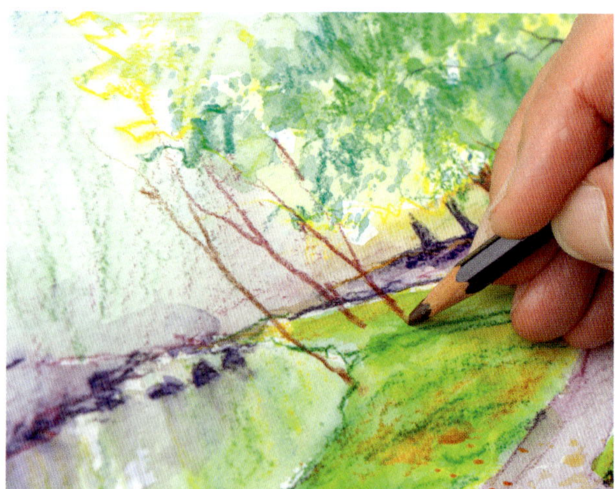

138

Here is my reference photograph that was the inspiration for this demo.

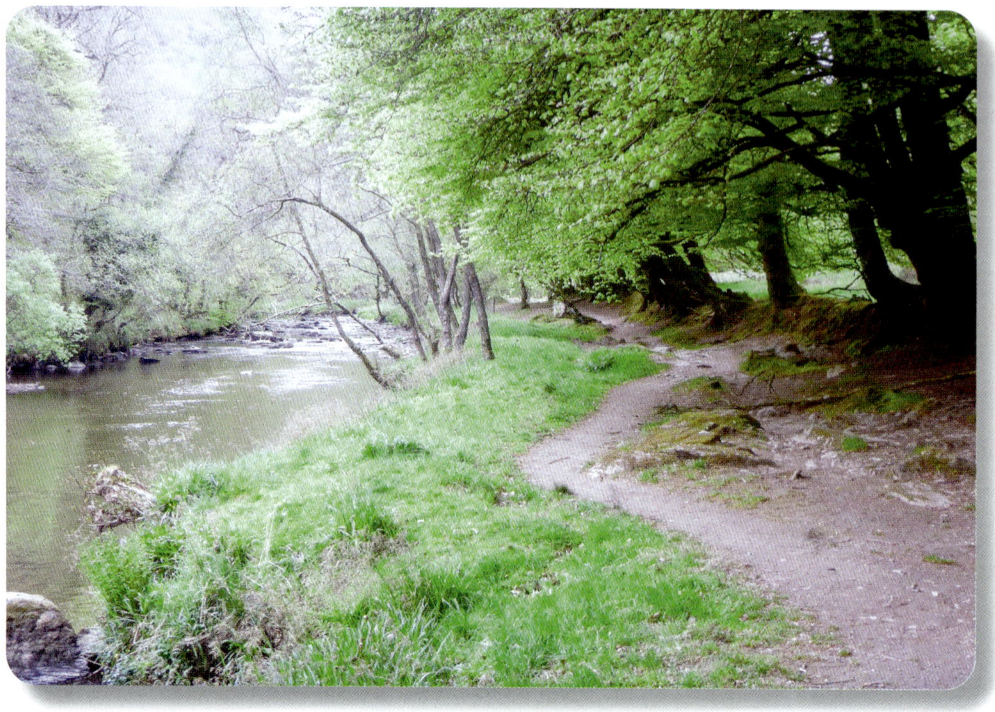

I enjoyed that! This is a really uplifting, upbeat style of painting.

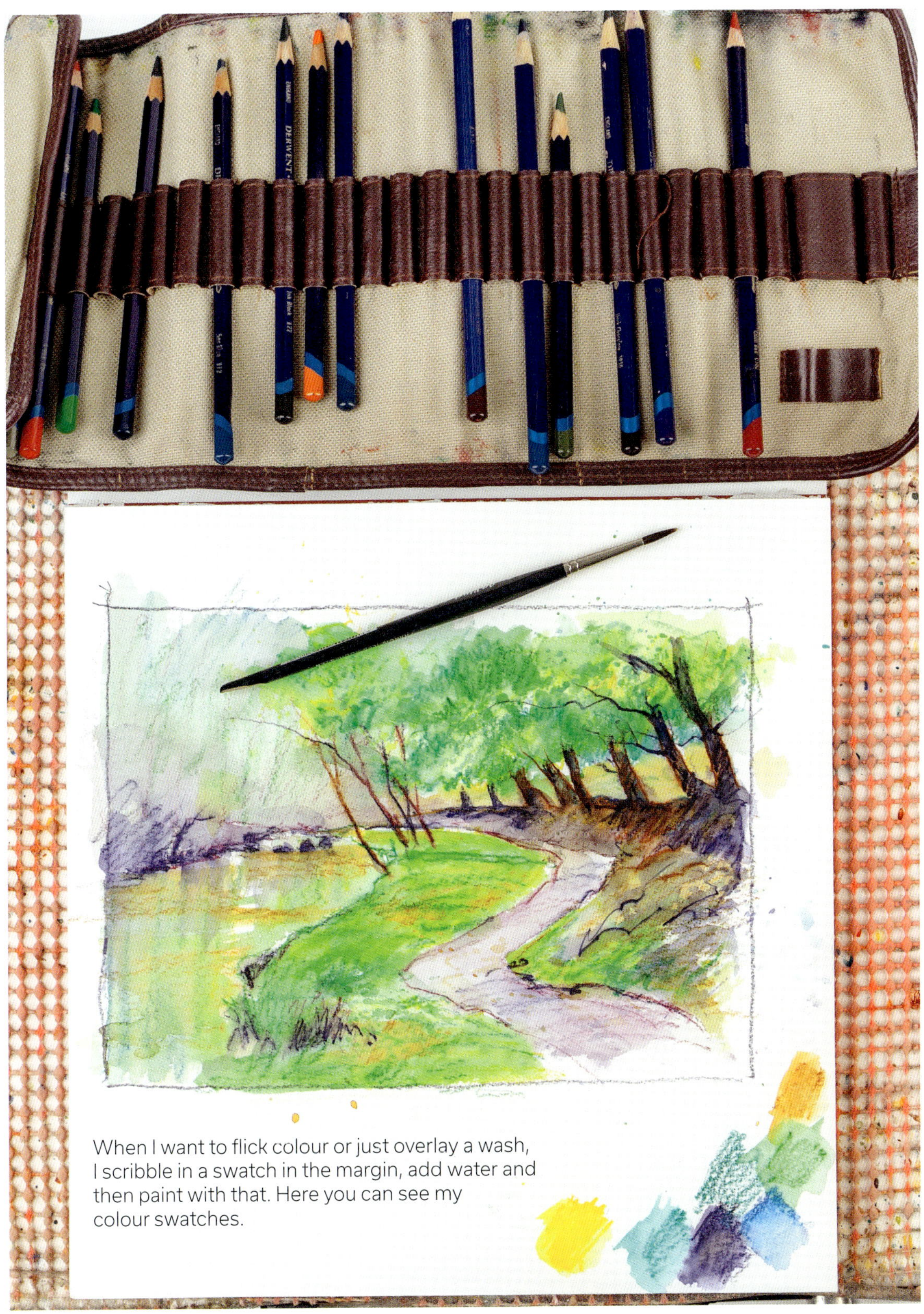

When I want to flick colour or just overlay a wash,
I scribble in a swatch in the margin, add water and
then paint with that. Here you can see my
colour swatches.

Sketching indoors

With all the best intentions you can set out for an outdoor sketching session, only to find that the weather has a different idea. Embrace the experience – sometimes the unexpected can provide you with a weallth of other sketching opportunities. If you really have to abandon the outdoor excursion, head for shelter inside and discover that sketching interiors can also be a treat!

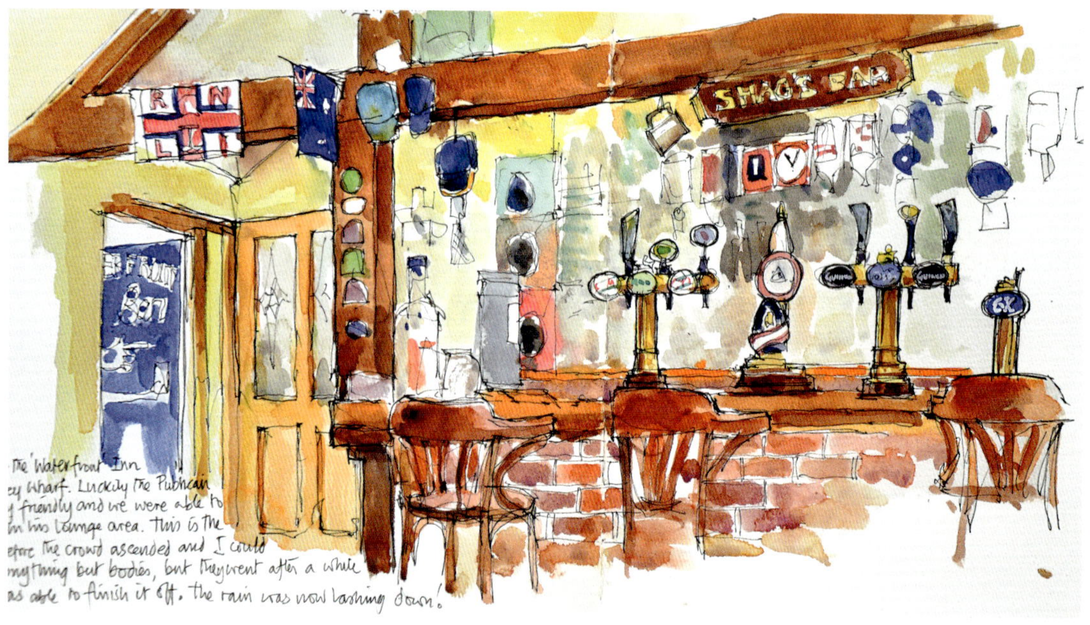

I took a group to paint on the canal one day only to be rained on incessantly. We took shelter in the canal-side pub. As it happened, the owner was a really friendly guy and said we could paint in his bar as it was quiet midweek. So we did a pub interior...and here it is.

Some interiors such as the incredible bar at El Pimpi in Malaga, Spain, just cry out to be painted. This lunchtime was fairly quiet so we were able to set up at one of the tables to sketch this scene.

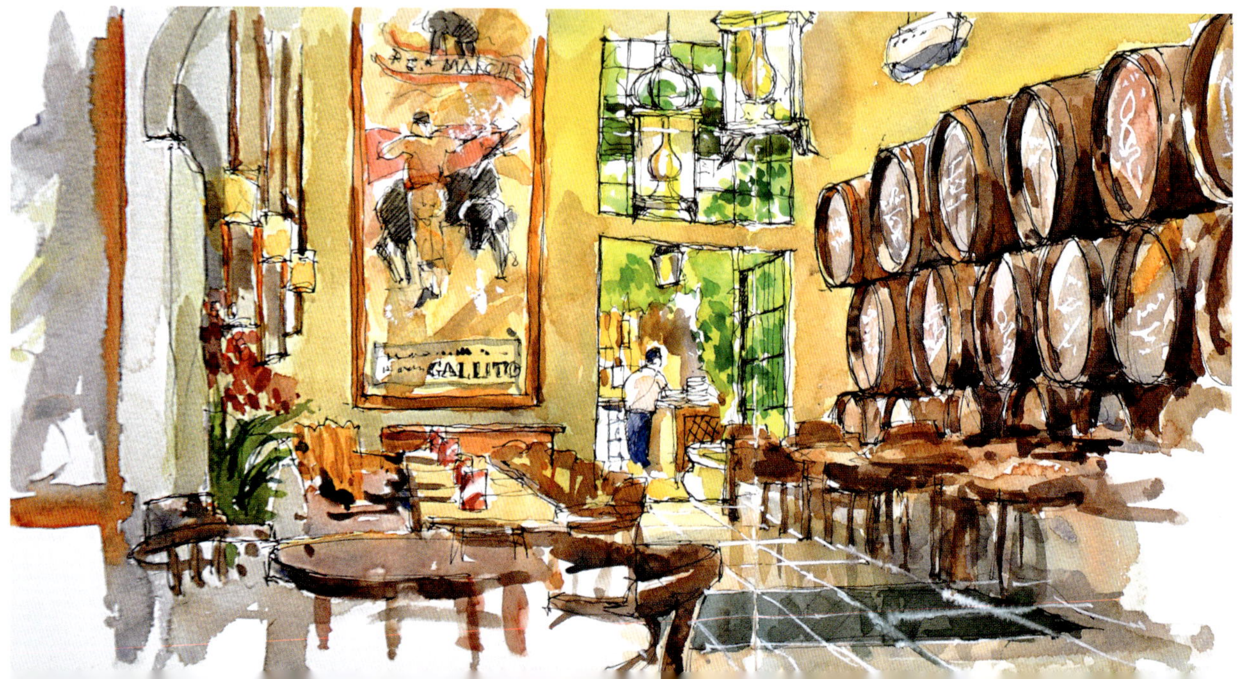

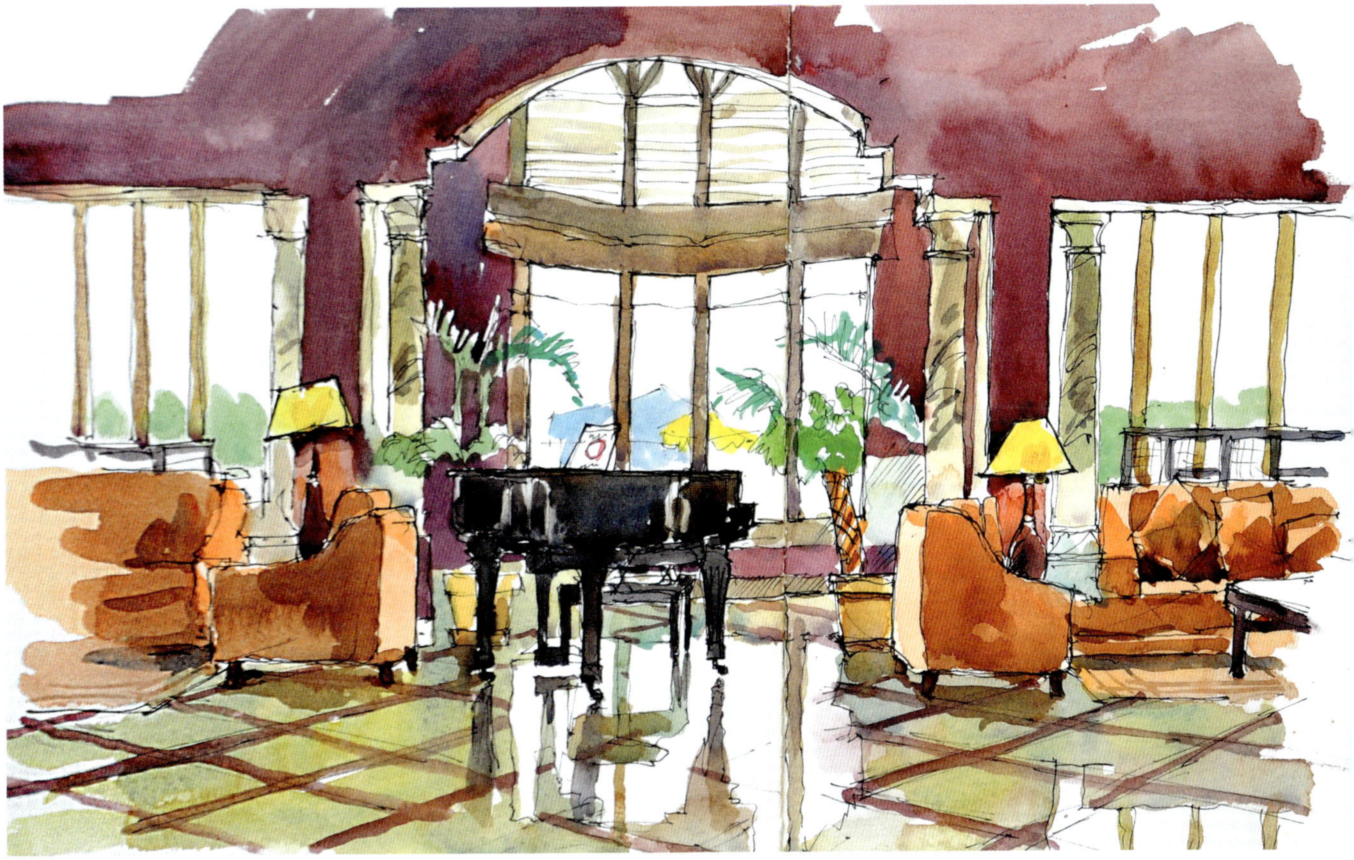

The lobby of our hotel in Tunisia had these huge windows and a lovely grand piano
set on a marble floor which gave off great reflections. The manager allowed us to
sit around to paint this view, which was quite striking.

Not exactly an interior but this
Souk in Tunis certainly feels
like one with its labyrinthine
covered alleyways. I did this
sketch as a demo to my group
on our painting trip, and it was
well received.

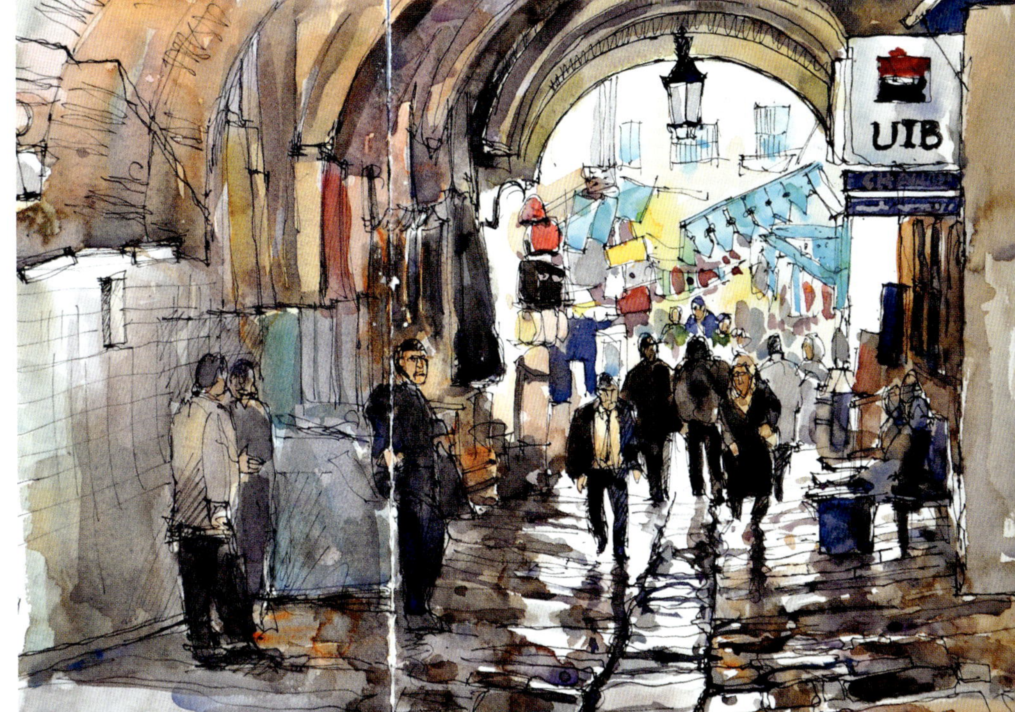

Afterword

I hope you have enjoyed my book and if you have never experienced the joy of painting *en plein air*, maybe I have given you the boost to have a go. If you're already out there with your sketchbook and paints, I hope it will provide practical help and inspiration to carry on. Throughout this book I have been focusing on the way I sketch outdoors and the results can be a bit 'rough and ready', but my aim is that they embody the essence of the scene in front of me and are great fun to do.

So pack up your gear and get painting outdoors!

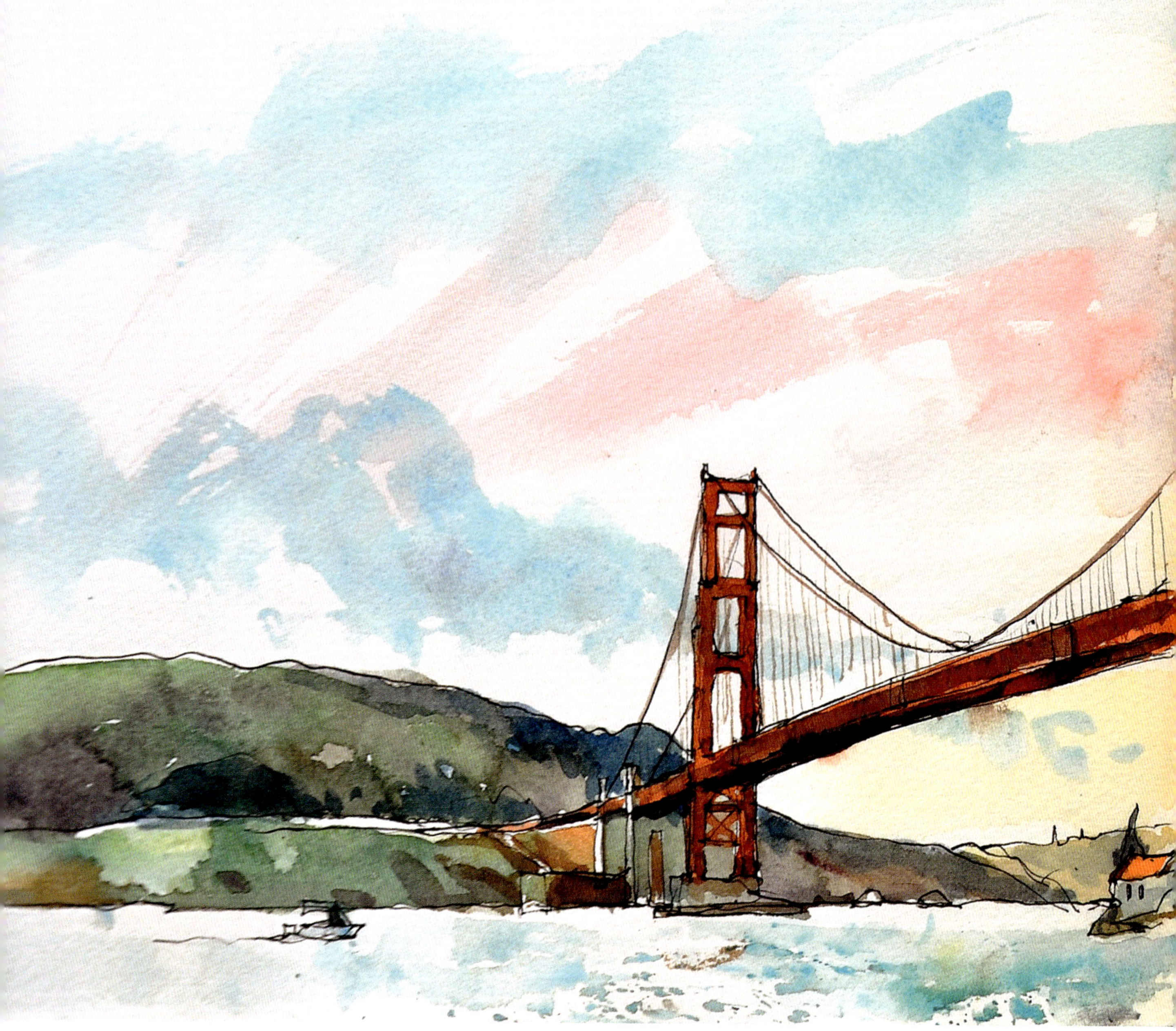

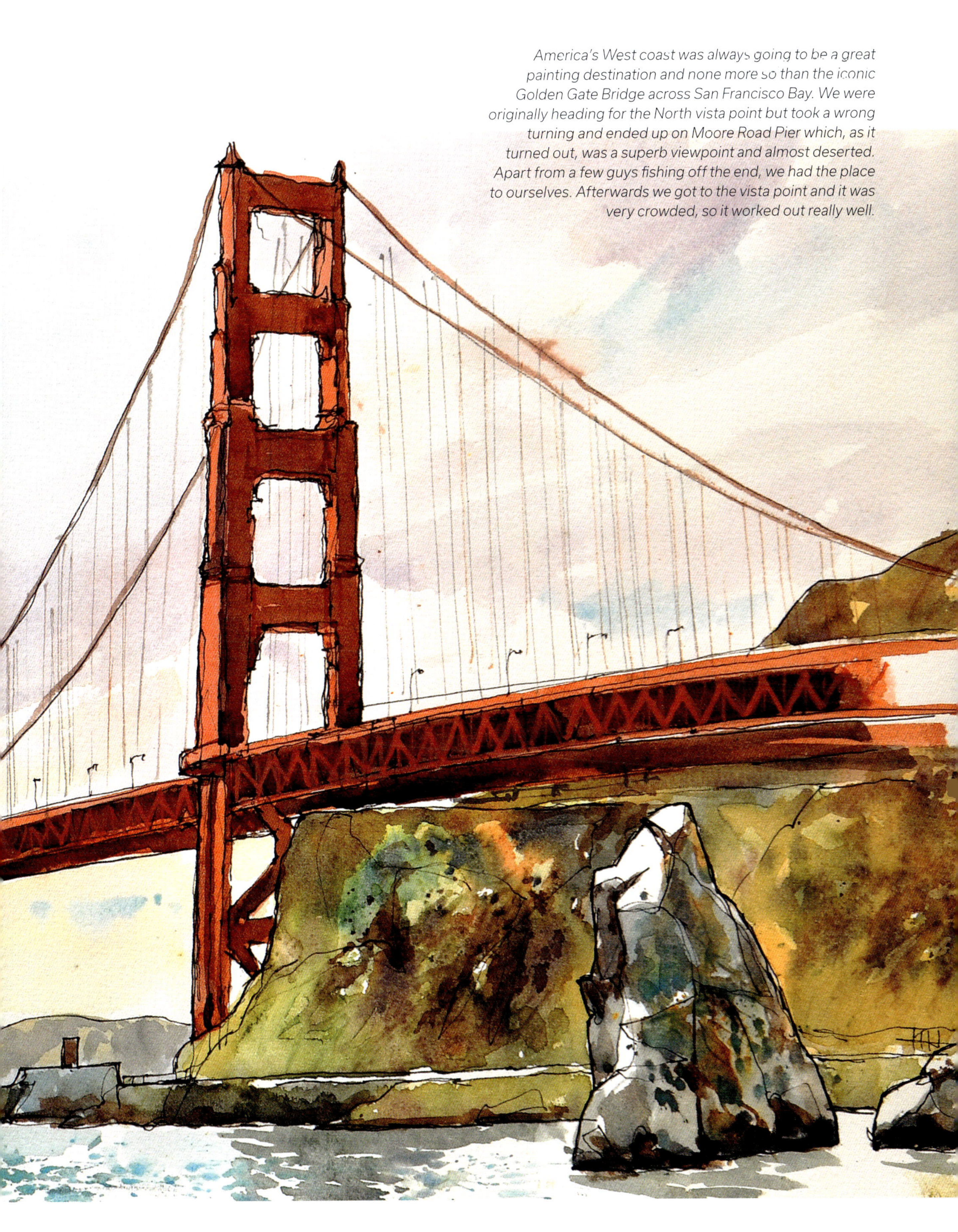

America's West coast was always going to be a great
painting destination and none more so than the iconic
Golden Gate Bridge across San Francisco Bay. We were
originally heading for the North vista point but took a wrong
turning and ended up on Moore Road Pier which, as it
turned out, was a superb viewpoint and almost deserted.
Apart from a few guys fishing off the end, we had the place
to ourselves. Afterwards we got to the vista point and it was
very crowded, so it worked out really well.

Index